Teaching Olaudah Equiano's *Narrative*

TEACHING OLAUDAH EQUIANO'S *NARRATIVE*

Pedagogical Strategies and New Perspectives

Edited by Eric D. Lamore
Foreword by Vincent Carretta

THE UNIVERSITY OF TENNESSEE PRESS / KNOXVILLE

First Edition.

The paper in this book meets the requirements of American National Standards Institute / National Information Standards Organization specification Z39.48–1992 (Permanence of Paper). It contains 30 percent post-consumer waste and is certified by the Forest Stewardship Council.

Library of Congress Cataloging-in-Publication Data

Teaching Olaudah Equiano's *Narrative:* pedagogical strategies and new perspectives / edited by Eric D. Lamore; foreword by Vincent Carretta.

p. cm.

Includes bibliographical references and index.

ISBN 978-1-57233-868-5 (hardcover) — ISBN 1-57233-868-7 (hardcover)

1. Equiano, Olaudah, b. 1745. Interesting narrative of the life of Olaudah Equiano.
2. African literature (English)—Study and teaching.
3. Slave narratives—History and criticism.
4. Slavery in literature.

I. Lamore, Eric D.

PR9340.A53T43 2012
820.9'9607—dc23
2012005294

For Ricia

Contents

Part 3
Pedagogy, African American Studies, and *The Interesting Narrative*

Part 4
Pedagogy, American Studies, and *The Interesting Narrative*

Foreword

On 9 February 2009 Westminster Abbey commemorated with a plaque the 250th anniversary of the baptism of Gustavus Vassa (Olaudah Equiano) in St. Margaret's Church. He was the first, and remains the only, person of African descent to receive that honor from the Abbey. Westminster Abbey's decision to recognize Equiano's significance was a significant step in the recuperation of the man widely recognized as the founder of the genre of the African American slave narrative and increasingly acknowledged as an influential figure in the movement to abolish the transatlantic slave trade. Westminster Abbey's commemoration of Equiano was one of the most public events in the renaissance of interest in him and his writings during the last thirty-five years.

Olaudah Equiano, also known as Gustavus Vassa (1745?–1797), published *The Interesting Narrative of the Life of Olaudah Equiano, or Gustavus Vassa, the African. Written by Himself* in London in 1789. It is a spiritual autobiography, captivity narrative, travel book, adventure tale, slave narrative, economic treatise, apologia, and argument against the transatlantic slave trade and slavery. According to Equiano, he was born in 1745 in what is now southeastern Nigeria, where fellow Africans kidnapped and enslaved him when he was about eleven years old. He reports that Europeans bought him and forced him to endure the transatlantic Middle Passage from Africa to the West Indies. Equiano writes that he was soon taken to Virginia. There he was purchased by an officer in the British Royal Navy who renamed him Gustavus Vassa, which remained his legal name for the rest of his life. Equiano spent the next eight years with his master in London and at sea during the Seven Years' War. His master sold him into the horrors of West Indian slavery at the end of the war in 1762.

Equiano was able to save enough money to buy his own freedom in 1766 and to begin a series of voyages of commerce, adventure, and discovery to North America, the West Indies, the Mediterranean, the Middle East, and the North

Pole. His travels enabled him to observe and comment on the many varieties of eighteenth-century involuntary servitude. Equiano converted to Methodism upon returning to London from his voyage towards the North Pole in 1773. He became an outspoken opponent of the transatlantic slave trade during the 1780s, first in letters and book reviews in London newspapers and then in his autobiography. Equiano married an Englishwoman in 1792, with whom he had two daughters. One of his daughters survived to inherit the sizeable estate he left at his death on 31 March 1797.

Equiano was a remarkably successful businessman as well as a masterful rhetorician. He was able to keep the profits from the sale of his book because he never sold his copyright, which he saw through an impressive nine editions. Baptismal and naval records that say Equiano was born in South Carolina cast doubt on Equiano's story of his birth and early years. They suggest that he may have drawn on the experiences of others to invent his purported African birth and much-cited account of the Middle Passage to supply the abolitionist movement with the first-person victim's description it needed to advance its crusade to end the transatlantic slave trade.

Unauthorized editions of Equiano's *Interesting Narrative* were reprinted during his lifetime in Russia, Holland, Germany, and New York City. Several more editions of Equiano's autobiography appeared in altered and often abridged form during the twenty years after his death. British and American opponents of slavery briefly cited and sometimes quoted Equiano throughout the first half of the nineteenth century. The inscription on the recently discovered gravestone of Equiano's only child who survived to adulthood assumes that "Gustavus Vassa the African" was still a familiar figure in 1857. But Equiano and his *Interesting Narrative* seem to have been forgotten on both sides of the Atlantic for more than a century after 1857. The declining interest in the author and his book may have been due to the shift in emphasis from the abolition of the British-dominated transatlantic slave trade to the abolition of slavery, particularly in the United States, following the outlawing of the transatlantic trade in 1807. Paul Edwards's publication of a facsimile edition of *The Interesting Narrative* in 1969 initiated the renaissance of interest in Equiano and his writings.

In recent decades, historians, literary critics, and the general public have increasingly recognized Equiano as one of the most accomplished English-speaking writers of African descent. Several modern editions are now available of Equiano's autobiography. He is the subject of two recent biographies: James Walvin, an eminent historian of slavery and the slave trade, published *An African's Life: The Life and Times of Olaudah Equiano, 1745–1797* in 1998; my own *Equiano, the African: Biography of a Self-Made Man* first appeared in 2005.

The canonical status of *The Interesting Narrative* has been acknowledged by its inclusion in the Penguin Classics series. Excerpts from the book now appear in every anthology and on any website covering American, African American, British, and Caribbean history and literature of the eighteenth century. The most frequently excerpted sections are the early chapters on his life in Africa and his experience on the Middle Passage crossing the Atlantic to America. Indeed, it is difficult to think of any historical account of the Middle Passage that does not quote his purported eyewitness description of its horrors as primary evidence. Interest in Equiano has not been restricted to academia. He has been featured in television shows, films, comic books, and books written for children. The story of Equiano's life is part of African, African American, Anglo-American, African British, and African Caribbean popular culture.

Teaching Olaudah Equiano's Narrative is a fitting and important contribution to the widespread recognition of Equiano as a major author and historical figure. Appropriately interdisciplinary in scope, this collection of strong essays is the first book devoted to the pedagogical challenges and opportunities Equiano's autobiography offers to teachers and their students. Publication of this book is as noteworthy an acknowledgment of Equiano's significance as the plaque in St. Margaret's Church.

Vincent Carretta

Acknowledgments

I am grateful to Scot Danforth, director of the University of Tennessee Press, for expressing interest in this volume, to Kerry Webb, acquisitions editor at the University of Tennessee Press, for all of her generous time, and to Gene Adair, manuscript editor at the press, for his careful work on the book. The press found two superb readers to evaluate the manuscript of *Teaching Olaudah Equiano's* Narrative. I have no doubt that the comments from these readers enhanced this volume.

I am indebted to Vincent Carretta for his meticulous reading of the manuscript and for contributing the foreword.

I wish to thank Marion Rust, the chairperson of "Teaching Equiano's *Narrative*," the title of a panel at the 2008 American Society for Eighteenth-Century Studies, for inviting me to participate on this conference panel. This opportunity motivated me to complete this book.

I would also like to extend my thanks to all the contributors whose valuable intellectual work appears in this volume. Thank you for teaching me about Equiano's *Narrative* by consistently calling my attention to additional layers of complexity found in this text.

I would be remiss if I did not acknowledge the generous time that Ricia Anne Chansky invested in reading parts of this manuscript and in hearing me talk again and again about teaching Equiano's *Narrative.* This volume is dedicated, with love, to her because of her unwavering support.

Finally, thank you to E.J. and M.K. for making me smile.

* * *

For permission to reprint previously published articles, I am grateful to the following authors and rights holders:

Srinivas Aravamudan. "Equiano Lite." *Eighteenth-Century Studies* 34:4 (2001): 615–19. © 2001 The American Society for Eighteenth-Century Studies. Reprinted with permission of The Johns Hopkins University Press.

Sarah Brophy. "Olaudah Equiano, Autobiography, and Ideas of Culture." *1650–1850: Ideas, Aesthetics, and Inquiries in the Early Modern Era* 17 (2010): 249–70. Copyright © 2010 AMS Press, Inc. All right reserved. Reprinted with permission of AMS Press.

Tess Chakkalakal. "I, Hereby, Vow to Read *The Interesting Narrative.*" *Captivating Subjects: Writing Confinement, Citizenship, and Nationhood in the Nineteenth Century.* Eds. Jason Haslam and Julia M. Wright. 86–112. © The University of Toronto Press, 2005. Portions of this essay are reprinted with permission of The University of Toronto Press.

Adam Potkay. "History, Oratory, and God in Equiano's *Interesting Narrative.*" *Eighteenth-Century Studies* 34:4 (2001): 601–14. © 2001 The American Society for Eighteenth-Century Studies. Reprinted with permission of The Johns Hopkins University Press.

Roxann Wheeler. "Domesticating Equiano's *Interesting Narrative.*" *Eighteenth-Century Studies* 34:4 (2001): 620–24. © 2001 The American Society for Eighteenth-Century Studies. Reprinted with permission of The Johns Hopkins University Press.

Introduction

Eric D. Lamore

Critical readings of *The Interesting Narrative of the Life of Olaudah Equiano, or Gustavus Vassa, the African. Written by Himself* far outweigh analyses that examine the teaching of this eighteenth-century text. Currently, teacher-scholars have access to scholarly essays that focus on the authenticity of the author's African origins, the implications of this authenticity debate, the appropriate generic classification(s) for the narrative, the usefulness of applying colonial and postcolonial theory to read the *Narrative,* the legitimacy of placing the narrative in a given literary canon or canons, and the purpose of Equiano's use of religious and secular rhetorics in the *Narrative,* among other relevant topics. Clearly, these critical interpretations of Equiano's text offer pertinent commentary on the *Narrative* for teacher-scholars as they prepare to bring all or parts of the text into the classroom. However, meaningful teaching of the *Narrative,* or any other text for that matter, calls for more than just assigning scholarship to students or articulating significant points found in scholarly articles in classroom discussions. With this observation in mind, we may conclude that while several exciting and varied investigations exist to enrich teacher-scholars' understanding of Equiano and his eighteenth-century text, these readings of the *Narrative* do not offer a pedagogical model to work with and against in their classrooms. Until now, no volume exists that discusses ways to share pedagogically this multifaceted narrative with diverse students across the curriculum.

Even though Equiano and his 1789 narrative are frequently discussed topics in a variety of intellectual fields, the successful teaching of the text remains an underexplored topic.[1] In searching pedagogical scholarship for help in teaching Equiano, we discover three significant patterns. First, teacher-scholars seldom focus solely on the teaching of Equiano's *Narrative* in pedagogical articles, usually referencing his text only briefly as one among others taught in the fields of early American studies, African American studies, and autobiography studies. Second, these articles often do not contain adequate discussion of the pedagogical strategies that teacher-scholars can use when exploring the contents of the eighteenth-century narrative with their students. Third, some investigations of teaching Equiano do not explore fully the justifications for teaching the narrative in a given pedagogical context.[2] Given such limitations in the scholarship on teaching Equiano, it is clear that this is a pedagogical topic in need of further exploration.

Teaching Olaudah Equiano's Narrative remedies this gap by focusing explicitly on the identification of classroom spaces in which teacher-scholars currently assign this seminal text. This volume blends new readings of Equiano's *Narrative* with relevant justifications for why this eighteenth-century text matters in the contemporary moment. Furthermore, the contributions found here purposefully tackle the pedagogical problems that accompany the teaching of this text and the specific strategies that instructors can employ to ensure that students understand this multilayered narrative and the cultural and historical contexts that helped shape and continue to shape this popular text. Although the authors of these diverse essays draw on theories and texts from different disciplinary fields, we discover throughout this volume a uniform argument which holds that by including this work as an integral part of their courses, teacher-scholars enhance their students' learning in a variety of important ways, not the least of which is improving their understanding of the dynamics of the early Atlantic World. On yet another level, this book strives to articulate why this eighteenth-century book remains fresh, relevant, and important to contemporary students, regardless of whether they are literature majors, non-majors, undergraduates, or graduate students studying Africa, the Caribbean, the Americas, Great Britain, the Arctic region, or Europe.

The *Narrative* enhances courses because it is, on one hand, a text that allows our students to explore a plethora of pertinent topics: Equiano's strategic representations of his Eboe nation, the dynamics and geography of the eighteenth-century slave trade, the economic dimension of the slave trade, the representations of Africa and Africans in the European imagination, transatlantic travel in the early Atlantic World, and the Middle Passage. Careful teaching of this literary text also requires instructors to discuss with their students such topics as apologias for the eighteenth-century transatlantic slave trade, the Seven Years' War, the presence of the "talking book" in African American and Afro-British literary texts, Equiano's rigorous book tour, debates over the slave trade in the British Parliament, the role of the Judaeo-Christian religious tradition and the Bible in debates on slavery, the representations of slavery in the eighteenth-century Caribbean, and representations of Afro-British figures in eighteenth-century art. Equiano's disputed claim concerning his birth in Africa, moreover, allows the teacher-scholar to address, in the space of the classroom, the significance of archival work and the rhetorical moves found in academic argumentation.

As this listing of discussion topics clearly indicates, instructors possess the unique opportunity to place Equiano's *Narrative* in a wide variety of literary, historical, and cultural contexts. This list, on the other hand, risks embracing a reductive pedagogical coverage model that ultimately minimizes the intricacy of his text. (This is a problem that can apply to virtually any text for that matter.) Equiano's consistent interrogation of boundaries—whether racial, geographic, national, generic, or cultural—provides additional layers suitable for classroom discussion that test the stability of the text and the overall effectiveness of the pedagogical coverage model mentioned above. It is largely because of this interrogation that teachers frequently assign the *Narrative* in various pedagogical contexts and that scholars continue to revisit this multidimensional literary text by placing it in newly discovered contexts.

Equiano's *Narrative* is available in many forms suitable for classroom use. Portions from it appear in popular textbooks such as *The Longman Anthology of British Literature, The Norton Anthology of American Literature, The Heath Anthology of American Literature, The Norton Anthology of African American Literature,* Vincent Carretta's *Unchained Voices: An Anthology of Black Authors in the English-Speaking World of the Eighteenth Century,* Myra Jehlen and Michael Warner's *The English Literatures of America, 1500–1800,* Carla Mulford's *Early American Writings,* Adam Potkay and Sandra Burr's *Black Atlantic Writers of the Eighteenth Century: Living the Exodus in England and the Americas,* and Susan Castillo and Ivy Schweitzer's *The Literatures of Colonial America* (Drexler and White 19).

For instructors who prefer to analyze the autobiography more extensively, various complete versions are available: Shelly Eversley's Modern Library Classic edition, Angelo Costanzo's Broadview edition, Vincent Carretta's Penguin edition, Robert J. Allison's Bedford Series in History and Culture edition, Werner Sollors's Norton Critical edition, Paul Edwards's *Equiano's Travels* (both the 1967 edition and the 1996 edition with an introduction by S. E. Ogude), Joslyn T. Pine's Dover Thrift edition, and Henry Louis Gates Jr.'s *Classic Slave Narratives.* Dodo Press, Coffeetown Press, Barnes and Noble, NuVision Publications, Bibliolife, and Echo Library also sell affordable editions of the *Narrative,* and the Kindle edition offers more technologically savvy readers an electronic version of the text.

This sampling of anthologies and the literary marketplace underscores the current interest in and popularity of Equiano's *Narrative.* Nonetheless, assigning portions from it—or all of it—first requires teacher-scholars to confront critical questions. Why, in the first place, should we require our students to read this work as opposed to another literary, cultural, and theoretical text? How should a teacher-scholar properly contextualize and frame the *Narrative* for her or his undergraduate and graduate students? What pedagogical strategies do teacher-scholars need to employ in the classroom to make this literary text, one originally published by a former slave in London in 1789, relevant for our twenty-first century students? And, what do our contemporary students gain by immersing themselves in a work that comments upon the slave trade, the institution of slavery, and an interconnected eighteenth-century transatlantic and transnational world that at first glance appears remote from their own experiences?

Part 1 of this volume, "Foundational Discussions on Teaching *The Interesting Narrative,*" features Adam Potkay's, Srinivas Aravamudan's, and Roxann Wheeler's essays from the 2001 forum "Teaching Equiano's *Interesting Narrative,*" first published in the academic journal *Eighteenth-Century Studies.* These essays are included here for key reasons. First, they provide an essential contextual framework for readers—whether they are seasoned teacher-scholars who have taught the *Narrative* in a variety of pedagogical contexts or undergraduate or graduate students who are reading the eighteenth-century life narrative for the first time—to understand fully the teaching of Equiano's *Narrative* and the ramifications of our pedagogical decisions. These essays, moreover, serve as a springboard for the other essays in the volume, which productively complicate Potkay's, Aravamudan's, and Wheeler's arguments as well as deliberately advance the scholarly conversation on the successful teaching and reading of Equiano's text. Taken together, all of the essays included here provide the teacher-scholar with a thorough resource to adopt in a variety of undergraduate and graduate courses.

In Part 1, Potkay, Aravamudan, and Wheeler disagree on the appropriate way to frame Equiano's narrative for contemporary students and the significant contexts that helped give shape to the construction of this literary text. In his frequently cited essay "History, Oratory, and God in Equiano's *Interesting Narrative,*" Potkay argues that postcolonial readings of the narrative deliberately dismiss and obscure other, more meaningful dimensions found in the *Narrative.* Teachers of eighteenth-century British literature commit to a more responsible pedagogy, according to Potkay, when they invest time in the classroom discussing the role of oratory in the eighteenth century and Equiano's discussions of religion and religious commitment.

In the next two essays, Aravamudan and Wheeler respond to Potkay's frustrations with postcolonial readings of the *Narrative* and his proposal for a pedagogy that analyzes the intersection of eighteenth-century oratory and religion. In "Equiano Lite," Aravamudan accuses Potkay of focusing narrowly on the presence of religious conversion in the *Narrative,* and he encourages readers to find additional layers beyond ones that openly celebrate Equiano's commitment to Calvinism. Potkay's dismissal of postcolonial readings of the narrative, Aravamudan argues, results in a failure to acknowledge the extent of the political and cultural work Equiano accomplishes in the *Narrative,* the narrator's multidimensional political self, and the complexity found in Equiano's relationship to religion.

As the title of the second response, "Domesticating Equiano's *Interesting Narrative,*" indicates, Roxann Wheeler holds that Potkay's pedagogical proposal reacts too strongly to the global, transatlantic, transnational, and interdisciplinary turns found in the field of eighteenth-century studies. According to Wheeler, Potkay's push for a renewed emphasis on oratory and religion endorses a "little England" mentality that too narrowly frames the contexts relevant for twenty-first-century literary and cultural studies. Wheeler notes that teacher-scholars uncover valuable layers of seminal British literary texts, including Equiano's *Narrative,* when they teach these works not as products of an isolated island culture but as ones immersed in transatlantic, transnational, and global contexts.

Part 2 of the volume moves from the foundational essays by Potkay, Aravamudan, and Wheeler to focus on "Special Topics in Teaching *The Interesting Narrative.*" Unlike the latter parts of the volume that identify a particular field of study from which to examine the 1789 *Narrative,* Part 2 embraces the multilayered nature of the eighteenth-century literary text and provides teacher-scholars with the opportunity to engage with pedagogical proposals and ideas that do not clearly fall into the fields of African American studies or American studies. In the first essay in Part 2, Sarah Brophy discusses her interaction with her students in a cultural theory classroom as they read the narrative alongside several other literary and theoretical texts from the Enlightenment to the contemporary moment, focusing on competing conceptions of the term "culture." Brophy proposes in her "Olaudah Equiano, Autobiography, and Ideas of Culture" that this diverse grouping of texts allows instructors to focus on how the narrative embraces and simultaneously reworks ideas of culture to offer engaging discussions on Equiano's subjectivity and his relationship to capitalism.

Jessica L. Hollis's "Flat Equiano: A Transatlantic Approach to Teaching *The Interesting Narrative,*" the second essay in Part 2, interrogates the effectiveness of using spatial metaphors from the field of colonial and postcolonial studies in the classroom. Hollis argues that contemporary understandings and usages of vertical spatial metaphors from this field do not adequately reflect the dynamics and interplay of the eighteenth-century world. A more productive pedagogical approach, according to Hollis, lies in the use of a horizontal spatial metaphor that works to ensure that students understand the transatlantic exchanges found in the early Atlantic World, especially concerning the critical categories of slavery, race, and citizenship.

Tess Chakkalakal's "Finding a Home for Equiano" also outlines a specific pedagogical problem concerning the teaching of the *Narrative.* Chakkalakal's students become frustrated with Equiano's text when it departs from the typical conventions of the African American slave narrative. To remedy this dilemma, Chakkalakal invites teacher-scholars to approach the *Narrative* as a performative text that actively works to connect the writer and the reader. In particular, Chakkalakal articulates how she focuses on the representations of marriage in the *Narrative* to offer her students a more nuanced understanding of the different layers of protest against the institution of slavery found in Equiano's text.

Emily M. N. Kugler's "Loving the Unstable Text and Times of Equiano's *Narrative:* Using Carretta's Biography in the Classroom" completes Part 2 of this volume. In this essay, Kugler discusses the ways in which she incorporates Vincent Carretta's *Equiano, the African: Biography of Self-Made Man* into her classroom. This seminal text, Kugler states, offers students necessary insights into the complex debates on slavery, Equiano's representation of himself and of his African nation, the frontispiece from the 1789 first edition, and the author's formation of a unique Afro-British identity. When instructors allow students to engage with

Carretta's biography, Kugler claims, they become more invested in learning about the eighteenth-century transatlantic world, and they see a clear model in Carretta's work concerning the logistics of scholarly exchange and how one successfully enters into scholarly conversations.

Essays by Angelo Costanzo, John Saillant, Phillip M. Richards, and Cedrick May constitute Part 3 of the volume, "Pedagogy, African American Studies, and *The Interesting Narrative.*" These four established scholars reflect on their extensive experiences teaching Equiano's narrative and propose that there are additional ways to approach the *Narrative* in the African American studies classroom beyond its status as an eighteenth-century slave narrative. In Costanzo's essay, "When Young Minds Read Equiano's *Narrative,*" this veteran teacher and scholar encourages a self-reflective approach to teaching the *Narrative.* He outlines his experiences reading the *Narrative* for the first time when African American literary texts started to enter postsecondary curriculums in the early 1970s.

As Costanzo maintains, the early chapters of Equiano's narrative, in which he describes his youth in Africa, contain appropriate subject matter that engages contemporary students who seek to transition from adolescence to adulthood. Costanzo encourages instructors of Equiano, however, to move from this student engagement with the early chapters to discussions of the text's religious and abolitionist rhetoric. Although contemporary students may find the early African chapters more interesting, Costanzo submits, a responsible pedagogical approach to the *Narrative* should introduce them to the historical, religious, social, and economic layers of the eighteenth-century world that determinatively shaped Equiano's literary text.

Similar to Costanzo's argument, John Saillant, in his "'Profitable Reading': Literacy, Christianity, and Constitutionalism in Olaudah Equiano's *Interesting Narrative,*" calls for a more complex pedagogical approach to the narrative that does not focus solely on the early African chapters. For Saillant, an additional pedagogical mishap occurs when teachers of Equiano introduce and analyze the literary text as a spiritual autobiography, a slave narrative, or a text that punctuates the writer's otherness in the eighteenth century. All of these common interpretations and pedagogical approaches, Saillant maintains, overlook Equiano's placement of two petitions—one to the British Parliament and one to the Queen of England—in his *Narrative.* To position pedagogically the *Narrative* as an extended petition, according to Saillant, allows contemporary students to understand the significance of acquiring literacy in Equiano's text and in other seminal works found in the canon of African American literature. The representations of reading and writing in a number of canonical African American literary texts, Saillant states, allow for the creation of the self and arm the writer with the appropriate tools to enter into the public sphere and fight for both abolitionism and the rights of African Americans.

Throughout his "Equiano and One Canon of African American Literature," Phillip M. Richards calls for a greater understanding of the history of African American studies and African American literary criticism and theory in the contemporary literature classroom. Drawing upon Gerald Graff's pedagogy of teaching the conflicts, Richards urges teacher-scholars to introduce students to the competing responses concerning the relationship between African American literary texts and Western literary and cultural expressions. While Richards submits that some African Americanists have argued for acknowledging the uniqueness of the African American literary text and even its antagonistic relationship to Western literature and culture, he urges that readings of Equiano's *Narrative* cannot ignore how white patronage, the commodification of the African American literary text, and the incorporation of elements from popular literary and cultural texts helped give shape to the *Narrative.* These contexts, Richards proposes, provide students of African American literature with the appropriate lens through which to develop a better understanding of Equiano's place in the African American literary canon.

In his "Metaphysics of Presence in Olaudah Equiano's *Narrative,*" Cedrick May focuses on the famous "talking book" scene found in the text. As May states, instructors need to move beyond teaching this scene as one that illustrates an illiterate young African boy "speaking" to the book and holding his ear to the book and waiting for the book to "talk" back. According to May, this scene represents a crucial philosophical and theological layer in the *Narrative* in which Equiano draws upon his extended knowledge of Western classical rhetoric and Christian hermeneutics, and Equiano offers his readers a unique representation of black subjectivity and engagement with the Bible that aims to show them the incompatibility of Christianity with the institution of slavery. Additionally, May argues that this pedagogical proposal intellectually challenges all contemporary students, including the ones who do not subscribe to a particular religious tradition. As May outlines, this critical investigation provides his students, regardless of their views on religion or their experiences studying the Bible, with a more sophisticated understanding of the role religion plays in the *Narrative.*

Part 4 of the volume, "Pedagogy, American Studies, and *The Interesting Narrative,*" includes five essays that examine Equiano's narrative in this final pedagogical context. Equiano's place in anthologies such as *The Norton Anthology of American Literature* and *The Heath Anthology of American Literature* situates the *Narrative* as a significant part of the American literature survey course. In the first essay, "'Neither a Saint, a Hero, Nor a Tyrant': Teaching Equiano Comparatively," Keri Holt reflects on how she places the narrative alongside Benjamin Franklin's *Autobiography,* another staple of the American literature survey course. This careful and in-depth comparative approach concentrates on the key elements that surface in these writers' texts: the significance of hard work or industry, the rags-to-riches narrative, invocations of Christianity, the language of commerce, and participation in the public sphere, among others. Holt proposes that when these texts are analyzed alongside one another, we productively complicate our students' understanding of the representation of identities in early American literature, and they gain a more nuanced understanding of the difficulties that New World Africans faced in negotiating the dynamics of the early Atlantic World.

Michael Pringle's "Equiano's *Interesting Narrative* and the Difficulties of Teaching the Early American Literature Survey Course" provides insight on the interdisciplinary interplay between the fields of literary studies and history in his classroom. According to Pringle, the authenticity debate over Equiano's African origins—the question of whether or not the writer was born in Africa, as he states in the *Narrative,* or in South Carolina, according to Vincent Carretta's discovery of ship logs and a baptismal record—provides instructors with the perfect opportunity to interrogate the disciplinary boundaries of "literature" and "history." Pringle finds that his classroom discussions on Equiano's African origins helpfully push his students to struggle over the limitations of approaching the eighteenth-century literary text as either a "historical" or "fictional" text. The result of this analysis, as Pringle states, allows his students to discover the interplay of "fiction" and the social and political work found in Equiano's *Narrative* and teaches them to understand the implications of establishing rigid disciplinary boundaries in an early American literature course.

Unlike Pringle, who values the authenticity debate in the undergraduate American literature survey course, Lisa M. Logan holds in her "The Difference Teaching Equiano Makes: Notes on Teaching *The Interesting Narrative* in the Undergraduate American Literature Survey" that the debate over Equiano's African origins encourages her students to approach the narrative in a reductive way. In

Logan's estimation, students who wish only to understand the "truth" concerning Equiano's African origins fail to attend to how the multiple layers of the text—the frontispiece to the 1789 edition, the dedication page, the writer's extensive transatlantic travels, and the symbol of the ship, among others—actively work to dismantle national, generic, and disciplinary boundaries. Attending more fully to Equiano's embrace of difference and the reasons behind his consistent interrogation of binary logic throughout his text, Logan maintains, counters discussions that only focus on the authenticity debate.

While most of the essays in the volume focus on the place of the narrative in a specific course that mainly privileges literature, Abby Chandler's "Captives, Slaves, and Writers: Teaching *The Narrative* of Olaudah Equiano as Captivity Narrative" describes this instructor's use of the narrative in a specific sequence from an American history course. Chandler assigns her students sections from the *Narrative* because the text effectively bridges cultural events and literary texts found in the seventeenth, eighteenth, and nineteenth centuries. Placing the *Narrative* alongside captivity narratives of the New England Puritans allows students to grasp the conventions of this popular colonial genre, readers' interest in encountering the other, representations of gender in the United States and the early Atlantic World, and the deliberate goals of the authors and editors who contributed to this genre of literature. The impressive flexibility of the *Narrative,* according to Chandler, lies in the teacher's ability to use the text as one that also guides students in understanding the differences between colonial slavery and nineteenth-century slavery in the United States, the agency of Africans and African Americans in dismantling the institution of slavery before the nineteenth-century abolitionist movement, and the ways in which Equiano's literary text anticipates several of the conventions found in the African American slave narrative.

My essay, "Transatlantic Transformations: Olaudah Equiano's *Narrative* and Caryl Phillips's *Cambridge,*" the final piece in Part 4, offers an investigation of the transatlantic and transnational dimensions of the *Narrative* in the American studies classroom. I discuss a pedagogical proposal that outlines the ways in which Caryl Phillips, a contemporary Afro-British and Caribbean author, rewrites the eighteenth-century narrative in his 1991 novel, *Cambridge.* Analyzing Equiano's *Narrative* alongside Phillips's *Cambridge* allows instructors to move beyond the geographical parameters of the United States to discuss the role that Africans played in dismantling the slave trade and representations of slavery in the Caribbean. Furthermore, this comparative analysis invites students to investigate how several key elements from Phillips's contemporary text critique the logic in the *Narrative* and continue to shape our understanding of the eighteenth-century narrative.

Even though the contributors to this volume address the teaching and critical reading of the *Narrative* in the fields of eighteenth-century studies, postcolonial and colonial studies, African American studies, and American studies, it should be noted here that in collecting these essays I do not suggest that this project exhausts the ways that scholars currently teach the *Narrative.* Further reflections on the teaching of the narrative in the canons of African literature, early Anglophone Caribbean literature, and early black British literature stand as necessary projects that would continue to improve our understanding of how instructors successfully teach this literary text in the contemporary classroom.

Teaching Olaudah Equiano's Narrative assists teacher-scholars in constructing relevant, purposeful, and educational experiences for their students when they collectively explore the contents of the 1789 narrative. I hope that this volume both encourages teachers of Equiano to develop meaningful pedagogical strategies for teaching this text in historical, literary, cultural, intellectual, and pedagogical contexts that are not outlined in this volume and further motivates them to continue to construct educational moments that make this seminal eighteenth-century text relevant for our contemporary students.

Notes

1. The significant exceptions are three essays in an *Eighteenth-Century Studies* forum on "Teaching Equiano's *Interesting Narrative*"; Sarah Brophy's "Olaudah Equiano and the Concept of Culture," included in *Teaching Life Writing Texts*; and two essays found in Michael J. Drexler and Ed White's *Beyond Douglass: New Perspectives on Early African-American Literature.*

2. The contributions of Amy E. Winans, Pattie Cowell, David S. Shields, and Gregory Eiselein in Carla Mulford's volume, *Teaching the Literatures of Early America,* are good examples of essays that only briefly mention the teaching of Equiano in a larger comparative project.

Similarly, Michael W. Young's "The Many Voices of Creation: Early American and Canadian Travel Writing" and Gary Totten's "Teaching Travel Writing as

Life Writing" touch upon the teaching of Equiano's *Narrative,* but both of these chapters from Miriam Fuchs and Craig Howes's book, *Teaching Life Writing Texts,* leave the reader with more questions than answers. For instance, several parts from Equiano's *Narrative*—the writer's disputed representation of himself as an African, the calculated presentation of his Eboe nation, and the discussions of multiracial equality between different cultures in the Americas and Europe—fit perfectly into Young's stated pedagogical goal: exploring representations of self and nation in early America. However, Young does not explore these dimensions of the *Narrative* in his essay but only mentions that *The Norton Anthology of American Literature* includes portions from Equiano's eighteenth-century literary text (199). And, despite Totten's nod to the "transcultural negotiation of identity" (54) found in the *Narrative* and his repeated use of the terms "American" (53, 54, 56) and "United States" (54, 56, 57), he does not address how or if he teaches the extensive parts of the *Narrative* that comment on cultures and peoples outside of the United States. Another limitation found in Totten's article appears when readers discover that he never quotes from the *Narrative* in his essay, thereby making it difficult for other teacher-scholars to identify, in their own primary texts, where this author sees discussions of Equiano's transcultural identity appear in the narrative.

In this same book, Sarah Brophy offers a rare concentrated discussion on teaching the narrative in her "Olaudah Equiano and the Concept of Culture." In this valuable essay, Brophy addresses how she pedagogically approaches the text in an undergraduate cultural studies course and an undergraduate American literature survey. Brophy, as I explain above, attends more fully to the theoretical underpinnings of her pedagogy when she teaches the *Narrative* in her contribution to this book.

Another recently published text that references the teaching of Equiano's *Narrative* appears in the introductory essay, "Canon Loading," in Michael J. Drexler and Ed White's coedited volume, *Beyond Douglass: New Perspectives on Early African-American Literature.* Drexler and White offer more instructive commentary on teaching Equiano in this essay than the ones found in the two books referenced above. They outline the problems that surface when instructors focus solely on the "two poles of origin and fulfillment, foundation and capstone" (1) in early African American literature. Drexler and White point out that concentrating solely on the works of Phillis Wheatley, Olaudah Equiano, Frederick Douglass, and Harriet Jacobs results in the deliberate ignoring of the "consistent constellation of secondary figures" (1) in the early African American literary canon and "privileg[es] representative extremes over nuanced complications" (2) found in this same literary canon. Readers of this essay would benefit from an in-depth discussion on the pedagogical strategies these teacher-scholars use to prevent their students from falling into the critical trap of perpetuating the troubling generalizations Drexler and White caution their readers to avoid. Nevertheless, the contributions to this volume embrace the editors' argument for understanding Equiano in more complicated ways and seek to meet their challenge to offer teacher-scholars different ways to teach the eighteenth-century narrative that move beyond the positioning of Equiano as either "generic eyewitness" (12) or "idiosyncratic speaker" (12) in the classroom.

Finally, Drexler and White include Vincent Carretta's essay "Early African American Literature?" in their book. Like Brophy's essay in *Teaching Life Writing Texts,* Carretta's contribution to *Beyond Douglass* is a rare, concentrated treatment of the successful teaching of Equiano. In this essay, Carretta uses the genre of autobiography to reflect on his first encounters with the *Narrative,* the often frustrating exchanges with some Americanists who firmly position the text in the canons of American and African American literatures, and the discovery of the significant documents suggesting that Equiano was likely born in South Carolina. Carretta proposes that the incorporation of a transatlantic and transnational pedagogical approach more fully prepares our students to understand the complexities found in the early Atlantic World. In light of this proposition, several essays in this volume extend Carretta's call for a transatlantic and transnational approach to the teaching of Equiano and mirror the way in which he usefully blends textual evidence, references to relevant scholarship, original argumentation, and reflections on the implications of his arguments in his writing about the teaching of Equiano.

Works Cited

Allison, Robert J., ed. *The Interesting Narrative of the Life of Olaudah Equiano, Written by Himself.* Boston: Bedford/St. Martin's, 1995.

Baym, Nina, gen. ed. *The Norton Anthology of American Literature.* 6th ed. New York: Norton, 2003.

Carretta, Vincent. "Early African American Literature?" *Beyond Douglass: New Perspectives on Early African-American Literature.* Ed. Michael J. Drexler and Ed White. Lewisburg, PA: Bucknell UP, 2008. 91–106.

———. *Equiano, the African: Biography of a Self-Made Man.* Athens: U of Georgia P, 2005.

———, ed. The Interesting Narrative *and Other Writings.* Rev. ed. New York: Penguin, 2003.

———, ed. *Unchained Voices: An Anthology of Black Authors in the English-Speaking World of the Eighteenth Century.* Lexington: U of Kentucky P, 1996.

Castillo, Susan, and Ivy Schweitzer, eds. *The Literatures of Colonial America.* Malden, MA: Blackwell, 2001.

Costanzo, Angelo, ed. *The Interesting Narrative of Olaudah Equiano, or Gustavus Vassa, the African. Written by Himself.* Peterborough, Ont.: Broadview, 2001.

Cowell, Pattie. "Figuring Multicultural Practice in Early American Literature Classrooms." *Teaching the Literatures of Early America.* Ed. Carla Mulford. New York: MLA, 1999. 63–74.

Damrosch, David, and Kevin J. H. Dettmar, eds. *The Longman Anthology of British Literature.* 3rd ed. New York: Pearson, 2006.

Drexler, Michael J., and Ed White. "Canon Loading." *Beyond Douglass: New Perspectives on Early African-American Literature.* Ed. Michael J. Drexler and Ed White. Lewisburg, PA: Bucknell UP, 2008. 1–19.

Edwards, Paul, ed. *Equiano's Travels.* Portsmouth, NH: Heinemann, 1967.

———, ed. *Equiano's Travels.* African Writers Ser. Portsmouth, NH: Heinemann, 1996.

Eiselein, Gregory. "American Self-Fashioning and the Problems of Autobiography." *Teaching the Literatures of Early America.* Ed. Carla Mulford. New York: MLA, 1999. 229–42.

Eversley, Shelly, ed. *The Interesting Narrative of Olaudah Equiano, or Gustavus Vassa, the African. Written by Himself.* New York: Modern Library, 2004.

Gates, Henry Louis, Jr., ed. *The Classic Slave Narratives.* New York: Signet, 2002.

Jehlen, Myra, and Michael Warner, eds. *The English Literatures of America, 1500–1800.* New York: Routledge, 1997.

Lauter, Paul, ed. *The Heath Anthology of American Literature.* 5th ed. Boston: Houghton, 2006.

McKay, Nellie, and Henry Louis Gates Jr., gen. eds. *The Norton Anthology of African American Literature.* 2nd ed. New York: Norton, 2004.

Mulford, Carla, ed. *Early American Writings.* New York: Oxford UP, 2002.

Pine, Joslyn T., ed. *The Interesting Narrative of Olaudah Equiano, or Gustavus Vassa, the African. Written by Himself.* New York: Dover, 1999.

Potkay, Adam, and Sandra Burr, eds. *Black Atlantic Writers of the Eighteenth Century: Living the New Exodus in England and the Americas.* New York: St. Martin's, 1995.

Shields, David S. "The Literature of England's Staple Colonies." *Teaching the Literatures of Early America.* Ed. Carla Mulford. New York: MLA, 1999. 129–42.

Sollors, Werner, ed. *The Interesting Narrative of Olaudah Equiano, or Gustavus Vassa, the African, Written by Himself.* New York: Norton, 2001.

Totten, Gary. "Teaching Travel Writing as Life Writing." *Teaching Life Writing Texts.* Ed. Miriam Fuchs and Craig Howes. New York: MLA, 2008. 53–58.

Winans, Amy E. "Diversity and Difference in African American Writings." *Teaching the Literatures of Early America.* Ed. Carla Mulford. New York: MLA, 1999. 27–47.

Young, Michael W. "The Many Voices of Creation: Early American and Canadian Life Writing." *Teaching Life Writing Texts.* Ed. Miriam Fuchs and Craig Howes. New York: MLA, 2008. 195–200.

Part 1

Foundational Discussions on Teaching *The Interesting Narrative*

History, Oratory, and God in Equiano's *Interesting Narrative*

Adam Potkay

Increasingly, college students are coming into contact with at least parts of the work generally recognized as the capstone of eighteenth-century black writing—*The Interesting Narrative of the Life of Olaudah Equiano, or Gustavus Vassa, the African. Written by Himself.* In doing so, they are rediscovering a work that once was very widely read. First published in London in 1789, *The Interesting Narrative* was in Equiano's lifetime—he died in 1797—something of a "best-seller," enjoying a host of British editions that made its author a wealthy man, as well as American, Dutch, German, and Russian piracies that attested to its international cachet. The book remained in print until the end of the 1830s.[1] After that, *The Interesting Narrative* was not reprinted in English, in its entirety, until 1969, when Paul Edwards published his two-volume facsimile of the first edition, with a magisterial introduction and extensively researched notes.[2] Yet it was Henry Louis Gates's 1987 paperback edition, *The Classic Slave Narratives,* which first made Equiano's narrative widely available. Since then, six more editions of or including Equiano have appeared, all of them at student-friendly prices.[3] During the twelve-year period 1987–1999, excerpts of Equiano's *Narrative* have also been added to the textbook anthologies of English, American, and African American literature produced by Norton, Heath, Longman, and Blackwell.

Since we know that Equiano's *Interesting Narrative* is being taught, we may take this opportunity to ask: how do we teach it? What are, or might be, aspects of its classroom value to teachers in the fields of eighteenth-century British and American literature and history, African and African-American literature and history? With these concerns in mind, I offer a survey of the ways in which scholars and critics have written about Equiano over the past twenty years. The scholarly and critical literature is animated, I find, by three fundamental questions or points of contention. First, to what degree are historical and literary approaches to Equiano compatible? Conversely, to what extent are they at odds? Second, if we approach Equiano as primarily a literary text—and there are, I will suggest, good reasons for doing so—what precisely is "literary" about it? To borrow the title of a recent conference panel, what constitutes "the category of 'literature' in literary study today"?[4] Third and last, what is the relationship between literature, as we now conceive it, and religion—in Equiano's case, the Calvinist Methodism he accepted and sought to promulgate?

In framing and pursuing each of these three questions, I will test the limits of poststructuralist and especially of postcolonial (or "post/colonial") theory against *The Interesting Narrative.*[5] I will argue that Equiano's narrative supposes as a condition of its intelligibility a world very different from, and in many ways antagonistic to, the world inhabited by many of his recent critics: his is a Christian, an oratorical, even a colonial world. Postcolonial critics are apt to read back into the language of those colonized or displaced by empire signs of creolization, parodic subversion, or "talking back"—in Equiano's case, however, those signs are faint and all too easily exaggerated by those who, programmatically, seek them out.

The Competing Claims of Literature and History

Teachers of social and political history typically rely on documentary sources, autobiographies or memoirs among them, that are presumed to have "veridicality," or truth to fact.[6] Autobiography is a literary genre, of course, but it is one from which even literature professors are apt to crave veridicality. Though wont to remark upon autobiography's rhetorical aims and representational selectivity, most literature professors still value the genre's relation to "what's really out there." Teachers, as well as their students, will assume prima facie that an autobiography, however artful, is more mirror than lamp.

The claim for Equiano's *Interesting Narrative* as a reliable documentary source was eloquently made by Keith Sandiford, a pioneer in the literary study of, to quote the subtitle of his 1988 book, "eighteenth-century Afro-English writing." Sandiford writes, "Throughout the narrative, [Equiano] makes a conscious effort to delineate the principal incidents and experiences of his life as faithfully as memory would allow and to appraise his conduct with honest judgment and sober reflection. The result is a document both thoroughgoing and credible" (119).[7]

This is how Equiano begins his thoroughgoing and credible narrative—from Chapter 1:

> That part of Africa, known by the name of Guinea, to which the trade of slaves is carried on, extends along the coast above 3400 miles, from Senegal to Angola, and includes a variety of kingdoms. Of these the most considerable is the kingdom of Benin. . . . This kingdom is divided into many provinces or districts: in one of the most remote and fertile of which, I was born, in the year 1745, in a charming fruitful vale, named Essaka. (32)[8]

It may be noted here that Equiano does not always transcribe his sources very exactly. Equiano's authority in calculating the extent of the Guinea coast is Anthony Benezet, who had written that "the coast [extends] for three or four thousand miles"; Equiano conflates "three or four thousand" into "3400" (Potkay and Burr 251n1). Such are the frailties to which the pen is heir. Slips of this sort scarcely effect our general sense of Equiano's credibility.

As Equiano continues his description of life in Essaka, we find him no less credible because certain of his "sober reflections" now appear dated. For example, we think no less of his veracity for being unable to accept his Biblicist claim that the Igbo people derive from Abraham and Keturah, and so share a common ancestral root with the post-exilic Jews (Potkay and Burr 255n31).[9] We easily accept the weathering of opinions.

But recent scholarship has thrown into question more substantial portions of Equiano's account of his life, whittling away at the notion that Equiano made, in Sandiford's phrase, "a conscious effort to delineate the principal incidents and experiences of his life as faithfully as memory would allow." Some of the factual slips of his *Narrative* might be due to mistaken memory: for example, although he could not, as he claims, have seen the Methodist preacher George Whitefield in Philadelphia early in 1766—in point of fact, Whitefield was in England between July 1765 and September 1768—Equiano may have seen Whitefield preach on some other occasion.[10] Or perhaps he encountered Whitefield only in the pages of earlier black autobiographies: the man figures as a pivotal spiritual presence in the recorded lives of both Ukawsaw Gronniosaw (1772) and John Marrant (1785).[11] Should Equiano's encounter with Whitefield prove solely a textual one, we might still credit his assessment of the man and his influence, but with the recognition that the truths at which *The Interesting Narrative* aim are, at least in this instance, of a different order than that of factual record.

The question of whether or not Equiano saw Whitefield at a particular time or place may seem a minor matter. But consider this: what if Equiano were a native not of Africa but of South Carolina? What if his account of Igbo life in Essaka were an imaginative blend of the travel writings of Anthony Benezet and John Matthews along with the African oral history he may have heard as a boy? These possibilities are raised by Vincent Carretta in a recent article. Through archival research, Professor Carretta has discovered significant (though not conclusive) evidence that Equiano was indeed a native of South Carolina. The parish register of St. Margaret's Church, Westminster, records the baptism on February 9, 1759, of "Gustavus Vassa a Black born in Carolina 12 years old"; fourteen years later, South Carolina is given as Vassa's birthplace in the muster book of a ship on which Equiano is known to have served (Carretta, "Olaudah"). The very name "Olaudah Equiano" may have been assumed, rather than revealed, by a man who, as far as the record goes, was known up until the publication of his autobiography exclusively as Gustavus Vassa, and thought to be from the colonies, even by several contemporary reviewers of *The Interesting Narrative.*

Carretta's recent findings provide a further stumbling block for the already shaky historical-biographical reconstruction of Equiano's Igbo life undertaken by the Nigerian scholar Catherine Obianuju Acholonu, who surmised that Equiano was an ancestor of the Ekwealuo family of the village Isseke, Ihiala Local Government Area, Anambra State, Nigeria.[12] And yet, for literary critics and cultural historians of a certain stripe, the question of Equiano's origins or real identity will not matter at all. In some circles, "the author" has been dead for some time now. According to this line of reasoning, the interesting thing about *The Interesting Narrative* is its role in the cultural archive, its fusion at a more or less critical juncture of several available, interrelated discourses or historical "languages"—those of race, evangelicalism, abolitionism, travel, and political economy. An emphasis on *langue* over *parole,* structure over event, has enchanted Anglo-American scholarship since Thomas Kuhn's discrete "paradigms" of scientific research and the importation of Foucault's "archaeology" of discursive formations; the study of structuring languages attained full respectability with J. G. A. Pocock's influential "history of discourse." Within these *modi operandi,* the conscientious professor analyzes the warp and woof of "language" or "languages" in the text at hand, situating them in relation to shifting discursive paradigms. Foucauldians may also assess a discourse in terms of its complicity with or, if such is deemed possible, its contestation of power. These fundamentally poststructuralist approaches lie, it seems to me, at the heart of literary and historical interdisciplinarity as many have come to practice it in the past twenty years.

Yet few of us can really or finally transcend the customary world of authors and concrete events—especially when it comes to autobiography. Most historians, for all their demurrals, like professedly factual accounts to be factual, and most literary critics, for all their demurrals, like to attribute imaginative accounts to an orchestrating intelligence. Thus, Equiano's possible fabrication of his African past strikes me as a problem for which both literary critics and professional historians are likely to seek solutions.

The literary solution, to which I am inclined by disposition as well as by training, is simply this: whether or not Equiano is from Africa is beside the point because *The Interesting Narrative* is far less significant as a factual account of one man's life than as a rhetorical performance of considerable skill. Its purpose is to rouse an audience to a specific course of action. Equiano prefaced his *Narrative* with a petition to Parliament that makes his rhetorical aim perfectly clear: "Permit me with the greatest deference and respect to lay at your feet the following genuine Narrative; the chief design of which is to excite in your august assemblies a sense of compassion for the miseries which the Slave Trade has entailed on my unfortunate countrymen" (7). Autobiographical narrative is here expressly yoked to the purpose of persuasion. It is also, in the introductory paragraph of *The Interesting Narrative,* yoked to God's overarching plan for the universe and its creatures: "I regard myself," writes Equiano, "as a *particular favourite of Heaven,* and acknowledge the mercies of Providence in every occurrence of my life." And yet even this invocation of Providence serves, in part, to persuade his 1789 readers of the ills of the slave trade, as Equiano explains that he feels himself a "favorite of Heaven" only "when I compare my lot with that of most of my countrymen" (31).

The *narrative* portion of Equiano's life is indeed just one strand of the work titled *The Interesting Narrative,* for in his book Equiano employs a welter of persuasive modes—apologia, allegory, sermon, exhortation, jeremiad, and argument directed to economic self-interest—all aimed at the immediate political end of abolishing the slave trade and toward the ultimate end of abolishing slavery and ushering in a truly Christian and staunchly commercial millennium. William L. Andrews, in his classic study *To Tell a Free Story* (1986), rightly calls *The Interesting Narrative* "an oratorical autobiography whose vocation was as much the creation of an implied reader as the education of the narrator" (57). Knowing that Equiano may have doctored the account of his life to further his avowed rhetorical purposes does no more than make us shift the emphasis of "oratorical autobiography" to "semi-autobiographical oration" or "oration using autobiographical elements."

As such, it corresponds to the oration that classically educated eighteenth-century readers most admired—Demosthenes's *On the Crown.* To gage how highly Demosthenes's rhetorical art was esteemed, consider the public judgment of David Hume: Demosthenes's manner

> is rapid harmony, exactly adjusted to the sense: It is vehement reasoning, without any appearance of art: It is disdain, anger, boldness, freedom, involved in a continued stream of argument: And of all human productions, the orations of DEMOSTHENES present to us the models, which approach the nearest to perfection. (106)[13]

The scope of this verdict is simply stunning, and no less stunning for concerning an art that is generally underrated in our times. That oratory plays but a minor role in the category of "literature" today should lead us to ask: what have we lost?

The Category of "Literature" in Literary Studies Today

During the long eighteenth century, with the revival of classical republicanism and the popularity of Longinus's treatise on the sublime, oratory became the most celebrated of the literary genres. Its praises are sung from Fenelon to Voltaire, from Hume to John Quincy Adams. Great orations, Greek to contemporary, were widely disseminated through popular anthologies such as *The Forum Orator* (Boston, 1804) and the book which Frederick Douglass presents as pivotal in his own life, *The Columbian Orator* (Boston, 1797), which went through several editions and dozens of printings in the American antebellum period. In 1807 Lord Byron, the man destined to become the age's most celebrated poet, declared that in all things "the *Poet* yields to the *orator*" (27).[14]

Yet in the course of the nineteenth century it was oratory that yielded to poetry, particularly in the classroom and among cultivated readers. As M. H. Abrams argued so effectively in *The Mirror and the Lamp* (1953), Romantic literary theory dissociated the good poem from rhetorical or persuasive ends, seeing it instead as either an expression of its author's personality, or as a heterocosm, a self-sufficient entity constituted by its parts in their internal relations. "The still, sad music of humanity" does not try to convince us of anything; it is not there to persuade us; it stands, rather, as either an insight into its author or as a formal element of an autonomous poem.

This view of literature, based as it is upon Romantic and New Critical models of reading poetry, will now probably strike most professors as utterly unjust, not to mention antiquated and exploded. Allow me here to limit my remarks to the field of eighteenth-century British literature, as the immediate context of Equiano's *Interesting Narrative.* Eighteenth-century British literature classes have traditionally asked students to cultivate some appreciation for a wide variety of literary genres, most of them suasive, some argumentative, a few downright homiletic. The classic Tillotson/Fussell/Waingrow anthology, *Eighteenth-Century English Literature* (1969), includes as "literature" Latitudinarian Anglican sermons, "a serious call to a devout and holy life," moral philosophy, the modern philosophy of religion, and an historical analysis of the interconnections of Christian rise and Roman decline. While much of this religious and philosophical literature has (unfortunately) been jettisoned from literature syllabi in more recent years, the attendant definition of "literature" has not necessarily shrunk. Professors committed to the idea that analyzing gender, class, and race in texts of the past will serve the ends of social justice in the present have ushered into the classroom a plethora of new generic and subgeneric interests—in women's romances and novels, women's verse, working-class ballads, pamphlets, and bottom-up ephemera of all sorts. Perhaps most notable has been the renewed interest in travel writings, especially when the travels take white men or women into some "torrid zone."[15] Equiano himself has been examined by Geraldine Murphy, in her "Olaudah Equiano, Accidental Tourist," as a travel writer, one who employs the ethnographic or "imperial gaze" of the white traveler for his own self-legitimating and at least partially "dissident" ends.

Yet even Murphy's postcolonial analysis of Equiano as a travel writer is built on assumptions about his *rhetorical* ends. Travel writing, then, becomes but one more persuasive mode within Equiano's varied oratorical performance. Accordingly, might not the study of Equiano benefit from the study of other oratorical or polemical writings? I personally hope that the category of "literature" in literary studies today might come to encompass a renewed appreciation of oratory or oratorical norms.[16] Equiano's work might then be set alongside other late eighteenth-century oratorical or semi-oratorical masterpieces of "savage indignation," such as Jefferson's original draft of the Declaration of Independence, selected Parliamentary speeches of Pitt and Sheridan, Burke's *Reflections on the Revolution in France,* and the oration that so impressed Frederick Douglass, Arthur O'Connor's 1795 speech on Catholic Emancipation.[17] Indignation is what eighteenth-century readers most admired in oratory: Hume admired Demosthenes's "freedom, anger, disdain," and his friend Adam Smith got to the heart of the matter in his lectures on rhetoric and belles-lettres: "The passion which animates . . . [Demosthenes] in all his orations is Indignation" (194).

Equiano is another orator apt to "raise our Indignation"—at least, this is how he has been read, and presumably been taught, by William Andrews and those who have studied *To Tell a Free Story.* According to Andrews, "Equiano's reader is obliged to undergo a de-culturation process through which he divests himself of his insider's cultural myopia and accepts the complimentary value of the outsider's perspective" (57). For examples of this "de-culturation process," Andrews turns to Equiano's most rhetorical, sentimental, even homiletic passages. This is from Chapter 2 of *The Interesting Narrative:*

> I remember in the vessel in which I was brought over, in the men's apartment, there were several brothers who, in the sale, were sold in different lots; and it was very moving on this occasion to see and hear their cries at parting. O, ye nominal Christians! might not an African ask you, learned you this from your God? who says unto you, Do unto all men as you would men should do unto you? Is it not enough that we are torn from our country and friends to toil for your luxury and lust of gain? Must every tender feeling likewise be sacrificed to your avarice? Are the dearest friends and relations, now rendered more dear by their separation from their kindred, still to be parted from each other, and thus prevented from cheering the gloom of slavery with the small comfort of being together and mingling their sufferings and sorrows? Why are parents to lose their children, brothers their sisters, or husbands their wives? Surely this is a new refinement in cruelty, which, while it has no advantage to atone for it,

> thus aggravates distress, and adds fresh horrors even to the wretchedness of slavery. (61)

"O, ye nominal Christians!": Equiano here employs Whitefield's favorite stricture, which in turn harkens back to Jesus's denunciations of "scribes and pharisees, hypocrites!" and to the woes Isaiah prophesied for the "rebellious children" of Israel. Behind all of these lies the promise of divine vengeance. In this context, the question "might not an African ask you, learned you this from your God" signals not so much the perspective of a cultural outsider as a confirmation that the Christian universe knows no outside; it is all inclusive, and is itself the surety of eventual justice.

Here is another example of what Andrews calls Equiano's strategy of "deculturation," but what I would call oratorical indignation, learned from the best classical models:

> The small account in which the life of a negro is held in the West Indies is so universally known, that it might seem impertinent to quote the following extract, if some people had not been hardy enough of late to assert that negroes are on the same footing in that respect as Europeans. By the 329th Act, page 125, of the Assembly of Barbadoes, it is enacted, "That if any negro, or other slave, under punishment by his master, or his order, for running away, or any other crime or misdemeanor towards his said master, unfortunately shall suffer in life or member, no person whatsoever shall be liable to a fine; but if any man shall out of *wantonness, or only of bloody-mindedness, or cruel intention, willfully kill a negro, or other slave, of his own, he shall pay into the public treasury fifteen pounds sterling.*" And it is the same in most, if not all, of the West India islands. Is not this one of the many acts of the islands which call loudly for redress? And do not the assembly which enacted it, deserve the appellation of savages and brutes rather than of Christians and men? It is an act at once unmerciful, unjust and unwise; which for cruelty would disgrace an assembly of those who are called barbarians; and for its injustice and *insanity* would shock the morality and common sense of a Samaide or a Hottentot. (109)[18]

Compare to this Cicero's celebrated invocation of the crucifixion of a Roman citizen:

> Should I paint the horrors of this scene, not to Roman citizens, not to the allies of our state, not to those who have even heard of the Roman name, not even to men, but to brute-creatures; or, to go farther, should I lift up my voice in the most desolate solitude, to the rocks and mountains, yet should I surely see those rude and inanimate parts of nature moved with horror and indignation at the recital of so enormous an action. (Cicero, *Against Verres* 2.5.67; in Hume "Of Eloquence" 100–101)

It will, of course, prove easier for our students to identify with the anger of Equiano than with the indignation of Cicero—Equiano is, in certain ways, our contemporary. The wounds inflicted by chattel slavery and unjust racial laws have still not altogether healed. Indeed, the danger in teaching Equiano's rhetoric is that it may feed into an indignation *with* the past that our own age all too often self-righteously demands. As John Ernest has remarked, the problem with teaching slave narratives in general is the lure of "easy knowledge": that is, students may find in them no more than an opportunity to reaffirm their ethical self-images and to neglect in their moral outrage the type of things that we as teachers like to teach them—the nuances of historical context, the artistry of an author's presentation.[19] Students are automatically indignant that the past did not know what they do; to offset this, they need to be taught to appreciate the art of indignation *in* the past.

Otherwise, students are likely at some point to feel indignant not with, but at, Equiano. After his manumission Equiano, voluntarily and for profit, serves as a slave purchaser and overseer for Dr. Irving's central American plantation. And, turning from race to gender, Equiano is culpable of "patriarchal" comments. The following one occurs within his description of being transported, as a slave, from Essaka to the Guinea coast:

> All the nations and people I had hitherto passed through resembled our own in their manners, customs and language: but I came at length to a country, the inhabitants of which differed from us in all those particulars. I was very much struck with this difference, especially when I came among a people who did not circumcise, and eat without washing their hands. . . . Their women were not so modest as ours, for they eat, and drank, and slept with their men. (53–54)

Similarly, when Equiano arrives in England he

> was greatly amazed at their not sacrificing, or making any offerings, and at their eating with unwashen hands, and touching the dead. I also could not help remarking the particular slenderness of their women, which I did not at first like, and I thought them not so modest and shamefaced as the African women. (68)

What we need to recognize about these sentiments, however, is that they are not simply "patriarchal" in our contemporary, pejorative sense, but that Equiano offers them, quite literally, as Patriarchal sentiments. "I cannot forebear suggesting," Equiano remarks,

> the strong analogy, which . . . appears to prevail in the manners and customs of my countrymen, and those of the Jews, before they reached the Land of Promise, and particularly the patriarchs, while they were yet in that pastoral state which is described in Genesis—an analogy, which alone would induce me to think that the one people had sprung from the other. (43–44)

Religion: The Forbidden Topic

Equiano begins his life's journey among the Patriarchs, then finds himself enslaved in a strange land, and is finally liberated not only from literal captivity but, through grace, from the bondage of sin. In short, Equiano claims not only to have reenacted in his life the basic narrative pattern of the biblical books of Genesis and Exodus (itself an extraordinary and, as far as I know, an unprecedented claim), but also to have learned, through his Christian conversion or rebirth, to read Israelite history along with his own experience as an allegory of spiritual deliverance. As I have argued elsewhere, biblical hermeneutics provide the very framework for the narrative portions of *The Interesting Narrative.*[20] Since the gospel writers first presented Jesus as a new and greater Moses, Christian salvation has routinely been allegorized as freedom from Egyptian captivity. As George Whitefield put it,

> Let us consider ourselves . . . as persons traveling to a long eternity; as rescued by the free grace of God, in some measure, from our Egyptian bondage, and marching under the conduct of our spiritual Joshua, through the wilderness of this world, to the land of our heavenly Canaan. (111)

In *The Interesting Narrative,* Equiano recounts, tropologically, the freeing of his soul from the symbolic Egypt of carnality. As he elaborates at great length in Chapter 10,

> It was given me at that time to know what it was to be born again, John iii. 5. . . . When I considered my poor wretched state, I wept, seeing what a great debtor I was to sovereign free grace. Now the Ethiopian was willing to be saved by Jesus Christ, the sinner's only surety, and also to rely on none other person or thing for salvation. (190)

Yet Equiano's faith and the biblical pattern of his narrative are the elements of *The Interesting Narrative* most likely to be misunderstood or simply ignored by scholars of the past twenty years. Angelo Costanzo's 1987 study proves an exception, and Keith Sandiford's 1988 study a partial exception, to the rule of not taking Equiano's Christian commitments all too seriously. It is significant, however, that both of these works, though published in the 1980s, were based on Ph.D. dissertations completed in the 1970s.[21] Houston Baker's influential *Blues, Ideology, and Afro-American Literature: A Vernacular Theory,* published in 1984 by the University of Chicago Press, set the study of Equiano on a new and wholly secular direction. For Baker, "The *Life of Olaudah Equiano* can be ideologically considered as a work whose protagonist masters the rudiments of economics that condition his very life" (33). "[T]he narrator," Baker argues,

> having been reduced to property by a commercial deportation, decides during his West Indian captivity that neither sentiment nor spiritual sympathies can earn his liberation. He realizes, in effect, that only the acquisition of property will enable him to alter his designated status *as property.* (35)[22]

Four years after the appearance of Baker's book, Henry Louis Gates Jr. published *The Signifying Monkey,* a work concerned more with the literary than the economic self-possession of black writers, but equally uninterested in their Christian claims. Gates grounds the origin of a distinctly African-English literary tradition in "The Trope of the Talking Book," a scene of encounter between illiterate slave and unspeaking book that Paul Edwards had earlier traced back, through Equiano, to the 1772 narrative of Ukawsaw Gronniosaw.[23] Yet what Gates does not specify is that, in context, the book that won't speak to the young slave is not just any book, but rather the Bible, the book that explains what the black writer's former self wants to know—how all things came into being. The young Equiano, like the young Gronniosaw before him, would talk to books "to learn how all things had a beginning"; as mature authors, both men situate their early curiosity into origins as the first crucial step towards "worshipping God, who made us and all things" (Equiano 67–68).[24]

It was my desire to supply forgotten or neglected eighteenth-century contexts, especially religious ones, that led me first to write on Equiano, and then to edit, with my student Sandra Burr, a collection of eighteenth-century black writers. Indeed, I had planned to title our edition "Black Anglican Writers of the Eighteenth Century" until an *au courant* friend loaned me a copy of Paul Gilroy's *The Black Atlantic* and alerted me to the growing field of "circum-Atlantic studies." And so we ended up with *Black Atlantic Writers of the Eighteenth-Century,* a more timely and marketable title, but not necessarily a more apposite one. Gilroy's "black Atlantic" involves interculturation, the creolized and creolizing processes of a community-world. Eighteenth-century black writers, however, appear staunchly European in their writings—a point that is emphasized with considerable aplomb in a recent article by Tanya Caldwell. Caldwell effectively argues,

> Far from establishing himself and black Africans against Britain as a potential "new force," Equiano sees the danger of being perceived in this way and reveals the thoroughly European nature of his mind most convincingly when he proposes strengthening the system of which he is part by offering up Africa to the forces of British trade. (265)

The Interesting Narrative is, in conclusion, "profoundly British" (280).

I have grown somewhat uncomfortable with my one editorial nod to intercultural "hybridization." In the introduction to *Black Atlantic Writers,* I wrote:

> The Christian idiom of the pioneer black writers suggests at times—and especially in Equiano—the syncretic presence of distinctly African ideas. For example, as Paul Edwards and Rosalind Shaw have argued, the mature Equiano's belief in divine providence *is rooted in* the Igbo conception of *chi,* "an entity sometimes described as a 'personal god' responsible for the individual's destiny." (Potkay and Burr 3; emphases added)

I now see no reason for accepting a strong version of Edwards's and Shaw's claim; I would agree only that Equiano's belief in divine providence has loose parallels to the Igbo conception of *chi.* Yet noting this parallel serves only a political, and no real explicative, purpose.

Still, my nod to the invisible "chi" in Equiano's *Interesting Narrative* is just about the only thing palatable about our edition to a recent postcolonial reader of Equiano, Srinivas Aravamudan. His book, *Tropicopolitans,* comes from Duke University Press with, among other credentials, a blurb from Donna Landry: "*Tropicopolitans* might initiate a school of 'tropicalization' studies. In the emerging field of what we have learned to name Black Atlantic writing, Aravamudan has made two substantial contributions in his chapters on Equiano and Toussaint Louverture, in which each character is richly, contextually read." But one context that Aravamudan has no truck with is Equiano's Christianity. Aravamudan does not like either the universalist pretensions of Christianity or its basic tenet that *in interiore homine habitat veritas,* and so, in an effort to like Equiano, he decides that Equiano paid lip service to Christianity with a "sly civility" (286). The only evidence Aravamudan offers for this claim is an implied syllogism that emerges from his peculiar practice of contextual reading. Extrapolating from two books, one from 1698 and the other from 1811, Aravamudan premises that "new sailors were frequently subjected to ritual ablutions when ships crossed important nautical lines"; these ablutions are, in the text from 1698, referred to as "tropical baptisms." Now, given that Equiano was once a new sailor (second premise), he must have undergone a "tropical baptism" (although he never tells us about it in *The Interesting Narrative*). Moreover, by a logic that wholly eludes me, "as a rite of passage, it [the tropical baptism] both undercuts and reinforces religion through syncretic parody" and so "Equiano's maritime background inflects his evangelical performance"; his Methodism is consequently "qualified" and his adherence to the articles of the Church of England merely "nominal" (239–40). Aravamudan then proceeds to chide my figural reading of *The Interesting Narrative* for failing to pass beyond tropology, which concerns the conversion of the individual soul, and onto anagogy, which to his mind implies "a collective historical direction"—though how he comes to associate the Last Judgment with collective political experience is a mystery to be understood, if at all, only by those who derive their biblical hermeneutics from Fredric Jameson, as Aravamudan professedly does (243–44).

Another recent postcolonial critic, Helen Thomas, associates hermeneutics not with any biblical tradition so much as with African priests and magicians (the "Ah-affoe-way-cah") (233). Thus, when Equiano claims, in his Christian new birth experience, that "the Scriptures became an unsealed book," Thomas proposes that Equiano is here "blessed with the power of hermeneutics . . . , a power previously attributed to the Ibonic Ah-affoe-way-cah" (248). This previous attribution is not Equiano's, but Thomas's (233). Thomas claims that her goal is to read *The Interesting Narrative* as "a paradigm of cultural miscegenation": "Equiano's 'diasporic' text demarcates a narrative of cultural hybridity—a text propounding the synthesis of principal tenets of dissenting Protestantism with West African epistemology" (248). However, Thomas has little patience for "dissenting Protestantism." First, she discounts Whitefield's role in Equiano's tale, claiming that Equaino's

> account of Revd Whitefield "exhorting the people with the greatest fervor" is . . . curiously dismissive: he describes the Reverend as "sweating as much" as he did himself whilst a slave on Montserrat beach and declares that he is no longer at a loss to "account for the thin congregations" to which those divines preach. (246)

"Those divines" refers back to nothing in Thomas's text; in Equiano's text, it refers to ministers, presumably nonevangelical ones, who *lacked* Whitefield's mesmerizing "fervour and earnestness" (Equiano 132). It is thus puzzling to conclude, as Thomas does, that Equiano's account of Whitefield is an "ironisation of dissenting Protestantism" (246).

Still more puzzling is Thomas's later contention that towards the end of his tale Equiano rejects Christianity altogether. Grudgingly admitting that "Equiano's own spiritual 'conversion' is more or less completed by his account of his attempts . . . to 'convert' the Musquito Indians on the Dupeupy shore," Thomas nonetheless seeks signs of his "radical alienation of (or even rejection of) Christian ideology" (251). Can this point be inferred from either Equiano's failure to convert the Indians, or the respect he shows for their "customs and social mores"? Thomas seems to think it can—but this is, to put it mildly, quite a stretch. What is far clearer is Thomas's own disdain for "Christian ideology" as "interdependent upon colonial and racist ideology" (252). For Thomas, "Africa" and its vaguely defined "epistemology" are, by contrast, not only non-assimilationist but fundamentally, and beneficially, matriarchal. This, however, is a position that Thomas could and should defend on her own; it cannot, I think, reasonably be attributed to Equiano. Thomas suggests that "in Equiano's text" we may find "the attempted subordination of African matriarchy by patriarchal European society" (239); but if we may find this, then clearly we may find there anything else we wish.

The strained arguments of Aravamudan and Thomas, one hopes, will mark the outer limits of postcolonial theory's effort at refashioning Equiano in its own image. Perhaps Equiano's text has something to teach us, instead, about the proper limits of scholarship and, to end where I began, about the college classroom. One could attempt to convince a group of sceptical twenty-year-olds that Equiano really is not serious about the spiritual concerns he spends so much time telling us about. Or one could use *The Interesting Narrative* to bring to life for our students some of the religious experiences, biblical hermeneutics, and religious politics that are so crucial to all of the fields in which students are likely to encounter Equiano: African American Studies, Studies of the African diaspora, and British or American Eighteenth-Century Studies. Our students will, I think, be best served if we try to teach Equiano and other eighteenth-century black writers on something at least approaching their own terms—terms which are, historically, colonial, oratorical, and Christian.

Notes

1. On Equiano's wealth and fame, see Vincent Carretta's introduction to his edition of The Interesting Narrative *and Other Writings,* ix–xxviii. For a bibliography of editions and printings of *The Interesting Narrative,* see Adam Potkay and Sandra Burr, eds., *Black Atlantic Writers of the Eighteenth Century: Living the New Exodus in England and the Americas,* 162–64.

2. The rise of contemporary scholarly interest in Equiano's *Interesting Narrative* may be traced back to Paul Edwards's first published abridgment, *Equiano's Travels,* in 1967,

followed by his two-volume facsimile reprint of the original 1789 edition. A Swedish translation of *The Interesting Narrative* had earlier appeared in 1964.

3. Subsequent editions include Paul Edwards's abridgement, *The Life of Olaudah Equiano, or Gustavus Vassa, the African;* Potkay and Burr, eds., *Black Atlantic Writers of the Eighteenth Century: Living the New Exodus in England and the Americas* (contains an abridgement of *The Interesting Narrative,* 1814 edition); Robert J. Allison, ed., *The Interesting Narrative of the Life of Olaudah Equiano. Written By Himself;* Vincent Carretta, ed., The Interesting Narrative *and Other Writings;* Vincent Carretta, ed., *Unchained Voices: An Anthology of Black Authors in the English-Speaking World of the Eighteenth Century;* and, Werner Sollors, ed., *The Interesting Narrative of the Life of Olaudah Equiano.* Among the complete texts of *The Interesting Narrative* in print, only Carretta's Penguin edition and Sollors's Norton edition should be cited in published scholarly quotations. Carretta uses as his copy text the rare ninth edition of 1794, which contains Equiano's final changes; Sollors uses the first edition of 1789, which had a wider circulation in Equiano's lifetime. Scholars should avoid citing the editions of Gates, who uses an untrustworthy copy text (the 1814 Leeds edition), and Allison, who corrupts the New York edition of 1791 (itself a piracy of Equiano's second London edition) by, for example, silently inserting the penultimate paragraph from the fifth and subsequent editions.

4. This essay, which began as an invited talk at a convention of the American Society for Eighteenth-Century Studies held in Philadelphia, 12–16 April 2000, is organized around three topics drawn from sessions at that conference: "The Tensions of Interdisciplinarity: The Competing Claims of Literature and History"; "The Category of 'Literature' in Literary Studies Today"; and, "Religion: The Forbidden Topic."

5. Chris Bongie uses the word "post/colonial" to gesture towards "the (con)fusing energies of creolization" that connect the discourses of late eighteenth-century colonialism and "postcolonial" (used simply as a historical marker) period of the later half of the twentieth century. He limits the hyphenated "post-colonial" to "conveying the (purely ideological) hypothesis of a future that would be completely severed from colonialism" (12–13).

6. The concern with veridicality of sources has not, I think, been abated by the increasing doubts professional historians have felt since the mid-1960s about the

possibility of objective historiography. See Peter Novick, *That Noble Dream: The "Objective Question" and the American Historical Profession.*

7. See Keith A. Sandiford's *Measuring the Moment: Strategies of Protest in Eighteenth-Century Afro-English Writing,* a work based on the author's doctoral dissertation (U. of Illinois, 1979).

8. All references (hereafter cited by page number) to Equiano's text are to The Interesting Narrative *and Other Writings,* ed. Vincent Carretta.

9. Equiano bases his Igbo genealogy on the Old Testament exposition of John Gill (1763–1766).

10. Carretta, in a note (277n362) revised for the second printing of his Penguin edition of *The Interesting Narrative,* proves that Equiano and Whitefield were both in Savannah the week of 9 February 1765 and proposes that Equiano may have heard Whitefield preach there.

11. For annotated editions of the lives of Gronniosaw and Marrant, see Potkay and Burr, eds., *Black Atlantic Writers,* 26–105.

12. Acholonu's speculations on Equiano's African birthplace, although widely cited by literary scholars, are based on very tenuous evidence; see Paul Edwards's review of Acholonu's book in *Slavery and Abolition.*

13. The quotation is drawn from Hume's essay, "Of Eloquence"; on the transatlantic popularity of this piece, see my "Theorizing Civic Eloquence in the Early Republic: The Road from David Hume to John Quincy Adams."

14. Byron was just nineteen years old when he made this claim in a letter to his solicitor and friend, John Hanson; see *Byron: A Self-Portrait in His Own Words* (ed. Peter Quennell), 27.

15. The recent vogue for studying travel writing is largely indebted to Mary Louise Pratt's *Imperial Eyes: Travel Writing and Transculturation.*

16. It should be noted that oratory finds little favor today even among reaches of literate culture which are not identical to the professional public sphere. Witness, for example, the recent complaints about Ralph Ellison's *Juneteenth* for being, in the words of one reviewer, "too often homiletic, sentimental, and rhetorical" (Wood 38);

cf. Louis Menand's critique in *The New York Times Book Review* (6). Rhetorical is still often seen as what the truly literary is not.

17. O'Connor's speech, which Douglass found in Caleb Bingham's *Columbian Orator*, is incorrectly remembered by Douglass as "Sheridan's speech on Irish Emancipation" (369).

18. Carretta notes: "Equiano is probably trying to sound unbiased by using examples from the geographical and racial extremes of humankind, commonly thought to be neither Negroes nor Caucasians" (272n317); in eighteenth-century ethnography, the Tartar "Samaides" were grouped among the radically distinct peoples found in the polar regions.

19. MLA roundtable on teaching slave narratives, MLA Conference, Chicago, December 1999.

20. See my "Olaudah Equiano and the Art of Spiritual Autobiography" and the introduction to *Black Atlantic Writers.*

21. Angelo Costanzo, "The Art and Tradition of Black Autobiography in the Eighteenth Century" (Ph.D. diss., State U. of New York, Binghamton, 1976) would give rise to *Surprizing Narrative: Olaudah Equiano and the Beginnings of Black Autobiography.* Sandiford informs his reader in *Measuring the Moment* (9) that the book began as a Ph.D. diss., U. of Illinois, 1979.

22. Taking issue with Baker's "summary rejection of Christian discourse," the Marxist critic Joseph Fichtelberg argued that Equiano's piety and profit motive are deeply implicated—religion, for Fichtelberg, being epiphenomenal to Equiano's self-alienation within the capitalistic system.

23. Edwards, in his introduction to his 1969 facsimile reprint of the two-volume 1789 edition of *The Interesting Narrative,* compares the parallel instances in Equiano, Cugoano, and Gronniosaw of "talking to books" (1: xlvii).

24. My argument concerning the "talking book" topos is elaborated in "Olaudah Equiano and the Art of Spiritual Autobiography," 677–80.

Works Cited

Abrams, M. H. *The Mirror and the Lamp: Romantic Theory and the Critical Tradition.* Oxford: Oxford UP, 1953.

Acholonu, Catherine Obianuju. *The Igbo Roots of Olaudah Equiano: An Anthropological Research.* Owerri, Nigeria: AFA, 1989.

Adanson, Michel. *A Voyage to Senegal, the Isle of Goree, and the River Gambia.* London, 1759.

Allison, Robert J., ed. *The Interesting Narrative of the Life of Olaudah Equiano. Written by Himself.* Boston: Bedford/St. Martin's, 1995.

Andrews, William L. *To Tell a Free Story: The First Century of Afro-American Autobiography, 1760–1865.* Urbana: U of Illinois P, 1988.

Aravamudan, Srinivas. *Tropicopolitans: Colonialism and Agency, 1688–1804.* Durham: Duke UP, 1999.

Baker, Houston A., Jr. *Blues, Ideology, and Afro-American Literature: A Vernacular Theory.* Chicago: U of Chicago P, 1984.

Benezet, Anthony. *Some Account of Guinea, Its Situation, Produce, and the General Disposition of Its Inhabitants. With an Inquiry into the Rise and Progress of the Slave Trade, Its Nature, and Lamentable Effects. Also a Re-Publication of the Sentiments of Several Authors of Note, on this Interesting Subject; particularly an Extract of a Treatise, by Granville Sharp.* Philadelphia, 1771; rev. and exp., London, 1788.

Bongie, Chris. *Islands and Exiles: The Creole Identities of Post/Colonial Literature.* Stanford, CA: Stanford UP, 1998.

Byron, George Gordon, Lord. "Letter to John Hanson, April 2, 1807." *Bryon: A Self-Portrait in His Own Words.* Ed. Peter Quennell. Oxford: Oxford UP, 1999. 26–28.

Caldwell, Tanya. "'Talking Too Much English': Languages of Economics and Politics in Equiano's *The Interesting Narrative.*" *Early American Literature* 34.3 (1999): 263–80.

Carretta, Vincent, ed. The Interesting Narrative *and Other Writings.* New York: Penguin, 1995.

———, ed. *Unchained Voices: An Anthology of Black Authors in the English-Speaking World of the Eighteenth Century.* Lexington: UP of Kentucky, 1996.

———. Introduction. The Interesting Narrative *and Other Writings,* by Olaudah Equiano. New York: Penguin, 1995. ix–xxviii.

———. "Olaudah Equiano or Gustavus Vassa? New Light on an Eighteenth-Century Question of Identity." *Slavery and Abolition* 20.3 (1999): 96–105.

Costanzo, Angelo. *Surprizing Narrative: Olaudah Equiano and the Beginnings of Black Autobiography.* New York: Greenwood, 1987.

Douglass, Frederick. *Narrative of the Life of Frederick Douglass, an American Slave. Written By Himself. Classic Slave Narratives.* Ed. Henry Louis Gates Jr. New York: Signet, 1987. 323–436.

Edwards, Paul. Introduction. *Equiano's Travels.* Ed. Paul Edwards. Portsmouth, NH: Heinemann, 1967. vii–xix.

———. Rev. of *The Igbo Roots of Olaudah Equiano: An Anthropological Research,* by Catherine Obianuju Acholonu. *Slavery and Abolition* 20.3 (1999): 124–28.

———, ed. *The Life of Olaudah Equiano, or Gustavus Vassa, the African.* Harlow, UK: Longman, 1989.

Edwards, Paul, and Rosalind Shaw. "The Invisible Chi in Equiano's *Interesting Narrative.*" *Journal of Religion in Africa* 19.2 (1989): 145–56.

Equiano, Olaudah. The Interesting Narrative *and Other Writings.* Ed. Vincent Carretta. New York: Penguin, 1995.

Fichtelberg, Joseph. "Word Between Worlds: The Economy of Equiano's *Narrative.*" *American Literary History* 5.3 (1993): 459–80.

Foucault, Michel. *The Order of Things: An Archaeology of the Human Sciences.* New York: Vintage, 1973.

Gates, Henry Louis, Jr., ed. *The Classic Slave Narratives.* New York: Penguin-Mentor, 1987.

———. *The Signifying Monkey: A Theory of African-American Literature.* New York: Oxford UP, 1988.

Gilroy, Paul. *The Black Atlantic: Modernity and Double Consciousness.* Cambridge, MA: Harvard UP, 1993.

Hume, David. "Of Eloquence." *Essays, Moral, Political, and Literature.* Ed. Eugene Miller. Indianapolis: Liberty Classics, 1985. 97–110.

Kuhn, Thomas S. *The Structure of Scientific Revolutions.* Chicago: U of Chicago P, 1962.

Matthews, John. A *Voyage to the River Sierra-Leone, on the Coast of Africa; Containing an Account of the Trade and Productions of the Country, and of the Civil and Religious Customs and Manners of the People; in a Series of Letters to a Friend in England. By John Matthews, Lieutenant in the Royal Navy; During His Residence in that Country in the Years 1785, 1786, and 1787.* London, 1788.

Menand, Louis. Rev. of *Juneteenth,* by Ralph Ellison. *New York Times Book Review.* 20 July 1999. 4.

Murphy, Geraldine. "Olaudah Equiano, Accidental Tourist." *Eighteenth-Century Studies* 27.4 (1994): 551–68.

Novick, Peter. *That Noble Dream: The "Objective Question" and the American Historical Profession.* Cambridge, UK: Cambridge UP, 1988.

Pocock, J. G. A. *Virtue, Commerce, and History: Essays on Political Thought and History, Chiefly in the Eighteenth Century.* Cambridge, UK: Cambridge UP, 1985.

Potkay, Adam. "Olaudah Equiano and the Art of Spiritual Autobiography." *Eighteenth-Century Studies* 27.4 (1994): 677–92.

———. "Theorizing Civic Eloquence in the Early Republic: The Road from David Hume to John Quincy Adams." *Early American Literature* 34.2 (1999): 147–70.

Potkay, Adam, and Sandra Burr, eds. *Black Atlantic Writers of the Eighteenth Century: Living the New Exodus in England and the Americas.* New York: St. Martin's, 1995.

Pratt, Mary Louise. *Imperial Eyes: Travel Writing and Transculturation.* New York: Routledge, 1992.

Sandiford, Keith A. *Measuring the Moment: Strategies of Protest in Eighteenth-Century Afro-English Writing.* Selinsgrove, PA: Susquehanna UP, 1988.

Sollors, Werner, ed. *The Interesting Narrative of the Life of Olaudah Equiano, or Gustavus Vassa, the African. Written by Himself.* New York: Norton, 2001.

Smith, Adam. *Lectures on Rhetoric and Belles-Letters.* Ed. J. C. Bryce. Indianapolis: Liberty Classics, 1985.

Thomas, Helen. *Romanticism and Slave Narratives: Transatlantic Testimonies.* Cambridge, Cambridge UP, 2000.

Tillotson, Geoffrey, Paul Fussell, and Marshall Waingrow, eds. *Eighteenth-Century British Literature.* New York: Harcourt, 1969.

Whitefield, George. *Sermons on Various Subjects.* London, 1739.

Wood, James. Rev. of *Juneteenth,* by Ralph Ellison. *New Republic.* 28 June 1999. 38–42.

Equiano Lite

Srinivas Aravamudan

In Adam Potkay's essay, a vehemence about the importance of rhetoric in Equiano's *Interesting Narrative* is combined with a new twist on academic anti-intellectualism, whereby "a group of sceptical twenty-year-olds" is wheeled out to battle against "postcolonial theory's effort at refashioning Equiano in its own image" (611). While almost every single published work of scholarship on Equiano that I know registers the obvious fact that *The Interesting Narrative* appears to be a spiritual autobiography, does this mean that the text contains no other material worthy of classroom or scholarly discussion? Potkay is content with beginning and ending all further discussion by pointing to the Christian claims made in the text and to some of the classical rhetorical tools with which those claims are made. To hold that position about Equiano's worth is no crime, although some would call it poor teaching and perhaps also a disservice to cultural history. By this manner of accounting, the *Iliad* is about rescuing an abducted woman and the *Odyssey* a very long voyage.

However, all literary scholars may not be content with belaboring the obvious. Potkay's answer to the question "what is the relationship between literature, as we now conceive it, and religion?" vacuously reaffirms "the Calvinist Methodism [Equiano] accepted and sought to promulgate" (602). As Equiano's narrative is one about *conversion,* even a laconic undergraduate might wonder: conversion *from* what, *into* what? Deeming the conclusion to the process of conversion as the only significant meaning is greedy haste. Even and especially in the eighteenth century, there are other secular and religious worlds to discover in Equiano's text.

Potkay's narrow definitions of Christianity cannot bear very much reality. While Equiano's conversion might be a happy focus for evangelically minded students, it would be less than edifying to the historically and anthropologically curious and those who might profess other faiths or none at all. If Potkay is indignant that religion is an ignored category of analysis in literary studies today, he ought to lead the way to an expanded understanding of the category rather than a narrow reiteration. Potkay's knowledgeable student-skeptics—at least when postcolonial theory is at stake—appear naively ready to believe uninflected accounts of eighteenth-century black Christianity.

Potkay (and his student coeditor) decided to rename their anthology after having been lent a copy of Paul Gilroy's book, *The Black Atlantic,* by "an *au courant* friend" (609). The editors should clearly have stuck with the earlier, more limited, but far more honest title, "Black Anglican Writers of the Eighteenth Century," as the published *Black Atlantic Writers of the Eighteenth Century* misleads readers with the faulty premise that Christian writing by blacks is the only black writing worthy of attention. Taking a religion-friendly scalpel to *The Interesting Narrative* in that edition, Potkay and Burr dispense with the picaresque aspects of the text. While Potkay now regrets his then "editorial nod" (or marketing gimmick), he can no longer agree "that Equiano's belief in divine providence has loose parallels to the Igbo conception of *chi* . . . noting this parallel serves only a political, and no real explicative, purpose" (609).

Political purposes seem extraneous to real explication in Potkay's view of literature in general, much though he forgets the extent to which *The Interesting Narrative* in its appeal is also a political manifesto. The book's preface is addressed "To the Lords Spiritual and Temporal, and the Commons of the Parliament of Great Britain." Equiano's claim about his own work is that its "chief design . . . is to excite in [Britain's] august assemblies a sense of compassion for the miseries which the Slave-Trade has entailed on [his] unfortunate countrymen" (iii). By his own definition, Equiano is "an unlettered African, who is actuated by the hope of becoming an instrument towards the relief of his suffering countrymen" (Equiano iv). These concerns with "the inhuman traffic of slavery" convince many readers, including Houston Baker, Henry Louis Gates, and myself that religious salvation is not the be-all and end-all for this text. Potkay accuses postcolonial critics of programmatically seeking out signs of parodic subversion, creolization, and "talking back" by over-reading faint signs (602). It is worth asking him in response: was the preface faded in all the editions of Equiano that he read? Or did he hastily discount its relevance as there were not enough mentions of Christianity on the page? With blind willfulness, Potkay ignores most non-Christian signs, faded or otherwise. Obliviousness regarding the full gamut of what *was* eighteenth-century Christianity might have led him to assume too quickly a content that could be beneficially recontextualized with some historical reading.[1]

It amazes me that Potkay claims that my fifty-five-page chapter in *Tropicopolitans,* entitled "Equiano and The Politics of Literacy," "has no truck with . . . Equiano's Christianity." What I contest, rather, is the position that Equiano's Christianity represents a privatized evangelical vision with little theological and political content. I have considerable truck with, and discuss at great length and perhaps even *ad nauseam,* multiple aspects of religious analysis. To reiterate, I argue that the following points are crucially necessary for any reading of Equiano, religious or otherwise: the complex *evangelical* and *rhetorical* staging of the portrait; the trimming between Calvinism and Arminianism in Equiano's rhetoric; the biblical tropology and hermeneutics that is (despite Potkay's asseverations) a fourfold, not a threefold process; Equiano's unsuccessful encounter with the racist Bishop Robert who refuses to ordain him a missionary; the significance of Olaudah Equiano's reclaiming of an African name over and against his legal identity of "Gustavus Vassa"; and the multiple and complex ways in which religious fetishism and readerly agency inhabit the text and jostle for characterization and narrativization as "Christian," "African," and "literate." Furthermore, Potkay has misunderstood my rhetorical use of the "tropical baptism." To quote myself, "we can imagine Equiano as the maritime novice, undergoing tropical baptism by English literary history and emerging as sailor *and* writer" (Aravamudan 253). But the merits of my full-scale reading of Equiano's text—rather than that of a sectarian reaffirmation of his religion—can be assessed by others who may encounter *Tropicopolitans* more intimately than by hearing attacks on the generosity of a blurb on its back cover.

The plea for a renewed appreciation of oratorical norms in literature is less innocuous than it seems. It is one thing to ask for a renewed appreciation of oratory in literature; it is yet another matter to go about replacing the literary function of Equiano's text with an oratorical one. While oratorical views of Equiano are derived from William Andrews's *To Tell A Free Story,* Potkay proceeds to wrestle Equiano into the bogus genre of "savage indignation." This turns out to be a recipe for ideological evacuation. If a writer's transitive anger about politics can be taught as merely representing the rhetorical genre of anger, such a pedagogy reduces differences to the status of tropological variance within an infinite series of oratorical situations. Such a reduction of all angry eighteenth-century texts to formal functions of rhetorical structures learned from classical sources is as distorted an exercise as that of only annotating the biblical references in any given English literary text and thereupon redescribing all eighteenth-century literature as the sole product of biblical inspiration. To show that Edmund Burke's *Reflections on the Revolution in France,* Equiano's *Interesting Narrative,* and Jefferson's original draft of the Declaration of Independence share savage indignation is perhaps a useful formalist insight, but in Potkay's hands it seems to be the best way to dismiss any possibility that Equiano possesses any relationship of alterity to his audience: "In this context, the question 'might not an African ask you, learned you this from your God' signals not so much the perspective of a cultural outsider as a confirmation that the Christian universe knows no outside; it is all inclusive, and is itself the surety of eventual justice" (Potkay 606). Such an oratorical crib is based on the notion of an idealized, evangelical, and missionary Equiano, divorced from the other (also highly oratorical) functions performed by Equiano the labor organizer in Philadelphia, Equiano the inventor of the book promotion tour, Equiano the antislavery speech giver, and Equiano the associate of political radicals. These associates included English Jacobins such as Thomas Hardy (founder of the London Corresponding Society) and Irish Jacobins such as Samuel Neilson, Thomas McCabe, and Thomas Digges (Rodgers 73–89). That Equiano claimed to be a sincere, believing Christian is not in contention; it is the meanings of *that* Christianity, and that *claim,* which are not quite as obvious as we are being told that they are.

To reduce the anger of politics to the genre of anger is an ideological containment strategy and is likely ineffective pedagogically, as a transitive function has been rendered intransitive. This rendition actively fights the text and treats it blandly in the manner of a rhetorical "set speech." Students are bound to react differently to Burke, Jefferson, and Equiano out of a welter of their religious beliefs, political commitments, and historical knowledge (or ignorance). As teachers and scholars, we always need to (and always have) worked with this (dis)identification openly. Oratorical situations—just as pedagogical situations—work in part through the psychoanalytical structure of transference. These oratorical occasions cannot simply be classified and dismissed as the pastness of the past. The presence of the past has to be reinterrogated and recontextualized. Such an active response is what postcolonial methodologies enable in teaching and in scholarship. Perhaps Potkay has misunderstood the radical relevance of anger in its connection to politics. What comes across, at any rate, is *his* deeply felt anger toward—and intemperate dismissal of—postcolonial methodologies. I would respectfully suggest that Potkay resolve his anger by pedagogical experiment rather than scholarly backlash. Otherwise, he risks being classified in a genre of his own making.

Finally, Vincent Carretta's very recent speculations are not just beside the point for literary critics of Equiano even though Potkay deems that they are. A bizarre divorce between "facts" and "rhetoric" only allows an old-fashioned division of labor between history and literature. Equiano's possible South Carolinian ancestry is an extremely important avenue worth exploring. If Equiano's autobiography is willfully falsified, especially with respect to the childhood sections, terminological shifts from "oratorical autobiography" to "semi-autobiographical oration" or "oration using autobiographical elements" (Potkay 604) to explain this falsification will not suffice. What maintains the integrity of Equiano's much-touted conversion if there is such a convenient instrumentalization of fact in the text? Isn't the genre of spiritual autobiography compromised by the possibility of a strategic lie? But doesn't this possibility also enhance claims made by myself and others regarding the rhetorical and religious slipperiness of the text? These questions may be addressed more effectively, not as regarding truth, falsehood, or impersonation concerning religion, but regarding literary and political agency and Equiano's making do with the biblical fetish, or "factish," as I have argued in my book.

Where would Potkay draw the line on these questions, especially as he believes in policing "the proper limits of scholarship" (611)? When Potkay returns to his classroom, "teach[ing] Equiano and other eighteenth-century black writers on . . . their own terms . . . which are, historically, colonial, oratorical, and Christian," (611) will he merely open a page of the text, point to it with "savage indignation," as Equiano does in his famous frontispiece portrait, and allow his (or Equiano's) oratorical skills to take care of the rest? Rather than shedding new light on Equiano, as Carretta's research potentially does, Potkay's nostalgia for a time before postcolonialism runs the risk of reinstituting an eighteenth-century studies lightened of its historical and cultural burdens and whitened in the name of religion. Would we want to deliver our students to an Equiano Lite?[2]

Notes

1. For a start, Isabel Rivers's *Reason, Grace, and Sentiment: A Study of the Language of Religion and Ethics in England, 1660–1780.* While only volume 1, *Whichcote to Wesley,* was available when my book went to press, volume 2, *Shaftesbury to Hume,* has just been released. Potkay's students may also wish to acquaint themselves with Walter Pitts's *Old Ship of Zion: The Afro-Baptist Ritual in the African Diaspora,* which argues that most New World black Christianity was highly African in its practice until the second wave of the Evangelical revival in 1799.

2. We should remind ourselves of the differences between William Denton's painting and Daniel Orme's and Cornelius Tiebout's engravings of Equiano in the British and American editions respectively. See *Tropicopolitans,* 243–48.

Works Cited

Aravamudan, Srinivas. *Tropicopolitans: Colonialism and Agency, 1688–1804.* Durham: Duke UP, 1999.

Baker, Houston A., Jr. *Blues, Ideology, and Afro-American Literature: A Vernacular Theory.* Chicago: U of Chicago P, 1984.

Carretta, Vincent. "Olaudah Equiano or Gustavus Vassa? New Light on an Eighteenth-Century Question of Identity." *Slavery and Abolition* 20.3 (1999): 96–105.

Equiano, Olaudah. *The Interesting Narrative of the Life of Olaudah Equiano, or Gustavus Vassa, the African. Written by Himself.* London, 1789.

Gates, Henry Louis, Jr. *The Signifying Monkey: A Theory of African-American Literary Criticism.* New York: Oxford UP, 1988.

Pitts, Walter. *Old Ship of Zion: The Afro-Baptist Ritual in the African Diaspora.* New York: Oxford UP, 1993.

Potkay, Adam. "History, Oratory, and God in Equiano's *Interesting Narrative.*" *Eighteenth-Century Studies* 34.4 (2001): 601–14.

Rivers, Isabel. *Reason, Grace, and Sentiment: A Study of the Language of Religion and Ethics in England, 1660–1780.* Vol. 1, *Whichcote to Wesley.* New York: Cambridge UP, 1991.

———. *Reason, Grace, and Sentiment: A Study of the Language of Religion and Ethics in England, 1660–1780.* Vol. 2, *Shaftesbury to Hume.* New York: Cambridge UP, 2000.

Rodgers, Nini. "Equiano in Belfast: A Study of the Anti-Slavery Ethos in a Northern Town." *Slavery and Abolition* 18.2 (1997): 73–89.

Domesticating Equiano's *Interesting Narrative*

Roxann Wheeler

"The eighteenth century as a whole remains obstinately out of fashion," Pat Rogers lamented in the 1970s (ix). Over a decade later, that sentiment was the rallying cry of Felicity Nussbaum's and Laura Brown's *The New Eighteenth Century: Theory, Politics, English Literature* (1987). Arguing that resistance to contemporary theory was at the heart of our marginalization within English literary history, Nussbaum and Brown called for a new interdisciplinarity to renovate teaching and research (1, 21–22). While there has not been a revolution in our scholarly methods since then, eighteenth-century studies has been energized by a critical return to issues originally raised in the social histories of England by A. S. Turberville, A. R. Humphreys, and Roy Porter. Our field has also been invigorated by the introduction of new or previously overlooked facets of eighteenth-century life and literature, including studies of finance capital, stage performance, consumerism, maternity, and sensibility.[1] These books demonstrate that national and even regional studies bear intimate connection to events in France, North Africa, West Africa, the West Indies, East India, and North America. This wave of scholarship rightly assumes that neither eighteenth-century writers nor their world was bound by the island itself.

The expansion of interests in eighteenth-century literary studies is a distilled subtext of Adam Potkay's "History, Oratory, and God in Equiano's *Interesting Narrative*." Potkay's investigation of religion and oratory seems on the face of it a necessary reminder that there remains much to rediscover about our period.[2] As many of us routinely tell our students, in a century with an enticing array of secular temptations, religious literature was more widely read than travel writing, poetry, or novels: the Bible was the best selling and most widely debated book in England, and Bunyan's *The Pilgrim's Progress* was the most popular work of fiction (Watt 49–50). Arguably, it is the tension between religious belief and secular pursuits that is the most fascinating characteristic of the British Enlightenment. No doubt, reassessments of religion's role in everyday life and its relation to literary production and consumption, sexuality, sociability, nascent feminism, and colonialism will usher in a new era of scholarship.

While I value Potkay's suggestions for companion readings to Equiano's narrative, I do not endorse his dismissal of the suggestive findings of poststructuralist and postcolonial critics.[3] Besides providing us with astute interpretations of Equiano's ideological investments, these are the very critics who have assured *The Interesting Narrative* a secure position in our classrooms and scholarship. Potkay differs from these critics in that he wants to return English studies to a simpler, "purer" past, one that need not consider unequal relations of power in the eighteenth century or the politics of literary interpretation in the present, but one that features instead the tidiness of rhetorical power ("History" 607).[4]

Potkay intimates that eighteenth-century conceptions of social mobility, masculinity, patriotism, and even racial ideology are somehow less historically appropriate to understanding Equiano's *Interesting Narrative* than rhetorical structures of the Bible and classical oratory. In participating in the backlash against theory derived from Marxism, feminism, and civil rights, Potkay domesticates this political activist and former slave's narrative.[5] For example, if we focus primarily on biblical resonances in *The Interesting Narrative,* as Potkay proposes, we lose sight of an intriguing connection between Equiano's literary record of his faith and the institutional workings of the Church of England.[6]

Situating Equiano within an emerging Methodism in Britain or even within the politics of proselytizing a Christian identity in the colonies enhances an examination of his rhetorical power rather than detracts from it.[7] In the eighteenth century, Christianity was one of the most powerful of all hegemonic forces. Possibly its most significant aspect was that it gave rise to both radical and reactionary ideology. One example of the conflict between personal and social modes of consciousness is the tension between Equiano's voluntary conversion and the Church of England's stance on the slave trade and slavery. Formed in 1701, the Society for the Propagation of the Gospel in Foreign Parts was largely concerned with keeping wayward, fractious Britons within the purview of the Church and its official morality. Mostly unsuccessful in attempts to convert native Americans and Caribbean islanders, lukewarm if not hostile to converting slaves, the Church of England pursued a very different path in the history of the early empire than did the Catholic Church associated with Spain, Portugal, and France.[8] Compared to the power of the Catholic Church in the Americas, including its sheer number of converts, the lackluster mission of the Church of England outside of the British Isles (it was far more successful in parts of Scotland and Ireland) helped create a political, economic, and religious vacuum filled to an extent by Moravians, Quakers, Methodists, and Baptists. The Church of England's proslavery tradition, not to mention the influential slaveholding factions of the Quakers and other Dissenters, illuminates Equiano's faith in a way that is suppressed by *The Interesting Narrative* in regard to his own conversion, but revealed in his attempts to convert Miskito Indians.

A significant reason that new historicist, poststructuralist, and postcolonial theories have had such a general impact on our thinking is that they have helped scholars shift literary interpretation out of its "little England" context.[9] By situating *The Spectator, Gulliver's Travels, Pamela,* or Hume's essays in an international network of trade, especially the burgeoning slave trade and empire building, we retrieve, not obfuscate, aspects of eighteenth-century sensibility.[10] In regard to Equiano, Potkay cites the most theoretically reductive form of poststructuralism and its postcolonial manifestations as grounds for dismissing its analytical efficacy.

Arguably, the most suggestive colonial theory has not emanated from the field of English literature, which is as far as Potkay ventures. The most intellectually challenging versions of postcolonial theory have aimed to restore historical complexity to our understanding of the colonial world on both sides of the Atlantic. For example, anthropologists, cultural geographers, and historians have helped recover competing agendas between agents of colonialism and metropolitan politicians, and they have analyzed the varying responses to political conquest and cultural hegemony among the indigenous elite, their subordinates, and newly created colonial populations. Over a decade ago, feminist anthropologist Ann Laura Stoler warned against our presentist tendency to view the colonial situation and people in too unified and simplified a manner. Taking her cue from Stuart Hall, Stoler noted that racism, Christian identity, colonial administration, and slavery, for instance, vary in quality and intensity over time (Stoler 137).[11] This intellectual mandate is fulfilled in Nicholas Thomas's *Colonialism's Culture* (1994). Contrasting the missionary and secular approaches to trade, settlement, and human relations in Fiji, Thomas investigates the conflicts among various British colonial interests in the late eighteenth to twentieth century.[12]

In this vein, we enhance our understanding of Equiano's *Interesting Narrative* by comparing it to similar productions of his peer groups, not only the orators and Methodists, as Potkay urges, but also other sailors, servants, autobiographers, political activists, literary celebrities, even other "new" Britons.[13] This lateral juxtaposition provides much needed historical depth to our analysis of Equiano's literary performance, a depth that we have not explored as fully as the narrative structure and style. A recent essay that enables this kind of perspective is Christopher Brown's "Empire without Slaves," an examination of emancipation schemes that political orator Edmund Burke and Anglican clergyman James Ramsay, among others, circulated in the decade before Equiano writes. These schemes went beyond condemning slavery to offering alternatives to it (288).[14] Given that we have just begun to reap the benefit from this intersection of literature, history, and postcolonial theory in eighteenth-century studies, it seems premature to call for its abandonment.

In singling out biblical structures and oratorical cadences, Potkay recovers significant contemporary coordinates for analyzing Equiano's rhetorical performance, but in divorcing them from their historical and political milieus, he recommends the flattest version of Equiano, one that omits the most intriguing aspect of the dynamic between secular and religious elements in his writing. Potkay's interest in analyzing *The Interesting Narrative* in the context of religion has gone largely unheeded by critics. Why? First, Equiano's reliance on narrative structures culled from conversion literature, or even his faith, while significant, are likely not the aspects of his writing that motivate our pedagogical interest. Most of us teach Equiano because he is a literate former slave who is also a lively contemporary observer, political activist, businessman, and Christian. Second, Potkay's rejection of recent critical theory would have us return to the same terms of a debate already waged in *The New Eighteenth Century* and in the profession at large.[15] Rather than urging us to a much needed revision of religion's role in eighteenth-century literature, Potkay instead simply calls for a return to traditional habits of interpretation: he proposes neither a new formalism nor a *new* new historicism but an old intertextuality.

It is a sign of life within our field that we are waging battles over Equiano's narrative, but the larger stake as Potkay presents it is the abandonment of the past twenty-five years of theory. A vital field should not ignore a larger body of scholarship that energizes it: there is room for a plurality of approaches to teaching and research and for arguments about their terms of engagement. In our teaching and in forging a new generation of Equiano scholarship, it may be useful to recall the injunction to attend to the complexity of Equiano's relationship to English culture: "The temptation is strong in some criticism to tune in only one of Equiano's voices and to silence others" (Chinosole 52). New readings of Equiano are best served not by jettisoning lessons learned from postcolonial theory, but by refining and redefining the nexus of history, theory, politics, and literary interpretation.

Notes

1. On finance capital, see Baucom. On stage performance, see Roach. On consumerism, see Bhattacharyra, Brown, Kowaleski-Wallace, Mackie, and Sussman. On maternity, see Nussbaum. On sensibility, see Carey, Ellis, and Festa.

2. Potkay's interpretation of Equiano as a spiritual autobiographer appears in "Spiritual Autobiography"; Potkay and Burr examine Equiano's Calvinist inflected Anglicanism.

3. For instance, Aravamudan's is one of the more sustained considerations of Equiano's representation of his faith (238–53).

4. In his rich study of politeness, *The Fate of Eloquence in the Age of Hume,* Potkay divorces his intellectual interests and interaction with new historicism from its putative unitary political agenda because, he claims, against-the-grain interpretations of the Enlightenment and Enlightenment principles have led to the isolation of academic writers from a general public audience (12, 18–19, 226–27).

5. For studies that situate Equiano appropriately in a more international context, see Aravamudan, Brown, *Moral Capital,* Carretta, who provides a detailed account of his life, faith, and political activism, and Linebaugh and Rediker.

6. In privileging form over content, Potkay claims that we would benefit from juxtaposing Equiano's oratory to Thomas Jefferson's in an effort to appreciate the role of "savage indignation" in the political sphere. While this comparison would undoubtedly shed light on their shared modes of public address and their similar responses to political injustice, it is necessary to address their very different conception of the public sphere, citizenship, and race.

7. H. Thomas's is the most suggestive study to date. Fleshing out the structural, ideological, and publishing connections among spiritual autobiography, slave narrative,

and Romantic poetry, Thomas argues that black autobiographers not only imitate the structure and themes of radical dissenting Protestant narrative, but also that the authors revise them (182). See Stevens for a rich study of the biblical and secular imagery common to religious writing and poetry of the era. See Brown, *Moral Capital,* for the tension between Dissenters and Church of England religious commitments and anti–slave trade agenda.

8. See Stevens for the most compelling study of religious institutions, missionary goals, religious pity, and conflicts among metropolitan and colonial actors that enhance our understanding of Equiano's milieu and writing. See Brown, *Moral Capital,* and Carretta for specifics about Equiano's political activism and religious faith.

9. Other than encouraging students of eighteenth-century literature to consider literature's connections to commerce, slavery, and gender ideology, recent critical theorists, particularly feminists, have encouraged practitioners to disclose their major interpretive assumptions so that the very students whom Potkay cites as his own moral authority might be able to judge the choice of context for themselves.

10. These texts have all been traditionally treated as depicting domestic or national ideology; recently, they have been productively reinvestigated in light of empire building.

11. For the theoretical development of why we must study the historical variations in the intensity and quality of racism and colonialism, see Hall.

12. Thomas, like Stoler, supplies a rich theoretical critique of postcolonial theory as well as offers a historically nuanced example of his theoretical interests. See Stevens for a compelling investigation of the Atlantic context in this mode.

13. Suggestive readings of Equiano's *Interesting Narrative* in light of other contemporary writers and tropes may be found in Aravamudan, Boulukos, Festa, Linebaugh and Rediker, Nussbaum, *Limits,* and Wheeler. Equiano's narrative might usefully be examined in light of various Scots' narratives about the effects of English cultural and economic forces: James Boswell's *London Journal* (1762–63), servant James Macdonald, *Travels, in Various Parts of Europe, Asia, and Africa,* known today as *Memoirs of an Eighteenth-Century Footman* (1790), and soldier of fortune John Gabriel Stedman's *Narrative of a Five Years Expedition Against the Revolted Negroes of Surinam* (1796).

14. Brown's essay is vital to understanding the political constraints Equiano faces as he pens his narrative in the effort to halt the slave trade. The more detailed account is found in Brown's *Moral Capital.*

15. It is also worth recalling that critical treatment of Daniel Defoe's *Robinson Crusoe* (1719) modeled these interpretive struggles in reverse. In general, readings of the novel comparing it to spiritual autobiography and Puritan conceptions of the self in the 1960s gave way to interpretations based on Marxist critiques of capital in the 1970s and finally to colonial readings in the 1980s.

Works Cited

Aravamudan, Srinivas. *Tropicopolitans: Colonialism and Agency, 1688–1804.* Durham: Duke UP, 1999.

Baucom, Ian. *Specters of the Atlantic: Finance Capital, Slavery, and the Philosophy of History.* Durham: Duke UP, 2005.

Bhattacharyra, Nandini. *Reading the Splendid Body: Gender and Consumerism in Eighteenth-Century British Writing on India.* Newark: U of Delaware P, 1998.

Boulukos, George. *The Grateful Slave: The Emergence of Race in Eighteenth-Century British and American Culture.* Cambridge: Cambridge UP, 2008.

Brown, Christopher. "Empire without Slaves: British Concepts of Emancipation in the Age of the American Revolution." *William and Mary Quarterly* 56.2 (April 1999): 273–306.

———. *Moral Capital: Foundations of British Abolitionism.* Chapel Hill: U of North Carolina P, 2006.

Brown, Laura. *Ends of Empire: Women and Ideology in Early Eighteenth-Century English Literature.* Ithaca, NY: Cornell UP, 1993.

Carey, Brycchan. *British Abolitionism and the Rhetoric of Sensibility.* Basingstoke, UK: Palgrave Macmillan, 2005.

Carretta, Vincent. *Equiano, the African: Biography of a Self-Made Man.* Athens: U of Georgia P, 2005.

Chinosole. "Tryin' to Get Over: Narrative Posture in Equiano's Autobiography." *The Art of Slave Narrative: Original Essays in Criticism and Theory.* Ed. John Sekora and Darwin Turner. Macomb, IL: Western Illinois UP, 1982. 45–54.

Ellis, Markman. *The Politics of Sensibility: Race, Gender, and Commerce in the Sentimental Novel.* Cambridge, UK: Cambridge UP, 1996.

Festa, Lynn. *Sentimental Figures of Empire in Eighteenth-Century Britain and France.* Baltimore: The Johns Hopkins UP, 2006.

Hall, Stuart. "Gramsci's Relevance for the Study of Race and Ethnicity." *Stuart Hall: Critical Dialogues in Cultural Studies.* Ed. David Morley and Kuan-Hsing Chen. London: Routledge, 1996. 411–40.

Humphreys, A. R. *The Augustan World: Society, Thought, and Letters in Eighteenth-Century England.* 1954. New York: Harper & Row, 1963.

Kowaleski-Wallace, Elizabeth. *Consuming Subjects: Women, Shopping, and Business in the Eighteenth Century.* New York: Columbia UP, 1997.

Linebaugh, Peter, and Marcus Rediker. *The Many-Headed Hydra: Sailors, Slaves, Commoners, and the Hidden History of the Revolutionary Atlantic.* Boston: Beacon, 2000.

Mackie, Erin. *Market à la Mode: Fashion, Commodity, and Gender in* The Tatler *and* The Spectator. Baltimore: The Johns Hopkins UP, 1997.

Nussbaum, Felicity. *Limits of the Human: Fictions of Anomaly, Race, and Gender in the Long Eighteenth Century.* Cambridge, UK: Cambridge UP, 2003.

———. *Torrid Zones: Maternity, Sexuality, and Empire in Eighteenth-Century English Narratives.* Baltimore: The Johns Hopkins UP, 1995.

Nussbaum, Felicity, and Laura Brown. Introduction. *The New Eighteenth Century: Theory, Politics, English Literature.* Ed. Felicity Nussbaum and Laura Brown. New York: Methuen, 1987. 1–22.

Porter, Roy. *English Society in the Eighteenth Century.* 1982. London: Penguin, 1988.

Potkay, Adam. *The Fate of Eloquence in the Age of Hume.* Ithaca, NY: Cornell UP, 1994.

———. "History, Oratory, and God in Equiano's *Interesting Narrative.*" *Eighteenth-Century Studies* 34.4 (2001): 601–14.

———. "Olaudah Equiano and the Art of Spiritual Autobiography." *Eighteenth-Century Studies* 27.4 (1994): 677–92.

Potkay, Adam, and Sandra Burr, eds. *Black Atlantic Writers of the Eighteenth Century: Living the New Exodus in England and the Americas.* New York: St. Martin's, 1995.

Roach, Joseph. *Cities of the Dead: Circum-Atlantic Performance.* New York: Columbia UP, 1996.

Rogers, Pat. *An Introduction to Pope.* London: Methuen, 1975.

Stevens, Laura. *The Poor Indians: British Missionaries, Native Americans, and Colonial Sensibility.* Philadelphia: U of Pennsylvania P, 2004.

Stoler, Ann Laura. "Rethinking Colonial Categories: European Communities and the Boundaries of Rule." *Society for Comparative Study of Society and History* 31 (1989): 134–61.

Sussman, Charlotte. *Consuming Anxieties: Consumer Protest, Gender, and British Slavery, 1713–1833.* Stanford, CA: Stanford UP, 2000.

Thomas, Helen. *Romanticism and Slave Narratives: Transatlantic Testimonies.* Cambridge, UK: Cambridge UP, 2000.

Thomas, Nicholas. *Colonialism's Culture: Anthropology, Travel and Government.* Cambridge, UK: Polity, 1994.

Turberville, A. S. *English Men and Manners in the Eighteenth Century.* 1926. New York: Oxford UP, 1957.

Wheeler, Roxann. *The Complexion of Race: Categories of Difference in Eighteenth-Century British Culture.* Philadelphia: U of Pennsylvania P, 2000.

Watt, Ian. *The Rise of the Novel: Studies in Defoe, Richardson, and Fielding.* 1957. Berkeley: U of California P, 1965.

Part 2

Special Topics in Teaching *The Interesting Narrative*

Olaudah Equiano, Autobiography, and Ideas of Culture

Sarah Brophy

In a debate published in *Eighteenth-Century Studies* in 2001, Adam Potkay, Srinivas Aravamudan, and Roxann Wheeler heatedly disagree regarding the way in which *The Interesting Narrative of Olaudah Equiano* should be framed for students. Potkay, coeditor with Sandra Burr of the volume *Black Atlantic Writers of the Eighteenth Century: Living the New Exodus in England and the Americas,* seems to recant his earlier interest in diasporic writing, taking issue with what he sees as the tendency of postcolonial criticism to privilege evidence of resistance; in fact, he insinuates that critics tend to manufacture evidence of Equiano's resistance to acculturation and that the problem with contemporary criticism is largely that it does not pay enough attention to rhetorical conventions and cannot admit that Equiano was a wholehearted Christian. Potkay argues that

> Equiano's narrative presupposes as a condition of its intelligibility a world very different from, and in many ways antagonistic to, the world inhabited by many of his recent critics: his is a Christian, an oratorical, and a colonial world. Postcolonial critics are apt to read back into the language of those colonized or displaced by empire signs of creolization, parodic subversion, or "talking back"—in Equiano's case, however, those signs are faint and all too easily exaggerated by those who, programmatically, seek them out. ("History" 602)[1]

It is apparent that Potkay's argument turns on questions of culture, in that a defense of capital "C" Culture (culture as a tradition conceived of as offering a universal model for identity) is being pitched against the reformulation of culture as "cultures" in the plural, where the concept is loosened from its moorings in an Anglo-European tradition and rearticulated to address questions of social justice, history, and identity formation, in this case in the context of the African diaspora. Responding to Potkay, Aravamudan contends that "the presence of the past has to be reinterrogated and recontextualized," arguing that to reduce Equiano's narrative, as Potkay does, to the "rhetorical genre of anger" is to "evacuate" its significance as "a political manifesto" (616–17). Wheeler agrees with Aravamudan, taking the position that Potkay "domesticates" Equiano by ignoring "unequal relations of power in the eighteenth century" and "the politics of literary interpretation in the present," and emphasizing instead the "the tidiness of rhetorical power" (620–24). But neither Potkay nor Aravamudan nor Wheeler clearly defines the stakes of the complicated and changeable term "culture," a consideration which allows us to make connections between the desires of readers, past and present, and the complex, self-conscious staging of ideas of culture in Equiano's narrative.

Reading the narrative as a document knowingly occupied with ideas of culture (including an awareness of some of the emerging concept's internal contradictions) may allow teachers to reposition recent debates about Equiano's identity as well as the pedagogical controversy. When Vincent Carretta points to the narrative's indebtedness to European travel literature about the west coast of Africa, as well as its ambiguity about the narrator's age at the time of his captivity and about his name, he suggests that this reading puts the "author's rhetorical ethos" into question, raising the problem of whether we can accept Equiano's, or Gustavus Vassa's, testimony as an accurate, verifiable first-hand account of slavery ("Olaudah" 97). Voices on opposing sides of the identity debate draw attention to the *Interesting Narrative*'s status as *cultural* testimony, but work with strikingly different concepts of autobiographical evidence, memory, and cultural comparison. In his 2005 biography of Equiano, Carretta notes that baptismal and naval documents suggest Equiano's birthplace was South Carolina (*Equiano* 2). Carretta highlights that even if *The Interesting Narrative* does not qualify as "straightforward autobiography" (*Equiano* 8), it remains significant as the culturally representative biography of a self-identified "African," fashioned for the purposes of the abolitionist movement (3): "A combination of personal experience, conflated sources, recovered memory, and the power of suggestion should not be surprising in a work that may be as much the biography of a people as it is the autobiography of an individual" (7–8). Paul Lovejoy, by contrast, argues that "the most reasonable conclusion in assessing whether or not Vassa was born in Africa or in America is to believe what Vassa claimed" (339). He argues that the narrative reflects Equiano's childhood acculturation as Igbo and fluency in the language, and points out that Equiano and others repeatedly defended in public his claim to have been born in Africa (332, 329, 330). In prioritizing internal (textual) and circumstantial evidence over the baptismal and naval records, Lovejoy draws attention to the non-straightforwardness of a narrative that relies on childhood memory and that engages in sophisticated forms of cultural comparison:

> [A] careful reading of the linguistic, geographical and cultural details provided by Vassa leaves little doubt that he was born in Africa, and specifically in Igboland. In methodological terms, written documentation confronts oral sources and traditions, as related through the memories of an individual and filtered with acquired information through a variety of sources. (325)

Such contrasting engagements as Lovejoy's and Carretta's readings should make scholars and teachers keenly aware of how our reading *methods,* particularly our concepts of evidence and our ideas of individual and collective significance, allow us to make meaning out of the narrative's complexities. I want to suggest that by stepping outside of some of the assumed frameworks of literary studies, while remaining attentive to historical context, rhetorical strategy, narrative structure, and figurative language, we can work towards a better grasp of what was at stake for Equiano in publishing this text and take the discussion a step further as we consider the conceptual challenges it poses to us, its legatees. What happens, in other words, when we consider that another subject is being accounted for in *The Interesting Narrative,* namely that the book is *about culture* as much as it is about individual identity?

Working from this premise, my chief pedagogical strategy is to position *The Interesting Narrative* as taking up received and emergent ideas of culture, reworking them in order to mobilize its complex abolitionist argument. In the context of a course on cultural theory, I pursue with my students a meta-critical and discursive exploration of Equiano's autobiographical strategies, reading them both as self-conscious engagements with ideas of the cultural and as unconscious, interested investments in dominant concepts of culture.[2] A "cultural" reading of the text has been offered by Helen Thomas, who considers how *The Interesting Narrative*'s "bicultural tactics" make it possible for Equiano to "achiev[e] a creolised (re)construction of 'himself,'" as well as to create an effective political intervention intended, ultimately, to address Parliament in the most strenuous possible terms. While Thomas's suggestion that the narrative "offers a subtle critique of the relationship between power and the mechanisms of discourse itself" corroborates the possibility of reading the text as a commentary on culture, her particular focus explicates the narrative's endeavor to fuse "principal tenets of radical dissent with significant elements of African epistemology," so that beliefs including fortune and spirit possession are read as signifying, equally, in both frames of reference (226–28, 254). My main concern here is, rather, to tease out the secular dimensions of the narrative, specifically, the way various notions of culture combine, in this narrative, to constitute working concepts (and the ideology) of the "individual." A major line of inquiry is the role that culture plays in determining who can legitimately claim subject status and in shaping how this is attempted, whether the struggle occurs within a national or diasporic frame of reference. Two questions arise from this contrapuntal approach to teaching *The Interesting Narrative.* First, if we acknowledge the text's complicated relationship with ideas of culture, then does the identity debate continue to matter in the same way? Second, given that ideas of culture are never disinterested (and most *especially interested* when claiming their universality), is it really responsible or even possible to set the bounds of "proper" or legitimate readings?

The introductory (second-year) cultural theory course in which I teach Equiano is titled "Concepts of Culture"; its mandate is to examine debates about culture from the Enlightenment to the present. I begin the semester by highlighting Raymond Williams's attempt to define in his *Keywords* the term "culture" and how this critic draws attention to the contradictory meanings of the term, pointing to its early modern "roots" in the idea of tending natural growth, to its associations with the cultivation of human character, and to its dominant meaning for nineteenth- and early- to mid-twentieth-century critics: the arts considered as the source of Matthew Arnold's "sweetness and light" (87–93). Equally important in Williams's view is the coevolution of the anthropological sense of a culture as "a whole way of life" and, subsequently, the growing awareness of a multiplicity of world cultures, a shift in meaning which, as Terry Eagleton has argued in his *The*

Idea of Culture, gave rise to the characteristic postmodern use of the term "culture" to refer to group identities and allegiances of all kinds. In Eagleton's explication of the culture wars of the 1980s and '90s, the continuing tensions between "Culture" and "culture" (as identity) become clear. Where Culture "cherishes" the individual and posits "a direct relation between the individual and the universal," culture as identity emphasizes "the mediation of the historically particular" (55). The transit (and clash) between the two modes is mediated, significantly, by the modern nation-state, which allows us to imagine the unification of the particular and universal, because it offers a vision of ethnic ties rationally disciplined by the state (57–58). It is also mediated by the idea of the representative individual, who is at once ordinary and an exceptional, heroic model for others to follow.

I also introduce students to Gayatri Spivak's analysis of culture in *A Critique of Postcolonial Reason,* an argument with a more polemical twist and a different assessment of culture that focuses on colonialism and globalization. According to Spivak, from the Enlightenment to the present European imperialism has attempted to make Culture its special but exportable property, and to rationalize and maximize its spread. Significantly, in both colonial and neocolonial definitions of culture, the "native informant" is "denied autobiography" (6).[3] Spivak argues that subaltern personal narratives are not permitted to qualify as legitimate or representative within the "Eurocentric" tradition, except after being framed by an expert interpreter or by virtue of their seeming alignment with a model of heroic individualism. Too often approached as either as repositories of scientific fact (and hence as valuable as resources for constructing a natural history of the human) or as one-dimensional political tracts, subaltern personal narratives are typically seen as in need of being "mediated by the dominant investigator or field worker" (6, 153).

Spivak's analysis is germane to my project because she draws attention to how the positivist framework governing reception works to preclude the possibility of reading subaltern personal narratives as strategic, motivated, and contestatory speech acts. In other words, autobiography is differentially distributed: while the privileged are assumed to engage in inventive self-exploration in their personal narratives, the "native informant" is required to be objective and to provide empirical evidence that can be used to classify group identities. Thus, Spivak poses a challenge to practitioners of literary and cultural studies; she asks that we "keep focusing on the traces of the heterogeneous" rather than allowing the dominant matrix of culture to be simply naturalized and the "native informant" to be conceptualized as "a 'blank,' generative of a text of cultural identity that only the West (or a Western-model discipline could inscribe)" (6).[4]

Bearing in mind Spivak's challenge to read for heterogeneity and for discursive connections across historical periods and movements, I do not wish simply to hold up *The Interesting Narrative* as evidence of "early" resistance to imperialism, but, rather, I am interested in looking at how the text fabricates a strong myth of individual adaptability in which capitalism is naturalized and redeemed, while it simultaneously (though fitfully) questions this framework. To highlight an unexpected (and unexpectedly productive) interpretive layer in *The Interesting Narrative*'s account of personal and cultural identity, let us begin with a revealing intertext from the more recent past, E. D. Hirsch's 1987 book, *Cultural Literacy*, a text that makes a powerful but ultimately disingenuous case for the central value of the Anglo-European tradition in national education today. Disclaimers notwithstanding, Hirsch's definition of "cultural literacy" as "the network of information that all competent readers possess" proposes a rather static, narrow, and utilitarian definition of culture, one that disavows the particularity of the dominant tradition by emphasizing that any individual, including those from minority groups, can ascend to power by mastering and putting into practice the dominant culture's codes, which are posited as a shared value system if not as entirely stable (2). Hirsch's book exemplifies how invocations of "personal merit" in theories of culture mask in-built hierarchies and exclusions (12). It provides us with an overtly conservative assessment of multinational capitalism's impact on individuals as both enabling and destabilizing.

For students, Equiano's narrative is a provocative example to juxtapose with Hirsch's text: *The Interesting Narrative* tells a story of the acquisition of literacy, cultural literacy, and freedom and in this sense seems to confirm a trajectory of individual transcendence. One temptation is to read the narrative for the consolidation of identity and agency—and to read it as a guide, à la Hirsch, outlining the "cultural literacy" an individual needs to acquire to become successful. Certainly, this is the path that Potkay advocates when he insists that the only legitimate reading of Equiano is one that understands and appreciates his mastery of the *rhetoric* of outrage. Simultaneously, though, the narrative testifies (sometimes deliberately, through irony, and sometimes unconsciously, through contradiction) to how the discourses of racialization and enslavement (which denied literacy and reason to Africans) complicate the project of self-fashioning. In order to assess this text's rhetorical and political positioning, it is imperative that we attend carefully to the coexistence of these two contradictory ways of conceptualizing the self-in-culture.

We focus on Equiano's construction of himself as an exceptionally fortunate and gifted individual, "*a particular favourite of Heaven*" (Equiano 31; emphasis in original) as he says, who manages to survive the violent gulf between cultures in the era of the slave trade, to make his way to and through the metropolitan center of the Black Atlantic: London. The sequence of Equiano's adventures in the Royal Navy is of primary importance in establishing him as a successful and fortunate individual, though this sequence is often underplayed in the practices of assembling anthologies, perhaps since the debates about the authenticity of Chapter 1 have become a primary focus in Equiano criticism. Asking students to read the text in full allows them to encounter the depiction of the navy by Equiano as a meritocracy that is also a microcosm of capitalism, in which he, like his master, Captain Pascal, can define himself as *homo economicus.*

In the book's first half, Pascal's rise through the ranks on account of his courage and discernment is carefully recorded and held up as a model. Not only does he feel "attachment and gratitude" to Pascal, but Equiano's improving fortunes are directly linked to his master's promotions, as in the event of Pascal being appointed to the command of a fire-ship, which entails Equiano's rise to the position of steward (84). Under Pascal's command, Equiano develops the character attributes that precipitate his later success as an entrepreneur. For one, he becomes "a stranger to terror of every kind," an attribute which makes him "in that respect at least, almost an Englishman" (77). At the same time, a growing Calvinistic belief in predestination is interwoven with his struggle to survive by his wits. Through a combination of heaven's favor, occasional opportunities to better his education and resources, and his own "dexterity," Equiano survives innumerable battles and begins to gain recognition and a measure of privilege, prosperity, and friendship amongst his fellows (90). As my students are ready to point out, E. D. Hirsch might well applaud Equiano's mastery of the culture's common vocabulary and his application of this "cultural literacy" to economic ends.

To challenge the students' inclination to fall into the interpretive trap of praising Equiano as an exceptional individual, I draw their attention to the fact that a fetishization of the narrative characterized its reception in the period, suggesting that this fetishization persists today. The medallion reprinted as the frontispiece in an early-nineteenth-century edition of the narrative, which shows a slave in a position of supplication asking, "Am I Not a Man and a Brother?", is reproduced in Henry Louis Gates Jr.'s edition of the 1814 text.[5] The origin of the emblem as a trinket produced and distributed by Wedgwood in support of the abolitionist cause allegorizes the sentimentalized commodification of Equiano's narrative. While the words articulate a claim of equal rights, the figure's posture of supplication outlines a power dynamic, in which the subaltern can only better his plight by addressing the wealthy and courting their sympathy: the appeal is to the individual who will buy this lozenge and display it as a personal decoration. Taken as an allegory of publication and reception, this image and its accompanying text are enclosed within and framed by the logic of consumer culture, which is willing to champion protest but only if that protest conforms to an established, nonthreatening protocol for representing difference, one that keeps social hierarchies, especially those of race, intact. Readings that overvalue Equiano's mobility and successful acquisition of literacy and trading acumen participate in this sentimentalized commodification, albeit at a remove.[6] We want the narrative to yield the story of a heroic individual, and not to be a discontinuous, self-contradictory essay, in order that readers can continue to function as patrons of an unambivalently triumphant text.

But what if, along with naming the engagement with ideas of culture as one of the text's primary aspirations, we consider avowed fictionalization as an autoethnographic writing strategy? A key theoretical reading in my cultural theory course is Mary Louise Pratt's "Art of the Contact Zone." Like Françoise Lionnet, who defines autoethnography as the self-reflexive writing of the story of a self-in-culture (115), Pratt points to the resistant orientation of autoethnography, identifying it as a mode of writing that contests the reductive, limiting definitions of "colonial others" that metropolitan texts produce. For Pratt, the autoethnographic text is one "in which people undertake to describe themselves in ways that engage with representations others have made of them." She continues:

> Thus if ethnographic texts are those in which European metropolitan subjects represent to themselves their others (usually their conquered others), autoethnographic texts are representations that the so-defined others construct *in response to* or in dialogue with those texts. . . . Such texts often constitute a marginalized group's point of entry into the dominant circuits

> of print culture. It is interesting to think, for example, of American slave autobiography in its autoethnographic dimensions, which in some respects distinguishes it from the Euramerican autobiographical tradition. (608–9)

After grappling with Pratt's emphasis on dialogue and contestation, my students are ready to pursue the possibility that Equiano's narrative testifies, in a critical and often canny fashion, to the contradictory subjective experiences that the black Atlantic has generated for displaced and racialized people.[7] Recognizing the self-conscious, sustained engagement with ideas of culture in this text allows us to reframe the questions that have been raised about the reliability of *The Interesting Narrative* as a historical document; moreover, tracing ideas of culture through the narrative reveals that there is something much more complicated at work in the text than aspirations to acceptance and integration. I highlight the fact that some of the most unabashedly "invented" aspects of the text are crucial to the project of mapping and potentially challenging the exclusion of displaced and racialized people from the matrix constituted by Western European (primarily Anglophone) manners, customs, religion, and literacy.[8] Accordingly, our class discussions highlight four key tropes in *The Interesting Narrative,* tropes that expose the patterns of exclusion that characterize the purportedly neutral and open matrix of eighteenth-century Atlantic modernity.

First, we consider how the narrative relativizes Anglo-European culture by contrasting it with what is, by the narrator's admission, a fictionalized and idealized account of African cultures, specifically that of the Eboe. There is abundant evidence that the fictionalization of Chapter 1 is an avowed strategy. In the notes, we are referred directly by the author to the sources that inform the portrait: Thomas Clarkson's *Observations on a Guinea Voyage* and Anthony Benezet's *Some Historical Account of Guinea* (Equiano 231nn42–43). Then, at the beginning of Chapter 2, an address to the reader expresses the wish that the author will not be judged as having "trespassed on [the reader's] patience" (46). The suggestion that "the love of one's country" can "be real or imaginary, a lesson of reason, or an instinct of nature" introduces a subtle element of indeterminacy to this reframing of Chapter 1: if the account is "imaginary" (though perhaps it is not), then the desire to imagine oneself as affiliated, originally, with a nation along with the desire to remember and describe this possibility, are accounted for as impulses that are both natural and rational (46). Equiano anticipates the development of an "anthropological" sense of cultures in the plural, as "ways of life." Unlike a late-nineteenth- or early- to mid-twentieth-century anthropologist, however, he resists the typical hierarchizing that posits literate, technologically developed societies as most evolved and oral cultures as melancholy vestiges of a vanished past. In his account of the Eboe, Equiano insists on a definition of the arts as including music, dance, and oral poetry in addition to literature, and he characterizes the culture in the following way: "we are almost a nation of dancers, musicians and poets" (34). Only Swift's Houyhnhnms rival the cleanliness and rationality of the Eboe, who are constructed to exemplify the classical ideal of an agriculturally based, honorable warlike society, one where trade is limited to basic provisions, where modesty reigns, and where rituals of purification are elaborately developed.

Furthermore, in Equiano's text, temporal distinctions are creatively collapsed by the tactic of aligning the Eboe of Benin with two nonfictional societies: "the Israelites in their primitive state," whose government by wise patriarchs and whose rituals are held up admiringly (44), and with the Greeks he has met in Smyrna, whose festive dances Equiano compares enthusiastically with those of the Eboe (242n44). Acknowledging the imaginative elements of the portrait by noting that it is an "imperfect sketch my memory has furnished me" (or perhaps protecting himself against charges of inaccuracy by emphasizing memory's inherent limitations), Equiano offers the analogy between the Eboe and the Israelites not with the aim of verifying a genetic or even a historical connection, but rather because the comparison itself promises to help "remove the prejudice that some conceive against the natives of Africa on account of their colour." Spanish and Portuguese settlements in "the torrid zone" are cited here as well, because "they shew how the complexions of the same persons [that is, persons who share customs and language] vary in different climates" (44–45).[9]

Second, I ask students to consider the importance of the discussion of beauty in Chapter 2. I note that Equiano elaborates the strategic separation of culture from race, opening up the exploration of culture into the field of aesthetics before returning to the central issue: slavery's infringement on human rights. In his summary of the "character" of the Eboe people, Equiano argues that "in regard to complexion, ideas of beauty are wholly relative," noting, for example, that during his travels in Africa he saw several children of lighter complexion and assumed them to be "deformed" (38). This point contrasts with other aesthetic theories of the period, notably Edmund Burke's argument in the *Philosophical Enquiry* that a horror of blackness inheres in our natural faculties. Burke uses the example of a blind boy, whose sight is restored by a cataract operation, noting that the physician

> Cheselden tells us, that the first time the boy saw a black object it gave him great uneasiness; and that some time after, upon accidentally seeing a negro woman, he was struck with great horror at the sight. The horror in this case, can scarcely be supposed to arise from any association. (144–45)

Where Burke's attempt to establish a universal aesthetics that confirms social order inadvertently betrays confusion and panic regarding difference, Equiano's response to difference is notably unflustered, and stresses that the perception of attractiveness or ugliness is a function of custom. The angry passage that concludes Chapter 1 of *The Interesting Narrative* picks up on this chain of argument by emphasizing that "inferiority," like "deformity," is only apparent, the result of an unthinking response to superficial differences:

> Are there not causes enough to which the apparent inferiority of an African may be ascribed, without limiting the goodness of God, and supposing he forbore to stamp understanding on certainly his own image, because "carved deep in ebony"[?] Might it not naturally be ascribed to their situation? When they come among Europeans, they are ignorant of their language, religion, manners, and customs. Are any pains taken to teach them these? Are they treated as men? Does not slavery itself depress the mind, and extinguish all its fire, and every noble sentiment? But, above all, what advantages do not a refined people possess over those who are rude and uncultivated? Let the polished and haughty European recollect that *his* ancestors were once, like the Africans, uncivilized and even barbarous. Did nature make them inferior to their sons? And should *they too* have been made slaves? Every rational mind answers, No. (45; emphasis in original)

This passage makes a reasoned case for "inferiority" as only apparent if examined closely, as the result, in other words, of an unjust "situation": the systematic barring of Africans from "language, religion, manners, and customs," in addition to the dispiriting effects of forced labor and the "brutal cruelty" inflicted on slaves (56). The text thus criticizes racialization, analyzing it as an elaborate system of social and economic difference based on skin colour, to which it juxtaposes a discussion of culture defined in terms of "manners, customs and language" (53). Labeling Europeans as "polished" and "refined," Equiano boldly extends the critique; moreover, he plays on an emerging anxiety in the period, namely the problem of "over-civilization" (the expansion of trade and industry, both at home and abroad, and the escalating accumulation of wealth in the middle classes) which threatens to corrupt the body politic unless tempered by genuine cultivation (42–49).[10] Anticipating nineteenth-century critics such as Coleridge and Arnold, Equiano insinuates that "civilization" without culture leads to arrogance, abuse, and social disorder. The Romantic, reformist bent of *The Interesting Narrative*'s invocation of culture thus begins to become clear for students: culture is held up as a force that will potentially transform the text's addressees into rational, cultured individuals who will be able to see the injustice of the slave-trade and slavery as currently conducted.

Third, I have students analyze how European claims to the achievement of a higher degree of civilization are deflated in the passages that attribute cannibalistic appetites to the white sailors and slave traders that Equiano encounters. Upon being "tossed up to see if I were sound by some of the crew," Equiano reports that he wondered whether he had "gotten into a world of bad spirits, and that they were going to kill me" (55). Parodying the irrational reaction to difference he has already noted in European representations of Africans, he suggests that "their complexions too differing so much from ours, their long hair, and the language they spoke, (which was very different from any I had ever heard) united to confirm me in this belief" (55). The pointedly humorous portrait of the pallid, hairy Europeans exposes the chain of associations by which Europeans extrapolate from fear of differences in appearance (an aesthetic judgment) into the more specific dread of cannibalism (a moral judgment). Once he has a chance to talk with fellow captives Equiano inquires "if we were not to be eaten by those white men with horrible looks, red faces and long hair" (55). Equiano's repetition of this (mis)perception highlights the ironic gap between the slave traders' claims to civility and the "barbarism" of their trading practices. Here the underlying point is that the Europeans are more than metaphorically cannibalistic: their trading practices, and the larger system to which they supply forced labor, do in fact consume human beings.[11] Later, when he sails to England for the first time with Captain Pascal, the trope is repeated:

> He [Pascal] used often to tell him [Equiano's friend and tutor, Richard Baker] jocularly that he would kill and eat me. Sometimes he would say to

> me—the black people are not good to eat, and would ask me if we did not eat people in my country. I said, No: then he said he would kill Dick (as he always called him) first, and afterwards me. (65)

Joking reversals of cannibalism become even more unsettling when they are spoken by the man who owns and names "Gustavus Vassa." While he rehearses the stereotypical association of cannibalism with the torrid zones, Pascal, in a telling contradiction, then attributes it to himself in a way that underscores his power over Gustavus Vassa's very life. As our narrator notes, the possibility of a resort to cannibalism is not entirely unlikely on this "very long passage" with its "very short allowance of provisions" (64). Taken together, this chain of references serves to undo a progressivist account of culture by questioning the "apparent superiority" (to revise Equiano's phrase) of Europeans: how can they continue to claim cultural superiority while they continue to trade in, and exploit, slaves? Given the ironic tenor of the references to cannibalism, the narrative can be considered as a significant account of the relationship between ideas of culture, including notions of monstrosity and cannibalism, and as a critique of the self-justifying "logic" of the predatory economic system that is slavery.

Fourth and finally, we trace the trope of the "talking book," identified by Henry Louis Gates Jr. as a central recurring trope in slave narratives. The "talking book" is vital both in Equiano's staking of a claim to literacy and for mobilizing a critique of literacy being withheld from slaves:

> I had often seen my master and Dick employed in reading; and I had a great curiosity to talk to the books, as I thought they did; and so to learn how all things had a beginning: for that purpose I have often taken up a book, and have talked to it, and then put my ears to it, when alone, in hopes it would answer me; and I have been very much concerned when I found it remained silent. (Equiano 68)

The scene demonstrates several layers in this text: his youthful eagerness for knowledge, his exclusion from anything but a haphazard education, and the mystification in which the white world cloaks itself and its technologies. As Gates argues, implicit in the emphasis on the book's refusal to speak is Equiano's highlighting of his own status as object: "Under the guise of the representation of his naive self, he is naming or reading Western culture closely, underlining relationships between subjects and objects that are implicit in commodity cultures" (*Signifying* 156).

Through the inclusion of such details in his narrative, Equiano testifies to psychological truths and aspects of self-transformation that are not strictly possible to document: the experience of being categorized and treated as object and the process of establishing subjectivity. This is certainly the case later in the narrative, when the Bible speaks to him: "the Scriptures became an unsealed book, I saw myself as a condemned criminal under the law, which came with its full force to my conscience" (189–90). With the experience of conversion, "the word of God was sweet to my taste, yea sweeter than honey and the honey comb. Christ was revealed to my soul as the chiefest among ten thousand" (190). Here, the trope of the talking book, and its promise of access to literacy, cultural literacy, and power, becomes reality, for who can hope to document a conversion experience, to verify its empirical "truth"? This experience is "unspeakable" and also "undeniable" (190). The significance of Equiano's narrative thus exceeds our conventional notions of autobiography as it aspires to bear witness to more than "the facts" and more than can be strictly called his own experiences. That this trope appears in earlier narratives (those of Marrant, Gronniosaw, and Cugoano), and can be placed in the realm of fictionalization, does not detract from its critical functions in Equiano's autobiography. While Gates's primary aim in *The Signifying Monkey* is to identify an African American tradition, his reading is also valuable for drawing out Equiano's focus on critiquing, and insinuating himself into, the discourses and practices of Western culture. As Gates concludes: "if Cugoano names the trope, Equiano names his relation to Western culture through the trope" as well as "his relation to his three antecedent authors" (156).

If the text posits a critique of culture through its use of irony and metaphor, as the four examples cited above suggest, then that critique exists in uneasy tension with the story of successful acculturation that my students are all to eager to see in the book. I guide my students towards recognizing a contradiction here in the narrative's argument about culture; Equiano articulates two seemingly opposed positions, charting the process of acculturation and the development of subjectivity while strenuously criticizing the corruption of slave-trading and slave-owning nations. Rather than interpreting this contradiction as undermining the text's "rhetorical ethos," I suggest to my students that this double agenda be regarded as both explicable and significant: it is intrinsic to Equiano's version of capitalism.

At several points, Equiano is compelled to extend his discussion beyond the realms of economics and literacy and to engage with the concept of culture even more directly than he does in the autoethnographic opening chapters, in the discussion of aesthetics, and in his reworking of the tropes of cannibalism and the talking book. What I want to argue here is that the analysis of slave traders' and owners' behavior hinges on the intertwining, in Equiano's worldview, of the cultural and the economic. As is shown repeatedly in the behavior of Equiano's masters, Captain Pascal, Captain Doran, and Mr. King, as well as in a range of other instances he cites of slave traders and slave masters, white men who own slaves feel free to fail to carry out promises made to a slave and to exploit not only slaves' labor but the products of their leisure time. In Chapter 5, Equiano summarizes what he has witnessed during his captivity in the West Indies after Pascal surreptitiously sells him to Doran. Placed on an equal plane with the many acts of brutality (including "wanton" murder, which would be fined in some jurisdictions, and the sale by planters of their children by black women slaves, which is not recognized in any fashion by the law) is the plight of "a poor Creole negro," who was rarely able to enjoy the rewards of his leisure-time fishing since white men, including his master, "take [the fish] away from him without paying him" (109–10).[12] The narrative's juxtaposition of this repeated, systematic theft with acts of extreme violence against slaves in the West Indies implicitly makes the point that, on a fundamental, philosophical level, the infringement on a man's right to profit by his own labor is in itself morally problematic and in need of "redress" (109–10). While the example of the fisherman is of strategic value for the way it draws attention to the full range of exploitative property relations slavery entails, it clearly resonates personally and ideologically as well: Equiano sees the right to reap the benefits of one's own labor, and particularly one's ingenuity, as fundamental to being human.

Following in the same vein, the subsequent argument that the slave trade and slavery are corrupt is formulated through an opposition of meritorious and meretricious economies: "Surely this traffic cannot be good, which spreads like a pestilence, and taints what it touches" (111). Equiano measures current practices, which bring dishonor, and figuratively damage and contaminate the society against a more honorable and productive standard: a form of liberalism, I point out, in which every man, regardless of the color of his skin, is free to work for his own profit but must refrain from excessively exploiting others. Then, he turns the critique upon slave owners and traders themselves, arguing that Western norms do not adequately check men's greed: "I will not suppose that the dealers in slaves are born worse than other men—No; it is the fatality of this mistaken avarice, that it corrupts the milk of human kindness and turns it into gall" (111). Reading Equiano's tone for its multiple valences is crucial here, and so I invite my students to analyze the language very closely. The tenor of these remarks is at once sarcastic, pointedly critical in its isolation of "avarice" as a central problem, and self-incriminating: for, crucially, it is Equiano's own involvement in the local transport and sale of slaves in the West Indies that allows him to accumulate the money to buy his manumission.

In the rhetorically powerful passage that concludes this chapter, Equiano passionately denounces the asymmetries and inequities in the imperial economy and the concepts of culture that undergird it:

> When you make men slaves you deprive them of half their virtue, you set them in your own conduct an example of fraud, rapine, and cruelty, and compel them to live with you in a state of war; and yet you complain that they are not honest or faithful! You stupify them with stripes, and think it necessary to keep them in a state of ignorance; and yet you assert that they are incapable of learning; that their minds are a barren soil or moor, that culture would be lost on them. (111–12)

With reference back to Raymond Williams on culture from their earlier reading for the course, my students are prepared to see how the metaphors that animate the concept of culture (derived from agriculture, through an analogy between the tending of natural growth and the tending of human development) are used here in a creative, albeit problematic, way. Equiano plays with the instability that is built into the concept of culture through its instantiating organic metaphor; as Eagleton points out, the term "culture" contains within it a dialectic between "what we do to the world and what the world does to us" and so emphasizes the intertwining of "realist" and "constructivist" perspectives on the formation of human character and civil society (2). For Equiano, the minds of slaves are only "barren" because they are excluded from culture, and commerce, when justly conducted, has an inherently "cultivating" impact on individuals and nations.

Significantly, the passage concludes with a quotation from Book 2 of *Paradise Lost,* which not only serves as proof of Equiano's mastery of the English language and its literature, but indirectly threatens insurrection by asking, in Milton's words, "What peace can we return? / But to our power, hostility and hate" (*Paradise Lost,* Book 2, 335–36, cit. in Equiano 112). Equiano's gloss on the passage again draws attention to his belief that commerce can be a positive and morally invigorating force, not least because it is a vehicle for personal cultivation and prosperity.[13] On the basis of necessary links between commerce, individual freedom, and individual and societal cultivation (where the right to engage in commerce on one's own behalf and freedom are really one and the same), Equiano proposes that rebellion can be circumvented (and the whole society strengthened) by owners' "changing your conduct, and treating your slaves as men" (112).

My cultural studies approach endeavors to bring into view *The Interesting Narrative*'s engagement with ideas of cultivation, commerce, self-development, and abolition in the late eighteenth century. I wrap up our study of Equiano's narrative (and anticipate the following unit on empire and culture in the nineteenth century) by emphasizing that Equiano both does and does not see the limitations of hinging his self-definition as a Christian, literate, British subject on his claim to exemplify *homo economicus.* His state of being inside and outside ideology, of simultaneous knowingness and blindness, is, significantly, inherent in his contradictory embrace of individualism and capitalism. Accordingly, when we ask ourselves—and our students—questions about *The Interesting Narrative*'s transcultural situation and its critical engagement with ideas of culture, the text comes into view as an ambivalent intervention in the concept of culture itself. A cultural reading does not, by any means, render the identity debate irrelevant. Indeed, whatever our awareness of the fictionalized dimension of Equiano's autobiography, it is the traces of a lived life that allow readers to identify and empathize with the collective trauma to which Equiano's tale testifies.

It is precisely its charting of the struggle to articulate subjectivity—and to make subjectivity legible within the terms of Western culture—that makes it possible for *The Interesting Narrative* to circulate meaningfully in our contemporary classrooms and academic debates. But the demand for the heroic individual (and for the heroic individual's consistency) that a cultural reading reveals does make the identity debate problematic, particularly because the differential distribution of autobiography noted by Spivak clearly has not dissipated. It seems that Equiano, like Spivak's gendered subaltern, is always vanishing from the universalizing forms of culture that are mobilized in order to fix him in place and to support imperialism's various justificatory narratives of (self-) development and modernization. If we pay more attention to the narrative's self-implication in these contentious matters, then we may be chastened in our quest to establish, test, and retest the identity of the *Interesting Narrative*'s author and more attentive to the narrative's complex critique of culture at the moment of its emergence in the "heart of the Enlightenment" (Eagleton 11).

Notes

1. Potkay singles out Srinivas Aravamudan's and Helen Thomas's readings for emphasizing "cultural hybridity," and in particular for suggesting that Equiano's account of Protestantism is significantly ironized (610). Labeling these arguments "strained," he records his hope that they "will mark the outer limits of postcolonial theory's effort at refashioning Equiano in its own image" and concludes by remarking that "[p]erhaps Equiano's text has something to teach us, instead, about the limits of proper scholarship" (611).

2. See Brophy, "Olaudah Equiano and the Concept of Culture." This earlier version of my argument discusses why and how I teach the book in two specific types of undergraduate courses, one an introduction to cultural theory and the other an American literature survey. The present, longer essay, explores more fully the theoretical underpinnings of my case for framing students' encounters with the text in terms of contested, historically mutable definitions of "culture."

3. Spivak uses the term "native informant" to mark the (im)possible subjectivity of the subaltern within European frameworks for imaging "humanity" and "culture," and, more specifically, to reference the way the figure is required, displaced, and foreclosed in many canonical Western texts (xi).

4. Spivak reads some critics (including Eagleton along with Jameson and Lentricchia) as overemphasizing the decentered subject, arguing that theirs is not an innocent mistake but rather an "interested misreading" (322). Since no cultural explanation is merely descriptive, we must ask, too, whether Eagleton's account assembles a too tidy, even nostalgic view of the nation-state and its forms of imperialism in opposition to transnational capitalism and its forms. Eagleton writes, for example, that "the problem is that our modes of politics and forms of culture have come adrift, in an age where one ideal resolution of the two—the nation-state—is increasingly under siege"

(*The Idea of Culture* 61). Spivak wants us to question a tendency to construct the past as stable and the present as entirely decentered.

5. See this visual image under the title *The Interesting Narrative of the Life of Olaudah Equiano, or Gustavus Vassa, the African. Written by Himself* in Gates's *The Classic Slave Narratives* (15). Gates chooses to reprint the altered 1814 text and therefore does not include the portrait of Equiano holding the Bible by William Denton (Equiano 315). For readings of the Wedgwood slave medallion as offering women of the period an opportunity to combine humanitarian concern with "feminine" acts of consumption and display, see Kowaleski-Wallace (37–39) and Sussman (127). Sussman suggests that the medallion exemplifies abolitionism's tactic of "reconfiguring" consumption as agential, expressive, and potentially ethical. While throughout the eighteenth century women's consumerism was regarded with anxiety (out of a suspicion that it heightened Britain's economic dependence on its colonies) (9), in this new "compassionate" form consumption harmonized with, and reinforced, white British women's claims to domestic authority and virtue (127).

6. Mobility, financial success, and toughness are emphasized, for example, in Gretchen Holbrook Gerzina's "Mobility in Chains: Freedom of Movement in the Early Black Atlantic." While this reading draws productively on new work on travel writing, seamanship, and black sailors' writings of the eighteenth century, its impulse is notably psychological in emphasis. Gerzina's questions are keyed to the heroic individual:

> What did mobility require in terms of opportunity, personal characteristics, and skills? What were the dangers and benefits of movement? In what ways do their writings combine religion with travel, myths of domestic origin with self-determinism? What notions of the literary hero or heroine become possible when mobility is combined with literacy? (44)

By contrast, Sonia Hofkosh and Tania Caldwell both emphasize the interplay of freedom and restriction in the matrix of eighteenth-century Anglo-American culture. Hofkosh concentrates on the mediating effect of Romantic individualism, and Caldwell focuses on Equiano's conflicted relation to the English language as well as to political and economic ideologies of the period.

7. For a more thorough discussion of the Black Atlantic, see Paul Gilroy's seminal text *The Black Atlantic: Modernity and Double Consciousness.*

8. This way of proceeding has implications not only for interpreting written texts but also for how we think about the genealogy of cultural studies and its formation as (anti-)discipline. As Handel Kashope Wright argues, accounts of the history of cultural studies need to be questioned for a prevailing "exclusivity and Eurocentrism": "in articulating, accepting and disseminating a singular, definitively Anglocentric origin of cultural studies [i.e., the Birmingham Centre], we all participate in the negation / denial of Other origins" (357). It is a central premise of my discussion that Equiano can be considered amongst the plethora of African (including diasporic) "literary and cultural works" that, as Wright points out, constitute "'always, already' a heuristic [and performative] form of cultural studies" (360). Spivak similarly challenges the received Anglo-American academic and sometimes masculinist genealogy of cultural studies, in the hope of fashioning a more heterogeneous conception of "transnational cultural studies" (*Critique of Postcolonial Reason* 104, 414).

9. As Thomas points out, "Equiano endeavors to destabilize theoretical configurations of polygenesis and racial difference by means of a strategic narrative of cultural hybridity and racial fluidity"; moreover, the focus on rituals "serves to endorse a comparison between Ibo and Jewish culture and, more importantly, to erode the ideological and epistemological boundaries between African culture and the west" (231–32).

10. Coleridge, for instance, worries that

> civilization itself is but a mixed good, if not more a corrupting influence, the hectic of disease, not the bloom of health, and a nation so distinguished more aptly to be called a varnished than a polished people; where this civilization is not grounded in cultivation, in the harmonious development of those qualities and faculties that characterize our *humanity.* We must be men in order to be citizens. (42–43)

See also Matthew Arnold, *Culture and Anarchy and Other Writings.* Arnold worries about the tendency to associate industrialization, particularly the personal accumulation of profit, with "greatness and welfare," and argues for Culture as a corrective to this "Philistine" view of civilization:

> what an unsound habit of mind it must be which makes things like coal or iron as constituting the greatness of England, and how salutary a friend is culture, bent on seeing things as they are, and thus dissipating delusions of this kind and fixing standards of perfection that are real! (64–65)

11. Valuable extended readings of the trope of cannibalism have been offered by Charlotte Sussman and by Mark Stein. As Sussman persuasively argues with respect to the rhetoric of consumer boycotts of sugar in the period,

> The abolitionist accusation of English cannibalism enacts a kind of paranoid reversal . . . as a result of their improper consumption of colonial products, British consumers are themselves transformed into the savage cannibals they had once fantasized about as existing only on the colonial periphery. (*Consuming Anxieties* 116)

Looking more specifically at Equiano's use of this strategy, Stein makes the important further point that "by mimicking colonial discourse (in lodging accusations of cannibalism) and by translating one form of anthropophagy into another, Equiano stresses the *tropicality* of cannibalism. Equiano's textual tricksterdom dislodges cannibalism from the realm of the real to suggest that its foremost existence is discursive" ("Who's Afraid of Cannibals?" 143).

12. While an analysis of gender is not the focus of this essay, it is nonetheless important to note how Equiano's claims to belonging and legitimacy in the worlds of seafaring and trading are frequently played out in scenes of male bonding, in which virility is enacted by men through a triumphing over the relatively more vulnerable bodies of women. For example, Thomas reads Equiano's ambivalent testimony to his implication in the sexual exploitation of female slaves, observing that his narration of these scenes "underlines an important recognition of his own 'lack' of power"

(239–40). For a wide-ranging discussion of triangulated male power relations in the period, see Eve Kosofsky Sedgwick, *Between Men: English Literature and Male Homosocial Desire.*

13. Sussman contends that Equiano's narrative concludes by emphasizing "utopian hopes for free-market capitalism" (including arguments that emphasized Africa's potential as a market), pointing out that such hopes were the basis "of much of the abolitionist appeal in England" before the failed experiment of the Sierra Leone colony (195–96).

Works Cited

Aravamudan, Srinivas. "Equiano Lite." *Eighteenth-Century Studies* 34.4 (2001): 615–19.

Arnold, Matthew. *Culture and Anarchy and Other Writings.* Ed. Stephen Collini. Cambridge, UK: Cambridge UP, 1993.

Brophy, Sarah. "Olaudah Equiano and the Concept of Culture." *Teaching Life Writing Texts.* Ed. Miriam Fuchs and Craig Howes. New York: MLA, 2008. 270–76.

Burke, Edmund. *A Philosophical Enquiry into the Origins of Our Ideas of the Sublime and the Beautiful.* 1757. Ed. James T. Boulton. London: Routledge, 1958.

Caldwell, Tania. "'Talking Too Much English': Languages of Economics and Politics in Equiano's *The Interesting Narrative.*" *Early American Literature* 34.3 (1999): 263–82.

Carretta, Vincent. *Equiano, the African: Biography of a Self-Made Man.* Athens: U of Georgia P, 2005.

———. "Olaudah Equiano or Gustavus Vassa? New Light on an Eighteenth-Century Question of Identity." *Slavery and Abolition* 20.3 (1999): 96–105.

Coleridge, Samuel Taylor. *On the Constitution of Church and State.* Vol. 10 of *The Collected Works of Samuel Taylor Coleridge.* Ed. Kathleen Coburn. Princeton, NJ: Princeton UP, 1976.

Eagleton, Terry. *The Idea of Culture.* Oxford, UK: Blackwell, 2000.

Equiano, Olaudah. The Interesting Narrative *and Other Writings.* Ed. Vincent Carretta. Rev. ed. New York: Penguin, 2003.

Gates, Henry Louis, Jr., ed. *The Classic Slave Narratives.* New York: Mentor, 1987.

———. *The Signifying Monkey: A Theory of African-American Literary Criticism.* New York: Oxford UP, 1988.

Gilroy, Paul. *The Black Atlantic: Modernity and Double Consciousness.* Cambridge, MA: Harvard UP, 1993.

Hirsch, E. D. *Cultural Literacy: What Every American Needs to Know.* Boston: Houghton, 1987.

Hofkosh, Sonia. "Tradition and *The Interesting Narrative:* Capitalism, Abolition, and the Romantic Individual." *Romanticism, Race, and Imperial Culture, 1780–1834.* Ed. Alan Richardson and Sonia Hofkosh. Bloomington: Indiana UP, 1996. 330–44.

Holbrook Gerzina, Gretchen. "Mobility in Chains: Freedom of Movement in the Early Black Atlantic." *South Atlantic Quarterly* 100.1 (2001): 41–59.

Kowaleski-Wallace, Elizabeth. *Consuming Subjects: Women, Shopping, and Business in the Eighteenth Century.* New York: Columbia UP, 1997.

Lionnet, Françoise. *Autobiographical Voices: Race, Gender, Self-Portraiture.* New York: Cornell UP, 1989.

Lovejoy, Paul. "Autobiography and Memory: Gustavus Vassa, alias Olaudah Equiano, the African." *Slavery and Abolition* 27.3 (2006): 317–47.

Potkay, Adam, and Sandra Burr, eds. *Black Atlantic Writers of the Eighteenth Century: Living the New Exodus in England and the Americas.* New York: St. Martin's, 1995.

———. "History, Oratory, and God in Equiano's *Interesting Narrative.*" *Eighteenth-Century Studies* 34.4 (2001): 601–14.

Pratt, Mary Louise. "The Arts of the Contact Zone." *Ways of Reading.* Ed. David Bartholomae and Anthony Petrosky. 5th ed. Boston: Bedford/St. Martin's, 2002. 605–18.

Sedgwick, Eve Kosofsky. *Between Men: English Literature and Male Homosocial Desire.* New York: Columbia UP, 1985.

Spivak, Gayatri Chakravorty. *A Critique of Postcolonial Reason: Toward a History of the Vanishing Present.* Cambridge, MA: Harvard UP, 1999.

Stein, Mark. "Who's Afraid of Cannibals: Some Uses of the Cannibalism Trope in Olaudah Equiano's *Interesting Narrative.*" *Discourses of Slavery and Abolition: Britain and its Colonies, 1760–1838.* Ed. Brycchan Carey, Markman Ellis, and Sara Salih. Basingstoke, UK: Palgrave Macmillan, 2004. 136–53.

Sussman, Charlotte. *Consuming Anxieties: Consumer Protest, Gender, and British Slavery, 1713–1833.* Stanford, CA: Stanford UP, 2000.

Thomas, Helen. *Romanticism and Slave Narratives: Transatlantic Testimonies.* Cambridge, UK: Cambridge UP, 2000.

Wheeler, Roxann. "Domesticating Equiano's *Interesting Narrative.*" *Eighteenth-Century Studies* 34.4 (2001): 620–24.

Williams, Raymond. "Culture." *Keywords: A Vocabulary of Culture and Society.* Oxford, UK: Oxford UP, 1983. 87–93.

Wright, Handel Kashope. "Take Birmingham to the Curb, Here Comes African Cultural Studies: An Exercise in Revisionist Historiography." *University of Toronto Quarterly* 65.2 (1996): 355–65.

Flat Equiano: A Transatlantic Approach to Teaching *The Interesting Narrative*

Jessica L. Hollis

In a 2001 forum on teaching *The Interesting Narrative,* Roxann Wheeler emphasizes the need to contextualize Equiano's work within its historical and political milieus. Arguing against approaches to the narrative that focus exclusively on eighteenth-century investments in oration and spiritual autobiography, Wheeler reminds us that such readings restrict our understanding of not only *The Interesting Narrative* but the eighteenth century as well. In her words, these latter analyses lead to the "*flattest* version of Equiano," while those that place the work within a broader range of period texts provide "a *depth* that we have not explored as fully as the narrative structure and style" (622; emphases added). The language of horizontality and verticality employed here ("flattest" and "depth") is, of course, intended to convey disparate degrees of interpretation, and I call attention to it not to disagree with Wheeler's point, which I affirm. Rather, I want to use it, though somewhat differently, as a starting point for reconsidering some of the ways scholars and teachers have spatially understood *The Interesting Narrative* and, more generally, have conceptualized relationships between the different geographical areas and peoples of the eighteenth-century Atlantic World.

Spatial and spatializing concepts have become almost a given in the way we introduce the eighteenth-century Atlantic World to our students: empire-colony, center-periphery, metropole-province. Certainly, these couplings have provided a useful framework for highlighting the often exploitive and unequal power relations between European nations and other parts of the Atlantic that became more solidified during this period. Likewise, they have helped critics explicate the efforts of those subjugated to resist the systems that restricted them. Further, given they were used by eighteenth-century Europeans to describe how different sides of the Atlantic were connected, they have also been a fruitful means of recovering how individuals understood and experienced these connections in this period. However, as scholars have argued recently, eighteenth-century usages of these terms did not always carry the same connotations as they do within much recent criticism—particularly a certain, influential strain of postcolonial studies. They did not, that is, always convey a hierarchal relationship between Europe and the rest of the Atlantic.[1] Indeed, the vertical power structure implied by the critical usage of these binaries too often fails to recognize adequately the much more complex power dynamics that defined eighteenth-century Atlantic relations. Their continual usage, likewise, risks reemphasizing a reductive verticality *because* dichotomous implications of dominance/subjugation continue to obtain to them.

In this sense, I concur with Adam Potkay's caveat about reading Equiano's narrative (and the eighteenth-century Atlantic World) singularly in terms of postcolonial critique (though I disagree with him on other points, which I discuss below). But I also agree with Roxann Wheeler that the "most challenging versions of postcolonial theory have aimed to restore historical complexity to our understanding of the colonial world on both sides of the Atlantic" (621). Nonetheless, vertical resonances of spatial concepts employed within postcolonial studies indicate that this is one area in need of redirection. Not surprisingly, Wheeler asserts that "the most suggestive colonial theory has . . . emanated from . . . cultural geographers," among others, for it is, indeed, these geographers who are currently engaged in redressing the spatialities of postcolonial studies (621).[2]

A decidedly horizontal conceptualization of—or a "flat" approach to—the eighteenth-century Atlantic, then, potentially offers a counter-framework for teaching *The Interesting Narrative,* and, I argue, one that allows for a richer exploration of Equiano's experiences. As some readers may discern, the title for this article is a play on "Flat Stanley," an international literacy tool that takes the form of a cut-out, paper doll–like boy that is mailed by elementary-school students to places around the world. The Flat Stanley project, while very diverse in its ultimate manifestations,[3] is basically designed to help children learn geography and about different places by way of this virtual traveler-visitor who can be mailed in an envelope to distant family members, friends, or even strangers. The task of these hosts is to continue a journal begun by Stanley's sender, which describes her or his "home life." The host family's portion of the journal records the places he sees, people he meets, foods he eats, and anything he learns about his new home; then, Stanley and the journal are either sent back to the "home family" or on to another host family.

I invoke "Flat Stanley" to emphasize a particular kind of relationship between people and places and between people *in* different places. Flat Stanley is, of course, subject to his senders and receivers, much like Equiano is a great deal of the time. Nonetheless, the concept of the Stanley project is that of a constant traveler who experiences the world by way of more or less equal partners (home and host "families") who participate in a shared endeavor (the exchange of information and experience about new places and people). Stanley's travels, then, are determined either by social and familial networks or by curiosity about unknown places and people, and in each case exchange is the goal. The sense of travel, experience, and place that "Flat Stanley"—or *flatness,* more generally—evokes, I suggest, is one that can redress some of the problems current approaches to *The Interesting Narrative* have created. Specifically, this "flatness" both highlights and counterbalances the vertical frameworks that have been employed to read Equiano's narrative. Thus, I argue, a flatter or *transatlantic* approach to the narrative, which emphasizes movement and exchange among different areas of the Atlantic as a defining feature of eighteenth-century life and literature, is a more fruitful one than those that frame the work in terms of imperialism or colonialism.

Below, I discuss in more detail some of the limitations that spatial concepts such as center-periphery impose on our understanding of *The Interesting Narrative* in the context of my most recent experience teaching the work. Then, I propose how a transatlantic rubric more fruitfully allows us to acknowledge and come to terms with the narrative's incorporation of the varied and changing nature of eighteenth-century ideas about slavery, race, and citizenship and Equiano's position with respect to these terms.

Given the horizontal/vertical contrast I am setting up, I do want to stress that I am interested in examining the way *spatial* concepts and *spatializing* gestures are employed to examine the relationships between different parts of the world (both now and in the past). Certainly concepts such as Homi Bhabha's use of "hybridity" have worked to complicate strictly dichotomous understandings of the power dynamics that characterize relationships between colonizer and colonized. However, given that spatial conceptualization is still a significant factor in our analysis of Atlantic (and now global) relations—and, as I will show below, in our students' understanding of them—ongoing critical evaluation of its usage is necessary. I also want briefly to call attention to the nonetheless "flattening" connotations of some of the pairings noted above. On one hand, they *do* suggest a radiation outward rather than upward. Empire spreads out to cover vast territory, and "center-periphery" conjures up images of spokes on a wheel branching out from an interior midpoint. Thus, these binaries imply a horizontal spatiality. On the other hand, what radiates outward from the center is power, whether it be cultural, political, economic, or physical. Any flattening connotation they might evoke, then, does not level out power relations among geographical areas but instead verticalizes them.

This observation is not to ignore that scholars over the last few decades have invigorated binaries such as center-periphery with much more interpretive complexity. Most famously, perhaps, Mary Louise Pratt's exploration of "transculturation" in *Imperial Eyes* and Joseph Roach's "circum-Atlantic" approach attempt to account for the various configurations of power that occur through cultural contact, appropriation, and exchange. These scholars illustrate some of the intricacies of Atlantic encounters, highlighting the processes of mutual influence as well as the failure and rejection of influence in both directions. However, as both the main part of Pratt's book title and her notion of a Eurocentric "planetary consciousness" indicate, the controlling energies of "empire" are ultimately paramount. This is the case *despite* Pratt's expressed wish not to concede autonomy to the metropolis in her analysis nor to "simply reproduc[e] the dynamics of possession and innocence" that she finds depicted at times in the texts she examines (5–6). So, we can see how the traditional spatializing gestures of these concepts continue to haunt some of our most influential scholarship despite our best efforts to avoid reductiveness in using them as framing rubrics.

These hauntings, not surprisingly, find their way into our classrooms as well. They do so both via our own immediate use of terms such as "empire" to describe our courses and their themes and our students' pre-established familiarity with these concepts. This type of surfacing became starkly apparent to me recently, when I taught Equiano's narrative in a theme-based, lower-level undergraduate literature course at the University of Kentucky. With a main title of "Literature and Identities" and "modernity" as an overarching theme, the course explored how identities were formed in the context of processes such as urbanization, imperialism, and transnationalism. The course focus and texts were chosen by me, and we covered works from *The Tempest* to Willa Cather's *Alexander's Bridge* to Tsitsi Dangarembga's twentieth-century Zimbabwean novel, *Nervous Conditions.* Given the transnational (not to mention historical) scope of the course, we used individual editions of these works, including the W. W. Norton edition of the 1789 text (first printing) of *The Interesting Narrative,* rather than an anthology. Current anthologizing of Equiano's narrative, indeed, counters the tranatlanticism of the work that I wanted to emphasize as a defining feature of imperialism. Although British/English and American literary anthologies (Norton, Heath, Longman), in their literary and historical overviews, have complicated the national and imperial frameworks that their titles intimate, such works nonetheless keep such categories alive. We would do well to find other forms of organization; however, including Equiano's text in a world literature anthology as Bedford does, while maintaining American anthologies (and including *The Interesting Narrative* there as well), does little to address the emphasis on national literatures. Longman's *Transatlantic Romanticism: An Anthology of British, American, and Canadian Literature, 1767–1867* seems a step in the right direction. However, the subtitle undercuts its initial gesture towards a transatlantic orientation even though the organization of the content does not adhere to the tripartite nationalization.[4]

Although I included the word "imperialism" in the course description for my class, I strove *not* to employ the spatial concepts of postcolonial studies as framing rubrics in my lectures, focusing instead on terms like "fluidity" and "flows" to avoid emphasizing a top-down approach to Atlantic interchange. Despite these efforts, however, students seemed to migrate towards "empire" as an orienting touchstone. I found that even those undergraduate students least familiar with literary studies and the eighteenth century understood the basic concept of empire as one of political and cultural domination and recognized narratives such as Equiano's autobiography as illustrative of that aspect of eighteenth-century Atlantic relations. The slave trade and its deracinating and dehumanizing effects on black Africans are historical events that my students associated with the period, even if they had not encountered (or simply could not remember having encountered) period texts that provide accounts of these events or could not distinguish between eighteenth- and nineteenth-century forms of slavery and the slave trade. Likewise, they appeared to have been nurtured to express what Adam Potkay has referred to as a kind of self-righteous indignation at Equiano's plight and the brutal treatment of dark-skinned individuals by Europeans more generally.[5]

Thus, my students easily accepted Equiano's narrative as an abolitionist text and the status of all black individuals as inferior and as property (or at least potential property) in the Atlantic World. That is, though they saw this status of blacks as unjust and recognized Equiano's efforts to redress it, they nonetheless accepted it as really the only one available to Equiano and his fellow black Atlantics. These are not surprising conclusions, given some of the framing and reoccurring elements of Equiano's narrative: he addresses his work to political leaders of Great Britain (as well as "spiritual" leaders),[6] states that bringing attention to the suffering of his enslaved "countrymen" is the objective of his narrative, and repeatedly reminds his readers that he is vulnerable to a range of violations even after he acquires his freedom, including loss of property, physical violence, capture and, most important, re-enslavement.

Indeed, for my students, Equiano's recurrent identification with other black Africans in the later parts of his narrative only solidified his subjugated status in the Atlantic World. While they did read Equiano's claims to Englishness as indicating his genuine feelings and experience of the person he had become, they also saw the repeated references to his continual vulnerability as evidence of his inability to appropriate this cultural and national identity. For instance, they noted that in the same chapter (Chapter 4) that Equiano represents himself as happily and successfully acclimating to his "new [British] countrymen" (Equiano 56), so much so that he considers himself "almost an Englishmen" (56), he is also reminded that he ultimately has little power over his fate. Upon returning to London after fighting in the Seven Years' War, Equiano is taken by surprise when Captain Pascal asserts his power over Equiano: "[A]ll in an instant, without having before given me the least reason to suspect any thing of the matter, he forced me into the barge; saying, I was going to leave him, but he would take care I should not" (68). Equiano experiences his vulnerability even more when Pascal quickly sells him to Captain Doran, who likewise makes his power felt:

> Captain Doran said I talked too much English; and if I did not behave myself well, and be quiet, he had a method on board to make me. I was too well convinced of his power over me to doubt what he said; and my former sufferings in the slave-ship presenting themselves to my mind, the recollection of them made me shudder. (69)

My students observed not only Equiano's claims to a proto-Englishness in the first part of this chapter but also his extended descriptions of his military activities, contending that the sense we get of Equiano here is of a soldier not of a slave. Thus, they argued, the selling of Equiano, coming quickly on the heels of these experiences, underscored his lack of control over his fate. In other words, they sensed Equiano's vulnerability even more in the context of his preceding representations of himself as relatively self-willed. They also pointed out a parallel between these passages and those detailing Equiano's manumission and his immediate experiences as a free man. Within two pages of the narrative Equiano is freed from slavery and threatened with flogging without recourse to "judge or jury," a situation that he has seen in "many instances . . . of the treatment of free negroes" (106–8). The continued threats Equiano experiences illustrated for my class that the dominating group did not fully accept him and thus his identification with this group was more tragic than anything. For them, Equiano's felt experiences of Englishness did not signify agency because ultimately he was subject to the proprietorship of his masters and to laws (or lack of them) that denied him personal rights.

I understood my students' desires to emphasize the unjust treatment of African Atlantics in their reading of *The Interesting Narrative.* As one member of the class put it (and I will have to paraphrase here), "if we read Equiano's claims to Englishness as successful, then, we assume he has overcome the whole slavery system, which ascribes too much power to him and leaves us thinking such an accomplishment was possible." I also understood they were coming from an understanding of empire as referencing vertical power relationships. However, I also wanted the class to recognize and grapple with the much more complex representations of agency and subjugation that Equiano's narrative offers. To counteract this reading of Equiano as utterly powerless and objectified, I pointed the class to moments when Equiano negotiates his relative powerlessness. I noted his recurrent success as a trader and employee aboard trading ships (while also bringing attention to his participation in the slave trade) and moments when Equiano reports defending himself against his white oppression. For example, Equiano manages to extract due payment from whites despite their attempts to assert that no black individual need be remunerated. At times, Equiano's negotiations are relatively passive, as when he simply waits out his debtor:

> I had lent my captain some money . . . but when I applied for it, though I urged the necessity of my occasion, I met with so much shuffling from him, that I began at last to be afraid of losing my money, as I could not recover it by law: for I have already mentioned, that throughout the West Indies no black man's testimony is admitted, on any occasion, against any white person whatever, and therefore my own oath would have been of no use. I was obliged, therefore, to remain with him till he might be disposed to return it to me. Thus we sailed from Martinico for the Grenades. I frequently pressing the captain for my money to no purpose . . . At last, however, with a great many entreaties, I got my money from the captain. (122)

Here, Equiano seems to succeed by simply wearing on his captain's patience.

At other times, Equiano is much more active in his applications, though he usually obtains the help of white men in these situations. In one example I noted, Equiano and another black man band together with whites in a similar situation.

> A white man, an islander, bought some goods of me to the amount of some pounds, and made me many fair promises as usual, but without any intention of paying me. . . . when I asked him for my money he threatened me and another black man he had bought goods of, so that we found we were like to get more blows than payment. On this we went to complain to one Mr. M'Intosh, a justice of the peace; we told his worship of the man's villainous tricks, and begged that he would be kind enough to see us redressed: but being negroes, although free, we could not get any remedy; . . . Luckily for us[,] however, this man was also indebted to three white sailors, who could not get a farthing from him; they therefore readily joined us, and we all went together in search of him. When we found where he was, I took him out of a house and threatened him with vengeance; on which, finding he was likely to be handled roughly, the rogue offered each of us some small allowance, but nothing near our demands. This exasperated us much more; and some were for cutting his ears off; but he begged hard for mercy, which was at last granted him, after we had entirely stripped him. We then let him go, for which he thanked us, glad to get off so easily, and ran into the bushes, after having wished us a good voyage. (129)

While this passage indicates that Equiano does not always manage to obtain everything due to him, it does illustrate his efforts to assert himself against exploitation. Thus, it helped stress to students that agency need not depend upon acquiring the explicit goal of an action. The description of Equiano's debtor in the last few lines of this passage, in fact, indicates that Equiano and his companions are recompensed in non-monetary ways: their exploiter has lost all sense of power. Equiano also successfully talks his way out of confrontations, as seen in this passage:

> [W]hile I was a little way out of the town of Savannah, I was beset by two white men, who meant to play their usual tricks with me in the way of kidnapping. As soon as these men accosted me, one of them said to the other, "This is the very fellow we are looking for that you lost:" [*sic*] and the other swore immediately that I was the identical person. On this they made up to me, and were about to handle me; but I told them to be still and keep off; for I had seen those kind of tricks played upon other free blacks, and they must not think to serve me so. At this they paused a little, and one said to the other—it will not do; and the other answered that I talked too good English. I replied, I believed I did; and I had also with me a revengeful stick equal to the occasion; and my mind was likewise good. Happily[,] however[,] it was not used; and, after we had talked together a little in this manner, the rogues left me. (121)

Just as Equiano defends himself verbally here, I proposed, Equiano's narrative itself is a form of "talking back" to the oppressors.

This approach, however, ended up producing an unintended consequence. While my initial goal for the course was to de-emphasize vertical power relationships, pointing to these instances where Equiano *resists* oppression resulted in reaffirming vertical power relationships; Equiano, from below, strives against a still dominant oppressor from above. Just as the students' readings of *The Interesting Narrative* fit nicely with the hierarchical power dynamics that postcolonial spatial terminology (center-periphery, metropole-province, empire-colony) was meant to describe and critique, so did my counter reading. Thus, my efforts also failed to bring attention to the narrative's complex representation of agency by relying on a rubric that opposed agency and subjugation as binaries. In some sense I had inadvertently fallen into the trap that Adam Potkay notes many critics of *The Interesting Narrative* have, that of "read[ing] back into the language of those colonized or displaced by empire signs of creolization, parodic subversion, or 'talking back'" (602). However, while Potkay finds such strategies a problem because "in Equiano's case . . . those signs are faint and all too easily exaggerated by those who, programmatically, seek them out," the examples above and many others in the narrative illustrate that these signs are quite evident in the narrative (602). Though I agree that emphasizing these forms of resistance and the power dynamics they suppose to the exclusion or subordination of all other considerations is limiting, I do not suggest that we entirely abandon the analysis of power in the study of *The Interesting Narrative,* or the eighteenth century and race more generally, which Potkay's emphasis on religion in Equiano's work seems to suggest. Most notably, Potkay points out the presence of "patriarchy" in the narrative only to highlight its "Patriarchal" sentiments, sentiments that appear to matter only as far as Equiano's religious faith and the biblical pattern of the narrative are concerned (608–9). No doubt, the biblical context here is significant but it need not become a focus that, again, excludes other considerations. Indeed, given that Equiano proposes "the excite[ment] . . . of compassion for the miseries which the Slave Trade has entailed on [his] unfortunate countrymen" as the "chief design" of *The Interesting Narrative,* exploring the power dynamics of "patriarchy" as well as "Patriarchy" seems unavoidable (7). Potkay himself points out the parallels between slavery in Equiano's work and in the Old Testament; yet, discussion of power relationships is absent.

Teaching *The Interesting Narrative,* then, requires a conceptual framework that anticipates and counters both my students' approaches to Equiano's experiences and my strategies for responding to them. In other words, a framework that does not understand Equiano simply in terms of resistance and oppression is needed. Srinivas Aravamudan has alerted us to the problem that such an account of black subjectivity produces. Conceptualizing Equiano's agency in relation to his treatment by and resistance to his white masters, Aravamudan insightfully argues, requires domination to exist in order for black selfhood to be imagined; Equiano's status is wholly dependent upon his subjugation and enslavement, and we fail to allow that he exists as a subject outside these parameters. In essence, we affirm his status—and that of other Atlantic Africans—as non-subjects who must strive for subjectivity, rather than recognizing they are already subjects. However, Aravamudan argues,

> [c]ommon sense would grant that slaves were already political and psychological subjects of the human community despite their masters' treatment of them as chattel and commodity and continued to be subjects both before and after they were coerced into the Middle Passage and the work of the plantation. (271)

Equiano's narrative grants this point as well. We are, after all, introduced to Equiano through his life as a child in Africa and given a sketch of the social and political structures of his community as well as that of other African communities (chaps. 1 and 2). For instance, we learn that one mode signifying status and political position entails corporeal marking:

> This mark is conferred on the person entitled to it, by cutting the skin across at the top of the forehead, and drawing it down to the eye-brows; and while it is in this situation applying a warm hand, and rubbing it until it shrinks up into a thick weal across the lower part of the forehead. (20)

And, we see that Equiano very early on has strong emotional attachments, to the extent that he breaks the rules of his community:

> Every woman too, at certain times, was forbidden to come into a dwelling-house, or touch any person, or any thing we ate. I was so fond of my mother I could not keep from her, or avoid touching her at some of those periods, in consequence of which I was obliged to be kept out with her, in a little house made for that purpose, till offering was made, and then we were purified. (28)

In my latest experience teaching *The Interesting Narrative* at Ohio University, I encouraged my students to analyze this rebellion against restrictive village laws with later moments when Equiano notes the injustice of colonial and national laws with respect to both enslaved and free Africans. Doing so demonstrated that his subjectivity is in some way consistent throughout his text, thus making it possible to conceptualize him, whether as a slave or a vulnerable free black, as determined by something more than just power relationships manifested after his enslavement.

To illustrate how we might prepare students to acknowledge Equiano's various subject positions throughout *The Interesting Narrative,* the remainder of this essay will focus on strategies for implementing a transatlantic approach in the classroom. Some of these I employed in the class noted above, others I have implemented in later classes, at both upper- and lower-division levels. I typically begin my eighteenth-century classes by emphasizing forms of movement and exchange among different areas of the Atlantic as a defining feature of eighteenth-century life and literature. For instance, rather than reading J. Hector St. John de Crèvecoeur's early essays about colonial life as U.S. literature, a transatlantic approach draws attention to a number of geographically diverse elements of this work: the writing of the series of essays in *colonial* New York but their initial publication in *London* in 1782, *after* the U.S. Declaration of Independence and under the title *Letters from an American Farmer* (emphasis added); Crèvecoeur's birth in France, travel to Canada, move to New York, conversion to a British subject, and ultimate return to France; the author's dedication of the letters to the French natural historian Raynal, whose work the author says inspired his own, and the *English* gentlemen he supposedly writes the letters for; and, some of the lesser studied letters, such as the description of Nantucket, which points to that settlement's dependence on both east-west and north-south transatlantic travel and exchange. Such focus on the mobility of ideas, people, and objects counters approaches that retroactively employ national boundaries and cultural divides to understand the period and that see spatial distance as an impediment to any kind of meaningful transatlantic influence.

In this context it is not difficult to see how or why *The Interesting Narrative* can and should be taught as a transatlantic text rather than as part of a *single* national literature, *multiple* national literatures, or even continental literature (e.g., British, American, Nigerian, and African). In the course of his narrative, Equiano moves from one part of the Atlantic to another numerous times, in both east-west and north-south directions and has no real "home base." Yet, despite Equiano's mobility and his lack of British subjecthood, approaches to the narrative in the Western academy have traditionally oriented it nationally and imperially. The recent controversy over Vincent Carretta's research on Equiano's birth has brought new attention to *The Interesting Narrative*'s place within not only U.S. literary histories but African ones as well; likewise, the graphic depictions of slavery in the colonies and Equiano's description of the Middle Passage have located it within American and African American traditions, particularly that of the slave narrative. On the other hand, the narrative's publication (and supposed composition) in England and Equiano's eventual settlement there have been used as grounds for its place in the British literature corpus, while the British slave trade debate that the text invokes has similarly situated the work within studies of British imperialism. And, I think it is safe to say that this is how the work has traditionally been taught. The various British and American literature anthologies attest to this fact, as does the continuing distinction between British and American literature courses in English department curricula at most schools. Moreover, seminal scholarship by critics such as Chinua Achebe, Henry Louis Gates Jr., Houston A. Baker Jr., and Keith Sandiford as well as Carretta affirm the work's place within various American, British, and African traditions.[7] While I do not want to suggest that these are unimportant contexts for understanding Equiano's narrative, identifying them as the ultimate defining feature of the work suppresses the much more obvious transatlantic elements of *The Interesting Narrative.* Avoiding the use of the anthologies mentioned above, of course, is sometimes not an option or not a feasible one for either our students or us, due to costs of materials in other forms (individual texts or numerous photocopies). Likewise, curricular changes are infamously protracted processes, thus ensuring that national distinctions will continue to characterize course options at many institutions. Though we should work toward making these changes, more important immediate tactics are needed. Classroom strategies such as emphasizing the transatlantic nature of the eighteenth century through the structure and publication of *Letters from an American Farmer* or Equiano's travels are one option.

Practical teaching strategies that can orient students towards a more transatlantic perspective on Equiano's narrative include preceding students' reading of the work with a presentation on the routes of slave ships and shipping routes in general. Doing so highlights the interconnectedness and interdependency of various Atlantic locations. This pedagogical strategy could take the shape of student presentations, which could be staggered along with the reading schedule for Equiano's narrative. In a class I recently taught, presentations illustrated the Atlantic triangulations of these routes, from Britain to Africa to the colonies and back to Britain, and even wider itineraries from the East Indies to Africa to the colonies and back to Britain. Students identified the cargoes that organize these routes (imported raw materials from the colonies to Britain; traded, raw, and manufactured goods from the East; exported goods from Britain to Africa; and enslaved persons from Africa to the colonies). This identification of specific cargo alongside that of ship routes showed how the movement of *goods* becomes a perpetuating cycle, one that creates the need for its own repetition. Thus, students saw the slave trade as part of an Atlantic and even geographically broader system of commerce that continued to fuel it. This contextualization also provided a means for understanding Equiano serving on a slave ship even after his manumission.

Additionally, since Equiano says little about how long his many trips take, providing students with more explicit information about (or simply emphasizing) the approximate time it took to travel from different points in the Atlantic gives them a sense of how much time Equiano spends on the Atlantic Ocean itself rather than docked or semi-settled in one place or another. Thus, they have a better understanding of the extent of his unrootedness in any physical place. Before they start reading, I ask my students to take note of any mention in the text of the temporal length Equiano's ocean voyages take. I also ask them to pay attention to how much textual space is devoted to events that take place on the ocean (and on a ship) versus land. I provide them with excerpts from Daniel Defoe's *Moll Flanders* (1720), which describes transatlantic voyages from England to the North American colonies of approximately one month, and from Gottlieb Mittelberger's *Journey to Pennsylvania* (1756), which notes variations in time for such voyages from "eight, nine, ten, or twelve weeks . . . if the wind is unfavorable" and seven "given the most favorable winds" (20). We compare these to some of Equiano's calculations for transatlantic voyages to and from England to the colonies (thirteen weeks [47], ten weeks [72–73]) as well as his shorter transatlantic trips (three weeks from Savannah, Georgia to Montseratt in the West Indies [96–97]). Together, these estimations and the attention to conditions that impended travel (weather) provide a richer sense of how much time Equiano spends traveling and how much space he covers. They protract the textually collapsed time and space that we see in passages like this one: "I shipped myself as a steward with Capt. William Robertson of the ship *Grenada Planter,* once more to try my fortune in the West Indies; and we sailed from London for Madeira, Barbadoes, and the Grenades" (129).

We also map Equiano's travels to develop a better sense of how many times he crisscrosses the Atlantic, the distance of his trips, and how often his travel is voluntary rather than forced, unobstructed rather than impeded. The Norton Critical Edition of *The Interesting Narrative* contains a map of Equiano's various landings as well as a possible route for his initial forced travel in Africa, and geographer Miles Ogborn has mapped routes for all of Equiano's travels (Carey). But students can still be asked to map the circumstances of each trip in relation to these maps. With the aid of these existing cartographic projections, students can use Google Maps to insert balloon comments onto their own maps. Since Equiano's individual trips are so numerous, assigning individual students or pairs to particular legs of his journeys is essential for more fully understanding Equiano's Atlantic travels. Finally, in one instance, some students could not understand Equiano's willingness to go back to sea and particularly back to the West Indies after he has landed in England as a free man, so we also looked closely at Chapter 3, which describes Equiano's experiences as a young boy in the Atlantic. Well over half of the chapter is devoted to Equiano's life on the water. We considered this episode as a formative moment in Equiano's life and a reason for his "roving disposition" later in life (130).

These tactics orient students to Equiano's movement within the Atlantic rather than encouraging them to think automatically in terms of, on one hand, national literature (which an initial emphasis on the narrative's place of composition and publication would do) or, on the other hand, a center-periphery imperialism that looks out from the center (which an initial emphasis on the slave debate would). And, given the vivid description Equiano provides of his experiences, there seems to me little danger that students will lose sight of these as effects of a violent and dehumanizing imperialism. Indeed, in highlighting Equiano's travel experiences, students see that because of the enslavement of Africans via European imperialism, he faces dangers (including re-enslavement) almost *everywhere* in the Atlantic, even after he has obtained the most official form of freedom available to him.

Once (or as) students become oriented to Equiano's almost continual travel from a transatlantic perspective, focusing on his identification with different places and groups of people—England, the English, Europeans, Africans, and Africa—allows us to explore how the narrative addresses questions that preoccupied eighteenth-century thinkers and that have recently garnered renewed, intense interest among academics and non-academics alike. Namely, how is belonging, citizenship, patriotism, and/or loyalism defined? Although the American Revolution had already taken place and the Constitution ratified when *The Interesting*

Narrative appeared, these were questions that still preoccupied both sides of the North Atlantic as American and European expansion continued and the French Revolution reverberated in England and the newly formed United States.

A comparison of the passages where Equiano makes a claim to some sort of belonging coupled with an awareness of his lack of any kind of official citizenship, nationality, or subjecthood within the British empire illustrates how the narrative challenges the grounds of more official forms of these affiliations and how it proposes a sense of multiple belonging. Even before he receives manumission, Equiano learns that free blacks possess no rights that others enjoy in the West Indies: "[t]hey live in constant alarm for their liberty; and even this is but nominal, for they are universally insulted and plundered without the possibility of redress; for such is the equity of the West Indian laws, that no free negro's evidence will be admitted in their courts of justice" (90). Likewise, Equiano's experiences show that whether enslaved or nominally free, blacks have little recourse at the center of the empire. Despite experiencing baptism and hearing that "the law of the land" insures that he cannot be sold after working for his master, Equiano is sold in England (69), and he later fails to preserve another free man living in England from being re-enslaved (136–37). Yet, drawing attention to Equiano's comment that his "heart" is in England (106, 112, 119) alongside his references to both the people of Africa and the English as his "countrymen" (19, 29, 40–43, 56, 75, 124, 155, 175) allows students to see that the narrative proposes different *modes* of affiliation: affection for a clearly defined place (England), whether rooted in it or not, and a sense of belonging to a group of people, whether living amidst them or not. Here the *OED* entry for "country" is useful for furthering discussion. The first definition connects the term strictly to land, rather than to any sense of political, governmental, national, religious, or ethnic space. In this case, sharing the same physical space is a basis for connection. Thus, students can consider how Equiano's use of the term "countrymen" rather than or in addition to references to nationality seeks to redefine the grounds of affiliation against limited forms of nationality and imperial subjecthood that deny him personhood.

Alongside these passages from the narrative, we also read the first few paragraphs of "Crisis I" from Thomas Paine's earlier *The American Crisis* (1777). Paine's discussions of lawfulness, freedom, and slavery in the context of the colonies' revolt against Britain provide further grounds to explore Equiano's position with respect to the law versus his attachments to Africa and England. Paine's attack on Britain's claim to "right[fully]" tax and "BIND [the colonies] in ALL CASES WHATSOEVER" questions the law, which would deny the colonies some form of independence and redress for abuses. This comparative reading exercise highlights a wider cultural and discursive context for Equiano's experiences. Equiano's narrative illustrates that such questions were not confined to those of European descent nor isolated from the South or from Africa. Similarly, the first several pages of Richard Price's *A Discourse on the Love of Our Country* (1790), a response to Edmund Burke's *Reflections on the Revolution in France* (1790), provides both corresponding and competing notions of national affiliation found in Equiano. Price's text (available via Eighteenth-Century Collections Online) denies that physical or political geography determines one's home country. This point highlights Equiano's attachment to *both* Africans and the English as his "countrymen." And, while Price also upholds the "law," "government," and civil polity as the grounds of affiliation, he also makes a distinction between just and unjust laws, and thus provides an opportunity to reexamine Equiano's critique of law in the colonies as a comment on the *lack* of just laws as much as it is a comment on the injustice of existing ones. Finally, in an excerpt from *The Rights of Man* (1791–1792), another response to Burke, Thomas Paine asserts that the "rights" of citizens do not exist "in this or in that person, or in this or in that description of persons, but that [they exist] in the whole; that it is a right resident in the nation" (4). This observation allows us to see Equiano's attachment to England as one that in theory provides him with the protective affiliation that he otherwise lacks.

At this point, a discussion of the publication of *The Interesting Narrative* in England and its role in the slave trade debate is productive without risking a top-down imperial orientation. We reconsider the narrative as strictly arguing for an end to the slave *trade* and contemplate how the elements of the narrative call for the end of slavery itself. We begin at the ending of the narrative, with Equiano's participation in the failed, white-led philanthropic expedition to Sierra Leone and his subsequent proposal for a commercial intercourse between Britain and Africa. Here I ask students to think about two points: 1) the different ways these projects suggest that resident Africans and those who are returned can be self-sufficient in their "own" country and 2) the roles these projects envision for Africans and returnees. The Sierra Leone project, which endeavors to send Britain's black poor back to Africa and thus is in the vein of other poor relief efforts from this period, fails because of both the initial lack of supplies afforded to those who undertake the voyage and a lack of foresight. As a result,

> at last, worn out by treatment, perhaps, not the most mild, and wasted by sickness, brought on by want of medicine, clothes, bedding, &c. they reached Sierra Leone just as the commencement of the rains. At that season of the year it is impossible to cultivate the lands; their provisions therefore were exhausted before they could derive any benefit from agriculture. (173)

We compare this image of what appears to be unrealized *agriculture* to Equiano's vision for mutual *commercial exchange* between Africa and Britain that appears a couple of pages later. The difference between potentially self-sufficient agriculturalists (the Sierra Leone Project) and Europeanized consumers is easily recognized when reading these passages in class, but I also push my students to compare these roles with that of the enslaved individual, particularly in regards to agency. My goal here is to highlight the relative passivity of the Europeanized African consumer to the (still only potential) more active farmer. I point out that consumption need not be a passive act, but ask my students to think about who has agency in the relationship that Equiano describes. We look at Equiano's use of "insensibly" (177), which suggests both a natural process on one hand, but an unreflective one on the other. We also examine the rather ironic use of "demand" (177) to describe Africans' apparent desire for "manufactures." The passage presents this "demand" not as an expression of self-assertion on the part of Africans but of opportunity for British trade. Other instances where agency is emphasized in the section allow for these analyses: British manufacturers "facilitate and expedite" (177) the end of the slave trade; Africans "double themselves" (178) in population; and "[c]otton and indigo grow" (178) in Africa. No longer commodities themselves, in Equiano's scheme, Africans become an exponentially growing population of passive consumers of British goods as well as a passive source of raw materials. Following Potkay's urging to address Equiano's oratorical skills, we also discuss Equiano's need to appeal to a white readership and their interests in suggesting such a relationship between black Africans and white Britons, one that emphasizes African submissiveness and pliability and British action and control, rather than potential productiveness and wealth for Africans. Thus, students see how commercial interests facilitate a sense of racial difference and inequality.

This attention to Equiano's use of oratory (or rhetoric) then allows us to reconsider what he argues for in this passage and in *The Interesting Narrative* as a whole. I highlight Equiano's comparison between "the Aborigines of Britain" (177) and eighteenth-century Africans, which suggests a progressive civilizing process that Britain has already completed and that Africa is only beginning. And, I juxtapose this analogy to his later description of slavery: "Tortures, murders, and every other imaginable barbarity and iniquity, are practiced upon the poor slaves with impunity" (177). Placing these passages side by side allows students to see that Equiano invokes the trope of progressive civilization with Africans in the early stages of development to emphasize the continuing slave trade as evidence of a *lack* of development among *the British*. Thus, Equiano's depiction of Africans as nascently civilized can be understood as a well-planned rhetorical move rather than just an attempt to appeal to and appease white readers. Moreover, though Equiano's parting proposal restricts itself to a scheme for ending the extraction of Africans from the continent by making them a pool of consumers for British exports, and, thus suggests an end to the slave *trade* rather than slavery itself, the description of slavery noted above alludes to the conditions of slavery generally. Equiano does follow this statement with an expression of hope that "the slave trade will be abolished" (177); however, given our previous analysis, students begin to see how Equiano's speech-like proposal potentially works more complexly and radically.

To further the point that Equiano's proposal and his overall narrative can be read as making an argument against slavery and not just the slave trade, I provide some general background on the slave trade debate. Here I pay particular attention to arguments that emphasize the detrimental effects slave abolition would have on the British economy and the idea that ending the slave trade was the first step (because more easily attained) towards total abolition. This context helps students see again how Equiano manipulates the focus of the debate to argue against the institution as a whole. While Equiano does not directly address the effects of *abolition* on economy, his proposal envisions an alternative basis of Britain's economy where Africa and Africans are concerned. That is, Equiano's plan imagines a future for blacks outside the system of slavery altogether. Likewise, although Equiano's appeal to ending the slave *trade* takes a position more palatable to many white Britons, his references to the brutalities of slave life extend his argument to include the institution itself.

Next, we read the first two pages from the excerpt titled "The 1791 Debate in the House of Commons on the Abolition of the Slave Trade" in the Norton edition of *The Interesting Narrative.*[8] This excerpt summarizes part of William Wilberforce's 1789 House of Commons speech against the slave trade; this text focuses on Wilberforce's description of the atrocities of the "bloody traffic" ("From 'The 1791 Debate'" 284) and on his argument that the slave population in the colonies would not decline but would increase if the slave trade ended. Cut off from their ready supply from Africa, Wilberforce maintains, slaveholders would be inclined to treat their existing slaves better, and thus the slave population would reproduce itself and thrive in the colonies. We compare this summary excerpt with the Norton's extract from Thomas Clarkson's *An Essay on the Slavery and Commerce of the Human Species, Particularly the African* (1786). This excerpt begins with a summary of the Quaker opposition to slavery, then reflects on "divine writings" (Clarkson 278), poetry, and festivals as sources for proving the original equality of all men, and finally addresses the slave *trade.*

I use these two passages to illustrate that while emphasis was placed upon ending the slave *trade* in the debates (Wilberforce's argument shows that continuing slavery and abolition of the *trade* could go hand in hand), the structure of the Clarkson excerpt suggests grounds for the injustice of slavery itself. Though trafficking becomes the ultimate focus, the first parts of the Clarkson excerpt advocates for abolition. What at first seems to be only persuasive foundations for Clarkson's more explicit argument about the slave trade functions, like the earlier excerpt from Equiano's narrative, as a declaration against the entire institution. Moreover, Wilberforce's comments force us to contend with a different meaning of Equiano's comments about the brutality of slavery in his proposal. In the context of Wilberforce's argument about the improved condition of enslaved persons in the colonies, Equiano's lament becomes once again a reference to ending the slave trade. We consider the possibility of reading Equiano's comment as a purposely elliptical reference to Wilberforce; by avoiding Wilberforce's direct cause-effect connection between the end of the slave trade and the alleviation of the atrocities of slavery itself, Equiano, once again, manipulates the terms of the slave trade debate to extend his appeal to complete abolition.

With these examples in hand, we consider how Equiano's narrative as a whole can be read in a similar way. Having already read the culmination of the narrative as more than a call for the end of trafficking Africans across the Atlantic, we look back at other parts of Equiano's work that likewise can be read as exceeding this plea. For instance, Equiano's vivid descriptions of the treatment of enslaved persons in the colonies and his persistent references to threats to his freedom from various white men even after he obtains manumission reminds his readers that the ills of slavery are not confined to the *trafficking* of Africans from one side of the Atlantic to the other. Indeed, the treatment he receives after manumission highlights the extent of the institution's reach; as long as Africans are enslaved, no person of African appearance is safe from its injustices.

Ending a discussion of the narrative on this point—one similar to that my students initially made about Equiano's experiences—might seem counterintuitive, given my goal of avoiding binary frameworks that conceptualize him as victim or active resistor. However, my aim is not to deny Equiano's vulnerability in a world controlled mainly by white men, but rather to consider his vulnerability in the complex circumstances in which it occurs. This last consideration, indeed, highlights that complexity. Equiano writes from a position of relative safety and agency but focuses on a variety of situations in which he was utterly subjugated (bound and beaten), treated kindly but controlled, enslaved but seemingly free as any white man, and relatively free to travel and trade in the Atlantic. Students come to this point after thoroughly considering the transatlantic nature of *The Interesting Narrative;* they have viewed it more horizontally than vertically. This flatter orientation provides them with a richer context in which to read these allusions to Equiano's (and all black Atlantics') persistent vulnerability.

Notes

1. See, for instance, Edward Larkin's discussion of conceptions of "empire" in the late eighteenth-century Atlantic World.

2. Wheeler does not mention individual geographers, though she does refer to anthropologists, whom she argues have also produced some of the "most suggestive colonial theory." However, some intriguing work by geographers on spatial conceptualization can be found in a recent critical exchange that has been dubbed "the scale debate." See *Transactions of the Institute of British Geographers,* vols. 30 (issue 4), 31 (issues 2 and 3), and 32 (issues 1 and 2) for this exchange that begins with Sally Marsten,

John Paul Jones, and Keith Woodward's "Human Geography Without Scale." For a less pointed and extended series of articles on this issue, see *Antipode: A Radical Journal of Geography,* vols. 37 (issues 2, 4, and 5) and 38 (issue 2).

3. While the original "Flat Stanley" is a Caucasian boy, the project encourages children to create their own versions of Stanley. Some choose to model their Stanleys after themselves, changing his gender, nationality, skin color, etc. See http://www.flatstanley.com/ for examples of his different manifestations.

4. Of course, as teachers we can (and do) try to counteract the emphases such anthologies suggest in their titles, but, ultimately, I believe their orienting structures are difficult to overcome. An instructor might well use the Longman anthology to teach a course that does not focus specifically on Romanticism as a literary period or movement, but I think this choice would require a constant battle against the title of the anthology.

5. Potkay, emphasizing Equiano's use of "oratorical indignation"—his ability to raise indignation in his readers—asserts that

> [i]t will, of course, prove easier for our students to identify with the anger of Equiano than with the indignation of [ancient rhetoricians]—Equiano is, in certain ways, our contemporary. The wounds inflicted by chattel slavery and unjust racial laws have still not altogether healed. Indeed, the danger in teaching Equiano's rhetoric is that it may feed into an indignation *with* the past that our own age all too often self-righteously demands. . . . Students are automatically indignant that the past did not know what they do; to offset this, they need to be taught to appreciate the art of indignation *in* the past. (607; emphasis in original)

6. The Norton edition of the 1789 text includes this address after the title page. In his edition of the narrative, Vincent Carretta notes that the address appeared in the first and second editions (239n2).

7. See, for instance, Chinua Achebe's "Work and Play in Tutuola's *The Palm Wine Drinkard,*" Henry Louis Gates Jr.'s *The Signifying Monkey: A Theory of African-American Literary Criticism,* Houston A. Baker Jr.'s "Figurations for a New American

Literary History: Section V." in his *Blues, Ideology, and Afro-American Literature: A Vernacular Theory,* and Keith Sandiford's *Measuring the Moment: Strategies of Protest in Eighteenth-Century Afro-English Writing.* For a more extensive bibliography of scholarship that places *The Interesting Narrative* in different literary traditions, see George E. Boulukos's "Olaudah Equiano and the Eighteenth-Century Debate on Africa."

8. Werner Sollors identifies the source of this excerpt as *The Annual Register, or A View of the History, Politics, and Literature for the Year 1791* (Equiano 283).

Works Cited

Achebe, Chinua. "Work and Play in Tutuola's *The Palm Wine Drinkard.*" *Okike* 14 (1978): 25–33.

Aravamudan, Srinivas. *Tropicopolitans: Colonialism and Agency, 1688–1804.* Durham: Duke UP, 1999.

Baker, Houston A., Jr. *Blues, Ideology, and Afro-American Literature: A Vernacular Theory.* Chicago: U of Chicago P, 1984.

Boulukos, George. "Olaudah Equiano and the Eighteenth-Century Debate on Africa." *Eighteenth-Century Studies* 40.2 (2007): 241–55.

Carey, Brycchan. Home page. "Olaudah Equiano's Travels." (Reproduction of map from "Global historical geographies, 1500–1800," by Miles Ogborn. *Modern Historical Geographies.* Ed. Brian Graham and Catherine Nash. Harlow, UK: Longman, 1999.) 10 Apr. 2010 <http://www.brycchancarey.com/equiano/map1.htm>.

Carretta, Vincent, ed. The Interesting Narrative *and Other Writings,* by Olaudah Equiano. Rev. ed. New York: Penguin, 2003.

Clarkson, Thomas. "From *An Essay on Slavery and the Commerce of the Human Species, Particularly the African.*" 1786. *The Interesting Narrative of the Life of Olaudah Equiano, or Gustavus Vassa, the African. Written by Himself.* Ed. Werner Sollors. New York: Norton, 2001. 277–81.

"Country." Definition 1a. *Oxford English Dictionary.* 10 Apr. 2010 <http://dictionary.oed.com>

Crèvecoeur, J. Hector St. John de. *Letters From An American Farmer.* 1782. Ed. Susan Manning. Oxford: Oxford UP, 1998.

Defoe, Daniel. *Moll Flanders.* 1722. Ed. Paul A Scanlon. Toronto: Broadview, 2005.

Equiano, Olaudah. *The Interesting Narrative of the Life of Olaudah Equiano, or Gustavus Vassa, the African. Written by Himself.* Ed. Werner Sollors. New York: Norton, 2001.

"From 'The 1791 Debate in the House of Commons on the Abolition of the Slave Trade.'" *The Interesting Narrative of the Life of Olaudah Equiano, or Gustavus Vassa, the African. Written by Himself.* Ed. Werner Sollors. New York: Norton, 2001. 283–87.

Gates, Henry Louis, Jr. *The Signifying Monkey: A Theory of African-American Literary Criticism.* New York: Oxford UP, 1986.

Larkin, Edward. "The Cosmopolitan Revolution: Loyalism and the Fiction of an American Nation." *Novel: A Forum on Fiction* 40.1–2 (2006): 52–76.

Mittelberger, Gottlieb. *Gottlieb Mittelberger's Journey to Pennsylvania in the Year 1750 and Return to Germany in the Year 1754.* 1756. Trans. Carl Theodor Eben. Philadelphia: John Jos McVey, 1898.

Paine, Thomas. *The Rights of Man.* 1791–1792. Ed. Daniel Edwin Wheeler. New York: Vincent Park, 1908.

———. *The American Crisis.* 1777. *British Literature, 1640–1789: An Anthology.* Ed. Robert Demara Jr. Oxford, UK: Blackwell, 1999. 844–47.

Potkay, Adam. "History, Oratory, and God in Equiano's *Interesting Narrative.*" *Eighteenth-Century Studies* 34.4 (2001): 601–14.

Price, Richard. *A Discourse on the Love of Our Country.* London: George Stafford, 1790.

Pratt, Mary Louise. *Imperial Eyes: Studies in Travel Writing and Transculturation.* New York: Routledge, 1992.

Roach, Joseph. *Cities of the Dead: Circum-Atlantic Performance.* New York: Columbia UP, 1996.

Sandiford, Keith. *Measuring the Moment: Strategies of Protest in Eighteenth-Century Afro-English Writing.* Selinsgrove, PA: Susquehanna UP, 1988.

Wheeler, Roxann. "Domesticating Equiano's *Interesting Narrative.*" *Eighteenth-Century Studies* 34.4 (2001): 620–24.

Finding a Home for Equiano

TESS CHAKKALAKAL

What is the appropriate context to teach Equiano?[1] Part of the challenge and joy of reading and teaching the *Narrative* lies in finding the right course for it. I have taught or studied Equiano in a number of different courses, from Romantic Autobiography, Introduction to Africana Studies, Eighteenth-Century Black British Writing, Postcolonial Literature to African American Literature, the Slave Narrative, and Early American Literature. Equiano finds a home in all these courses, but students often struggle with the text's cosmopolitanism. The *Narrative,* as the subsequent sections of this essay illustrate, speaks to multiple genres and disciplines. While students are often excited by the text's multiplicity, that excitement soon turns to frustration when they realize that Equiano does not conform to their generic or racial expectations. Part of their frustration lies, I think, in Equiano's departures from the familiarity of the conventions of the African American slave narrative. His freedom is acquired by purchase rather than escape. This fact alone suggests that Equiano accepted the terms of his enslavement. As this essay argues, Equiano's protest against the conventions of his time operate more subtly, asking students to come to terms with the rhetorical strategies embedded in the *Narrative.* In my experience teaching the *Narrative,* I have found in its rhetoric of marriage—as a social, political, and racial institution—a way of understanding the structure of Equiano's protest, a protest that artfully resists the racial, generic, and national categories upholding the institution of slavery.

When Olaudah Equiano first published the story of his life in 1789 under the title, *The Interesting Narrative of the Life of Olaudah Equiano, or Gustavus Vassa, the African. Written by Himself,* it received considerable attention from English reading audiences.[2] Read as spiritual autobiography, captivity narrative, travel book, adventure tale, narrative of slavery, economic treatise and apologia, the

Narrative appealed to various tastes and consequently was a bestseller in its day.[3] A key difference, however, between Equiano's *Narrative* and those by later, more familiar slave authors such as Frederick Douglass and William Wells Brown is its internationalist—rather than nationalist—perspective.

Introducing Equiano to students in literature classes requires them to come to terms with the text's "foreign" identity. That it is a text premised on the paradoxical experience of "foreign citizenship" is made clear when Equiano refers to himself as "almost an Englishman" (77) and recognizes his difference from the Europeans among whom he lives throughout the text. Equiano asserts that difference when he begins his narrative as "an unlettered African" (7) and considers Africans—not Europeans—to be his countrymen. To help them understand the stakes of the text's identity, I have students engage with the critical controversy surrounding Equiano's *Narrative.* A number of the *Narrative*'s twentieth-century readers have commented upon the implications of its author's dual identity. S. E. Ogude, for instance, questions Equiano's claim to an African identity; he contends that Equiano's British sources for his description of Africa make the place a virtual fiction. Carretta's more recent groundbreaking historical research extends Ogude's claims by suggesting that Equiano "was born in South Carolina [and] constructed an African identity to support the British one he embraced as a free man" ("Defining" 386). Carretta's evidence effectively challenges Wilfred D. Samuels's, Paul Edwards's, and Dwight McBride's readings of the *Narrative,* which are predicated upon Equiano's beginning in Africa and, in McBride's words, "presenting himself in the narrative as living proof of the African's ability to reason and to master European forms of philosophy and cultural production" (135). The tension between the identities (European versus African) raises a number of interpretive problems. Most important, it raises the problem of classifying Equiano's *Narrative* and being attentive both to history and to the author's intentions. While most critics attempt to solve the problem Equiano's *Narrative* raises by looking *outside* the text, I encourage students to perform a close reading of the *Narrative* to discover for themselves the rhetorical strategies its author employed.

Genre and Identity

The *Narrative* differs from, for instance, sentimental, spiritual, and autobiographical narratives. While those genres can elide the difference between the author and reader in order to achieve a union or identification, Equiano's *Narrative* retains a distinction between the two to maintain a distance between the writer's life and its reader's. That is to say, the *Narrative* does not simply tell a story of a single individual's struggle from slavery to freedom in order to gain sympathy from his reader to further the cause against slavery. Instead, Equiano *translates* the experience of captivity into a language that will be understood by an audience for whom such experiences are entirely foreign and, in doing so, the *Narrative* relies on the reader's *different* experiences to negotiate the author's own. This aspect of the *Narrative* allows students to engage, rather than identify, with Equiano's unfamiliar experiences. The *Narrative* presents students with a catalogue of experiences that occur as the result of an encounter between the African and the European. Seeing himself as both, rather than either European or African, Equiano transforms the terms upon which citizenship is defined.

Drawing upon Henry Louis Gates's extensive study of the African American literary tradition, I have students consider what it means to read Equiano's *Narrative,* in Gates's terms, as a "black text"—a generic category that operates according to both literary conventions and authorial identity. By identifying common tropes, issues, and structural devices in various works by black writers, Gates makes these otherwise neglected texts more readily accessible to readers. What students learn from engaging with Gates's theory of the African American literary tradition is that it does not apply to the *Narrative,* whose immense popularity proves that it did not suffer from such problems. Examining the history of its publication against such theories of the text reveal a story about the author that moves well beyond such racial signifiers. As Equiano was directly involved in the publication and dissemination of his *Narrative,* his book reached readers throughout Great Britain and the United States, and it was eventually translated into several languages. Gates elides these historical details, its fictional account of Africa, and the author's occupation and economic status in order to turn the *Narrative* into a "prototype" of the African American slave narratives which he, and others, consider to be "the locus classicus of Afro-American literary discourse" (Baker 39). Examining the strategic uses of the *Narrative* enables students to understand its importance to broader questions of literary form.

Extending Gates's reading of Equiano's "subaltern" status, students turn to the relationship between autobiography and the slave narrative forms. In his essay "'I Was Born': Slave Narratives, Their Status as Autobiography, and as Literature," James Olney offers students a quick reference guide to distinguish the slave narrative from other forms of autobiography. Olney explains that the most obvious distinguishing mark is that it is an extremely mixed production typically including any or all of the following: an engraved portrait or photograph of the subject of the narrative, authenticating testimonials, prefixed or postfixed poetic epigraphs, snatches of poetry in the text, and poems appended. In spite of these differences, Olney goes on to construct a master outline for the slave narrative (151). Such lists, of course, cannot help but have a reductive effect on analysis; in the case of slave narratives, texts are typically read as instances of authorial biography. For critics committed to the generic category of the slave narrative, the value of the *Narrative* lies in the ways in which it upholds the conventions they have identified. In doing so, the *Narrative* facilitates the construction of a coherent community out of ex-slaves and literary "Others." I then pose questions to the class concerning the *Narrative*'s form.

What is gained and what is lost by identifying Equiano's *Narrative* as a slave narrative? The most common response has been to explore the specific ways in which slavery has influenced the author's life. In other words, the slave narrative, as a category, functions as a black version of the *bildungsroman.* Reading Equiano's *Narrative* as a slave narrative considers it through the subject's struggle from slavery to freedom, from illiteracy to literacy, and, finally, from childhood to adulthood. Such a reading depends on a linear, teleological mode of reading that the *Narrative* resists. Equiano's argument against slavery depends upon intertwining the disparate experiences of the reader with the author's to break down the difference between the European and African. For this reason, Equiano repeatedly inserts into his *Narrative* details far removed from his experience.

And it is such details that set the *Narrative* in opposition to specific generic conventions of the slave narrative that are so central to the development of an African American literary tradition. The question students inevitably ask after engaging with the *Narrative*'s complex rhetorical modes is: why are we reading Equiano in a course explicitly about "African American Literature"? To this question I can offer no easy answer. In fact, part of the point of turning to a text like Equiano's is to trouble the very category of African American Literature. Instead, the question concerning Equiano's identity raises another broader question about the discipline itself: what are the origins of African American Literature? By reading Equiano in this way, students are forced to turn to other literary traditions and thus realize that the history of literature and the people who write it is itself a kind of fiction.

Realizing the insufficiency and inaccuracy of the slave narrative to classify the *Narrative,* we examine other critical paradigms for reading Equiano. Alongside the slave narrative form, the *Narrative* has been classified as a prototypical "captivity narrative." In his introduction to *American Captivity Narratives: Olaudah Equiano, Mary Rowlandson, and Others,* Gordon M. Sayre argues that "the captivity phenomenon arises out of encounters between unfamiliar peoples, generally as a result of European imperialism in the Americas and Africa" (5). Importantly, Sayre marks the territory of captivity as narrating an encounter between unfamiliar peoples. According to Sayre, the captivity narrative necessarily regards this encounter as a hostile one wherein "two cultures brought into conflict are so foreign to one another that an individual forced into the midst of the other community regards the new life as a kind of imprisonment" (5). However, for Equiano, the new life he encounters as a result of his imprisonment is filled with multiple possibilities for self-improvement. Using Equiano's text as central to the definition of the captivity phenomenon distorts the *Narrative.* Sayre's definition is disproportionately invested in Equiano's account of his birth in and capture from Africa. Although this account may initiate the *Narrative,* it is actually a very brief section of the text and Equiano offers little commentary on the circumstances of his capture. Nonetheless, Equiano does find himself in something of a double bind. On the one hand, he enjoys his experiences of travel and trade that afford him multiple sources of increasing his wealth and acquiring new skills. On the other hand, these same encounters hold him captive and subject to unfair treatment. Teaching students to be suspicious of critical lenses that elide facets of the text to further the critic's own theoretical program encourages students to read the *Narrative* on its own terms, without the aid or distortion of contemporary critical theories. That is not to say, however, that we should approach the *Narrative* untheoretically. But theory should deepen our reading of the *Narrative* rather than skim over its distinguishing features, those that set it apart from current critical paradigms. It is for this reason that we embark upon a "close-reading" of the *Narrative.*

For many students, among the most illuminating parts of Equiano's account of his encounters are those in which he suffers "ill usage" (116) at the hands of others, or witnesses others subjected to such suffering. Somewhere in the West Indies, a countryman of Equiano's saves money to buy a boat, which the governor, when he discovers that it is the boat of "a negro," seizes without payment in an act of "extortion and rapine" (102). In Montserrat, "a Creole negro" of Equiano's acquaintance is robbed of his fish by his master, and "can't go to any body to be righted" (110). In Santa Cruz, the oranges and limes that Equiano intends to sell are "plundered" from him by white men (118). In Charlestown, he recalls, upon selling a "puncheon of rum" to a gentleman, "being a negro man, I could not oblige him to pay me" though afterwards, the man pays him, but partly in useless copper dollars (128–29). Near the Bermudas, a captain boards Equiano's ship, insists falsely that a "mulatto man" whom all recognize to be free is a slave, and carries the man away for no reason other than that "might overcomes right" among such "infernal invaders of human rights" (121). Free blacks are stolen away in bondage even in Philadelphia, "plundered without possibility of redress" (122). And throughout the Caribbean, Equiano finds that if a slave collects a small portion of grass in his spare time, expecting to sell it in the market, "nothing is more common than for the white people on this occasion to take the grass from them without paying for it" (108). Having no legal means to redress the wrongs committed against him and his "countrymen," Equiano uses his *Narrative* as a means by which these acts of injustice can be addressed and made right. The *Narrative* attempts to negotiate the conflicts which arise between African and British subjects more equitably than Equiano experiences them.

By putting our close reading together with the contemporary critical readings, I invite students to locate the *Narrative* between, rather than within, particular discourses in order to consider the consequences of Equiano's captivating encounters on those very conventions that bind him to a single identity. Equiano's *Interesting Narrative* operates as a performance—a specific action or set of actions—whose mutual recognition between reader and author cuts across the determined status of both subjects, dissolving, ultimately, the boundaries which separate the European from the African. Reading the *Narrative*'s departures from the author's experiences, what I call its performative utterances, reveals a set of terms that accounts for the conventions Equiano operates within and also attends to those moments in the *Narrative* when the author attempts to find a way out of them. By engaging the *Narrative* as a literary performance, students can begin to grapple with the fictional elements of the autobiography, elements that speak specifically to the historical particularity of Equiano's antislavery argument.

Miscegenous Marriages

Equiano's *Narrative* is motivated by a desire to extinguish the difference between African and European identities. However, he cannot achieve his task without the participation of his reader. The experience of reading Equiano's *Narrative* involves Americanizing the European reader and Europeanizing Africa; and it is a process predicated on intercourse between reader and author. I use the term intercourse here to distinguish it from discourse, as the latter would imply that the *Narrative* contributes to an already existing set of conventions whether they be those of British, African, or African American literature. The term "intercourse," instead, refers to a relationship that comes into being as the result of a singular action between individuals, acted out most explicitly and publicly through marriage ceremonies. In terms of the *Narrative,* the marriage ceremony functions as an encounter that holds the possibility for infinite gain. To help students theorize the *Narrative* on its own terms, I turn to Tilottama Rajan's conception of autonarration. As a concept, autonarration is less interested in establishing or participating in a literary tradition than in understanding how and why some literary texts fall outside tradition.

Rajan characterizes autonarration as "a genre characterized by its transgressive miscegenation of private and public spaces [and] part of a larger discursive formation characteristic of romanticism" (153). Rajan further notes that although it is "not exclusively a women's genre, its use tends to put the writer in a female subject-position" (153). The subject of autonarration is usually female, Rajan argues, because it is the female subject who must negotiate her relationship between representation and experience without relying on the constative or performative utterance: "either as it was, or as it becomes through the act of writing" (160). Rajan rightly assumes that the social constraints surrounding the telling of a woman's life story impel an articulation in two different media of "life" and "text," as if one requires the supplement of the other (159). She goes on to describe autonarration as "a specific form of self-writing, in which the author writes her life as a fictional narrative, and thus *consciously* raises the question of the relationship between experience and its narrativization" (160; emphasis in original). By emphasizing the word "consciously," Rajan draws our attention to the importance of women's writing that manipulates personal experience to serve broader sociopolitical interests. Rajan contends that critics of women's life-writing have failed to recognize the presence of the author's consciousness at work because women had no place thinking about or participating in political affairs; instead, their influence was restricted to the home. Reconsidering women's life-writing as autonarration foregrounds its national scope.

Rajan's definition of autonarration can be adapted to address the eighteenth-century black subject who must negotiate a comparable tension between experience and representation. Most important, autonarration recognizes the ways in which a disjunction exists in the formulation of consciousness outside dominant discourses. Working in the mode of autonarration, rather than autobiography, students can begin to understand how a text, written by a former slave in the eighteenth century, participates in public life. While the miscegenation Rajan refers to in her reading of eighteenth-century memoirs by women operates primarily figuratively, miscegenation, for Equiano, is a literal matter.

We see Equiano, in both his private and public life, as a vocal advocate of interracial marriages. These texts in which Equiano addresses his views on interracial marriage are significant ones that need to be discussed in the classroom to understand more fully Equiano's views on this topic. For instance, I present to students his response to an article by James Tobin denouncing miscegenation in which Equiano expresses the benefits of "the mutual commerce of the sexes of both Blacks and Whites" (Equiano 329). Equiano's letter on intermarriage (which was published in the *Public Advertiser* on 28 January 1788), when considered alongside his explicit references to this type of union throughout the *Narrative,* allows students to grasp more fully Rajan's formulation of autonarration both figuratively and literally.

Because Rajan's notion of autonarration arises out of a branch of linguistics that J. L. Austin terms the performative function of language, I use this time as an opportunity to introduce students to Austin's theory of performance. Doing so, I suggest, enables students a more contemporary entry point into a text that is otherwise rooted, quite firmly, in the late eighteenth century. In *How to Do Things with Words,* Austin defines performative utterances by suggesting that they are utterances that are neither true nor false, but rather words that in their utterance perform a specific action. In order to elucidate this concept, Austin provides a series of instances that would constitute performative utterances, the first of which is the marriage vow. Austin explains that the words "I do" uttered in the course of the marriage ceremony are an action and are considered to be a performative element of language because the utterance performs an action by changing the status of the marrying couple; but the words do not have the same meaning outside of the context of the marriage ceremony. While there are a number of such performative utterances in daily life, the marriage ceremony is exemplary because it is both contractual (through the utterance the couple affirms a promise) and declaratory (the vow uttered by each participant changes the status of the other). The marriage ceremony, instrumental to Austin's theory of performativity, has since enabled contemporary cultural critics to analyze and subvert instances of racist, homophobic, and sexist practices in daily life.

It would hardly be an overstatement then to claim that in using the marriage ceremony in 1789 to promote social change, Equiano was far ahead of his time. The relationship between reader and author of the *Narrative,* in effect, functions as a transgressive miscegenation. Equiano foregrounds problems concerning the reading and writing of his autobiography by describing his own struggle to become literate. To imitate the "wisdom of white people," Equiano turns to books "so [as] to learn how all things had a beginning" (68). He draws a direct link between his turn to books and a desire to participate in white institutions and practices. However, the now-famous passage relating a "curiosity to talk to books" (68) is immediately followed by an incident in which the author becomes aware of color distinctions. Equiano realizes that he can never acquire the wisdom of white people because he is black; thus he "began to be mortified at the difference in complexions" (69). The books Equiano reads teach him to discern differences in complexions, a practice which does not bode well for him as a black man.

Equiano's reader, both in his time and ours, would not necessarily experience the same sense of mortification. Moreover, it is unlikely that most of my students would consider racial difference in relation to the experience of reading at all. How, then, are students able to grasp what the act of reading meant for Equiano? Equiano makes this connection by relating the events of his own life in which he suffers "instances of ill usage" (116) at the hands of whites. Such scenarios trouble the connection between white readers and the *Narrative.* White readers would be equally mortified by the position white subjects occupy in the *Narrative.* Reading, in Equiano's terms, becomes a mortifying experience for both black author and white reader as each comes to recognize the limitations of these categories. As

Equiano aims to produce an experience of mortification in his reader, he creates a situation in which the two, despite historical, racial, and perhaps even ideological differences, are able to find common ground.

Equiano further bridges the difference between himself and his reader by drawing upon a personal experience that would be familiar to his reader: the marriage ceremony. He uses the marriage ceremony as a vehicle to change the reader's perception of the author. In the *Narrative,* different versions of the marriage ceremony negotiate the gap between the author's African and European identities as he writes as neither a British nor an African subject, but as both at once. Through an extended discussion of marriage laws and practices, Equiano shows how his life as both African and British is mortifying. By highlighting the role marriage plays in the *Narrative,* I have found that students experience the kind of mortification Equiano models in his *Narrative,* not as a result of sympathy or identification with Equiano, but because they mirror Equiano's outrage when he is treated, as he so often is, as someone to whom the law does not apply.

The marriage ceremony attempts to correct this discrepancy. First, Equiano uses its depictions to represent the ways in which the actions or inactions of the one affect the other. Second, Equiano's reading of these marriage ceremonies plays upon its contractual, progenitive, and performative conventions to create the conditions for African-British subjects like himself to be recognized and protected by the law.

To focus on such a reading in the classroom requires that we attend to the fact that marriage marks the beginning, middle, and end points of Equiano's life. First, he articulates his earliest memories by describing the "mode of marriage" practiced by the people in Benin when he was a child (33). A second marriage ceremony marks the midpoint of the *Narrative.* Equiano is now a young man working on a ship that has docked in the West Indies where he and his owner have stopped to acquire more slaves for England. The marriage Equiano describes on this occasion is an interracial union between a black free-woman and a white man. Not surprisingly, the third, and final, description of a marriage ceremony occurs in London when he "chanced once to be invited to a Quaker's wedding" and concludes the *Narrative* (225). As a witness to these three ceremonies, that is, as someone who is allowed to participate but must remain silent at them, Equiano offers his reader an African-British perspective that is crucial to the success of his *Narrative.* His presentation of the marriage ceremony advances the movement against slavery and racism by dissolving the difference between African and British identities.

Because Equiano's views on marriage are unique to his experience as a well-traveled black man in the eighteenth century, analysis of the rhetorical function of marriage in the *Narrative* requires a brief discussion in the classroom of common perceptions of marriage and interracial unions of the period. As my students and I discuss, marriage practices in late eighteenth-century England were a matter of some concern. To distinguish between their contemporary notions of marriage and eighteenth-century ideas about marriage, I use short critical articles, such as Carolyn D. Williams's "Another Self in the Case: Gender, Marriage, and the Individual in Augustan Literature," that helpfully summarize the politics of marriage during Equiano's time. Williams points out that the "idea of marriage in which [man and woman] become 'one flesh,' became increasingly alarming in the eighteenth century" (104). The "one flesh" clause of the marriage contract was met with alarm, as it put women and men on equal footing.

The egalitarian possibilities of marriage in terms of gender met with similar alarm in matters of race as well. Outlining attitudes towards interracial unions in his *Black and White: The Negro and English Society, 1555–1945,* James Walvin shows the opposition blacks and whites had to overcome before they could form relationships with one another. Walvin explains that "alarm, rather than curiosity was the most common response to miscegenation" (54). He cites Edward Long, a popular polemicist in the 1770s, who describes miscegenation as a "venomous and dangerous ulcer that threatens to disperse its malignancy far and wide, until every family catches infection from it" (qtd. in Walvin 55). Walvin concludes from his study of various texts from the period that "[t]here can be no doubt, that by a substantial and influential section of English society, miscegenation was regarded as a threat to the structure of that society" (55). These critical and historical sources help students to move beyond more current ideas about interracial marriages. While most students are familiar with the famous *Loving v. Virginia* decision and some are even familiar with movies like *Guess Who's Coming to Dinner* (1967) and the 2005 remake, *Guess Who,* students are less familiar with the political import of such relations. For Equiano, interracial marriage constitutes an opportunity to imagine a society predicated upon racial and sexual equality.[4]

The disjunction between Equiano's African and European identities necessitates a transgressive miscegenation that becomes the form through which the

Narrative is written. Thus, Equiano opens the *Narrative* with the following disclaimer: "It is, therefore, I confess, not a little hazardous, in a private and obscure individual, and a stranger too, thus to solicit the indulgent attention of the public" (31). His self-identification as a stranger alludes to his foreign status, which, by the time he writes his *Narrative,* can only be discerned by skin color. In the *Narrative,* Equiano reveals his reasons for claiming an allegiance to Africa even though there is little evidence to support his claim that he was born there. Equiano understands his African identity through encounters in which he is treated unfairly. By including the above disclaimer at the start of his *Narrative,* Equiano marks his entry into a potentially transgressive discourse that crosses the boundaries that separate his African and European identities in order to redress the wrongs he has suffered. Equiano crosses the line between Africa and Europe, fiction and truth, to legitimize his African-British identity. He recounts his past experiences of injustice to supplement his present situation, and gives each of his experiences of injustice a sense of relevancy and immediacy for his non-African readers.

Equiano is able to describe marriage ceremonies because he has served as an exemplary witness to them. While his experience of Africa rests largely on his presence at a specific ceremony, he draws numerous conclusions concerning the inner workings of that society from it. His description of the mode of marriage practiced in Benin in 1745, the supposed place of his birth and childhood, outlines an equitable system of justice far removed from his experience of living in England and provides him with the means by which he can begin to imagine a way of life very different from his own. Marriage, in this context, complicates an otherwise simple system of relations within a community that has "little commerce with other countries" (32). While most African men, in Equiano's recollection, respect and believe in the absolute authority of the law as decided by the "chief men"—one of whom Equiano claims is his own father—the laws governing the "honour of the marriage bed" are a notable exception to their principle of justice (33). "Of this," Equiano explains, "it was only when the laws of marriage were broken that Africans condoned the practice of slavery" (33). In other words, slavery signifies a transgression of law, but is not in and of itself a legally sanctioned institution.

From this notable exception to African justice, Equiano presents his childhood in Africa as a scene out of a typical English pastoral. According to Equiano, the Eboe live peacefully and enjoy the prosperity of a fertile countryside. Much of this information does not come from the author's own recollections but from an earlier text written by an Englishman, whom Equiano acknowledges in a footnote.[5] The description of the laws which govern the sanctity of "the marriage bed" to "most of the nations of Africa" stands out as a point of intersection between the African and European continents, for both geographical and cultural spaces use the law to determine an individual's status (33). Attending to this significant point prepares students to recognize the prominent role of marriage as both a legal and spiritual matter in the text. In addition, when students understand this point they are more fully prepared to examine how Equiano formulates an argument against the institution of slavery based on his observations and discussions of marriage.

Equiano prefaces his description of the first marriage ceremony by recounting an instance of adultery. As an explicit sign of a breach in the marriage contract, adultery was punished by slavery or death. Interestingly, the specific instance of adultery that instigates Equiano's account of the marriage ceremony involves an extenuating circumstance. Although the practice was to kill or enslave anyone found guilty of committing adultery, Equiano centers his discussion on a situation where the guilty party was "spared on account of the [married couple's] child" (33). Does Equiano recount the exception merely to prove the rule? More likely, the specific exceptionality in this case prepares his reader for a series of exceptions. As he begins to outline aspects of the marriage ceremony, he adds a brief comment in parentheses that offers the possibility of a marriage that diverges from the stipulated laws governing the practice: "Their mode of marriage is thus: both parties are usually betrothed when young by their parents (though I have known the males to betroth themselves)" (33). Because Equiano knows of some men who marry outside the "usual" law, acting on their own desire without interference from parental bodies, he shows the possibility of individual agency despite the constraints of convention.

It is through these two exceptions to the "mode of marriage" that Equiano inserts his "I." Although he is not an active participant, he asserts his presence by showing that ritual practices are malleable and prone to making exceptions. The marriage ceremony usually involves two participants, a man and a woman, but Equiano subverts this cross-gender dyad by inserting a third "I." As witness to the union between the other two, the third "I" becomes the broker of knowledge. For this reason, the marriage ceremony Equiano describes pays particular attention to the witnesses, those whom Equiano calls "their friends":

> On this occasion a feast is prepared, and the bride and bridegroom stand up in the midst of all their friends, who are assembled for the purpose, while he declares she is thenceforth to be looked upon as his wife, and that no other person is to pay any address to her. This is also immediately proclaimed in the vicinity, on which the bride retires from the assembly. (33)

Although the terms, "their friends," "the vicinity," and "the assembly" are different, each of these terms is used to describe the same persons: witnesses. The iterative effect of this triple naming proffers the third with a multiple and varied perspective denied to the marrying couple. Although it is the man and woman—husband and wife—around whom the ceremony revolves, Equiano's interpretation of this marriage ceremony renders their presence virtually incidental. Note that the "bride retires from the assembly" and then is "brought to her husband" (33). Husband and wife are able to do nothing without the consent and intervention of the witness. By first pointing to the possibility and knowledge of exceptions to marriage customs and then shifting focus from the couple to the witnesses, Equiano's rendering of the marriage ceremony shows how he, as witness and writer, possesses the ability to constitute the speech-act; hence, marriage opens up the possibility to write his life in the form of the *Narrative.* With this new-found ability, Equiano writes a new law by using the terms of the old one.

After recounting a number of Africa's "cultural events," Equiano acknowledges his distance from the events. The events do not provide information concerning the author's "life," but are significant because "such reflections as these melt the pride of [European] superiority into sympathy for the wants and miseries of their sable brethren, and compel them to acknowledge, that understanding is not confined to feature or colour" (45). Whereas Equiano had been formerly "recollecting" events in his life, he is now seen *reflecting* upon the circumstances of his life. The shift from recollection to reflection marks the author's self-conscious movement from his personal experience of racism towards mutual and fair exchange. Beneath Equiano's reading of the marriage ceremony lurks the possibility of the event as invention. In his meditations on marriage or, more accurately, on the exceptions to the laws which govern the practice, the *Narrative* manifests a life which does not conform to the constraints it has been assigned.

At the *Narrative*'s midpoint, Equiano forewarns his reader of a structural shift. After relating the circumstances of his captivity and subsequent enslavement, the chapter opens with a helpful summary: "In the preceding chapter I have set before the reader a few of those many instances of oppression, extortion and cruelty, to which I have been a witness in the West Indies; but, were I to enumerate them all, the catalogue would be tedious and disgusting" (113). After having enumerated a long list of instances of "oppression, extortion and cruelty," Equiano decides "that it cannot any longer afford novelty to recite them; and they are too shocking to yield delight either to the writer or the reader. I shall therefore hereafter only mention such as *incidentally* befel myself in the course of my adventures" (113; emphasis added). Up until now, the incidents of the *Narrative* have been organized randomly. From this point on, however, Equiano relates only those events which "incidentally befel" him. I have students note the double meaning implied by the adverb. Samuel Johnson's *Dictionary of the English Language,* published in 1755, offers two definitions: "Beside the main design; occasionally." While the second meaning relates to the occurrences of Equiano's encounters, the first meaning relates specifically to the structure of the text. Equiano marks the midpoint of his *Narrative* by declaring the import of the digression; that is to say, this *Narrative* relates not only what happens to its author but also what goes on around him, those events which stray from the central subject: the life of the author.

Like the ceremony in Benin, Equiano describes the wedding at St. Kitts because it is an exception. On this occasion, however, there can be no doubt: it is the exception that breaks the rule. Equiano's description of this particular ceremony is the most rigorous of all his accounts:

> While I was in this place, St. Kitts, a very curious imposition on human nature took place. A white man wanted to marry in the church a free black woman that had land and slaves at Montserrat: but the clergy-man told him it was against the law of the place to marry a white and a black in the church. The man then asked to be married on the water, to which the parson consented, and the two lovers went in one boat, and the parson and clerk in another, and thus the ceremony was performed. (119)

Using methods of close reading, I call upon students to point out the different ways in which this passage fits in with Equiano's larger project to bridge the gap between his African and British identities. Moving the interracial couple from the firm ground of prejudice to the unstable waters of interracial union makes it possible for the author to express his opinion of "the law of the place" that prohibits a white and black to marry in the church. Equiano uses the wedding scene he has drawn for his reader to convey his thoughts: "[t]he reader cannot but judge of the irksomeness of this situation to a mind like mine" (119). This situation leaves his mind "hourly replete with inventions and thoughts of being freed" (119) and leaves him more confused and desperate than the incidents of injustice that he experiences directly. Where the marriage ceremony had previously signified the power of the witness to create the conditions necessary for union, in St. Kitts marriage laws restrict relations between black and white. Recording the wedding at St. Kitts, performed *in spite of* legal restrictions, makes Equiano a passive accomplice in this illegal act. The appeal to the reader directly following this incident transfers some of his guilt onto the reader.

Following our close reading of the passage, I then solicit more personal responses from students to this moment in the text. Why does the wedding at St. Kitts cause the author such agony? Should the problem of interracial union be so pivotal in the author's desire for freedom? Students often have mixed responses to such questions. For some, Equiano's position on marriage seems not to go far enough. For others, Equiano places too great an emphasis on the wedding. "What do weddings have to do with the real problem of slavery?," one student asks. Equiano provides a lengthy explanation and justification for his silent participation in the illegal ceremony. But what of the *Narrative*'s reader? Since there is no loss of life or injury caused by this wedding, the stakes in the reader's judgment and position are low. The stakes are raised, however, with the entry of the "mulatto-man" (121) into the *Narrative.* Shortly after the interracial marriage ceremony, Equiano introduces Joseph Clipson, also known as the mulatto-man. Equiano is careful to mention that Clipson was "born free in St. Kitt's, and most people on board knew that he served his time to boat building and always passed for a free man" (121). Whether Clipson is the product of the earlier interracial union is difficult to prove. But Clipson's moniker indicates his relation to *some* interracial union in St. Kitts, one that is considered illegitimate and leaves Clipson vulnerable to "infernal invaders of human rights" (121). As Equiano relates Clipson's fate, it becomes increasingly difficult for students to remain passive in their judgment of those who break the laws prohibiting interracial unions:

> [Clipson] was forcibly taken out of [the] vessel. He then asked to be carried ashore, before the secretary or magistrates, and these infernal invaders of human rights promised him he should; but, instead of that, without giving the poor man any hearing on shore, or suffering him even to see his wife and child, he was carried away, and probably doomed never more in this world to see them again. (121)

Could these "infernal invaders of human rights" include those who choose to do nothing to protect interracial unions and their progeny from the imposition of slavery and captivity? Whatever the response to this question, the student must reconsider her or his relationship to the text. As the product of an interracial union, Clipson embodies the danger of interracial relationships, particularly those of a sexual nature. Although Equiano never comes into direct contact with Clipson, he feels it necessary to relate Clipson's circumstances. The import of this episode rests on its "very cruel" nature and because it "filled [Equiano] with horror" (121). This segment of the *Narrative* further shows the injustice of a culture that refuses to legitimate and respect the interracial relationship, a relationship, Equiano contends in his January 28, 1788, letter to James Tobin in *The Public Advertiser,* that "would yield more benefit than a prohibition" (Equiano 329) to both blacks and whites. Reading the marriage at St. Kitts in conjunction with the Clipson episode suggests the narrator's purpose is not just to present the author's life or even enumerate the horrors of slavery. Rather, Equiano uses these episodes to foreground his *Narrative* as breaking a law that governs marriage and thus prohibits mutual commerce between African and British subjects.

Shoring Up Equiano's Marriages

These instances of the marriage ceremony, alongside the Clipson episode, exhibit the inextricability of marriage and the formation of Equiano's *Narrative.* The marriage ceremony, as Equiano presents it, is paradigmatic of "a potentially transgressive discourse" and "claim[s] a presence and immediacy that is impossible in narrative as an account of the past" (Rajan 153). It is this generic feature of Equiano's *Narrative* that distinguishes it from other eighteenth-century narratives written in the autobiographical mode and makes it, in Rajan's useful terms, an autonarration. The legal and progenitive aspects of marriage Equiano outlines help our contemporary students to understand the broader sociopolitical purpose of the *Narrative.* Equiano's interpretation of Benin's marriage practices indicates the importance of the marital contract in determining human relations, while his description of the marriage at St. Kitts shows that the terms of the contract are in the best interests of neither the marrying couple nor the society surrounding them. As such, Equiano illegitimates the law by recording (and thereby legitimating) a union that has been deemed improper by legal codes, but not, importantly, banned by the church. The parson does, after all, agree to marry the couple, albeit outside the walls of the church. The *Narrative*'s explicit support of the marriage can therefore be seen as engaging in an attempt to change the law so that it operates for the mutual benefit of both black and white. The third and final instance calls upon the performative elements of the marriage ceremony to give Equiano's *Narrative* meaning beyond elucidating the author's identity and historical circumstance. It is here that Rajan's notion of autonarration is crucial in helping students think through the relationship between the author's identity in his own time and ours.

The third and final representation of marriage takes place in London in 1785. Like Equiano's previous examples, this ceremony is noteworthy because it is atypical. In this instance, the ceremony does not reflect the conventions practiced by most people living in England at the time. The mode of marriage practiced in England in 1785 would have followed the conventions of the Anglican Church as established by the monarch and bishop. The marriage custom that becomes associated with England by the *Narrative* is a London Quaker wedding. The inclusion of the Quaker wedding (which Equiano also chooses for his own marriage to the white Englishwoman Susanna Cullen) in the final pages of the *Narrative* makes clear Equiano's rhetorical use of the marriage ceremony. Carretta's textual note accompanying the incident reiterates this fact: "by inserting the letter of thanks to the Quakers and his description of the Quaker wedding, both set in London, Equiano has digressed from the chronology of his narrative" (297n631). Again, it is by way of the digression that Equiano involves his reader in the progression of the events.

By situating the author/reader relationship through a scene of an atypical marriage arrangement, Equiano forces the reader to assess her or his own identity and the ways in which it has changed through her or his engagement with a subject who is treated unjustly by the law. Equiano inscribes the wedding vow as well as describes it. Noting that "the man audibly declares to this purpose" (225), Equiano's account of the general event indicates that the vow can be read as well as heard. In order for this passage to have its full affect, I have students read it aloud in class.

Reading the vow in the context of Equiano's *Narrative* gives it its performative effect and the reader and Equiano are hereafter united by the law. Describing the event, Equiano declares: "Friends, in the fear of the Lord, and before this assembly, I take this my friend, M.N. to be my wife, promising, through divine assistance, to be unto her a loving and faithful husband until it shall please the Lord by death to separate us" (225). The "I" of this passage is Equiano, but the identity of the "wife" remains unknown. Equiano uses the initials "M.N." to denote the other rather than a proper name, leaving the other's identity ambiguous. Equiano also made a number of revisions to this particular passage. Carretta explains that the first five editions of the *Narrative* contain the lines "promising, through divine assistance to be unto her a loving and faithful husband till death separate us" (297n632). In the following four editions, Equiano changes this line to read "promising, through divine assistance to be unto her a loving and faithful husband until it shall please the Lord by death to separate us" (297n632), giving the Lord, rather than any mortal man, the right to separate the couple. The Quaker wedding vow, fully inscribed, becomes the model for the interpretive process as a dialogue in which the text mediates a series of differences within and between author and reader so that the two might experience, in Equiano's terms, "mutual commerce." He further writes that "[a] commercial intercourse with Africa opens an inexhaustible source of wealth to the manufacturing interest of Great Britain, and to all which the slave-trade is an objection" (234). The marital contract bears economic fruit as Equiano ends his *Narrative* explaining the mutual benefit of African-British relations.

The marriage vow marks an intercourse between reader and author. Since Equiano's vow must be simultaneously read and heard to have its desired effect, the *Narrative*'s reader provides the necessary context for the event. Unlike Rajan's female subject, "who must negotiate her relationship between representation and experience *without* relying on the constative or performative utterance" (153; emphasis added), the African-British subject employs both at once. It is with the utterance of the wedding vow that the *Narrative* performs a "transgressive miscegenation." As the relationship between reader and author is couched in the terms of the wedding ceremony, this miscegenous relationship is granted the stamp of legitimacy otherwise not recognized and protected by the law.

Although Equiano does not speak in this instance, he does write. In the Quaker ceremony, the witnesses are not merely silent spectators at the event. Instead, they are to sign their names to the marriage certificate that endorses the couple's union. The presence of the witness is necessary to the union. It is not surprising, then, that of the marriage ceremonies Equiano witnesses, it is the Quaker mode of marriage that he "highly recommend[s]" (226). The Quaker ceremony not only upsets the *Narrative's* chronology, but it provides the context and principle by which the incidents of the *Narrative,* as well as the reader's position in those incidents, must be assessed.

In marked contrast to the scenes of abuse Equiano suffers, the exchange of vows between subjects within the context of the marriage ceremony represents a collaboration between reader and author. Whereas Equiano and his fellow slaves are without recourse when they are treated cruelly by the "infernal invaders of human rights," he finds in the marriage ceremony a contract that shields him (and his countrymen) from their actions. Moreover, if one of the subjects breaks a vow, as was the case in the first marriage Equiano describes, the community will be called upon to decide upon the just punishment. In this way, the marriage ceremony enables Equiano to imagine a relation to his countrymen and system of exchange far removed from the restrictions and practices of slavery. Since students are often curious about how Equiano's own marriage may have influenced the writing of his *Narrative,* it is worth noting that Equiano makes little mention of his own wedding and subsequent marriage to Cullen. He writes only that he was married to "Miss Cullen, daughter of James and Ann Cullen" on April 7 after hearing the debate in the House of Commons on the Slave Trade (235). There is little evidence to suggest that either Equiano or Cullen encountered any opposition to their union and, as his will makes evident, he benefited greatly from it.[6]

Like much of the *Narrative,* Equiano's account of the marriage ceremony has little to do with his personal experience. Instead, the marriage ceremony provides Equiano with a vehicle to produce both a critique and legal end to slavery. His representation of different ceremonies calls into question the ways in which interpersonal relationships are regulated by peculiar institutions and calls for such regulations to be dismantled. The descriptions and reproductions of marriage ceremonies throughout the course of the *Narrative* help students to understand the connections between its fictional elements and its argument against slavery. Reading the *Narrative* as an act of textual miscegenation rather than within the confines of particular historical, generic, or national literary categories makes more sense in relation to the terms of Equiano's project. Equiano concludes his *Narrative* advocating a union between Britain and Africa through "economic intercourse" (234). Such a union is predicated, it would seem, upon terms for mutual exchange between these subjects that Equiano's *Narrative* establishes through witnessing the dissolution of difference between African and British subjects. Equiano's methodical insertions of marriage within his *Narrative* cause a rupture in the chronology of his life story. These ruptures represent the ways in which Equiano resists racial and other interpellative discourses that attempt to relegate him to the margins of political life.

The slave narrative's emphasis on communal utterances and collective tales elides the distinctive features of Equiano's consciousness; this *Narrative* offers the possibility of imagining a life outside the confines of his experience as black and oppressed. Equiano's *Narrative* is *not,* ultimately, a prototypical slave narrative, a British eighteenth-century personal narrative, or a captivity narrative. Despite efforts to incorporate the text as foundational to old and new traditions, the *Narrative* must be read as a text that imagines a life apart from conventions committed to continuing or establishing tradition, thus conceptually evading captivity itself.

But without participating in tradition, what establishes the use and truth value of Equiano's eighteenth-century text for students reading it for the first time in the twenty-first century? This is a question with which I conclude our study of Equiano's *Narrative.* Equiano's efforts to rewrite his life on his own terms must still confront the fact of his blackness. Equiano's *Narrative* is interested in addressing the contradictions and fissures within both African and British legal systems by engaging readers in free exchange and intercourse with the circumstances of his life. Rather than make Equiano into a representative of a particular race, we might instead use Equiano as a vehicle in the classroom to understand the difference between the author's time and our own.

Notes

1. A different version of this essay, titled "I, Hereby, Vow to Read *The Interesting Narrative,*" appeared in the collection *Captivating Subjects: Writing Confinement, Citizenship, and Nationhood in the Nineteenth Century,* edited by Jason Haslam and

Julia M. Wright. Though I am grateful to the editors for the opportunity to find an audience for my reading of Equiano's *Narrative,* the collection's critical commitment to the "captivity narrative" form and nineteenth-century history resulted in certain false formulations that I aim to correct here.

2. Nine editions were printed in Great Britain during the author's lifetime, and a first American edition appeared in New York in 1791. In his introduction to The Interesting Narrative *and Other Writings* (1995 edition), Vincent Carretta reprints some of the favorable reviews the *Narrative* received upon its first publication. All further page references to Equiano's *Narrative* will be to Carretta's edition and appear parenthetically in the body of the essay.

3. Equiano's exceptional wealth can be observed most vividly in the will he composed on 28 May 1796. Carretta informs us that "at a time when fewer than 5% of the male population had enough assets to merit writing a will, and when perhaps no other person of African descent in Britain left a will," Equiano left his surviving daughter 950 pounds—the equivalent of $120,000 today (Carretta, "Defining" 398).

4. For an extended discussion on Equiano's thoughts on interracial marriage, see his letter to James Tobin published in the *Public Advertiser* reprinted in The Interesting Narrative *and Other Writings,* 328–30.

5. Equiano's note reads, "See Benezet's *Account of Guinea* throughout." See also Carretta's additional note for a brief description of Benezet (241n43).

6. According to Equiano's will, through his marriage to Susanna Cullen he acquired "Two Acres of Copyhold Pasture Ground with the Appurtenances" (Equiano 354).

Works Cited

Austin, J. L. *How to Do Things with Words.* Cambridge: Harvard UP, 1962.

Baker, Houston A., Jr. *Blues, Ideology, and Afro-American Literature: A Vernacular Theory.* Chicago: U of Chicago P, 1984.

Carretta, Vincent. "Defining a Gentleman: The Status of Olaudah Equiano or Gustavus Vassa." *Language Sciences* 22.3 (2000): 385–99.

———. Introduction. The Interesting Narrative *and Other Writings.* New York: Penguin, 1995. ix–xxviii.

Edwards, Paul. "Three West African Writers of the 1780s." *The Slave's Narrative.* Ed. Charles T. Davis and Henry Louis Gates Jr. New York: Oxford UP, 1985. 175–98.

Equiano, Olaudah. The Interesting Narrative *and Other Writings.* Ed. Vincent Carretta. New York: Penguin, 1995.

Gates, Henry Louis, Jr. *The Signifying Monkey: A Theory of African-American Literary Criticism.* New York: Oxford UP, 1988.

Guess Who. Dir. Kevin Rodney Sullivan. Columbia Pictures, 2005.

Guess Who's Coming to Dinner. Dir. Stanley Kramer. Columbia Pictures, 1967.

Johnson, Samuel. *A Dictionary of the English Language.* London: Times Books, 1979.

McBride, Dwight. *Impossible Witness: Truth, Abolitionism, and Slave Testimony.* New York: New York UP, 2001.

Ogude, S. E. "Facts into Fiction: Equiano's *Narrative* Reconsidered." *Research in African Literatures* 13.1 (1982): 31–43.

Olney, James. "'I Was Born': Slave Narratives, Their Status as Autobiography, and as Literature." *The Slave's Narrative.* Ed. Charles T. Davis and Henry Louis Gates Jr. New York: Oxford UP, 1985. 148–75.

Rajan, Tilottama. "Autonarration and Genotext in Mary Hays's *Memoirs of Emma Courtney.*" *Studies in Romanticism* 32.2 (1993): 149–76.

Sayre, Gordon M. Introduction. *American Captivity Narratives: Olaudah Equiano, Mary Rowlandson, and Others.* Boston: Houghton, 2000. 1–17.

Samuels, Wilfred D. "Disguised Voices in *The Interesting Narrative of Olaudah Equiano, or Gustavus Vassa, the African.*" *Black American Literature Forum* 19.2 (1985): 64–69.

Walvin, James. *Black and White: The Negro and English Society, 1555–1945.* London: Penguin, 1973.

Williams, Carolyn D. "Another Self in the Case: Gender, Marriage, and the Individual in Augustan Literature." *Rewriting the Self: Histories from the Renaissance to the Present.* Ed. Roy Porter. London: Routledge, 1997. 97–118.

Loving the Unstable Text and Times of Equiano's *Narrative:* Using Carretta's Biography in the Classroom

Emily M. N. Kugler

When it came out, Vincent Carretta's *Equiano, the African: Biography of a Self-Made Man* prompted news reports attempting to make sense of an academic controversy for non-academic readers. Headlines such as the *Guardian*'s "Author casts shadow over slave hero" (Younge) or the *Washington Times*'s "New biography challenges iconic slave's account" (Manning) create the idea that Carretta's biography constitutes a possible delegitimization of Olaudah Equiano and his *Narrative,* regardless of whatever nuances are included in the articles themselves. In a good representation of this trend, *U.S. News and World Report* writer Nell Boyce presents Carretta's book as an attack on the legitimacy of teaching Equiano's *Narrative* in the university:

> Equiano's narrative has become a staple of African-American literature and history, one that professors routinely rely on to convey the pain of slavery to their students. But now a University of Maryland English professor has turned up evidence that Equiano may not have endured the middle passage—indeed, he may not have set foot in Africa. His likely birthplace? South Carolina. (Boyce)

The ominous "but" implies an end to the use of the *Narrative* in the classroom and points to a central question in teaching Equiano's work. Are we merely teaching his autobiography in order "to convey the pain of slavery"?

Some of our students might assume the answer is yes, and their assumption would be supported by the way they have likely encountered the text. Frequently, the *Narrative* is included in anthologies of world, U.S., and British literature, but just as frequently, the excerpts in these publications focus on the opening chapters dealing with Africa and the Middle Passage. I believe this is a dangerous truncation of the work. In its similarity to the eighteenth-century stereotype that women authors could only write from experience and lacked the masculine power of a creative imagination, this simplification of the *Narrative* presents the danger of sending students the message that its author only has value as a witness and as an African victim of the slave trade. Becoming like the famous figure on the Wedgwood "Am I Not A Man and a Brother?" medallion, he represents a larger issue of slavery, rather than being treated as an author of a complicated work and an equal to other figures of that era. Yet Equiano, even in his own account, hardly lived the life of a typical slave. His actual enslavement takes up less than half of the *Narrative.* Rather than give only an account of his enslavement, Equiano provides a story that focuses as much if not more on the transformations that occur after his emancipation. The *Narrative* is concerned largely with the creation of an identity that would provide for its narrator a sense of agency, security, and community—all of which he finds in England.

To bring out the richness and scope of the *Narrative,* students need to learn the historical context of the text. For this purpose, Carretta's biography (even in excerpts) is an effective pedagogical tool for transforming students' experience with the *Narrative.* Through this text, students can better appreciate Equiano as a skilled eighteenth-century author whose work illustrates the ambiguities of the slavery debate in context of multiple articulations of British identity. This approach introduces students to the complexities of the era as well as to the discussions in the fields of literary and historical studies today.

Equiano as Author: The Aesthetics of Eighteenth-Century British Politics

The most pedagogically useful aspect of Carretta's *Equiano* is his treatment of the author as a talented writer capable of creating a narrative that was both politically and financially successful. In my classes, I try to emphasize the contradictory and unstable presentation of slavery and identity both as a means for discussing the artistic complexity of the piece as well as to link the text to the multiple debates surrounding slavery at the close of the eighteenth century. Carretta's *Equiano* provides a useful model for reexamining the opening chapters (so often the only part included in anthologies) as the work of a gifted author, which fits with my approach to the text. Carretta presents Equiano as embodying the eighteenth-century ideal of a self-made man, a concept popular on both sides of the Atlantic:

> In the sense of raising himself from poverty and obscurity, Equiano was a more self-made man than [Benjamin] Franklin, and he was as successful during his lifetime as Franklin in marketing that image of himself. . . . Equiano rose from being property in the eyes of the law to being the wealthiest person of African descent in Britain. (Carretta xvii)

In this light, Carretta's thesis that Equiano was actually born in the Americas reinforces rather than undermines the *Narrative*'s appeal as a model of self-creation since, if true, "he invented an identity to suit the times" (Carretta xvii). Regardless of whether or not Carretta's argument about the birthplace is correct, his emphasis on the concept of identity as constructed resonates with the *Narrative* and the era that produced it.

One useful way to use Carretta's text is in the examination of the opening chapters of the *Narrative.* These chapters skillfully introduce and invert concepts of the Self/Other binary in ways that can be incorporated into college classes of every level. By comparing the vision of Britain in the book's Dedication with the description of Africa (Essaka) in the opening chapter, students can quickly see how Equiano creates an identifying link between his white British audience and his African persona. They may differ in some practices (polygamy, women warriors) but share ideals (one god, the high value they place on industry, chastity, and cleanness); they also culturally excel in ways the *Narrative* makes easily recognizable to late eighteenth-century Britons, as the Igbo (Eboe) society constitutes "almost a nation of dancers, musicians, and poets" (Equiano 14). Equiano diminishes the Igbo's otherness for his readers who belong to the middle class and above: they do not resemble plantation slaves or, for that matter, lower-class Britons.

But the *Narrative* further complicates the identification of the readers with their narrator by expanding this affiliation to the undermining of European/African and Civilized/Uncivilized binaries with his description of a confused, kidnapped child: the readers' perspective is with young Equiano, and they are made to see the European slave traders as alien:

> I was now persuaded that I had got into a world of bad spirits, and that they were going to kill me. Their complexions too, differing so much from *ours,* their long hair, and the language they spoke, which was very different from any I had ever heard, united to confirm me in this belief. (31; emphasis added)

The readers are included in the narratorial "ours," marking the white European slave traders as markedly different from the African/Reader Self the *Narrative* creates.

Indeed, little physical description is given of these first Europeans, thus preventing readers from relating to them rather than to the African "I" telling the story: when they are described as "white," it is in the context of their possible cannibalism, something to which presumably few of the white British readers could relate, as the young Equiano wonders "if we were to be eaten by those white men with horrible looks, red faces, and long hair" (31). The slave traders are further distanced from the readers by the violence they inflict on others regardless of race as they brutally flog sailors. Naively the child Equiano asks, "if these people had no country, but lived in this hollow place, the ship" (32), but the adult author has already separated them from the readers: rhetorically, their strangeness and brutality render them country-less because they do not represent the marks of civilization and British values the readers see in Equiano.

The addition of Carretta's biography to this reading helps students better grasp why this identification was crucial to the abolitionist movement:

> [Equiano's] representation of Igboland challenged images of Africa as a land of savagery, idolatry, cannibalism, indolence, and social disorder. Proponents of the slave trade argued that enslavement by Europeans saved Africans from such evils and introduced them to civilization, culture, industry, and Christianity. (Carretta 5)

Without this significant historical context, Equiano's assertion in the Dedication seems to undermine the political efficacy of the *Narrative:*

> By the horrors of that trade was I first torn away from all the tender connexions [*sic*] that were naturally dear to my heart; but these, through the

> mysterious ways of Providence, I ought to regard as infinitely more than compensated by the introduction I have thence obtained to the knowledge of the Christian religion, and of a nation which, by its liberal sentiments, its humanity, the glorious freedom of its government, and its proficiency in arts and sciences, has exalted the dignity of human nature. (Equiano 2)

Yet, when the historical context Carretta provides is given, the subtler political moves of the *Narrative* become highlighted for students. For example, Carretta argues that in these opening chapters, Equiano creates a new vision of the Igbo people: whereas eighteenth-century accounts such as the one by missionary Georg Andreas Oldendorp in 1777 refers to "cannibalism and human sacrifice by the Igbo[,] . . . Equiano speaks with the voice of an Igbo protonationalist proud of his homeland, no doubt aware that if he could rehabilitate the reputation of the Igbo in particular, he would rehabilitate the reputation of Africans in general" (Carretta 310). Rather than as a lesser group, the way slave traders of the day saw them, Equiano presents them as a superior and desired ethnic group (Carretta 311–13).

Going beyond the eighteenth-century debate over slavery, Carretta points out that Equiano's vision of the Igbo as a nation is more than simply a designation by those on the coast for those on the inland; instead, it predates any actual nationalism (Carretta 312). Equiano's view of a Pan-African continent (rather than a diversity of cultures) and his choice of selecting the name Equiano to create an African identity are also worth exploring with students. In my experiences teaching this text, students are often troubled by his seemingly pandering treatment of white Britons, exemplified by the Dedication's assertion that his sorrow as slave is "compensated" for by his introduction to British culture. The possibility that he creates a protonationalist identity and names himself befits Carretta's vision of him as a self-made man, and also draws attention to the loss of control Equiano experiences as a young slave when he cannot even control what name he is called (Equiano 38–39). His politicalization and major contributions to the abolitionist movement are rooted in his creation of a new identity that is both British and African (Carretta 328). He casts off his slave name to regain an African identity denied by European slavery and, in my view, creates a new kind of British identity independent of racial affiliation or nation of birth. Especially in its use of British identity, this pedagogical approach allows instructors to establish comparative connections that link the *Narrative* to later nationalist and ethnic solidarity movements, such as the West African Students' Union (WASU) and the National Congress of British West Africa (NCBWA) that emerged in the 1920s.[1]

The concept of identity, especially Equiano's eventual adaptation of a British one, intertwines with the relationship between the narrator and his readers. Expanding the identification of the readers with their narrator in the opening chapters, the *Narrative* also charts the politicization of a British citizen. Initially, Equiano only works for his own emancipation. Having earned almost enough to purchase his freedom, he goes on an additional voyage:

> After we had discharged our cargo there *we took in a live cargo, as we call a cargo of slaves. Here I sold my goods tolerably well;* but, not being able to lay out all my money in this small island to as much advantage as in many other places, I laid out only part, and the remainder I brought away with me neat. We sailed from hence for Georgia, and I was glad when we got there, though I had not much reason to like the place from my last adventure in Savannah; *but I longed to get back to Montserrat and procure my freedom,* which I expected to be able to purchase when I returned. (98–99; emphases added)

Many of my students fail to note that this final cargo includes slaves. Strangely, although Equiano highlights that "live cargo" means "slaves," he does not tie it overtly to his argument on slavery. Instead, this detail almost becomes buried in others. If we continue to acknowledge that the opening chapters set up an affiliation between Equiano and his readers, the passage makes more rhetorical sense: at this point he loses sight of the irony that this cargo represents because of all the other details filling his mind. His pursuit of funds is central to his quest for manumission, but this part of the *Narrative* can also be linked to his British readers' own aspirations to improve their positions economically and socially through enterprise, including their participation in the slave trade. This discussion allows even those who oppose his view on the slave trade to transcend these political differences through a shared pursuit of mercantilism and capital. Carretta's biography helps emphasize the chronology of the *Narrative,* as Equiano moves from concerns with his own freedom, to his involvement in individual legal cases involving the status of ex-slaves in London, to his eventual political commitment to the movement represented by his publicly taking the name Equiano as well as by his publishing the *Narrative.*

By focusing on the idea of self-fashioning as a key rhetorical tool for the *Narrative,* the historical debate surrounding the details of the Equiano's life becomes an asset for students as they explore the *Narrative* as a complex literary work. By setting up the opening of the text as a potentially unreliable or unstable narrative, this approach encourages students to pay attention to the other intricacies of Equiano's aesthetics and rhetoric. Once instructors establish this point in class, students can more easily grasp his contradictory role as the narrator. On one hand, Equiano must present himself as exceptional (both in his ability to buy his own freedom as well as a subject worthy of a biography) while at the same time presenting himself as the norm (which allows readers to transfer their perceptions of his rationality and sensibility onto the slaves in the West Indies).

As both a former slave and slave trader and a current social reformer, Equiano details an African childhood but presents himself as thoroughly European. The Dedication identifies him as African but suggests stronger loyalties to England. He refers to African slaves as his countrymen and shows how slavery has disrupted his own life, while at the same time he flatters Britons with claims of their superior culture, as he posits the seemingly paradoxical rhetorical strategy that the slave trade should be abolished because slaves (whom he represents) can appreciate the wonders of white, European (specifically British) culture, which he learned to appreciate as a slave. In asserting his cultural validity, he draws largely on the genre of spiritual autobiography, which usually presents one individual's story as potentially universal. However, I have found it fruitful to contextualize him in another genre as well: that of the African intellectual in Europe.

While readers are likely to recognize Leo Africanus, the most famous figure in this catalogue, it is important to acknowledge that there was also a tradition of African scholars in Europe. This established tradition of the African intellectual in Europe ultimately lends credibility to Equiano as an author. Carretta's *Equiano* offers a clear introduction to both the religious and racial context of the *Narrative* in its discussion of the visual parallels between the frontispiece Equiano uses in his 1789 edition of the *Narrative* and other portraits, such as those of Dutch Reformed Church preacher Jan Cornelis Sylvius and African-born New England poet Phillis Wheatley. With Equiano's portrait, Carretta notes, eighteenth-century readers

> confronted his dual identity as soon as they opened his book. The initial frontispiece presents an indisputable African body in European dress, and the title page offers us "Olaudah Equiano, or Gustavus Vassa, the African." To call him consistently by either the one name or the other is to oversimplify his identity. (Carretta 292)

The physical volumes of the *Narrative* were an extension of Equiano's self-fashioning of identity as he controlled all aspects of its publication (Carretta 301–2). Just as its narrator complicates readers' conceptions of their identity, the physical text presents a multifaceted persona for its author as a black Briton.

The dual nature of Equiano's persona and argument continues throughout the text as he lists the horrors of slavery (Equiano 74–80) and goes on to describe how, after he earns his freedom and receives manumission papers, the possession of additional money (possibly from that "live cargo") allows him to purchase and wear "superfine blue clothes" to dances (Equiano 102). Within a matter of paragraphs, Equiano can switch from calling for the immediate abolition of the slave trade, as he declares that "such a tendency has the slave-trade to debauch men's minds, and harden them to every feeling of humanity" (80) and "[s]urely this traffic cannot be good, which spreads like a pestilence, and taints what it touches" (80), to pleading simply for the better treatment of slaves, which will, in turn, result in a more passive workforce that is "faithful, honest, intelligent, and vigorous" (81) leading to "peace, prosperity, and happiness" (81) for the reformed slave owner.

The *Narrative* itself points to a complicated view of debates over British slavery, and many students are unaware of these significant proceedings. These debates entailed a more nuanced set of positions that extended beyond the stances of either pro or con, and the debates in Parliament on the slave trade reflected this complexity. Equiano's *Narrative* responds to that debate, but it was not a debate to end slavery but to end the trade from Africa. In the classroom, I have approached these contradictions as a means for discussing the changes that historical distance can create in our perceptions of an issue, pointing out that the issue Parliament was debating at the time of the *Narrative*'s publication was not whether or not to end slavery; instead, these proceedings were focused on the slave trade itself. The abolition of the trade attracted both supporters and opponents of slavery, and Equiano is in many ways attempting to reach the widest possible audience.

Carretta's *Equiano* augments this approach by laying out the multiple positions taken in the British slave debates, including the ameliorationist position the *Narrative* sometimes professes:

> Assuming that immediate and unilateral abolition of slavery by Britain would be commercially disastrous and that the trade continued because the West Indian slave population failed to be self-sustaining due to brutal conditions, opponents of the trade argued that were owners to ameliorate those conditions, slaves would be more productive, demographic longevity and fertility would increase, and consequently the transatlantic trade would no longer be necessary. (Carretta 97–98)

Many of my students are often unaware of the history of slavery outside of the United States and they frequently view the institution as a small problem that was solved neatly by the U.S. Civil War. British slavery debates provide the opportunity to show students a wider view of the world, introducing them not only to British history but also to the transformation of Saint-Domingue into Haiti, the aftershocks of the French Revolution, as well as a basic introduction to transatlantic studies. The enslavement of Africans in the transatlantic world does not stand as an isolated history: its creation and the attempts to abolish it are linked to other historical movements in a multitude of countries. One of the threads it touches upon is the ways in which British identity was being rearticulated in the decades that followed the creation of the United Kingdom of Great Britain in 1707.

The Narrative's Creation of a New (Black) British Identity

This transnational and transatlantic approach I advocate in the classroom is modeled for students within the *Narrative* itself. Equiano's own search for an identity that fits his emancipated life mirrors this larger cultural struggle to articulate a new British identity. Towards the end the *Narrative,* Equiano still debates where to settle both physically and spiritually. Turkey seems to offer a solution for him. Set outside of the transatlantic triangle of the British slave trade, the country offers an intriguing new start for Equiano. The "New" World of the Americas harbors the old dangers of a return to slavery, and the "Old" Ottoman Empire offers an escape from those dangers: Equiano presents Turks as generally "fond of black people" and kind to him despite the fact that they keep other Christians "separate, and do not suffer them to dwell immediately amongst them" (Equiano 125). Similar to the way I argue that a discussion of slavery needs to be discussed within a global context, the *Narrative* presents the creation of Equiano's identity as a free man as shaped by his travels and knowledge of a world outside of the triangle of the slave trade.

The Turkey episode, in particular, offers students an opportunity to bring out the nuances—as well as potential inconsistencies—of Equiano's objections to slavery. Although a move to Turkey would ensure Equiano's physical safety, it would also require an apolitical stance towards religion and slavery. Just as he presumably would ignore the segregation of other Christians in the country, so would he ignore the plight of other slaves: "I was surprised to see how the Greeks are, in some measure, kept under by the Turks, as the negroes are in the West Indies by the white people" (Equiano 126). The link between the Turkish enslavement of the Greeks and the British enslavement of Africans is brought out more by the cultural affiliation he constructs: "The less refined Greeks, as I have already hinted, dance here in the same manner as we do in my nation" (Equiano 126). Despite the intellectual links he makes between his past enslavement and the present situation in Turkey, he declares, "I liked the place and the Turks extremely well" (Equiano 126). For him to become politically engaged, he must find national and spiritual identities that reflect a sense of the present and future, rather than the past.

It is not until he finds a religious identity among Methodists that he truly makes Britain his home and becomes active in the abolitionist movement. Much like the geographic wanderings that bring him to Turkey and the North Pole before finding a physical home, his religious wanderings traverse multiple ideological spaces. Moving from "the neighbouring churches, St. James's, and others, two or three times a day, for many weeks" to Quaker meetings, Roman Catholic congregations, and Jewish communities, he links his religious search back to the earlier possibility of living in Turkey: "[F]inding those who in general termed themselves Christians not so honest or so good in their morals as the Turks, I really thought the Turks were in a safer way of salvation than my neighbours. . . . I determined at last to set out for Turkey, and there to end my days" (Equiano 135). But his switch to Methodism changes this position. He moves to England, becomes active in religious and abolitionist circles, marries an English-born woman, and writes the *Narrative.*

Again, Carretta's biography provides a useful tool for students to understand how Equiano's situation fits into the large context of the multiple articulations of British identity at this time. Carretta presents Equiano's wandering as a product both of his enslavement as well as part of an emerging British identity: "Enslavement had rendered him a man without a country, someone who seemed to define himself as much by movement as by staying in any one place for long. Slavery had controlled his mobility. Freedom meant that he could choose where and when to travel" (138), and these travels, as a means of self-fashioning, allow Equiano to experience "the working man's version of the grade tours taken by the sons of the wealthy to finish their education by traveling around Europe" (Carretta 138–39). These links made by Carretta can be useful in prompting students to think about connections within the text as a whole.

The Dedication, for instance, provides a fruitful example to link back to after discussing the *Narrative*'s closing chapters. That Britain, the introduction to which has "more than compensated" for his enslavement, is both highly praised for its "liberal sentiments, its humanity, [and] the glorious freedom of its government" seems at odds with Equiano's hope in the Dedication that divine intervention gives the Members of Parliament a "peculiar benevolence on that important day when the question of Abolition is to be discussed" (Equiano 2). The implicit charge that this "benevolence" is not normally part of the Members' hearts sets up a contrast between the ideals expressed in the Dedication and the political realities threatening abolitionist interests. I view the praise in the Dedication not so much as a depiction of how he perceived Britain's reality but of a potential Britain, where belonging is not marked by race or national origins but on a shared set of ideals and laws. In this light, the *Narrative* positions Britain as the place of present political struggles and future redemptive reform.

This possibility becomes easier for students to grasp if they understand the way Equiano's choice of religious identity fits into concepts of British culture. As Carretta points out, although Methodism was part of the Church of England—albeit an evangelical offshoot— "conservative Anglicans looked with suspicion on the 'enthusiastic' Methodists, whom they considered potential Dissenting separatists from the Church. . . . Methodist preachers were often physically assaulted as well as assailed in print" (Carretta 165). By becoming a Methodist, Equiano joins a community that was an established part of British culture through its membership in the state religion, but it was a marginalized, heterogeneous, populist, and reform-oriented group. Similarly, Equiano embodies British values of self-fashioning and industriousness, but he is still marginalized because of his race, national origin, and past enslavement.

This was a type of Christian identity that discouraged uniformity and a British identity that was conceived in the idea that to be British was to push for reform in the church, state, and secular world. Significantly for the case of Equiano, it was a movement that aligned itself more with British slaves than with British slave holders: "The evangelical Methodists saw all levels of society, including slaves, as potentially sharing in salvation" (Carretta 168). By rejecting the "New World" of the Americas as his past and an even older "Old World" of Turkey as a potential apolitical future, Equiano turns to what many U.S.-based and other students might view as the "Old World" of Europe in order to create a future where racial equality and personal fulfillment become a real possibility. Carretta's assessment of ex-slaves' preference for Britain over the newly formed United States supports this reading: "[M]ost of eighteenth-century blacks whose voices we can recover, either directly or through intermediaries, chose a British rather than American identity, taking advantage of the British promises of emancipation for refugee slaves of the colonial rebels (but not for refugees from loyalist masters)" (Carretta 215). Ironically, as the concept of a national identity for the United States emerged, a vision of British identity independent of race and national origin was being embraced by the black Loyalists. Although he never mentions the American War of Independence, Equiano expresses a similar belief that only as a Briton can he fashion a new identity as a freeman of African descent.

Carretta's *Equiano* as an Introduction to Current Scholarship

Certainly Carretta's biography is not the only source that offers historical context for the *Narrative* in an accessible way for students. Over the past two decades there has been a profusion of scholarship dealing with slavery, representations of race, and the eighteenth-century transatlantic world. Several of them are accessible to students both in terms of their physical availability as well as their approach to their subjects. Simon Schama's recent *Rough Crossing: Britain, the Slaves, and the American Revolution* and its BBC adaptation provide an excellent analysis of eighteenth-century slavery, the British abolitionist movement, and life for black Britons in the Empire, as well as of the Sierra Leone Company, with which Equiano was briefly affiliated. Gretchen Holbrook Gerzina's *Black*

London: Life Before Emancipation and (if the course's historical scope reaches back before the long eighteenth century) Kim F. Hall's *Things of Darkness: Economies of Race and Gender in Early Modern England* offer astute, accessible, and visual assessments of how blackness fit into British culture prior to Emancipation and how understandings and constructions of blackness shaped the reception of black Britons by their white counterparts.

Going beyond texts dealing with slavery, the concept of identity stands as a rich subject in current eighteenth-century literary and historical studies. Debbie Lee's *Romantic Liars: Obscure Women Who Became Impostors and Challenged an Empire,* for instance, provides an excellent way to initiate student discussion over how identity was constructed during this era, as well as to provide a context for the *Narrative*'s references to race, empire, and religion. Lee's profile of Joanna Southcott, for example, gives an interesting context of how Methodism was viewed and how it could be a source for challenges to the status quo. Although Southcott is hardly typical, her populist, woman-centered brand of religion provides an example of how religion was often linked to reform and other political issues. Like Equiano's status as an African and ex-slave, Southcott's background as a working-class, uneducated, unmarried woman made her both an unorthodox source of authority as well as an inspirational figure for those seeking to change society. In one instance, Southcott goes to a well-positioned clergyman to inform him that she believed herself to be a prophet and that he should help spread her message. His response lays out the assumed hierarchies of mainstream English culture at the end of the eighteenth century: "[T]he Lord would never have revealed it to you. There are a thousand in Exeter, whom I could point out, to whom the Lord would have revealed it before he would to you" (qtd. in Lee 35). Lee points out that it is "almost certain that Leach was referring to Joanna's status as an unmarried, uneducated, middle-aged, working-class woman" (Lee 35). Yet for many others in England, her lack of high status made her an inspirational figure:

> At the end of the eighteenth century, Devonshire's main industry—textiles, particularly wool—had reached an all time low through lack of demand, crop failure, and wars with France, and yet the cost of living was rising. Some had even rioted. Rural Devonshire dwellers were economically insecure; Joanna promised spiritual security. They were politically ineffective; Joanna promised them power. They were trapped and broken; Joanna

> promised them psychological transcendence. And she promised it soon. (Lee 37–38)

The profile's focus on a widespread desire in sections of the English populace to change accepted hierarchies and the religious communities they sought out to help facilitate these changes echoes the spiritual journey found in the *Narrative.*

Similarly, Lee's profile of Mary Willcocks, a.k.a. Princess Caraboo, explores the construction of knowledge, individual identity, and race in the context of the British Empire's Eastern swing away from transatlantic slavery towards the colonization of Asia. Lee argues that the persona Willcocks adopted "revealed both the falseness of this system of truth [at the root of Oriental studies in Europe], and how strong the desire to believe in such a system was to the Britons who created it" (Lee 187). Although not a false persona, Equiano adopts a public image that emphasizes his virtues and strengths according to the cultural standards in England; a connection could be made in the classroom between this move and the inverse one Willcocks performs by creating an identity out of European conceptions of Asian culture.

However, I choose to focus on Carretta's biography of Equiano for reasons other than providing historical context in the classroom. I teach sections of this text not only as an annotation to the *Narrative,* but also as a way of opening up present-day scholarship to students. The biography introduces them to the ways in which academics discuss, collaborate, build from, and argue against the work of their peers. And is this not what we are asking them to do in their own papers? Carretta's argument concerning Equiano's birthplace is clearly controversial to students regardless of their background. The explicit debatability of the biography makes them more aware of the other arguments Carretta makes. Rather than taking as fact Carretta's interpretation that the "innocent eye Equiano cast on the Greeks and Turks in Asia Minor contrasts sharply with the more experienced eye he cast on Europeans in the Mediterranean" (Carretta 140), they can debate whether or not they see this passage as an example of intentional authorial irony. This pedagogical strategy provides another professorial voice in the classroom other than my own, and it emphasizes what I want them to do in class discussions and in their papers: enter an on-going conversation on the *Narrative* and participate in the discussions found in the fields of transatlantic studies, eighteenth-century studies, literary studies, and more.

Carretta's biography is a key pedagogical tool for teaching the *Narrative* because it has elicited such a strong reaction from those studying Equiano. Carretta's text is beginning to have its own commentary history. If available, the film *The Extraordinary Equiano* can help supplement the use of Carretta's text.[2] The film includes scholars such as Carretta and Gerzina discussing the *Narrative,* its historical context, and the debate surrounding Carretta's thesis that Equiano was born in the Americas. The polite, reasoned assessments by the commentators clarify the scholarly stakes (as well as providing a useful behavior model for classroom debates). Another useful text is *Olaudah Equiano and the Igbo World: History, Society, and Atlantic Diaspora Connections* in which many of the essays directly refer back to Carretta's work. This text provides an excellent balance to Carretta, since, as the title implies, most of its authors disagree with the argument that Equiano was not born in Africa. As editor Chima J. Korieh explains, although Carretta's "discoveries raised important and legitimate concerns, [his] conclusions are problematic," and if they are correct, his "contention . . . does not alter Equiano's carefully constructed image of an Igbo world" (Korieh 6, 7). That Carretta's biography and the debate it prompted is not about the scholarly worth of the *Narrative* stands as an important position for students to grasp, and once this point is fully explored in the classroom, they will then be prepared to engage in more nuanced literary and historical analyses.

Returning to the *U.S. News and World Reports* article mentioned in the introduction, Boyce adds at the end that she finds the debate over Carretta's assertions "ironic—because Carretta really loves Equiano." I believe that in introducing our students to the scholarly conversations about the *Narrative* and other texts, we need to help them see the *lack* of irony in this position—that loving a subject as a scholar means questioning, prodding, and exploring its nuances rather than looking for one neat, all-encompassing reading. Given how infrequently scholarly work gets covered in the mainstream media, teacher-scholars need to be concerned with the rare cases when the spotlight actually focuses on academia because this coverage plays a large role in shaping public perceptions concerning the nature and relevance of our intellectual work. In "Who Killed Shakespeare? An Apologia for English Departments," Patrick Brantlinger outlines the dangers and annoyances English departments face when the curriculum of their classrooms and research of their faculty are misrepresented as unacceptably political:

> [I]n the neoconservative backlash against higher education, it's been absurdly easy to pick on English Departments. Millions of people, including trustees, journalists, and Woody [referring to then Indiana state representative Woody Burton], speak English, or some version of it. Many think they are experts, perhaps especially if they have taken that beloved Shakespeare course in the past. . . . [T]ell them an English Department contains Marxists, deconstructionists, or—God forbid!—feminists, or gay/lesbian theorists, and they are ready to call up the military. (686)[3]

Misrepresentations in the press can have severe consequences when we consider how dependent many institutions are on the opinions of the public and politicians for funding.

These threats to the financial well-being of colleges come in part from a lack of knowledge about what comprises scholarship in the humanities and social studies. Students' expectations of what we expect from them is also deeply influenced by the confusion over what goes on in academia. Our classes often must go beyond their specific topics to address what we mean when we refer to the word "scholarship" in the first place. One of the first steps I find in introducing students to literary or historical analysis lies in having them work beyond looking for a "moral" or some sort of pithy "life lesson." Equiano should be taught not to emphasize solely that slavery is horrible, as Boyce would like us to believe (surely there are other appropriate pedagogical methods for teaching this point), but because Equiano is one of the skilled authors of the era whose works carry aesthetic and historical merit separate from his role as a witness to genocide. Rather than neat, national histories, the *Narrative* offers a vision of a world where all boundaries, identities, and even history itself are ever-changing and contradictory.

Notes

1. For an excellent overview of British influence on Pan-Africanism, see Hakim Adi's "Pan-Africanism and West African Nationalism in Britain," which also links these later movements to the early activities of the Sons of Africa whose members included Equiano. This short article can help link the *Narrative* to later eras. If the course has time to look at the topic in more depth, Adi's book, *Pan-African History: Political Figures from Africa and the Diaspora Since 1787,* could also be assigned in full or in excerpts.

2. To the best of my knowledge, there are no copies of this documentary available for sale. To view it, one needs to find a recording from when it aired on BBC Two.

3. This article's argument is expanded upon in Brantlinger's similarly titled book *Who Killed Shakespeare? What's Happened to English Since the Radical Sixties.*

Works Cited

Adi, Hakim. "Pan-Africanism and West African Nationalism in Britain." *African Studies Review* 43.1 (2000): 69–82.

———. *Pan-African History: Political Figures from Africa and the Diaspora Since 1787.* New York: Routledge, 2003.

Boyce, Nell. "Out of Africa? New questions about the origins of a seminal slave narrative." *US News and World Report* 02 Feb. 2003. 30 Apr. 2009 <http://www.usnews.com/usnews/culture/articles/030210/10slavery_2.htm>.

Brantlinger, Patrick. "Who Killed Shakespeare? An Apologia for English Departments." *College English* 61.6 (1999): 681–90.

———. *Who Killed Shakespeare? What's Happened to English Since the Radical Sixties.* New York: Routledge, 2001.

Carretta, Vincent. *Equiano, the African: Biography of a Self-Made Man.* Athens, GA: U of Georgia P, 2005.

Equiano, Olaudah. *The Life of Olaudah Equiano, or Gustavus Vassa, the African.* 1789. Mineola, NY: Dover, 1999.

The Extraordinary Equiano. Dir. Chris Salt. Perf. Ariyon Bakare, Sam Hazeldine, and Josette Simon. BBC, 2007.

Gerzina, Gretchen Holbrook. *Black London: Life Before Emancipation.* New Brunswick, NJ: Rutgers UP, 1997.

Hall, Kim F. *Things of Darkness: Economies of Race and Gender in Early Modern England.* Ithaca, NY: Cornell UP, 1996.

Korieh, Chima J. "Mapping the Igbo-Atlantic Connection." Introduction. *Olaudah Equiano and the Igbo World: History, Society, and Atlantic Diaspora Connections.* Ed. Chima J. Korieth. Trenton, NJ: Africa World P, 2009. 1–20.

———, ed. *Olaudah Equiano and the Igbo World: History, Society, and Atlantic Diaspora Connections.* Trenton, NJ: Africa World P, 2009.

Lee, Debbie. *Romantic Liars: Obscure Women Who Became Impostors and Challenged an Empire.* New York: Palgrave Macmillan, 2006.

Manning, Stephen. "New biography challenges iconic slave's account." *Washington Times.* 24 Sept. 2005. 15 June 2009 <http://washingtontimes.com/news/2005/sep/24/20050924–111443–6717r/>.

Schama, Simon. *Rough Crossing: Britain, the Slaves, and the American Revolution.* New York: Harper Perennial, 2007.

Simon Schama's Rough Crossings. Dir. Steve Condie. Perf. Stephen Campbell Moore, Niall Macgregor, Joseph Marcell, Alice O'Connell, and Simon Schama. BBC, 2007.

Younge, Gary. "Author casts shadow over slave hero." *Guardian.* 14 Sept. 2005. 30 Sept. 2011 <http://www.guardian.co.uk/world/2005/sep/14/books.usa>.

Part 3

Pedagogy, African American Studies, and *The Interesting Narrative*

When Young Minds Read Equiano's *Narrative*

Angelo Costanzo

It is unlikely that present-day students will voluntarily pick up and read Equiano's *The Interesting Narrative.* The autobiographer's names of Olaudah Equiano and Gustavus Vassa not only look strange, but their pronunciations are also difficult to figure out without some instructional aid. Added to this difficult start is the narrative's eighteenth-century balanced prose, much of it presented in an elaborate and formal manner. This style appears foreign to most of today's young men and women, whose experiences with writing more often result not from intense study of eighteenth-century literary texts but from their interactions with the various electronic instruments they use to communicate with one another.

But fortunately many student readers first encounter Equiano's great work when they are assigned to read it in one of a variety of classes, whether this engagement occurs in the literature, history, sociology, or black studies classroom. Whenever I introduced Equiano's *Narrative* in my university-level African American literature class, I found that students would usually be faced with numerous hurdles in their readings of the autobiography. These same hurdles unfortunately often prevented them from completing their assignment(s) or, worse yet, turned them to resist Equiano's classic work itself.

The Interesting Narrative contains long stretches of religious and abolitionist rhetoric that many student readers find to be dull reading. The large number of scriptural verses Equiano cites and the detailed spiritual journey he dwells upon in his work contribute at times to the sense of boredom that many young readers experience while poring through his autobiography.

Luckily, most of the oratorical flourishes and the passages of moral sermonizing in Equiano's narrative appear in the later parts of his work. In the early sections of his account, Equiano uses a plain and vivid prose style to relate the details of his unusual life. And fortunately, it is that rhetorical choice by Equiano that helps students first starting their assigned reading to be drawn quickly into the mix of fascinating and shocking experience that characterizes much of his personal story.

In the first several chapters, Equiano describes his idyllic childhood life in Africa and how that innocent time came to a sudden end when he and his sister were kidnapped. Cruelly separated from his sister and sold into slavery, the youth was then transported to the coast where the slave ship awaited him and many other captured Africans. In a powerful passage, Equiano remarks that

> The first object which saluted my eyes when I arrived on the coast was the sea, and a slave ship, which was then riding at anchor, and waiting for its cargo. These filled me with astonishment, which was soon converted into terror when I was carried on board. I was immediately handled and tossed up to see if I were sound by some of the crew; and I was now persuaded that I had gotten into a world of bad spirits, and that they were going to kill me. Their complexions too differing so much from ours, their long hair, and the language they spoke, (which was very different from any I had ever heard) united to confirm me in this belief. . . . When I looked round the ship too and saw a large furnace or copper boiling, and a multitude of black people of every description chained together, every one of their countenances expressing dejection and sorrow, I no longer doubted of my fate; and, quite overpowered with horror and anguish, I fell motionless on the deck and fainted. (Equiano 69–70)[1]

Subsequently, Equiano graphically relates the agonizing voyage across the Atlantic followed by his brutal introduction to a life of slavery in the West. What especially makes this part of the narrative interesting is Equiano's startling manner of revealing to his readers the feelings of both fear and wonder he experienced while undergoing all these terrible events from this childhood ordeal.

Thinking about my own initial experience with *The Interesting Narrative* has helped me to understand what incentives teachers of Equiano's work can emphasize in the classroom for the benefit of their students, including those who might balk at reading the autobiography. As a graduate student many years ago, I accidentally came upon Equiano's account when I was searching for a research subject to explore. It was the early 1970s, when courses in black studies were being included in the curriculum offerings of many colleges and universities. The class I was taking was in early American literature, but the professor had listed Equiano's autobiography as a possible topic for a term paper project, probably as a goodwill gesture to campus activists' demands for the inclusion of African American contributions in their courses. I had never before heard of Olaudah Equiano and *The Interesting Narrative;* but since I had recently become interested in African American literary figures in my own teaching and scholarly career, my curiosity was aroused about this little-known eighteenth-century ex-slave and writer who had lived in several parts of the world.

Starting my reading of Equiano's work revealed to me a strange past time and place that drew my interest deeper and deeper into a mindset previously unknown to me. Looking back now, I realize that part of what cast its spell upon me then was the well-known eighteenth-century literary penchant for imagining a lost innocent world of primitivism. In describing his childhood life in Africa, Equiano paints an idyllic, if stereotypical, picture of his homeland in which noble men and women live and thrive in a natural environment. That is not to say, however, that this beautiful Eden lacks a framework of religious and moral societal tenets designed for the benefit of its inhabitants. Equiano makes it clear that although life in his African village is marked by simplicity and innocence, he considers the cultural and civic values and practices found in his ancestral home to be as worthy and effective as those that characterize many other societies, even those existing in the West. In fact, on moral grounds, Equiano imparts a sense of superiority of the Africans over Western men and women who have created an abominable institution in slavery, which stands in direct violation of their professed Christian principles.

Reflecting on my own experiences teaching the *Narrative,* I believe that most readers who begin to read Equiano's narrative become fascinated by the tranquil Edenic picture of African families living in a natural environment of earthly abundance and feeling somewhat secure within a well-structured, beneficent society. The land provides sustaining fruits and vegetables and the children play games until they come of age and are initiated into the adult world. But after

Equiano instills his readers with this highly pleasant mood, he severely shocks them with the description of how his childhood world was shattered when kidnappers invaded his village home to snatch away him and his sister.

Perhaps, the reason why this particular account resonates with young students is that they are reading the description of Equiano's lost world of joyful innocence at a crucial time in their own lives when they themselves are transitioning from the relative pleasures of youth to the formidable realities of the adult world. Even today, whenever I read Equiano's re-creation of his pleasant childhood days in Africa, I can recall my own feelings of delight when I recaptured for a brief moment the sense of a happy ideal existence.

Anyone who has studied the Equiano's autobiography knows that there are disputes in scholarly circles regarding his actual birthplace, the veracity of what he related about his African origins, and his extensive borrowings from contemporary sources.[2] These significant literary and biographical matters can and should be honestly examined in the classroom. At first, however, students reading the narrative need not think about the current hotly debated controversies to appreciate the remarkable literary re-creation Equiano skillfully sketches for us in the beginning chapters of his autobiography. Concern about the authenticity of the opening part of the life story and how it may affect the legitimate standing of Equiano's entire work can be laid aside until students complete their reading of *The Interesting Narrative.*

If what attracts many beginning student readers to the narrative is Equiano's idyllic depiction of an African existence shattered by the sudden evil intrusion of kidnapping and slavery, then what further draws them into Equiano's world are the many heart-wrenching incidents and strange encounters he describes in his account of the Middle Passage, along with his feelings of surprise and awe as he is forced to enter deeper and deeper into the Western world of slavery. Afterwards, students become absorbed in Equiano's vivid descriptions of his daring exploits at sea. And there is no doubt that most young minds and hearts are also affected by the deeply moving expressions delivered repeatedly by Equiano of his strong desire for freedom. This desire drives him to work hard at enterprises that will secure his eventual deliverance from slavery. Ultimately, all readers rejoice with Equiano when he purchases his manumission from a reluctant slave master; and those same readers marvel at Equiano's subsequent presentation of himself as a newborn figure who is able from then on to control more fully his destiny.

Admittedly, while reading the middle and later parts of the narrative, many students who were attracted to its early sections often lose interest and give up reading the autobiography. One reason for this decline in student interest is the increasing amount of space Equiano devotes to the details of eighteenth-century religious ideas and activities. After telling his readers about the unusual and startling adventures of his youth, Equiano begins dwelling increasingly on his spiritual explorations of Christian religious principles. He also sporadically inserts long polemical passages that earnestly plead support for the abolitionist cause. The religious and hortatory subjects do not always excite young readers, especially when Equiano allows the didactic topics to interrupt his narrative's flow of events. Here Equiano's manner of writing raises a problem for instructors who want to maintain their students' interest and involvement in the autobiography.

There is an effective approach to this problem. Students may be able to stick with their reading of Equiano's book if they are made to immerse themselves in the eighteenth-century world of the narrative. At the outset, of course, any study of Equiano's work should begin with an examination and appreciation of its literary elements and merits. Instructors should cover the spiritual autobiographical form that Equiano uses in inventing the slave narrative genre for which he has justly been given credit. A study of the narrative needs to include a thorough look at the various devices and methods Equiano adapted to his own purposes. Some of these devices, which lend depth and interest to the narrative, include the special uses Equiano makes of several prose traditions, especially those related to the picaresque hero, the verisimilitude style of writing, and the popular eighteenth-century view of primitivism.

Students will be intrigued to discover how Equiano portrays himself as a more justified picaro figure than the usual wayward character found in traditional picaresque writing, and they will most certainly be impressed by how Equiano employs Defoe-like matter-of-fact descriptive writing to impart a sense of credibility to the remarkable sights he witnesses during his life at sea. Also, the manner in which Equiano paints his African homeland in primitivistic hues heightens the contrast between his idyllic childhood existence and his agonizing life experience after being kidnapped and sold into slavery.[3]

In adding to the literary and autobiographical discussions of *The Interesting Narrative,* instructors can provide class assignments that deal with historical, religious, social, and economic issues and events. Visiting the eighteenth century can be an illuminating experience for many students when they begin to realize that many of today's ideas and beliefs are similar to those that were examined and agonized over by men and women of earlier times. This act of exploring the religious, political, and social climate of the eighteenth century can serve to open up the minds of young persons, to place them more fully into Equiano's world, and to enable them to see and understand how the founding blocks of present-day cultural ideals were shaped. Instructors can, for instance, explore and interrogate eighteenth-century ideals that not only deliver benefits for us now but also yield misguided notions that contribute to some of the unfortunate ills still prevailing among and within modern societies. On the one hand, there are the noble pursuits of liberty and equality that had their origins in the Age of Enlightenment, but on the other, there are the troublesome messianic impulses that have characterized many religious and political institutions for centuries.

Depending then on the interests of students, instructors can introduce the various study topics related to the complex struggles and events that occurred during Equiano's time in history. Students may be persuaded to conduct forays into the many eighteenth-century areas of thought dealing with economic practices, religious beliefs, political philosophies, slave institutions, and social and humanitarian ideals and efforts. Focusing on many of these subjects will help students to understand the particulars of Equiano's life story and to connect his experiences to the larger world in which he lived.

Instructors can assign their students in-depth study projects that examine the popular primitivism movement or the widespread support for both physical and spiritual freedoms; again, these eighteenth-century concepts and practices can be traced to present-day views and actions. After demonstrating how Equiano uses the Edenic ideal to reveal the extent to which Europeans are contaminating Africa, students can be expected to show how primitivism's idea of a once-natural and simpler world still exerts its power upon the modern minds of men and women. Another class assignment can involve a study of how Equiano's intense desire to be free from slavery and moral bondage reveals a universal human desire that continues to manifest itself in today's societies.

Probing into the eighteenth-century world can also allow student readers to explore and discern the depths of the human conditions that surrounded Equiano as he journeyed from his African homeland into the Western world of slavery and finally to a new life that he shaped for himself within white society. Students will want and need to learn how slavery and much of the rationale supporting its cruel existence were tied to the economic wealth of the European nations and their colonies in the Americas. Discussions of the role Africans themselves played in the capture and enslavement of fellow Africans might surprise young scholars, who will also be shocked to learn how many Christian followers twisted scriptural passages to justify slavery's existence. There are plenty of references to those practices to be found in Equiano's work, and students can be brought to consider how Equiano deals with the realities of African slavery and the devious pronouncements of hypocritical religious leaders. Equiano views African enslavement in an entirely different light than that of Western slavery; and in his study of Western religious beliefs, he wisely separates his high regard for Christian principles from the false teachings and actions of many of the members in the Christian churches.

The eighteenth-century world and how Equiano survives in it certainly attract the interests of those reading his classic autobiography. But there are at least two other topics that also absorb the attention of many readers. The first one relates to an understanding of the complex character of himself that Equiano creates in the narrative as he describes his perilous passage across and within the societies of the Western world. The second subject has to do with the fairly recent controversy questioning Equiano's place of birth.

William L. Andrews, Henry Louis Gates Jr., and the writer of this essay, among others, have discussed Equiano's presentation of himself in *The Interesting Narrative.*[4] In all autobiographical writing, the author commits an act of self-invention when she or he sets out to depict her or his character in the life story. Throughout his narrative, Equiano describes the worthy qualities that characterize the various types of self-made roles he assumes in his journey from slavery to freedom and beyond. Much has been made of his freedom-loving spirit combined with an entrepreneurial ethic and spiritual quest that give stature to Equiano's character through his autobiography. But upon closer scrutiny of this figure, readers can detect that the idealized narrative persona Equiano creates is marred by the contradictory behaviors and confusing ideas that are undeniably an important part of Equiano's everyday life. It is clear that in presenting his vision of himself in the narrative work, Equiano cannot avoid relating to his readers the ambiguous actions and thoughts in which he indulges at times.

Although Equiano writes vehemently in his narrative against slavery and the slave trade, he tells us that he purchased slaves in Jamaica for the plantation project he and his friend Dr. Irving were preparing to establish in Central America. And Equiano also relates that there were periods of time during his service at sea and on land when he worked as an overseer of slaves. He qualifies his unlikely actions in dealing with the slaves when he remarks that he always treated them kindly. Equiano writes that after he decided to quit Dr. Irving's plantation, "my poor countrymen, the slaves, when they heard of my leaving them, were very sorry, as I had always treated them with care and affection, and did every thing I could to comfort the poor creatures, and render their condition easy" (227). And at another point in the narrative Equiano softens his own image, compared to that of his overseer's image, when he describes how he was directly responsible for saving the lives of a group of slaves during a ferocious storm at sea. The captain ordered the enslaved blacks placed in the ship's hold and its hatches nailed down; this situation would certainly have doomed the slaves to a watery grave if the ship foundered. But Equiano stubbornly opposed the captain and luckily prevailed despite his cruel orders. Later, when the giant waves dashed the ship to pieces, the slaves were among the men rescued from the wrecked vessel.

The reader can find other examples of Equiano's contradictory ideas and actions about the subject of slavery. There is Equiano's mild treatment of slavery as it exists and is practiced in Africa. Moreover, what are readers to make of Equiano's apparent acceptance of slavery through a good part of his narrative? He even advises white slave masters on how they can increase their plantation profit by tempering the harsh treatment of their slaves. In this instance, however, student readers can easily see through Equiano's motive of wanting to ameliorate the plight of the enslaved men and women toiling on the sun-baked fields of the West Indian islands.

The *Narrative* contains additional instances of Equiano's puzzling acts and thoughts that students can find challenging as they discuss them in the classroom and conduct their research projects. One such example has to do with why Equiano early on abandons his notion of fleeing slavery and opts instead for earning the required sum to purchase legally himself out of bondage. Do his deep loyalties to the captains and other masters prevent Equiano from attempting a physical escape? And why does he develop such close relationships with his white masters? Are these bonds between master and slave solely the result of the roles the older men play as father figures in Equiano's young life? Lively classroom debates about Equiano's behavior and motivation usually prove fascinating to young people;

also, most students react positively to Equiano's acts, deeming them necessary survival techniques commonly used by many other slaves.

Other inquiries suitable for classroom discussion can be made into the nature of the long and tortured spiritual quest Equiano seriously conducts into the tenets of a number of religious faiths, mostly those held by various Christian churches. How important a role does his initial exposure to the Bible play, not only in his later spiritual struggles but also in his early determination to learn to read and write the white person's language? Is there an essential relationship between Equiano's learning about the liberating words in Scripture and his ever-rising desire for freedom that takes hold of him? Another question readers of the autobiography will want to consider is Equiano's early baptism into the Anglican faith. How important is that event for the young slave being led to St. Margaret's Church in London by the kind Guerin sisters?

As mentioned previously, there are many students who do not find Equiano's account of his religious journey to be of great interest. They are put off by the numerous biblical references and spiritual exhortations Equiano inserts into his narrative. It is no secret that young persons do not like to be preached to, especially in a manner that too easily attributes life events and experiences to omnipresent providential design. Perhaps, however, this problem might be solved if students are encouraged to immerse themselves in Equiano's eighteenth-century religious world of competing faiths and strongly held beliefs based on diverse interpretations of the Christian Bible. Delving into that world must include a study and understanding of one of the most popular religious literary genres of the time. Students should find it intriguing to see how Equiano takes the standard three-part pattern of the spiritual autobiographical form and adapts it to the slave narrative genre. Young minds will certainly appreciate how Equiano specifically describes his spiritual story of sin, conversion, and rebirth and parallels it with the account of his physical bondage, escape, and freedom.

In the popular conversion narratives of Equiano's time, the story line commences with an account of a sinful wretch enslaved by the devil's temptations who is suddenly struck by God's Word. This divine event sends the sinner on an agonizing conversion journey that culminates in his escape from evil into a new life of moral goodness. Equiano not only travels the same spiritual path but also journeys on a parallel road that takes him from bodily enslavement by white masters to a long, hard-fought struggle to escape bondage by purchasing his manumission. Once free, he is a reborn man who is now able to a greater extent to strengthen his character and develop his spiritual life.

Staying on the religious subject, students and their instructor might want to consider exploring a number of other matters that relate to Equiano's spiritual life. They can examine Equiano's reasons for ultimately choosing the Methodist faith. And they can try to figure out how Equiano is able to reconcile his commitment to Christian values with the African religious beliefs and practices he details at length in the opening part of his autobiography. A related discussion can focus on Equiano's favorable comparisons of the African religion to that of the Hebrews.

Then there is the passage in which Equiano graphically depicts the culminating experience of his spiritual conversion. Equiano's moving description of the mystical vision that appeared before him while aboard a ship in the Spanish port of Cadiz serves to impress upon readers the sincerity and authenticity of Equiano's long and often agonizing journey into the Christian faith. Here Equiano writes that after weathering a fit of despair, he began to ponder his spiritual condition when

> in this deep consternation the Lord was pleased to break in upon my soul with his bright beams of heavenly light; and in an instant as it were, removing the veil, and letting light into a dark place, I saw clearly, with the eye of faith the crucified Saviour bleeding on the cross on mount Calvary: the Scriptures, became an unsealed book, I saw myself a condemned criminal under the law, which came with its full force to my conscience, and when "the commandment came sin revived, and I died." I saw the Lord Jesus Christ in his humiliation, loaded and bearing my reproach, sin, and shame. I then clearly perceived that by the deeds of the law no flesh living could be justified. I was then convinced that by the first Adam sin came, and by the second Adam (the Lord Jesus Christ) all that are saved must be made alive. It was given me at that time to know what it was to be born again, John iii. 5. . . . The word of God was sweet to my taste, yea sweeter than honey and the honeycomb. Christ was revealed to my soul as the chiefest among ten thousand. These heavenly moments were really as life to the dead, and what John calls an earnest of the Spirit. . . . Now every leading providential circumstance that happened to me, from the day I was taken from my parents to that hour, was then in my view, as if it had but just then occurred. I

> was sensible of the invisible hand of God, which guided and protected me when in truth I knew it not: still the Lord pursued me although I slighted and disregarded it; this mercy melted me down. (205–6)

The image of the crucified Christ not only forcefully impacted Equiano's spiritual life but also strengthened his character and directs his way to a more purposeful end.

After conducting a thorough study and appreciation of *The Interesting Narrative,* teachers can then bring up for class examination and discussion the controversial topics of Equiano's birthplace and the veracity of his African story. Here students have the opportunity to observe and even to participate in cutting-edge research.[5] Academic research activity can reveal to students the important role ongoing scholarship plays in the quest for the truths and insights that contribute to the appreciation and understanding of the great works of literature.

Several writers have offered their opinions on the controversy surrounding Equiano's place of birth, but two major scholars—Vincent Carretta and Paul E. Lovejoy—have written extensively on the spirited debate. In his "Olaudah Equiano or Gustavus Vassa? New Light on an Eighteenth-Century Question of Identity," Vincent Carretta initiates the subject of Equiano's doubtful African origins when he discovered inconsistencies between what Equiano wrote in his narrative about Africa being his country of birth and two British documents that recorded Equiano's birth as having taken place in the American colony of South Carolina. Needless to say, if it is true that Equiano was born in America and not in Africa as he claims in his *Narrative,* then Carretta's findings cast serious doubt on the authenticity of what Equiano states in his autobiography. Of course, this problem brings up a host of concerns focusing on how Equiano's work should be evaluated and treated. Students here possess the opportunity to delve into much-written-about questions dealing with autobiographical veracity, creative license, and the higher truth that art claims.

Of course not all scholars agree with Carretta's tentative conclusions regarding Equiano's place of origin. In his "Autobiography and Memory: Gustavus Vassa, alias Olaudah Equiano, the African" and "Issues of Motivation—Vassa/Equiano and Carretta's Critique of the Evidence," to point out two examples, Paul E. Lovejoy stands as one of the writers who attempts to counter the claim that Equiano falsified his birthplace and much of the African part of his narrative.

One of Lovejoy's major ideas centers on the representation of an African mindset he sees in the narrative. Equiano demonstrates in the beginning parts of his autobiography an indigenous way of thinking about his life in Africa that Lovejoy believes helps to uphold the claim that the account of Equiano's African origins is authentic ("Issues" 1–5).

In familiarizing themselves with the differing ideas put forth by Carretta and Lovejoy, instructors would do well to assign these key articles from the issues of the journal *Slavery and Abolition* where these noted scholars present their findings and argue with one another. These essays can serve as jumping-off points for students who may want to consider the difficult task of figuring out how autobiographical truth and creative freedom can be applied to evaluating Equiano's *The Interesting Narrative.* Moreover, students examining the points of argument Carretta and Lovejoy bring to bear against each other's positions can be encouraged to deliver their own opinions on the soundness or lack thereof of the views held by each scholar.

However, amid all the tenuous evidence and opposing views, there is a strong probability that the questions surrounding Equiano's country of birth and the veracity of the early parts of the narrative will never be solved satisfactorily. Thus, students who choose to work on papers dealing with Equiano's African account (ironically, the initial part of the narrative that may have enticed them to read the autobiography) will be faced with the same dilemmas that have confronted other readers who have already learned of the controversy associated with Equiano's life story. Is *The Interesting Narrative* a clever hoax that should be relegated to the infamous list of fraudulent works of literary history? Or is Equiano, in his autobiography, to be seen as wisely using creative privilege and practical strategy to deliver a higher truth for the purpose of helping to destroy the unjust and brutal system of slavery? Or, ultimately, is the great narrative that Equiano wrote to be considered a remarkably factual and truthful telling of a kidnapped African's life in the eighteenth-century Atlantic World?

No doubt there is much to learn and explore in *The Interesting Narrative.* Students can first be drawn into the autobiography by reading Equiano's fascinating depiction of his African life and subsequently his trials and perilous experiences in the strange world of the West. The ensuing sections filled with spiritual and polemical matters may not fully appeal to today's young readers, but there are plenty of subjects in Equiano's work that instructors can choose from to arouse interest in the minds of their contemporary students. And not all of the topics open for consideration exist in the past, for even today, Equiano's autobiography continues to affect our thoughts about humanitarian, social, and spiritual issues. Furthermore, his work keeps challenging us to rethink our views about the best creative methods writers may be permitted to use in presenting the higher truths of a world they see mired in dark reality.

Notes

1. All citations from Equiano's work are from my edition of *The Interesting Narrative of Olaudah Equiano.*

2. The scholarly work of Vincent Carretta, Paul E. Lovejoy, and S. E. Ogude, among others, outlines these scholarly debates on Equiano's *Narrative.*

3. For a more comprehensive account of the picaresque hero, the verisimilitude style of writing, and the popular eighteenth-century view of primitivism and how these eighteenth-century literary traditions play an active part in Equiano's *Narrative,* see Angelo Costanzo (*Surprizing*); also, see the introduction to my edition of Equiano's *The Interesting Narrative.* Instructors searching for teaching guides might want to take an online look at my suggestions in the Heath Online Instructor's Guide to Olaudah Equiano's work in Paul Lauter's *The Heath Anthology of American Literature* ("Olaudah Equiano").

4. For a sampling of more thorough accounts of Equiano's construction and presentation of his self in the *Narrative,* see William L. Andrews, Henry Louis Gates Jr., and Angelo Costanzo (*Surprizing*).

5. The previously listed articles by Carretta and Lovejoy serve as excellent sources to introduce students to the contemporary scholarly debates on Equiano's *Narrative.* For a detailed comparison of the competing arguments concerning Equiano's birthplace, see Brycchan Carey's helpful analysis "Where Was Olaudah Equiano Born? (And Why Does It Matter?)" on his website.

Works Cited

Andrews, William L. *To Tell A Free Story: The First Century of Afro-American Autobiography, 1760–1865.* Urbana: U of Illinois P, 1986.

Carey, Brycchan. Home page. "Where Was Olaudah Equiano Born? (And Why Does It Matter?)" 1 Aug. 2009 <http://www.brycchancarey.com/equiano/nativity.htm>.

Carretta, Vincent. "Olaudah Equiano or Gustavus Vassa? New Light on an Eighteenth-Century Question of Identity." *Slavery and Abolition* 20.3 (1999): 96–105.

Costanzo, Angelo. Introduction. *The Interesting Narrative of Olaudah Equiano.* Ed. Angelo Costanzo. Rev. ed. New York: Broadview, 2002. 9–30.

———. "Olaudah Equiano." Heath Online Instructor's Guide. 1 August 2009 <http://college.cengage.com/english/heath/syllabuild/iguide/vassa.html>.

———. *Surprizing Narrative: Olaudah Equiano and the Beginnings of Black Autobiography.* New York: Greenwood, 1987.

Equiano, Olaudah. *The Interesting Narrative of Olaudah Equiano.* Ed. Angelo Costanzo. Rev. ed. New York: Broadview, 2002.

Gates, Henry Louis, Jr. Introduction. *The Classic Slave Narratives.* Ed. Henry Louis Gates Jr. New York: Signet, 1987. 1–14.

Lovejoy, Paul E. "Autobiography and Memory: Gustavus Vassa, alias Olaudah Equiano, the African." *Slavery and Abolition* 27.3 (2006): 317–47.

———. "Issues of Motivation—Vassa/Equiano and Carretta's Critique of the Evidence." *Slavery and Abolition* 28.1 (2007): 1–5.

Ogude, S. E. "Facts into Fiction: Equiano's *Narrative* Reconsidered." *Research in African Literatures* 13.1 (1982): 31–43.

"Profitable Reading": Literacy, Christianity, and Constitutionalism in Olaudah Equiano's *Interesting Narrative*

John Saillant

College students of the early twenty-first century will benefit from examining Olaudah Equiano's *Interesting Narrative* as a coming-of-age and coming-to-influence story of the late eighteenth century. As our students read in Afro-British and African American topics, we can show young men and young women how carefully Equiano read, how skillfully he drew from his readings and travels, and how adeptly he sought, in his maturity, to engage the political authorities of his time. The value of reading and writing was, of course, a prominent theme in early Afro-British and African American coming-of-age stories. It was also prominent in other eighteenth-century coming-of-age stories, such as Benjamin Franklin's *Autobiography.* But today students usually approach Equiano with an anachronistic assumption that he was expressing an African identity, not that he was a reader and a writer who understood influencing social and political power as part of a mature life. Indeed one reasonable way of looking at Equiano's narrative is that the frames at the beginning and end, in which he petitioned, first, Parliament and, second, the Queen, to move against the slave trade and slavery, were primary while the middle matter, in which he recounted his childhood and adulthood, was secondary, albeit more interesting to most of us today.

In this essay, I argue, as an alternative to our familiar conceptions of Equiano, that the leading elements of *The Interesting Narrative* were its petitions, supported both by its insistence on literacy and Christianity and by the constitutionalism of its approach to the abolition of the slave trade and slavery. Today we readily read *The Interesting Narrative* as a spiritual autobiography, an articulation of alterity, or an ex-slave narrative (all staples of Equiano studies), but these readings just as readily obscure the frames of his text and his exercise of a fundamental right in them. The right to petition was in the eighteenth century one of the most cherished rights in the Anglo-American tradition—a right that came to be exercised by black men and black women, free as well as enslaved, colonial as well as English, prerevolutionary as well as postrevolutionary. The right of subjects to petition the Crown was guaranteed in the 1689 Declaration of the Lords Spiritual and Temporal, and Commons, and the right of United States citizens to petition the federal government was guaranteed in 1791 in the United States Constitution. Indeed the language of the opening of *The Interesting Narrative,* addressing it to "The Lords Spiritual and Temporal, and the Commons of the Parliament of Great Britain," probably suggested to his readers that Equiano himself was familiar with the 1689 Declaration, though he could have learned these formal titles from other sources (Equiano 7–8).

To note that *The Interesting Narrative* was an extended petition is to situate it near the pinnacle of Anglo-American rights. Contemporaries of Equiano like Benjamin Franklin, Thomas Jefferson, and Thomas Paine all believed in the right to petition. Franklin endorsed a petition to the United States Congress requesting regulation of the slave trade. Jefferson's famed *Summary View of the Rights of British America* originated as a petition to the imperial powers. And Paine's *Common Sense* criticized George III's refusal to receive colonial petitions. A generous pedagogy of *The Interesting Narrative* should include both its African scenes and its goal of engaging and expanding a tradition of rights. And instruction in Afro-Briton and African American history and literature should include other examples of petitions written by black people of the eighteenth century and nineteenth century.

Today students' initial encounter with literacy as a theme in abolitionism is probably in Frederick Douglass's 1845 *Narrative.* In this text, readers learn that the young Douglass's first lesson in literacy, absorbed in late childhood, was that it would render him dissatisfied as a slave and lead him to yearn for freedom. His master in Baltimore, Mr. Auld, declared that Douglass's reading "'would forever unfit him to be a slave. He would at once become unmanageable, and of no value to his master. As to himself, it could do him no good, but a great deal of harm. It would make him discontented and unhappy'" (58). The lesson proved true as the ability to read sparked a sense of interiority and individuality in the young

Douglass that forever unsuited him for slavery. (I shall argue later in this essay that this sense should not be described as one of identity.) Once he learned to read, he discovered that American abolitionists were aiming for the end of the domestic slave trade and of slavery, and his *Narrative of the Life of Frederick Douglass, an American Slave,* published a little more than a decade after these years in which he started reading, was itself addressed to those in the United States who he thought had the capacity to end slavery—men with the power of suffrage who would force the issue of slavery into national politics. Two lessons for students in Douglass's *Narrative* are that he experienced a sense of maturity only as he learned to read and that literacy led him in his maturity to abolitionism.

If we move closer in time from Douglass to Equiano we see literacy as a theme again in David Walker's 1829–30 *Appeal.* In this text, Walker instructed literate black people to read aloud the *Appeal* to those who could not, and he presented education as not only a pragmatic way out of slavery but also as a daring path out of mental slavery. Black people should both gain marketable skills and free their minds from a sense of inferiority suited, as Walker saw it, only to slaves. Like Douglass after him, Walker understood the interiority and individuality gained from reading as the first step in liberation. The *Appeal* was corrosively critical of those who seemed to allow themselves to be enslaved mentally, and one of the signs of that enslavement was, he noted, a belief that education consisted of knowing the alphabet but not reading deeply in classical and modern texts and "the arts and sciences" (Walker 21).

One quarter of his *Appeal* was thus devoted to "our wretchedness in consequence of ignorance" (21). Walker himself was known to his contemporaries as an avid reader who, it seemed, talked like a book. William Lloyd Garrison wrote, for instance, "We are assured, by those who intimately knew him, that his *Appeal* was an exact transcript of his daily conversations; that, within the last four years, he was hurtfully indefatigable in his studies" (qtd. in Hinks 117). What has usually been unappreciated about the *Appeal* is its assumption that literacy is intertextuality, its reliance on the documentary history, widely available in Boston in the 1820s, of the American Revolution. The similarities of the *Appeal* to orally delivered sermons have been emphasized, but it also shares its form with early American newspapers and political pamphlets and its content with the writings of the Revolution.[1] Walker's notion of those who were empowered to end slavery were black people, who were to be freed by texts like his from mental slavery and who were indeed the audience of the *Appeal*—the *Coloured Citizens of the World*. The mental liberation gained through literacy would open, Walker believed, the door to the abolition of slavery.

A black woman, Betsy Swan, living in Massachusetts in 1822, though probably illiterate herself, emphasized to her sons the importance of reading. She spoke to a white minister, who saw her words disseminated in print. Swan used the occasion of the death of a son in his early teens to remind his older brothers of the value of literacy. She was probably thinking about their independence (the dying boy seems to have been abused by a man to whom he was apprenticed) but she also addressed their inner states insofar as reading would guide them on the path of Heaven (*Remarkable* 6, 8, 10, 16). Lemuel Haynes, writing in 1801 for the twenty-fifth anniversary of the Declaration of Independence, noted that an enforced "ignorance" was used to marginalize African Americans. He addressed the authorities charged with carrying on the legacy of the Revolution, pointing out to them that "true republicanism" (82) entailed education and the acceptance of blacks into a free American society. John Marrant's 1790 *Journal* was both a lesson to black people in a way to read or understand the Bible in accord with their interests and a justification to English religious authorities of his itinerancy among black refugees in Nova Scotia and probably of his plans for them that included removal to Sierra Leone.[2] Marrant himself died before the exodus of about twelve hundred black Nova Scotians to Freetown, but his own congregation went—man, woman, and child—and his writings probably sought to instill a biblically based consciousness in his black audience to encourage the migration even as they appealed to white Britons to support it. In 1773 John Quamine, a freedman who was seeking work as a Christian missionary—he instead soon became a mariner—reported to a sympathetic white minister, Ezra Stiles, that he was trying to teach himself to read to qualify himself for a mission post (Stiles 1:366). Quamine could have had sincere religious motivation, but he was also attempting, unsuccessfully, to find a way of supporting himself and his family through literacy instead of hard labor. He lost his life at sea as a mariner. This brief overview covering the years 1773–1845 reveals a model of literacy in which a sense of self and self-determination follow from a black person's reading. Equiano was one of the creators of this model, which is still, I shall suggest, relevant in the early twenty-first century.

Equiano provided some details about his education in literacy, but they seem improbable if we understand them as autobiographical. They record the history of someone with sparse tutoring in his adulthood who nonetheless became a careful reader, skilled writer, and well-to-do and well-connected author. A commonsense opinion is rather that he learned to read and write in his childhood but revised his own history in the service of his text. The true story of his education seems now forever lost. It is more useful to think about his presentation of literacy as it contributed to the abolitionist agenda of the narrative. This point broaches two major interpretive issues concerning Equiano. How much of the narrative do we believe? And is its primary goal to reveal a life story or to attack the slave trade and slavery? Vincent Carretta has shown that Equiano probably fabricated an African birth (8).[3] The reason was almost certainly that Equiano believed that an attack on the slave trade was best made by someone who had survived it and had become literate and Christian. Many elements of *The Interesting Narrative* invite skepticism insofar as they make more sense as abolitionism than as autobiography. His education in literacy is salient among these episodes.

Equiano's first memory of English was, he wrote, that it was fuller in words than were African languages. African languages were "easily learned," in part because they were not "so copious as those of the Europeans, particularly the English" (51). This was a commonplace about so-called primitive languages. But there was more than a civilizationist dismissal of seeming primitivism in Equiano's view of language and literacy. *The Interesting Narrative,* as an abolitionist and religious work, expressed Equiano's sense that the slave trade and slavery were most effectively challenged from a literate, Christian (and, we shall see, constitutional) perspective. After this initial encounter *The Interesting Narrative* gradually revealed the abolitionist power of literacy. The power of books at first seemed magical—the books actually spoke, it seemed, to whites—but soon it was shown to be ordinary yet essential to maturation (68). He himself desired to read and write, and he simultaneously received his first book and his first instruction in Christianity. "I had long wished to be able to read and write," he wrote, and he received as a gift a book he called "a guide to the Indians" (78). Reading led him to "the knowledge of God" (79). He noticed that reading Scripture aided others, and he "endeavored to improve" himself in reading and mathematics on ship (86, 91). Soon he was not only reading but comprehending the Bible as well as counting books among his possessions. People began writing to him, aiding him to gain his freedom, and he even began using poetry, including *Paradise Lost,* to corroborate his experience. In the short run he used his literary skills to gain a better position as a slave.

Equiano came to learn that others, even slaveholders, were *writing* in favor of the amelioration of slavery. "I have the honour," he stated,

> of knowing a most worthy and humane gentleman, who is a native of Barbadoes, and has estates there. This gentleman has written a treatise on the usage of his own slaves. He allows them two hours for refreshment at mid day; and many other indulgences and comforts; . . . so that by these attentions he saves the lives of his negroes, and keeps them healthy, and as happy as the condition of slavery can admit. (105–6)

From the perspective of the early twenty-first century, we readily condemn amelioration as a method of preserving slavery by making it seem more palatable. Equiano's understanding was, however, more nuanced than ours. He knew that in the late eighteenth century virtually all abolitionists would be converts who had once assumed the legitimacy of the slave trade and slavery, not, as in our own time, people who have never accepted slave trading and slaveholding. Indeed he was himself exactly such a convert, both in what are probably the fictional and the actual parts of his autobiography. For he wrote (probably as fiction) that he was born in Igboland in a slave-trading and slaveholding society and (probably as accurate personal history) that in the Americas he worked as a slave driver on ships transporting slaves in the coastal trade. Equiano understood that freedom was being born out of slavery in a process that could be quickened by literacy. Both ameliorationists and abolitionists were *writing* against slavery, and slaves themselves could reach out to liberty with literacy. Freedom and literacy were so closely joined in Equiano's mind that the original verse he added in *The Interesting Narrative* was self-referentially abolitionist:

> With thoughts like these my anxious boding mind
> Recall'd those pleasing scenes I left behind;
> Scenes where fair Liberty, in bright array
> Makes darkness bright, and e'en illumines day;
> Where no complexion, wealth, or station can
> Protect the wretch who makes a slave of man. (122)

The document that in *The Interesting Narrative* succeeds Equiano's various comments on literacy and his poem was his certificate of manumission, which he transcribed in full (137). Like his poetry, it was self-referentially abolitionist in that it was at once an expression of his liberation and a commentary on freedom.

The certificate was essential to his freedom. By "these presents," in other words, by these characters, words, and sentences, Equiano became free. It made sense that his manumission certificate used the language of British constitutionalism since his final attack on the slave trade would be constitutional. "Gustavus Vassa," gained, by the document, "all right, title, dominion, sovereignty, and property" in himself (137). It could hardly have been more obvious that freedom, literacy, and the constitution worked together. Having established the value of literacy and having quoted his certificate of manumission, Equiano was ready to show how reading and writing gave him a sense of self and made him an abolitionist. He read the Bible and he composed petitions—after his liberation, his story in large part comprised these two efforts that merged his freedom, literacy, religion, and constitutional rights.

Reading had more than pragmatic value for Equiano, for it gave him his sense of interiority and individuality as well as an opportunity to influence public affairs in his time. Carretta's recent biography deploys the term "identity," but this does not fit Equiano's narrative because the term inevitably implies to some modern readers disparate identities for African and for Anglo-American people (2–3, 8–9). Equiano saw some distinctions in identity as important—abolitionist versus slave trader or slaveholder, Christian convert versus nonbeliever, and literate versus nonliterate. Any difference between African and Anglo-American that he noticed was only a relatively trivial reflection of those other more fundamental forms of identity. "Interiority" and "individuality" better describe, for us today, the phenomenon Equiano evoked than does "identity." It was primarily his reading, in Scripture, that helped him become aware of his interiority and individuality. This awareness *was* a sense of himself as an African, yet *not* as an "other" but rather as a quintessentially biblical character, sharing traits of Joseph and Paul. The Bible seems to have confirmed the inmost structures of his existence and given him to himself after slavery had threatened to steal him away or alienate him from himself. The insight he garnered from reading is that he was not outside Judaeo-Christian history, confirmed by his assertion that Africans were likely descendants of the Israelites (44). Once he was placed in this history, he could appeal as an abolitionist to constitutionalism. This process was his "profitable reading" (183).

Equiano's worldly liberation occurred in Chapter 7; then Chapter 8 recounted God's providential dealings with him in difficulties caused by both racism and nature. Here he was, he understood in retrospect, one, like Joseph in Genesis and Exodus, a favored son whom God guided through tribulations to a status as savior of his own people. After his conversion in Chapter 9, Chapters 10 and 11 and the first part of Chapter 12 concentrated on his reading of the Bible. He reported that he found "heart-felt relief in reading my bible at home" (178). When all were "against" him, he wrote, "the only comfort I then experienced was in reading the Holy Scriptures" (181). Verses from the Bible appeared in his mind in his times of "agony," and he "had a great desire to read the Bible" (182). He began attending a Calvinist church after one of its congregants assured him that its focus was on Scripture, and there he received another book, "'The Conversion of an Indian'" (183–85). He continued reading the Bible, until a verse from the Bible, upon appearing in his mind's eye, even deterred him from suicide (187–89). Finally, while "reading and meditating on the fourth chapter of the Acts, twelfth verse," he was converted:

> The Lord was pleased to break in upon my soul with his bright beams of heavenly light; and in an instant, as it were, removing the veil, and letting light into a dark place, Isa. xxv. 7. I saw clearly, with the eye of faith, the crucified Saviour bleeding on the cross on Mount Calvary: the Scriptures became an unsealed book, I saw myself as a condemned criminal under the law, which came with its full force to my conscience, and when "the commandment came sin revived, and I died." I saw the Lord Jesus Christ in his humiliation, loaded and bearing my reproach, sin, and shame. I then clearly perceived, that by the deed of the law no flesh living could be justified. I was then convinced, that by the first Adam sin came, and by the second Adam (the Lord Jesus Christ) all that are saved must be made alive. It was given me at that time to know what it was to be born again, John iii. 5. I saw the eighth chapter to the Romans, and the doctrines of God's decrees verified, agreeable to his eternal, everlasting and unchangeable purposes. The word of God was sweet to my taste, yea sweeter than honey and the honey comb. (189–90)

After that moment he read his Bible with even more care and concern: "Now the Bible was my only companion and comfort; I prized it much, with many thanks to God that I could read it for myself, and was not left to be tossed about or led by man's devices and notions" (191). Reading was so important that he turned to the reader of his own text, addressing him or her with these words that were at once abolitionist and Christian: "The worth of a soul cannot be told—May the Lord give the reader an understanding in this" (191).

With this understanding achieved, Equiano offered some of his own verse to the reader—another literate act (194–97). Events in his life still elicited comparisons to the Bible. A scattering of references to Paul near the end of the narrative suggest that Equiano saw himself as a convert (like Paul) who had once persecuted God's people (Igboland was, he recounted, a slave-trading and slaveholding area and he worked in the New World slave trade) and who was after conversion a believer who added his own inspiration and interpretation to the Christian tradition (he was an author and abolitionist) (211, 221). Indeed *The Interesting Narrative* could well be described as an eighteenth-century revision of the Joseph and Paul figures into abolitionists.[4] Like Joseph and Paul, Equiano changed his name as he passed through God's plan for him: Gustavus Vassa became Olaudah Equiano just as Joseph became Zaphnathpaaneah (ts-ph-n-th p-'-n-ch) and Saul became Paul. At this point the logic of the narrative was revealed and fulfilled: it led to a petition asking for regulation of the British slave trade.

A review of the structure of the narrative is now in order so that his petitions can be understood and appreciated. *The Interesting Narrative* commenced, in the first two editions, with an address to Parliament, echoing, perhaps, the 1689 Declaration of Rights and envisioning that the narrative would lead the two houses to support "Abolition" (7–8). It then followed Equiano through a journey of African birth and capture, Anglo-American enslavement and acculturation, literacy and freedom, and, finally, conversion and political action through his petitions. It has hardly received modern attention, but the climax of the narrative in Equiano's mind as well as in its placement in the text was almost certainly his petition of 1788. "I had the honour of presenting the Queen with a petition on behalf of my African brethren," he wrote, "which was received most graciously by her Majesty":

> Madam, Your Majesty's well known benevolence and humanity embolden me to approach your royal presence, trusting that the obscurity of my

situation will not prevent your Majesty from attending to the sufferings for which I plead.

Yet I do not solicit your royal pity for my own distress: my sufferings, although numerous, are in a measure forgotten. I supplicate your Majesty's compassion for millions of my African countrymen, who groan under the lash of tyranny in the West Indies.

The oppression and cruelty exercised to the unhappy negroes there, have at length reached the British legislature, and they are now deliberating on its redress; even several persons of property in slaves in the West Indies have petitioned parliament against its continuance, sensible that it is as impolitic as it is unjust and what is inhuman must ever be unwise.

Your majesty's reign has hitherto been distinguished by private acts of benevolence and bounty; surely the more extended the misery is, the greater the claim it has to your Majesty's compassion, and the greater must be your Majesty's pleasure in administering to its relief.

I presume, therefore, gracious Queen, to implore your interposition with your royal consort, in favour of the wretched Africans; that, by your Majesty's benevolent influence, a period may now be put to their misery; and that they may be raised from the condition of brutes, to which they are at present degraded, to the rights and situation of men, and be admitted to partake of the blessings of your Majesty's happy government; so shall your Majesty enjoy the heart-felt pleasure of procuring happiness to millions, and be rewarded in the grateful prayers of themselves, and of their posterity.

And may the all-bountiful Creator shower on your Majesty, and the Royal Family, every blessing that this world can afford, and every fulness of joy which divine revelation has promised us in the next.

I am your Majesty's most dutiful and devoted servant to command,

Gustavus Vassa,

The Oppressed Ethiopian. (231–32)

The Interesting Narrative was an exercise in proving that its author possessed the moral and social authority as a convert and a British subject to present this petition. Much of what today we find most interesting in *The Interesting Narrative* was almost certainly intended to be a prelude to this political act. The last few pages of the narrative noted that the most likely path to the end of the slave trade and of slavery was their interdiction by Parliament operating as a "free" government led by those who supported "the cause of humanity, liberty, and good policy[,] and brought to the ear of the legislature designs worthy of royal patronage and adoption" (232–33). Indeed, if we pass over the motivations of abolitionists and politicians (which are sometimes easy to criticize) and focus on the constitutional process, this was precisely the process by which first the slave trade and then slavery itself were interdicted in the British Empire. Equiano, however, did not live long enough to see either outlawed.

Equiano was in the thick of abolitionism in the late eighteenth century. It is clear that he understood that any abolition of the slave trade or of slavery (or even amelioration of them) would originate in Parliament, not in colonial legislatures or among slave traders or slaveholders themselves. The fundamental matter was constitutional. How could Parliament interdict the slave trade or slavery when it had left virtually all legislation concerning them to colonial assemblies? In the British political tradition, the only answer to this question was that the supremacy and sovereignty of Parliament, with corroboration from the Crown, would allow British law to restrain or forbid slave trading and slaveholding (Brown 212–13, 241, 250). The distinctive contribution of Equiano and other contemporaneous black authors was to articulate the view of this constitutional process from the perspective of those who had weighty opinions about it but whose status as subjects who might participate in it was contested, to say the least.

Ottobah Cugoano was one of the "Sons of Africa" who, with Equiano, in 1787 cosigned a memorial to English abolitionist Granville Sharp (Carretta 256). Cugoano also promoted a constitutional solution. In 1787 he made a vivid appeal to the Crown and Parliament to end the slave trade and slavery. Appropriately, he began his call to the British state by casting himself as a citizen concerned with the strength of the empire. "Slavery and oppression . . . in its colonies," he argued, have caused "a world of debt at home" as well as a "long continued heavy annual load of taxes" (Cugoano 68). The slave trade, he continued, was "plunder" (69) and "war" (70), for which "money is wanted [and] the national debt becomes increased" (70). Such debt, he wrote, served only "to the further advantage of those who often occasioned it by their villainy" (70). The solution was, for Cugoano, the implementation of "one of the finest constitutions in the world" (70), the "British constitution" (70), which in his view was undermined by its protection of slave traders and slaveholders. Laws governing slave trading and slaveholding (thus allowing them) were "unconstitutional" (70), according to Cugoano, because men empowered by the commerce of slavery had hijacked the British government, depriving British subjects of their liberty and burdening the nation with debt. "[I]f these unconstitutional laws, reaching from Great-Britain to her colonies, be long continued in and supported, to the carrying on that horrible and wicked traffic of slavery" (70), he wrote, then he expected "the ruin and destruction" (70) of "the whole of the British constitution" (70). "There is very much wanted," he continued, "for regulating the natural rights of mankind, and very much wrong in the present forms of government, as well as much abuse of that which is right" (71). The constitution could be purified, implemented, and restored, Cugoano argued, if the "British legislature" would proclaim "the unlawfulness of slavery and commerce of the human species" and enforce "a total abolition of slavery" and a "universal emancipation of slaves" (98). Moreover, Cugoano envisioned a strong role for the British state in the postemancipation period. He advocated a state-designed program for Christianizing and educating freedmen and freedwomen, a British "fleet of some ships of war" (100) to stifle the slave trade on the African coast, the prosecution of the worst of the European slave traders ("crocodile settlers," he called them, "that should be called to a particular account for their murders and inhuman barbarities" [100]), and the replacement of some imperial functionaries, facilitators of the slave trade, with "faithful and good men" (100). It was the responsibility of "the noble Britons, and their August Sovereign" (101) to engender and order the postslavery empire, Cugoano asserted. Going back to one of the passages in Walker's *Appeal* that often confuses readers makes sense if we read it with the backdrop of Equiano's and Cugoano's words. Walker wrote, "The English are the best friends the coloured people have upon earth. . . . Though they have oppressed us a little and have colonies now in the West Indies, which oppress us *sorely*. . . . There is no intelligent *black man* who knows anything, but esteems a real Englishman" (43; paragraph break suppressed).

Equiano and Cugoano sought to lay to rest any lingering notions that the slave trade and slavery would be ended by local means as well as to demonstrate that blacks could be subjects in a postslavery society. They perceived both the intransigence of local slave-trading and slaveholding forces and the potential for a free multiracial society in a way that none of their white contemporaries could. It made sense that these black authors would turn to the well established and well respected right to petition government for redress of grievances. To situate fully

Equiano and Cugoano in the history of political thought, it is necessary to focus on how they were extending claims about the social contract and the supremacy and sovereignty of Parliament that derived from the Glorious Revolution into an argument for the inclusion of blacks in the British social contract and for the abolitionist power of Parliament. These arguments could hardly have appeared in the childhood scenes of *The Interesting Narrative.*

Anthologized versions of *The Interesting Narrative,* widely used today in teaching African American studies, typically present the childhood scenes Equiano wrote, with his address to Parliament that constituted the preface of the first two editions and thus immediately preceded the African chapters. They present neither his final petition nor other petitions written by black men and black women, although these documents were common before 1865. *The Norton Anthology of African American Literature,* for instance, should be supplemented. It offers only a slim view of Equiano's political life and brings forward the constitutional process only with the opening address to Parliament without the complement at the end of the work. It might even suggest to students that an African heritage was more potent than was a constitutional process in abolishing the slave trade and slavery—yet nothing could depart more from the meaning of *The Interesting Narrative,* which in fact noted that slaves were traded and held in Igboland and in adjacent areas. *The Norton Anthology of African American Literature* also anachronistically situates Equiano's African scenes after nineteenth-century and twentieth-century dialect transcriptions of oral folk tales, inevitably implying for some readers that Africa, childhood, and folklore are all of a piece (McKay and Gates 139–49, 187–213). Lisa Cohen Minnick has discussed a dichotomy between "limitation" and "liberation" that was suggested by late-nineteenth-century and early-twentieth-century representations of African American dialect. Today the pendulum has swung away from a view articulated by Richard Wright (representation of dialect is limiting) to one favored by Zora Neale Hurston (dialect can express liberation).[5] Yet the problem with *The Norton Anthology of African American Literature* is that by selecting Equiano's childhood scenes and juxtaposing them to folk tales transcribed in dialect it obliterates the liberation half of the dichotomy that occurs later in *The Interesting Narrative.* Equiano's maturity and political savvy disappear.

Students would benefit from a more complete exposition of *The Interesting Narrative.* To paint a general picture composed in more than ten years of teaching

The Interesting Narrative: many college students are fascinated by its childhood scenes because they confirm our common assumptions that diversity in personal identity is a good thing and that the slave trade and slavery are immoral. These assumptions are, thankfully, healthy and reasonable for our students, just as (to mention an author named in the previous paragraph) is the virtually universal student delight in Hurston's fiction.[6] But, because of the selection, students miss other aspects of *The Interesting Narrative* and of the process of the abolition of the slave trade and of slavery.

One omission is the insistence in *The Interesting Narrative* that a mature life is a literate and politically engaged life. The cost of this today is probably a less rewarding adulthood as well as a loss to the public sphere of the talents of some individuals. Another omission is its articulations of rights as based in both membership in society and constitutional traditions. The cost of this is certainly a misunderstanding of the sources of the rights we ourselves enjoy as well as an inability to comprehend the development of the tradition of rights. Today our notions of individual rights slice like a knife through any arguments in favor of trade or property in slaves, but Equiano knew that there were arguments on both sides of the Atlantic—including in Igboland for the slave trade and for slavery—and he knew he could not easily slice through them but would have to engage them politically and religiously. Equiano stood at the margin of the Anglo-American tradition of rights, addressing the questions of whether black men and black women could be members of society and whether individuals had a constitutional right to be free of enslavement.

A petition written by a black person was a provocative document worth studying today. College students should be provoked to think about their own rights, those of others, and the ways rights are strengthened or weakened in modern societies since the closing of the world's major slave-trading routes and the ending of the world's major slaveholding systems. Trade and property in slaves still persist, unfortunately, in some pockets of the globe, and new means of denying individuals rights crop up like weeds. Ironically in our own time a political immaturity that Equiano would probably have understood all too well has been fostered by the end of the major systems of trade and property in slaves as well as by an ideology of individual rights.[7] Rarely do we in the free world know about the remnants of slavery that persist, and only slightly less rarely do we understand that our natural rights are rooted in constitutional documents and would scarcely exist without them.

Notes

1. For discussion of orality, see Hinks, *To Awaken My Afflicted Brethren,* 173–75.

2. Marrant's use of the Bible to communicate a "back-to-Africa" message to his black auditors is discussed in John Saillant, "'Wipe Away All Tears from Their Eyes': John Marrant's Theology in the Black Atlantic, 1785–1808."

3. Elements of my essay here extend Carretta's skepticism about the truth of some parts of *The Interesting Narrative,* while attempting, like Carretta, to identify the purpose of the text, which I understand to be primarily abolitionist and religious.

4. Other critics of the slave trade and slavery made the same use of Joseph and Paul. See, for example, Thomas Clarkson, *An Essay on the Slavery and Commerce of the Human Species, Particularly the African, Translated from a Latin Dissertation, which Was Honored with the First Prize, in the University of Cambridge, for the Year 1785, with Additions,* 3rd ed., 37, 149–50.

5. See pp. 25–27 for a discussion of Wright and Hurston and pp. 149–52 for the dichotomy between limitation and liberation.

6. This observation about students and Hurston is based on more than a decade's worth of teaching introductory survey courses in African American studies, either as a history of African American literature or as an introduction to Africana studies.

7. An argument that after Equiano's generation abolitionists focused so intently on enslavement that they lost concern with other forms of subjugation appears in John Saillant, "Traveling in Old and New Worlds with John Jea, the African Preacher, 1773–1816."

Works Cited

Brown, Christopher Leslie. *Moral Capital: Foundations of British Abolitionism.* Chapel Hill: U of North Carolina P, 2006.

Carretta, Vincent. *Equiano, the African: Biography of a Self-Made Man.* Athens: U of Georgia P, 2005.

Clarkson, Thomas. *An Essay on the Slavery and Commerce of the Human Species, Particularly the African, Translated from a Latin Dissertation, which Was Honored with the First Prize, in the University of Cambridge, for the Year 1785, with Additions.* 3rd ed. Philadelphia: Joseph Crukshank, 1787.

Cugoano, Quobna Ottobah. *Thoughts and Sentiments on the Evil and Wicked Traffic of the Slavery and Commerce of the Human Species, Humbly Submitted to the Inhabitants of Great-Britain, by Ottobah Cugoano, a Native of Africa. Thoughts and Sentiments on the Evil of Slavery and Other Writings.* Ed. Vincent Carretta. New York: Penguin, 1999. 1–111.

Douglass, Frederick. *Narrative of the Life of Frederick Douglass, an American Slave, Written by Himself.* Ed. Benjamin Quarles. Cambridge, MA: Belknap–Harvard UP, 1960.

Equiano, Olaudah. The Interesting Narrative *and Other Writings.* Ed. Vincent Carretta. Rev. ed. New York: Penguin, 2003.

Haynes, Lemuel. "The Nature and Importance of True Republicanism: With a Few Suggestions Favorable to Independence. A Discourse, Delivered at Rutland, (Vermont,) The Fourth of July, 1801.—It Being the 25th Anniversary of American Independence." *Black Preacher to White America: The Collected Writings of Lemuel Haynes, 1774–1833.* Ed. Richard Newman. Brooklyn, NY: Carlson, 1990. 77–88.

Hinks, Peter P. *To Awaken My Afflicted Brethren: David Walker and the Problem of Antebellum Slave Resistance.* University Park: Pennsylvania State UP, 1997.

Marrant, John. "A Journal of the Rev. John Marrant, from August the 18th, 1785, to the 16th of March, 1790." *"Face Zion Forward": First Writers of the Black Atlantic, 1785–1798.* Ed. Joanna Brooks and John Saillant. Boston: Northeastern UP, 2002. 93–160.

McKay, Nellie Y., and Henry Louis Gates Jr., eds. *The Norton Anthology of African American Literature.* 2nd ed. New York: Norton, 2003.

Minnick, Lisa Cohen. *Dialect and Dichotomy: Literary Representations of African American Speech.* Tuscaloosa: U of Alabama P, 2004.

Remarkable Visionary Dreams, of a Mulatto Boy, in Northfield, Mass. By the Name of Frederic W. Swan, Aged Thirteen Years, Together with a Sketch of His Life, Sickness, Conversion, and Triumphant Death. Chesterfield, NH: Joseph Meriam, 1822.

Saillant, John. *Black Puritan, Black Republican: The Life and Thought of Lemuel Haynes, 1753–1833.* New York: Oxford UP, 2003.

———. "Traveling in Old and New Worlds with John Jea, the African Preacher, 1773–1816." *Journal of American Studies* 33.3 (1999): 473–90.

———. "'Wipe Away All Tears from Their Eyes': John Marrant's Theology in the Black Atlantic, 1785–1808." *Journal of Millennial Studies* 1.2 (1999): 9–15.

Stiles, Ezra. *The Literary Diaries of Ezra Stiles, D.D., LL.D., President of Yale College.* Ed. Franklin Dexter Bowditch. 2 vols. New York: Scribner's, 1901.

Walker, David. "Article II." *David Walker's Appeal to the Coloured Citizens of the World.* Ed. Peter P. Hinks. University Park: Pennsylvania State UP, 2000. 21–36.

Equiano and One Canon of Early African American Literature

Phillip M. Richards

The critically informed university teacher of Olaudah Equiano's *Narrative* faces or will face what is the deepest and most threatening impasse today in the field of literary studies. On the one hand, the black studies movement of the 1960s generated a set of influential critical paradigms that stressed the adversarial relationship of the Anglo-American black literary canon to a broader Western cultural continuity. This new canon adumbrated in works by critics such as Houston A. Baker Jr. and Henry Louis Gates Jr. sought to sustain a disciplinary tradition of black texts largely through linguistic continuities such as the "Blues Vernacular" or "Signify(ing)."

Another tradition of historically oriented literary critics, found in the work of such scholars as James Walvin, Paul Edwards, James Levernier, Mukhtar Ali Isani, David Grimsted, Christine Levecq, Charles Scruggs, Joanna Brooks, John C. Shields, Vincent Carretta, Philip Gould, Michael Drexler, and Ed White, among others, have pursued rigorous biographical, textual, intellectual, and comparative studies firmly grounding the origins of Anglo-African writers such as Equiano and Phillis Wheatley in Enlightenment and post-Enlightenment traditions. More and more, it appears that Equiano and Wheatley surface at a crucial moment in which British and continental writers' texts begin to engage in a critique of the Enlightenment as these authors (and the readers of these texts) become aware of the perspectives of non-Western cultures, the emergence of middlewomen and middlemen of color who act as go-betweens in an increasingly fluid Atlantic World, and when the development of subjectivity becomes a crucial issue within the Western literary tradition.

In his *Beyond the Culture Wars: How Teaching the Conflicts Can Revitalize American Education,* Gerald Graff has incisively argued to instruct our students in the ideological conflicts of contemporary literary critics. And in the case of Equiano, such instruction guides us to engage our students in the most profound questions raised by the black studies and multicultural movements. Do we discern in our growing awareness of black writers a separate literary continuity and consciousness, or are these writers and their texts simply one more involution in a broader, more expansive historical narrative of Western political discourse? If the second point holds true, then we owe it to our students to ground the canon of early black texts as rigorously as we can in the literary and cultural histories of the Enlightenment, Romantic, and post-Romantic periods. We must do so with a certain *sang froid* in regard to how this inquiry will validate or undermine the recently constructed oppositional, adversarial discourses of black studies and multiculturalism. For these "black" texts may simply be one more twisting and turning discourse in a larger tradition of non-Western appropriation of an essentially Western consciousness. The best starting place for this inquiry may be an examination of the Enlightenment process of "reading" and the conception of a "public sphere."

Literature courses inevitably create canons, which in turn have their own aesthetics. At the heart of contemporary, American college courses in literature—no matter how self-consciously avant-garde—remain now-traditional assumptions about the text, its relation to the reader, and reading habits themselves. Since the eighteenth century, critics in the Anglo-American tradition have casually assumed an aesthetic defining the interaction between the artistic object, the reader, and the fancy or imagination, and later on as a Coleridgean secondary imagination or transcendentalist higher reason. Even deconstructive and semiotic critics ground their initial linguistic manipulations with understandings of the text produced by what M. H. Abrams has called "disinterested" "contemplation" and reflection (Abrams 135). This aesthetic emerges from the capacity of the literary object to impinge upon and engage the subjectivity of each teacher and student. Romantic notions of creative imagination—in Coleridge's terms, the secondary imagination—often describe the engaged subjectivity's creation of a "secondary" world of art: a process of creation, comprehension, and re-creation that extends an individual literary text into a tradition.

From this perspective, the artistic observer reads the text as an inclusive entity, or, in romantic terms, an organic sphere of personae, conventions, idioms, imagery, symbols, and metaphors that constitute a distinctive world for the contemplation of the viewer. The artist who created paintings, fiction, and poetry had chosen and pursued a distinctive vocation in and of itself, apart from whatever professional status she or he might have as a preacher, political theorist, or philosopher. Like God, she or he produced a world, albeit an aesthetic, organic reality. Alternatively, the artist created a system of symbols through which the exterior universe might be seen, ordered, and interpreted. Within this symbolist world, the artist became the charismatic source of the meaning or related meanings of the universe. In both cases, the artist produced a reality and supra-nature that often approached the status of a secularized subjective system of belief.

The broad uniformity of this practice is an important issue to stress to beginning students of the African American literary tradition. From the start of African American literary criticism's entrance into the twentieth-century academy, black critics such as Sterling Brown, Arthur P. Davis, Houston A. Baker Jr., and Henry Louis Gates Jr. have shared a comprehensive understanding and evaluative criteria governed by these schema as they have been refined in the early twentieth century's linguistic turn. The New Criticism posited the existence of the literary work as an autonomous, interactive world. These formalists submitted this work to the norms of complexity of form, paradox, irony, richness of diction, symbolic depth, range of implied meanings, and the contemplative viewer's subjective sense of the literary text as an organic whole. These standards guided the early criticism of figures such as Brown, Davis, and Larry Neal.

Such codes have had much to do with the establishment of literary tastes in African American literature in the second half of the twentieth century. African American literature and its tradition of critical commentary originated in the late eighteenth century within a Neo-Romantic and Romantic discourse with clear links to twentieth-century formalism. In an important series of articles drawing explicitly on New Critical methodology (a critical method favoring verse forms), Arthur P. Davis persuasively established the importance of black writers such as Phillis Wheatley ("Personal Elements"), Countee Cullen ("The Alien-and-Exile Theme"), Langston Hughes ("Jesse B. Semple: Negro American"), and Richard Wright ("*Black Boy* by Richard Wright"). Davis coedited one of the discipline's founding anthologies, *Cavalcade,* and wrote *From the Dark Tower: Afro-American Writers, 1900–1960,* the central literary history of black American literature's integrationist era. In this body of work, Davis sought to establish the aesthetic worth of black American writing by appealing to New Critical standards of organic or symbolist form: complexity, paradox, irony, richness of diction, symbolic depth, range of implied meanings, and the text's status as an autonomously created, secondary world.

It is important that students see the continuities between the earlier and most recent practice of African American studies. Later critics such as Baker, Gates, Robert B. Stepto, Karla Holloway, and Deborah McDowell read the text's naively perceived message for underlying linguistic and semiotic structures or subversive counter-meanings grounded in the text's grammatical elements. These critics tended, however, to make so-called structuralist or deconstructive practice into the basis of an aesthetic of "blackness," often identifying semiotic and grammatical patterns with themes or interpreting the play of competing semiotic strands in the text as an essentially "black" rhetorical pattern such as the "Blues Vernacular" or "Signify(ing)," particularly in the years since the mid-twenties when black critics such as Brown, Davis, Baker, and Gates entered a highly visible formal discourse in the profession (Richards).

Whatever their claims to the contrary, it turned out that these avant-garde semiotic and deconstructive critics practiced a formalism too. In their readings of texts, thematic meanings often emerged directly from semiotic, grammatical, or inverted codes that functioned essentially as forms. And these semiotic readings, such as Baker's account of male sexuality in Ralph Ellison's *Invisible Man* or Gates's use of deconstruction as a rhetoric for Jean Toomer's psychology, simply imported the well-worn New Critical aesthetic standards of structural complexity, richness of expression, paradox, and ambiguity surreptitiously into the choice of canonical texts. Works characterized by *prima facie* simplicity such as the poetry of Langston Hughes, the blues verse of Sterling Brown, or the early fiction of James Baldwin did not by virtue of a traditional "straightforwardness" meet the aesthetic standards implicit in this new canonizing process.

Much of this calls into question the distinctiveness of recent attempts to articulate a back semiotics linked ultimately to a black consciousness. In the end, theorists interpreted the text's linguistic or rhetorical structures in order to dramatize a message, the text's mode of being, its symbolic vision, and an African American (male or female) sensibility. All of these methods translated claims about linguistic or grammatical structures into claims about meaning, sensibility, or subjectivity. A typical case in this procedure appears in Baker's reading of Olaudah Equiano's *Narrative,* the poetry of Phillis Wheatley, and other texts. A semantic field of "blackness" translates the semiotic term "black" into an explicitly aesthetic experience (Baker, *The Journey Back*).

According to Baker, the related sets of words and concepts for eighteenth-century blacks did, in order, stand in systematic opposition to a white American ordering of "reality." A neighboring lexical item of *Africa* for many blacks during the eighteenth century, for example, was home. Moreover, at a collocational level of language—on a plane, that is, where words come together to form meaningful constructs—phrases such as "intelligent black man" and "beautiful black woman" were semantic anomalies for many of the most talented white minds of the century. One might argue, therefore, that black Americans preserved their own concepts of experience despite the pressures of acculturation. One might additionally argue that blacks were able, as a result, "to introduce into the total *Sinnfeld* new dimensions of experience" (Baker 21).

In a wholly typical way, Baker translated black linguistic structures into structures of meaning, a "semantic" field and finally into an aesthetic evaluation. Aesthetic evaluations about beauty and intelligence are only applied to specific racial objects. Baker remains suspiciously silent about whether blacks also connect beauty and intelligence with whites, unless they have a certain "black consciousness." The reality of white attraction to blacks, apparent in the high miscegenation rates between white males and black women in the South, is obviously more complicated than Thomas Jefferson's claim. The sexual tastes and personal judgment of an avowed racist such as Jefferson seem to bear this out. Jefferson was clearly attracted to the black Sally Hemings, and he clearly thought his black acquaintance Benjamin Banneker to be an intelligent man. Baker's black aesthetic is grounded in a stipulation about white reading, a stipulation he will follow by the way in which black people and realities are understood by black people. Baker ignores, furthermore, that well established literary conventions of the "noble savage" and black heroes such as Oroonoko and black princess in the West Indies all turn on the conception of African human beauty.

Gates's seminal study *The Signifying Monkey* follows a similar strategy translating the arbitrary relationships between sign and signifier to "signifying" or "paradoxical" rhetoric, an ironic aesthetic posture not only of text to text but of writer to reader. Thus the author manufactures "signifying" or "ironic" relationships between arbitrarily constructed signs but translates those ironies into an aesthetic with its own ethos. This ethos is an aesthetic of wit based on the paradoxes, ambiguities, and indirect insult of rhetorical contests common to oral cultures, in particular the verbal jousting of lower-class black men. Gates's critical method significantly never dwells on the breakdowns of textual meanings created by deconstructive signifying forms of meaning. To emphasize the *aporia* Paul de Man found in his deconstructive readings of New Critical literary critiques (de Man 28) forces Gates to confront the nihilism implicit in his practice. This specter could only represent the dark side of the lower-class black culture of signifying that Gates romanticizes.

Gates, like Baker, sets forth a theory which stipulates assumptions of race. For the author of *Signifying*, blacks construct a system of communication and perception grounded in the ironic, parody of signifying. Black children learn—in a particular kind of socialization—how to "signify" upon others and to understand the ironic remarks of other black people. Gates avoids speculation about the social dysfunctions and breakdowns of communication that such a discourse would create in the black community. A wholly ironic form of communication would not only obscure understanding between black people but provide an important explanation for the highly unstable social and cultural world in which most blacks still live. The persistence of signifying as a feature of lower-class black society may well explain its instability, its lack of consensus, and its incoherence of moral, political, and social value. Significantly, Gates does not explore the moral and existential implications of this view.

Gates and Baker deploy semiotic and deconstructive critical methods to romanticize rather than demystify a traditional post-Enlightenment primitivism. Assuming a black critical subjectivity, these writers celebrate black literature with a simplified set of semiotic literary strategies. These strategies, for instance, celebrate Phillis Wheatley as the elegist for a lost African culture and as a prophet of a future black women's community. Or she is celebrated as an avatar of black consciousness grounded in African identity. These strategies demand, for their acceptance, a black audience requiring a therapeutic or symbolic payoff for their reading of works by black authors. Sympathetic white readers who adopted this protocol of reading thus encountered the communication between black texts and readers as observers who overhead the workings of an authentic African culture and thereby entered a world of "blackness."

Black critics have persistently canonized "literary" texts that invite the aesthetic transaction on which "black readings" are based. And this aesthetic, like that of "Signifying" or the "Blues Vernacular," emerges most clearly in the cultural rituals or performances of lower-class black life. Aiming at this so-called "authentic" black ethos, black literary critics have thus tended to find the "literariness" of black literature in wholly traditional Western literary tropes of invention, allusiveness, copiousness, punning, and paradox. As they worked to create the field of black literary studies, Gates and Baker made this ironic literariness a criterion for canonical African American writing. As a result, the canon has narrowed its inclusion of the slave narratives to the few texts, which fit the mold of playfulness, parody, fictive elaboration, and satire implicit in the aesthetic mold of signifying.

An important question in which to engage African American Studies students are the actual implications of the canonical motifs that the major shapers of disciplinary paradigms have advocated. Not only does this inquiry mean asking about the broad social and cultural consequences of an imputed "Blues Vernacular" or "Signify(ing)" discourse in African American culture, but it also means beginning to distinguish between canonical strategies that are more or less persuasive or plausible given a broad knowledge of the tradition.

Not all of these African American critics oversimplify the texts they study. One commentator, Robert B. Stepto, drew on the rhetoric, tropes, and themes of this black literariness in showing how slave memoirs absorb and reinterpret the rhetoric of their white patrons' authenticating documents. Although he never abandoned the structuralist dictum of a self-generating text, Stepto's interpretations of works such as Douglass's 1845 *Narrative* dramatized the creation of a black autobiographical voice. As he continued his historical narrative, Stepto went on to show the persistence of these and other interpretative tropes in late-nineteenth- and early-twentieth-century works by writers such as Booker T. Washington, James Weldon Johnson, and Richard Wright. In this interpretative strategy, *soi-disant* textual and literary data implicitly dramatize psychological styles. Like its other black semiotic descendents, Stepto's text *From Behind the Veil* would demonstrate how "empirical" features of a literary discourse eventually project an aesthetic ethos of autonomy and self-mastery in the black literary tradition. Similar to Gates and Baker, Stepto shows how black writers, ones supposedly trapped in white religious, political, and social conventions, acquired religious freedom. Unlike Gates and Baker, however, Stepto's narrative created a compelling historical interpretation of a black literary response to the pressures of white patronage and interpretation.

Stepto's narrative of the black writer's (or black writing's) acquisition of expressive freedom suggestively and subtly translated eighteenth-century notions of sensibility and romantic originality to African American literary works. Critics of black literature after him have largely imitated the trope of the black writer's autonomous expression articulated through ironic manipulation of convention. John C. Shields similarly placed Wheatley's work into the black tradition by pointing to her use of a subversive pastoral ("Phillis"). And postcolonial critics have elevated Equiano in their canons through their stress on his subversion and rereading of the spiritual autobiography.

The work of these critics is deeply suggestive about the relationship between so-called black and white Western traditions. These alleged adversary postures do not differ from the oppositional, political, social, and aesthetic gestures of Enlightenment art. The deconstruction of "white" writing by "black interpreters" does nothing more than repeat well-established genres of anti-pastoral, epyllion, mock-epic, as well as the satiric ode and lyric. No one can recognize these "mock" or "subversive forms" without reference to the author's evocation of the parodied genres. These oppositional strategies, however, cannot be differentiated from those appropriated by Thomas Paine in his *Common Sense,* Rousseau in his "Social Contract," and Montesquieu in his *Persian Letters.* These strategies that satirically or critically depict the political, cultural, and social institutions of a nation-state set forth doctrines of popular sovereignty and universal human dignity, as well as transcultural tastes, sensibilities, and reason. In doing so, these texts rewrite the travel narrative, epistolary novel, political treatise, biblical exegesis, and the emerging genre of ethnographic report. Notwithstanding, the strictures placed upon black intelligence by Jefferson, Kant, and Hegel, newly liberalized classificatory schemes of human nature, doctrines of transcendental reason, and a historical dialectic pushed other blacks such as David Walker, Frederick Douglass, and eventually W. E. B. Du Bois to an antiracist stance.[1]

Like much late eighteenth-century Anglo-European literature in general, African American expression often employed such manipulations of lyric, satire, elegy, memoir, and travel narrative for aesthetic purposes. This subversion, as Harold Bloom has shown, resulted more from a general Western response to the weight of a now burdensome literary tradition than a delusory liberation from Western tradition (*Anxiety*). No one, not even a black writer, can get outside of the history of Western culture. The black expression of such a possibility is in itself only the repetition of a post-Enlightenment, Romantic trope.

All of this commentary requires a reworking of our assumptions about the literary knowledge that our students must bring—or that conscientious professors must quickly adduce—when we study a late-eighteenth-century Anglo-African or black American text. Equiano's text was accessible for consumption in both the eighteenth-century British, Protestant, bourgeois, antislavery drawing room and the culturally anxious arena of the contemporary black studies classroom. As a narrative of a powerful imaginative sensibility, Equiano's memoir moves coherently from the subject's imputed royalty in Africa (significant biographical evidence uncovered by Vincent Carretta suggests that Equiano was born in South Carolina [*Equiano*]), to upper-class life in America, favored seamanship in the Atlantic, Christian conversion, life as a missionary, and finally the role of colonial administrator. He becomes a black Englishman whose African royal background prepares him for these relatively high positions. His conversion represents a psychological adjustment to his role as dependent on white patrons and the independent roles of entrepreneur, freelance explorer, and activist writer. In many ways, the text of Equiano represents a traditional narrative of the progress of civilization from pastoral to high commercial society. Indeed, Equiano defines his virtue by his capacity to resist the corruption of the luxurious eighteenth-century British consumer society of which he is a part.

These insights, which emerge quickly from the establishment of the necessary contexts for reading Equiano, allow us to challenge our students with new questions and, hopefully, new insights about the African-Atlantic tradition itself. On the other hand, the literary discourse of Equiano's strategies foreshadows the tactics with which future writers, ones gifted with the leisure for literary reflection, will exploit an audience for not only political sympathy but also for the perquisites of their aesthetic satisfactions. In these genteel, sentimental, "therapeutic" narratives, the slave narrator's advocacy of black "freedom" merges often with the white reader's sense of release from social restraint and her or his entrance into a world of self-invention. What makes this vicarious identification possible, along with various sentimentalist strategies, is the creation of a slave persona who is socialized as "white" and Western from the beginning of her or his narrative. The text directs the genteel white reader's literary sympathies towards a character that not only shares her or his superior ethnic status, but also displays a childlike capacity for endless, and endlessly, forgiven expression, self-invention, mimicry, trickery, and manipulation. Through this rhetorical tactic of attractive, vicarious childlike freedom, Equiano appeals not only to a moral revulsion against the white slave traders, but also manipulates the reader into a narcissistic attraction to Equiano himself. This manipulation of the reader's sympathy in effect celebrates the reader's power and privilege as a white Briton. And thus, Equiano is allowed to function as a moral lecturer while deferring to the system of privilege and to those who benefit directly from slavery.

Most important, this context requires us to explore the limitations of the interpretative insight of Equiano and other key early Anglo-African writers themselves. Equiano as an "implied author" also reinterprets the obvious psychological experience of capture by slave traders, again manipulating it by established symbols in eighteenth-century literary culture. The narrative's persona strikingly underplays the interior horrors of the slave trade: the presumptive ease with which an African takes on the monotheism of Protestant Christianity, the protagonist's lack of reflection upon his loss of autonomy under a master, and the absence of direct, displaced, or sublimated aggression directed toward the chattel owner. To a large extent, Equiano's conception of the book as commodity for the self-consoling gratification of an antislavery white audience shaped a literary strategy relying heavily on the well-known plot of the virtuous noble black savage who is removed from his African homeland, cultivated among materialistic whites, Christianized, and prepared for a fruitful life in the West.

From the narrative's beginning, Equiano pursued this strategy when he engages what Hutcheson or Shaftesbury would call the reader's "moral sense" by introducing himself as the chosen son of a distinguished chief of a divinely designated African nation. Indeed, Equiano tells his story from the perspective of the narrator formed by his experiences in the West: he has acquainted himself with the Protestant-Puritan concepts of eighteenth-century life. As Equiano, enchained with his fellow slaves, approaches the Atlantic coast, the indigenous blacks become more and more barbarous. Finally, in an ironic Swiftian judgment on the slave traders, the sailors aboard the slave ship appear in their white skins to be the savages, while the purest of the blacks—the narrator from the continent's interior—appears to be, in his blackness, the purest example of white civilization. Similarly, Equiano can place the African pastoral modes of life and that of commercialized luxurious societies on the circular scales of progress and decline. On the other hand, Equiano may present himself to his white cultivated reader again as a paradoxically whitened product of a civilization that emboldens him to subdue rebellious indigenous Caribbean "savages" by deploying a copy of the white man's Bible as a fetish.

I suspect that the consequences of such a contextual reading will be alarming to all but a few contemporary students of African American literature. Equiano, therefore, invites the eighteenth-century white reader to locate herself or himself as a black in an easily and comfortably shaped consumer culture, one grounded in a shared sentimental, political, and geographical worldview. It is this shared identification between reader and autobiographical subject that gives Equiano's *Narrative* its sentimental aesthetic power. For the African, the Enlightenment terms of reason, benevolence, human uniformitarianism, and Christian morality become aesthetic values. In the context of Equiano's autobiography, moreover, the public sphere's values of lucidity, polite conversation, genteel bearing, and attentiveness to fashion and philosophical high-mindedness are also deployed in the narrative persona for the pleasure, and significantly, the self-congratulation of the genteel, white, antislavery man of feeling, who is Equiano's ideal reader. Students who wish to reflect upon the elegance and erotic appeal of Equiano's frontispiece might well consider their implicit relationship to (and perhaps participation in) this ethos.

This point cannot be overstressed if the instructor is to challenge her or his class fully with the alterity—the cultural positioning—of the *Narrative* in relationship to the world of the early twenty-first-century class in black studies. Equiano is a congenial black studies text precisely because his aesthetic and rhetorical appeals to his white eighteenth-century audience also provides therapeutic comfort for a dislocated black twentieth-century bourgeoisie. The largely adolescent audience of the black literature college class can seize upon the black ex-slave's text as a sentimentally gratifying picture of African virtue. The benevolent eighteenth-century, middle-class, white Englishman was consoled by the imagery of stable, pastoral African culture, the Westernized African's cosmopolitan outlook, and his acquisition of a superficial mastery of the world. The aspiring black intellectual or student experiences a similar therapeutic boost from the same depiction.

An odd parallel thus exists between Equiano's white contemporaries and his future black twenty-first-century audience. Both are engaged in aesthetic consumption of travel narrative, moral reflection, and the dynamics of a liberal capitalist society. Equiano's ethnic, cultural, and economic experiences, as the Scottish Enlightenment's Lord Kames (Henry Home) might show, provide unifying aesthetic experiences as symbols of national, religious, and cultural solidarity not only in an increasingly fluid, late-eighteenth-century English society, but also in the recently integrated university community of alienated black students and academic intellectuals.

This shrewd packaging significantly diverted its Enlightenment audience—and perhaps the present-day African American intelligentsia—from more serious philosophical and political questions. Equiano comes to a traditional Calvinist conversion at a critical moment in the *Narrative* when he experiences the twin pull of his autonomous existence as an accomplished and responsible seaman and the reality of his subordination to a white master. However, the literary accounts of his adventures after these spiritual crises fail to link what appears to an existential and political crisis to his role as a participant in the British imperial enterprise. These literary strategies stem not only from Equiano's clear reliance on the plot strategies of popular art, but also on the political stance implied by his own search for freedom and independence. Believing in a predestinarian conception of God's redemptive history, Equiano does not question his role in the slave trade or military wars, or when he deludes the "natives" using the Bible as a fetish. Equiano's text speaks directly to the larger theological and philosophical questions raised by the Enlightenment thinkers themselves: what was the nature of a God whose laws were coincident with nature itself? How did the slave's self-consciousness itself come into being?

Given Equiano's immersion in a cis-Atlantic World of trade, why does he not pass judgment on the capitalist marketplace's dehumanization of black life into the raw material which enriches his work's leisure class and bourgeois, antislavery audience? The reduction of black people into slaves should be an unavoidable issue in a society where Equiano's polite class consumes labor intensive goods such as sugar, tobacco, cocoa, and china. One questions also Equiano's final identification with a British nationalism, a stance that coincides with slaveholding in the West Indies, military strength, and the creation of Equiano's African settlement as an imperial colony.

Equiano, as Vincent Carretta has shown compellingly, rises past slavery's limitations though engaging in opportunities provided by liberal capitalism. In the process, he not only becomes a part of a powerful colonial economy but also near his autobiography's end projects England's imperial ambitions as a means for African self-improvement. It is significant that the Equiano cultivated in middle-class, late-eighteenth-century British surroundings shows many of the same orientations of the young Frederick Douglass cultivated in early-nineteenth-century, middle-class, white, American antislavery circles. The forthright transcendence of slavery's limitations by Equiano's autobiographical subject is, like the *persona* of the first Douglass in his *Narrative,* not a subversive, revolutionary presence within slavery but an exemplary black, fit for assimilation into white society. The participation in the capitalist world he shared with ship captains, the Miss Guerins, and his assistants as a missionary and colonial administrator dramatized Equiano as a man drawn across racial boundaries by human sympathies. A similar strategy appears, as Vincent Carretta has argued, in the introduction to his edition of the letters of Ignatius Sancho, where Sancho, despite Jefferson's criticism of his lack of reflection, clearly functions at the center of an interracial community, where he is a man of good feeling. As such a benevolent black, however, he has made his peace with the oppressive, capitalistic system that is fueled by slavery.

Equiano's account of his intellectual development in the *Narrative* seals itself off from those Enlightenment and post-Enlightenment philosophical and political issues that drive David Walker in his *Appeal,* the Frederick Douglass of the 1855 *My Bondage and My Freedom,* as well as the later Douglass in his *Life and Times* to a discourse of revolt. Equiano's assertion of his humanity in the language of white patronage similarly echoes Phillis Wheatley's poetry, Jupiter Hammon's sermons, and the accomodationist rhetoric of Booker T. Washington (rhetoric also directed at northern and white philanthropic support).

Equiano's writing, like that of Wheatley, engages what Abram's would call the "disinterested" reader, one perusing a literary text as an aesthetic commodity in the leisure created by her or his surplus wealth. The sentimental discourse of Equiano's autobiography is the discourse of a polite public sphere that responds to sophisticated elements in these works such as sustained literary allusion, clear signaling of the text's generic constituents and their thematic implications, and carefully crafted (also frequently allusive) persona-speakers. While Wheatley handles Horatian, Ovidian, and Old Testament prophetic voices in her poetry, Equiano utilizes the persona of the captive African nobility transplanted to the Christian New World throughout his narrative, and Douglass casts himself as the cultivated literary orator in his text.

Like Equiano, the Douglass of the 1845 *Narrative* never seriously contemplates or encourages a mass black rebellion against whites. Douglass never really punches Covey in their famous fight. The ex-slave's attempt to follow Garrison's dictum of nonresistance results in an implausibly choreographed fight. Neither Equiano nor Douglass gives a detailed account of engaging with the ideas, books, or fellow activists and intellectuals who would help the writers shape their antislavery ideas. Equiano does not, as David Walker and Nat Turner do nearly forty years later, formulate an apocalyptic attack on slavery by the slaveholders themselves. Indeed the deepest paradox of their situation is that the patronage received by Equiano and Douglass from white friends, masters, and associates clearly provides them with the material and intellectual wherewithal to become authors. Both undergo a period of intellectual gestation that yields significant political activity, lecturing, and writing, and finally an autobiography. However, neither of them can develop the revolutionary ideas of a late-eighteenth-century Anglo-European Age of Revolution into an attack upon the state that maintains slavery.

Nonetheless, the critical aspect of the slave narrative is resistance to tyranny. This theme, though often related to the behavior of black slaves, was embedded in Anglo-American religious and political traditions. Since the time of the reformation, Puritan theologians had affirmed the right of revolt against princes who abused their office. Social contract theory was grounded in the right of revolution of a sovereign people whose rights had been abrogated by the state. Republican thinkers had similar strictures against tyranny. Furthermore, the strict moral and social norms of Puritanism often gave supposedly didactic moral literature such as criminal narratives and captivity stories a seamy side in which the protagonist's movement outside of his or her social norms opened up new possibilities of resistance to strict social norms in the enjoyment of forbidden pleasure or experience. The early British Puritan and Republican thinker's concern with the oppressed citizen's yearning for cathartic resistance, theories of resistance, and the nature of legitimate authority spoke directly to the most radical nineteenth-century black thinkers.

Clearly the difference between Equiano's *Narrative* and the *Appeal* is Walker's willingness to ignite a volatile mixture of republican, Protestant, sentimental, and romantic views. At the core of this willingness is Walker's conception of his narrator and audience as engaged in acquiring a racial self-consciousness: a sense of the place of blacks in America and in the world at large. A variant of self-consciousness has often been observed in the Douglass represented in the 1845 *Narrative.* However, by the 1850s, Douglass, Harriet Jacobs, and Martin R. Delaney write texts that self-consciously situate themselves as exemplary black Americans among a world of sympathetic British antislavery activists, the Irish poor, as well as a complex and broad range of northern and southern whites, including abolitionists and slaveholders. In the *Appeal,* Walker's *Notes*-like survey of different historical and national kinds of slavery, his awareness of the politics of colonization, his attention to the workings of a free black society, his distinctions between levels of learning, and his buried references to Jefferson, the authors of the *Federalist Papers,* and *Common Sense* point to a similar breadth of reference that has allowed him to identify himself first as a black American and second within a well-defined historical moment. One is tempted to see revolutionary visions as originary conceptions of the world, when, like American and African American Revolutionary discourse, these visions are radical realignments of exceptionally broad bodies of inherited cultural, social, and political traditions.

Equiano, nevertheless, was in the process of learning the meanings of liberty, corruption, tyranny, obligation, and contract in the various political contexts of his autobiographical experience. Indeed, one way of criticizing the autobiography on its own terms is that Equiano—though beset with situations in which his desire for autonomy is tested by dependence on a master—fails to bring his conception of a secular authority into a dialogue or debate with his internal, psychological conflict between his personal autonomy and dependence on God. No one observes the social mechanisms of his interaction with his masters more carefully than the slave narrator, but Equiano only gives the most cursory attention to what must have been a complicated arrangement or courtship preceding his marriage to a white Englishwoman.

Equiano similarly represses the development of a black political consciousness that would emerge from accounts of his interaction with politically radical black peers. We do not see him engaged in the reading, thinking, and reflecting from which his early antislavery work emerges. Significantly, his religious conversion does not direct him toward a resistance to slavery but rather to missionary work and later to a post as a colonial administrator. Although Equiano notes fiercely that he experiences none of the rights promised by the British constitution, he does not seek to enforce the social contract. And in that sense the autobiography is less rewarding than, say, Benjamin Franklin's *Autobiography,* which is continually engaged in defining an American identity in the contexts of religion, politics, continental military conflicts, family tradition, philosophy, the colony's provincial British culture, and the self-fashioning potential of various traditions of autobiography. Equiano's absorption of the volatile republican, liberal, Protestant ideologies of his day did not lead him to revolt. Ensconced within a world of genteel patronage, capitalist opportunity, and sentimental feeling, revolutionary vision is beyond him. This distinction might be forced upon the angry but acquiescent—scholars and students—with some force. This distinction, moreover, leads us directly back to the late twentieth-century world of black power from which the black studies movement largely emerged.

This reality was most cogently stated by the undervalued literary critic and political activist Julian Mayfield in his essay "You Touch My Black Aesthetic and I'll Touch Yours." In a prescient critique, he argued that although the gestures of black musical art might be imitated, no one would desire to imitate the phenomenon of black revolution for a consumer aesthetic or the entertainment world. And this reality divides the world of intellectually and aesthetically, serious writing from mere consumer or sentimental entertainment. The repression of the black power movement by various established mainstream political forces destroyed the revolutionary nationalist strand of the black power enterprise. What remained was a denatured cultural nationalism that has entered the university departments of English, history, and black studies. Revolutionary nationalists who rejected cultural nationalism for its vulnerability to co-optation had had, it turned out, earlier realized a large piece of the truth. Black studies scholars cannot pursue serious literary or political inquiry apart from intellectual perspectives that locate the central political, cultural, and philosophical issues implicit in a given text. A naïve presentation of Equiano's *Narrative* or Douglass's 1845 *Narrative* must confront the risk of identifying the text's consensual sentimentality: sentimentality aimed at an eighteenth-century consumer culture which is the ancestor of our own black middle-class, consumer orientation.

Rather than ponder the "blackness" of these narratives, one should perhaps begin to ponder the political significance of early black writers participating in the consensual sentimentality of a middle-class leisure culture, one indirectly built on capital linked to the suffering of black bondsmen. Reflection on these contradictions shows that the black art of sentimental consensus inevitably poses troubling political obstacles to aesthetic coherence.

To reflect on the contradictions of Equiano's *Narrative* as an Enlightenment text is ultimately to reflect on the distinctions between a sentimental, consensual literary tradition and a revolutionary one. This distinction significantly obtains in the difference between Douglass's 1845 Garrisonian *Narrative,* a text so fraught with the constraints of immediatist, abolitionist ideology, and the 1855 *My Bondage and My Freedom,* published in Douglass's own press, after he had run his own newspaper, *The North Star*, broken with Garrison, and effectively found his own political and intellectual voice (Andrews, Introduction xv–xxiii). Nearly fifty years later at the turn of the century, Du Bois would implicitly make this distinction when he differentiated between the accomodationist rhetoric of Booker T. Washington and the revolutionary spirit of figures such as Walker and Garnett.[2] (Du Bois was especially acute in distinguishing this literary spirit from the consensual sentimentality of Wheatley.)

> The liberalizing tendencies of the latter half of the eighteenth century brought, along with kindlier relations between black and white, thoughts of ultimate adjustment and assimilation. Such aspiration was especially voiced in the earnest songs of Phyllis [*sic*], in the martyrdom of Attucks, the fighting of Salem and Poor, the intellectual accomplishments of Banneker and Derham and the political demands of the Cuffes. (Du Bois 702)

This distinction between an interracially consensual discourse (whether sentimental or romantic) would predictably emerge again in Amiri Baraka (LeRoi Jones) who moved from an interracially grounded beat verse to the avant-garde poetry of the New York School poets to his later black, revolutionary art. The self-consciously critical engagement with an inevitably present Western culture will continue to be an enduring problem in studying African American art as black intellectuals still must confront the politics of their art simultaneously with its aesthetics.

Notes

1. On Enlightenment conceptions of black intelligence by major thinkers, see extracts from Comte de Buffon, Immanuel Kant, and Thomas Jefferson in *Race and the Enlightenment: A Reader* (ed. Emmanuel Chukwudi Eze).

2. See, in particular, Du Bois's account of the alternating phases of rebellious, conciliatory, and consensual phases in black thought and expression, beginning in the mid-eighteenth century and ending with the oratory and writing of Booker T. Washington. In connection with Washington, Du Bois writes, "Mr. Washington represents in Negro thought the old attitude of adjustment and submission" (703).

Works Cited

Abrams, M. H. "Art as Such: The Sociology of Modern Aesthetics." *Doing Things with Texts: Essays in Criticism and Critical Theory.* Ed. Michael Fischer. New York: Norton, 1989. 135–58.

Andrews, William L. Introduction. *My Bondage and My Freedom,* by Frederick Douglass. Ed. William L. Andrews. Urbana: U of Illinois P, 1987. xi–xxviii.

———. *To Tell a Free Story: The First Century of Afro-American Autobiography, 1760–1865.* Urbana: U of Illinois P, 1988.

Baker, Houston A., Jr. *Blues, Ideology, and Afro-American Literature: A Vernacular Theory.* Chicago: U of Chicago P, 1984.

———. *The Journey Back: Issues in Black Literature and Criticism.* Chicago: U of Chicago P, 1980.

Behn, Aphra. *Oroonoko.* Ed. Joanna Lipking. New York: Norton, 1997.

Bloom, Harold. *The Anxiety of Influence.* New York: Oxford UP, 1977.

Carretta, Vincent. *Equiano, the African: Biography of a Self-Made Man.* Athens: U of Georgia P, 2005.

———. Introduction. *Ignatius Sancho: Letters of the Late Ignatius Sancho, an African.* Ed. Vincent Carretta. New York: Penguin, 1998. ix–xxxii.

Davis, Arthur P. "The Alien-and-Exile Theme in Countee Cullen's Racial Poems." *Phylon* 14 (1953): 390–400.

———. "*Black Boy* by Richard Wright." *Journal of Negro Education* 14.4 (1945): 589–90.

———. *From the Dark Tower: Afro-American Writers, 1900–1960.* Washington, DC: Howard UP, 1974.

———. "Jesse B. Semple: Negro American." *Phylon* 15 (1954): 21–28.

———. "Personal Elements in the Poetry of Phillis Wheatley." *Phylon* 14.2 (1953): 191–98.

de Man, Paul. "Form and Intent in the American New Criticism." *Blindness and Insight: Essays in the Rhetoric of Contemporary Criticism.* 2nd ed. Minneapolis: U of Minnesota P, 1983. 20–35.

Douglass, Frederick. *Life and Times of Frederick Douglass.* New York: Citadel, 1983.

———. *My Bondage and My Freedom.* Ed. William L. Andrews. Urbana: U of Illinois P, 1987.

———. *Narrative of the Life of Frederick Douglass, An American Slave, Written by Himself.* Ed. David W. Blight. 2nd ed. Boston: Bedford/St. Martin's, 2003.

Du Bois, W. E. B. *The Souls of Black Folk. The Norton Anthology of African American Literature.* 2nd ed. Ed. Nellie Y. McKay and Henry Louis Gates Jr. New York: Norton, 2004. 692–766.

Eze, Emmanuel Chukwudi, ed. *Race and the Enlightenment: A Reader.* Cambridge, MA: Blackwell, 1997.

Gates, Henry Louis, Jr. *The Signifying Monkey: A Theory of African-American Literary Criticism.* New York: Oxford UP, 1988.

Graff, Gerald. *Beyond the Culture Wars: How Teaching the Conflicts Can Revitalize American Education.* New York: Norton, 1992.

Mayfield, Julian. "You Touch My Black Aesthetic and I'll Touch Yours." *The Black Aesthetic.* Ed. Addison Gayle Jr. Garden City, NY: Doubleday, 1971. 24–31.

Montesquieu, Baron de. *Persian Letters.* Ed. and trans. C. J. Betts. New York: Penguin, 1993.

Paine, Thomas. *Common Sense.* Ed. Isaac Kramnick. New York: Penguin, 1976.

Richards, Phillip M. *Black Heart: The Moral Life of Recent African-American Letters.* New York: Peter Lang, 2005.

Rousseau, Jean-Jacques. "On the Social Contract." *The Basic Political Writings of Rousseau.* Ed. and trans. Donald A. Cress. Indianapolis: Hackett, 1987. 141–227.

Shields, John C. "Phillis Wheatley's Subversive Pastoral." *Eighteenth-Century Studies* 27.4 (1994): 631–47.

Stepto, Robert B. *From Behind the Veil: A Study of Afro-American Narrative.* 2nd ed. Urbana: U of Illinois P, 1991.

Swift, Jonathan. *Gulliver's Travels.* Ed. Howard Erskine-Hill. Cambridge, UK: Cambridge UP, 1993.

Walker, David. *David Walker's Appeal.* Ed. Sean Wilentz. New York: Farrar, 1995.

Metaphysics of Presence in Olaudah Equiano's *Narrative*

Cedrick May

This essay is an attempt to deal with two related issues that occur frequently when literature teachers find themselves teaching a text containing a significant amount of religious content. *The Interesting Narrative of the Life of Olaudah Equiano, or Gustavus Vassa, the African. Written by Himself* is one of the most important pieces of writing in eighteenth-century transatlantic literature and one that overlaps the boundaries of several popular genres of the period. One genre it represents well is that of the spiritual autobiography. This essay provides teachers, ones who have little or no knowledge and training in Christian history and hermeneutics, with useful background information and methods for teaching this important aspect of Equiano's narrative. Though it is, in fact, a spiritual autobiography, Equiano's life narrative is first and foremost an antislavery argument. However, this argumentation is couched in a religious idiom often unfamiliar to teachers and students of today. Even for students who are familiar with the Bible and contemporary biblical interpretation, figuring out just what Equiano might mean at any given point in his text can still be a challenge, given the very distinct theological predispositions of the mid to late eighteenth century. What I provide here is a discussion for interpreting and understanding Equiano's autobiography so that the teacher of his text will be better able to conduct class discussions and prepare assignments that fully address these important, intersecting aspects of *The Interesting Narrative.*

Religion and Critique in Equiano's *Narrative*

The Interesting Narrative of the Life of Olaudah Equiano presents teachers with many challenges, as it is a text that does many things at once. It is representative of black autobiography, spiritual autobiography, slave narrative, ethnography, travel writing, history, antislavery polemic, and even possibly, ironically, of being a superb work of fiction.[1] It cannot be overemphasized to students that interpretation of this narrative relies on careful, close reading and a sense of history and context to get at any meaningful understanding of how the text operates as a cultural artifact. This essay will offer a reading of a small but significant portion of Equiano's *Narrative,* the "talking book" scene. A focus on this scene will help us understand the narrative as a subtle critique of Western nations that simultaneously practice Christianity and engage in the slave trade under the argument that the two institutions are compatible. Focus on this scene will also serve as a model for how teachers and undergraduate students might tease out the wealth of knowledge any given part of Equiano's *Interesting Narrative* might contain.

In the case of the scene I will focus on here, one of the dimensions that makes this particular part of Equiano's book so interesting is that some form of the "talking book" trope has appeared previously in black autobiographical texts of the eighteenth century, such as James Albert Ukawsaw's *A Narrative of the Most Remarkable Particulars in the Life of James Albert Ukawsaw Gronniosaw,* Quobna Ottobah Cugoano's *Thoughts and Sentiments on the Evil and Wicked Traffic of the Slavery and Commerce of the Human Species,* and John Marrant's *The Lord's Wonderful Dealings with John Marrant, A Black.* All of these works predate Equiano's *Interesting Narrative* in their use of the "talking book" trope. Equiano, however, reworks this trope within the context of his full autobiography to reveal a profound understanding of the Christian hermeneutical tradition, rhetoric, and black subjectivity within Western society. In doing so, Equiano further attempts to argue for a spiritual embodiment of textuality that was missing in his first encounters with the Bible. For Equiano, only an *embodied* text, one that "speaks" to the reader with a "corporeal" authority, will carry the rhetorical power to allow moral suasion, as a tactic, to move effectively his readers to right political action. This assumption about the nature of texts applies as much to the Bible as his own autobiography, and Equiano engages in a skillful act of what Henry Louis Gates Jr. refers to as tropological revision, a form of signifying that draws on both Equiano's African rhetorical background as well as his understanding of Western classical rhetorics and religion.

Equiano's "Talking Book" and *Logos*

Critics have long commented on the "talking book" scene in Equiano's *Interesting Narrative,* but there seems to be a longstanding misunderstanding of just what

Equiano is doing as a writer/reader of texts, including his own autobiography, particularly in its "talking book" scene.[2] The book that "refused" to talk back to him was the Bible, and the inclusion of this brief scene in the narrative underscores an important set of philosophical and theological problems Equiano wished to work through in his autobiography. On the surface, Equiano's autobiography is an attempt to bring coherence to the random events of life, but through a deeper reading into his text and an understanding of its context, it is possible to see that he is also choosing an order of events that will give him a stronger *moral* case and *ethical* argument against the slave trade.[3] As John Bugg has stated in his essay on Equiano's book tour, the narrative was "designed to sell," and, along with his book tour, meant to "convert sympathetic readers into political actors" (Bugg 1426). This political strategy would be no small feat for Equiano because the previous century of British and British-American evangelism sought to make it clear that slavery was consistent with Christianity and biblical scriptures. Plantation owners and other political actors, sympathetic to religion in general, nevertheless, needed convincing that the dissemination of Christian teaching to slaves would not undermine the control they exercised over their property. For them, economics trumped religion in the case of slavery, and it was clear that much of the Bible would put dangerous ideas about equality and freedom into their slaves' minds. The masters of slaves and others who profited from slave economies needed converting through a message and a theology that would assure them of the compatibility and usefulness of human bondage with Christianity and its spread to slaves. We see powerful religious leaders addressing these issues throughout the eighteenth century in texts such as Cotton Mather's *The Negro Christianized* (1706) and Edmund Gibson, the Lord Bishop of London's letters to his ministers and British plantation owners in the Americas (1727). Cotton Mather's theological perspective highlights the importance of Christianizing slaves for the sake of both the souls of the slaves and the masters:

> The greatest *Kindness* that can be done to any Man is to make a *Christian* of him. Your *Negroes* are immediately Raised unto an astonishing Felicity, when you have *Christianized* them. They are become amiable spectacles, & such as the *Angels* of God would gladly repair unto the Windows of Heaven to look upon. Tho' they remain your *Servants,* yet they are become the *Children* of God. Tho' they are to enjoy no *Earthly Goods,* but the small Allowance that your Justice and Bounty shall see proper for them, yet

> they are become *Heirs* of God, and *Joint-Heirs* with the Lord Jesus Christ. Tho' they are your *Vassals,* and must with a profound subjection wait upon you, yet the *Angels* of God now take them under their Guardianship, and vouchsafe to tend upon them. (*The Negro Christianized* 19–20; emphases and capitalization in original)

Mather does, however, approach the practical temporal and legal condition of the Christianized slave, issues that were, of course, of greater importance to masters of slaves:

> What *Law* is it, that Sets the *Baptized Slave* at *Liberty?* Not the *Law of Christianity:* that allows of Slavery; Only it wonderfully Dulcifies, and Mollifies, and Moderates the Circumstances of it. . . . Will the *Civil Law* do it? No: Tell, if you can, any part of *Christendom,* wherein *Slaves* are not frequently to be met withal. (26–27; emphases and capitalization in original)

Similarly, Edmund Gibson, the Lord Bishop of London, observes two decades later in a letter to plantation owners that the duty to bring slaves into the Christian fold is not a spiritual or legal obligation to change their condition as slaves under the law:

> But it is further pleaded, that the Instruction of Heathens in the Christian Faith, is in order to their Baptism; and that not only the *Time* to be allowed for Instructing them, would be an Abatement from the Profits of their Labour, but also that the *Baptizing* them when instructed, would destroy both the Property which the Masters have in them, as Slaves bought with their Money, and the Right of selling them at Pleasure; and that the making them Christians, only makes them less diligent, and more ungovernable. To which it may be very truly reply'd, that Christianity, and the embracing of the Gospel, does not make the least Alteration in Civil Property, or in any of the Duties which belong to Civil Relations; but in all these Respects, it continues Persons just in the same State as it found them. (*Two Letters* 10–11)

In both of the cases mentioned above, among others in their writings, they make clear that neither canon nor civil law prohibits the practice of slavery, and they set out guidelines for sensible lessons that ought to be taught to slaves as they are prepared for baptism. It is also possible to discern from these passages, and even more clearly throughout both of these texts, the anxiety that slave owners had toward the idea of either baptizing or giving lessons about Christianity to their slaves. The stated rationales that it took too much time out of their work schedule or made them unproductive were more likely canards; the more important concern being the issue of either the legal condition or the numerous places in the Bible where slavery is clearly shown to be unjust for those following God's covenant, such as the story of the Exodus in which Moses leads the Hebrews out of Egypt. Or, even more explicitly, some biblical laws require slave-owners not only to recognize the humanity of slaves, but to set them free should the master do bodily injury to them, such as in Exodus 21:26–27.[4] Lessons unmediated by masters, delivered by literate slaves, could lead to disquieting questions. Cotton Mather, therefore, cites specific lessons to be taught *to* slaves by masters, those employed by slave-masters specifically for the purpose, the master's children, "well-disposed and well-instructed *English Servants,*" or a catechized overseer. Nowhere does he suggest that the slaves, themselves, be allowed to lead religious instruction or even read the Bible.[5]

If Equiano's narrative were to counter over a century of proslavery theology and practice, he would need to construct a text that showed a truly Christian life in progress as well as a text that engaged with deep philosophical and theological questions relating to the matter of presence and authority. The Bible and Christianity, in his view, had been usurped for colonial ends. In Equiano's view, his *Interesting Narrative* would be a corrective and powerful argument to supplement efforts at moral suasion, the effort to convince the public and political powers that the slave trade was, indeed, a moral evil that needed to be abolished.

With these points in mind, the approach to reading his *Interesting Narrative* that I propose can help us to understand Equiano's text as a spiritual autobiography that also participates in a long philosophical struggle over the metaphysics of presence, the struggle to understand authority, subjectivity, and writing within a Christian tradition. Equiano understood the word, or rather the written "Word of God," differently than a contemporary, postmodern reader of the scriptures does today.[6] It is, of course, important to understand the ways eighteenth-century readers and writers understood religion, Christianity in particular, in British North America in order to appreciate fully the range of possible understandings of a particular text during that period. Equiano's understanding of text is grounded in Christian hermeneutics, an active belief in an authoritarian presence in the text of the Bible. His approach to thinking about the written text brings to light a philosophical struggle between the classical thinking on the primacy of speech to that of the written text.

Indeed, in the West, speech and oratory have enjoyed a privileged place in philosophy. In simplest terms, the presence of the *speaker* as an authority of his or her utterances, the ability to engage in dialectic and account for his or her speech, underlies this bias. It is a bias that has existed even at times when writing and literacy, in general, were required to be learned. But in ancient times, particularly as Christianity began to grow as a political and cultural influence in the West, a tension between the primacy of speech over text began to occur. Holy Christian texts, though written, were perceived to embody a presence that Platonists would have rejected. So while the general perception of the superiority of speech over the written word endured, Holy Scriptures, nevertheless, gradually acquired a metaphysical value not only equal with that of speech, but even superior to it.

This understanding of holy Christian texts begins during the first century of Christianity and can be initially seen in the received gospels. For instance, the writer of *The Gospel According to Saint John* proclaims, "In the beginning was the Word, and in the Word was God, and the Word was God. The same was in the beginning with God" (John 1:1–2). Here John specifically refers to the *spoken* word of God, an allusion to the first chapter of *Genesis* in which the Hebrew god created the world. But not much later in the chapter, John states, "And the Word was made flesh, and dwelt among us . . . full of grace and truth" (1:14). So, through these two passages, we can see that the writer of *John* appears to be educated within a Greek tradition of scholarship that values the importance of presence over that of a mere written word. This preference may be observed in the way that the spoken word and "flesh" come together to interact with humanity, to engage in discourses that are chronicled in the written text of *John.* Jesus is *logos*—the intelligible order of things, reason, and the truth. However, it is clear that at the time of the writing of *The Gospel According to Saint John,* the writer was speaking of Jesus in the person, not a textual representation of the Messiah. The text was still secondary to speech, but an alternative interpretation of *The Gospel According to Saint John* would be necessary to make the transcendent God and Christ into a more immediate spiritual presence less distant from the doings of humanity.

As the Christian church as an institution began to gain greater significance and power in the ancient world, the idea of a living divine presence in the immediate world became more important. The Word made flesh needed refashioning into textual form. But even in ancient times, Christian authorities struggled with reconciling the *logos* of the spoken word with the written. Indeed, Augustine of Hippo is very interested in the problems of authority, presence, and interpretation in one of his major works, *On Christian Teaching*. Here, Augustine begins his examination of language with the argument that, in addition to human teaching, the spiritual presence and "divine gifts" of God are required for a true understanding of biblical scripture (4–7). In other words, the written "Word of God" cannot simply be a supplement to an original speech act; the received scriptures must *be* as much the truth (*logos*) as "the word made flesh." The importance of spiritual intervention is central to Christian hermeneutics when it comes to understanding the written word; such understanding is a part of God's grace. In other words, unless one encounters the presence of God *through* scriptures it is not possible to have either true knowledge of the mysteries of the scripture or spiritual salvation. The text has not been anthropomorphized, but it is distinctly unique in that a presence, the presence of God, is understood to inhabit it.

There is a closing of the speech/text and presence/absence dualism, and Equiano taps into this trope of Christian hermeneutics as he constructs his own subject position through the telling of his narrative and toward the larger goal of forming an antislavery ethics.[7] It is at this point that we can begin to have a more complete appreciation of Equiano's encounter with the written "Word of God" as he relates the "talking book" scene. It is Equiano's assumption of a metaphysics of presence in speech *and* textuality, not naiveté, that is central to appreciating the full significance of the "talking book" scene within his narrative. The struggle over the metaphysical significance of text, and the assumption of *logos* as part of a text, is important to understanding Equiano's view of biblical interpretation, faith, and antislavery arguments relying on moral suasion in a discursive context where the question of just what a text, particularly a spiritual text, happens to be.

In the classroom, all of the issues presented above play well into discussions about narrative, religion, and identity as well as deepening student's understanding of the social and religious conflicts regarding slavery. On the first point, discussions about the primary importance of *narrative* in its many forms can help students to understand this important section of Equiano's book. Clearly, Equiano, along with many other writers before him, seized upon the "talking book" idea as a framework for understanding the power behind language and various forms of literacy. For Equiano, and Christians even more widely, language was understood to be a physical thing and that oral and written words could be transformative—though quite quickly it becomes apparent that the two cultures, Equiano's culture and that of those who enslaved him, understood oral literacy and written literacy differently. But *how* are they different? And how does Equiano reconcile his first encounter with writing with his later understanding of the first five verses of John 1:1–14? Further, why does he see borrowing the "talking book" idea and incorporating it into his own narrative as so necessary?

Another useful context for understanding Equiano's narrative revolves around the conflicting interpretations of Christianity's compatibility with the institution of slavery. At the university where I teach, undergraduates almost universally tell me that they have read little to nothing of any substance about transatlantic slavery. Aside from unfortunately narrow readings of the important autobiographies, such as the *Narrative of the Life of Frederick Douglass, an American Slave, Written by Himself* and Harriet Jacobs's *Incidents in the Life of a Slave Girl,* students are at a loss to discuss the institution of slavery and its powerful societal influence. Rather, they think of the cruel institution as some vague form of racism. As a corrective, I have my students read a variety of both proslavery literatures by prominent historical figures as well as the antislavery writings in order to give them a better sense of what people at the highest levels of government and religion were thinking. By incorporating these texts into the classroom, I engage them in discussions about the *institutional* nature of the transatlantic slave system and how it imposed certain ideological structures on the ways religion was being practiced and spread and its influence on biblical interpretation. Students have remarked to me how they learn so much more about slavery as a result of seeing what writers on both sides of the issue were saying to one another. In fact, students have mentioned in discussions how perplexed they are at many of the proslavery arguments, the logic being used to advance their cause and such ideas as the mark of Cain and Canaan, which most of them have never heard of before. These discussions can really only happen when these texts and concepts are introduced in relation to Equiano's own narrative and when they highlight a remarkable degree of borrowing, intertextuality, and, importantly, the narrative nature of biblical writing itself.

The "Talking Book" and Tropological Revision

> I have often seen my master and Dick employed in reading; and I had a great curiosity to talk to the books, as I thought they did; and so to learn how all the things had a beginning: for that purpose I have often taken up a book, and have talked to it, and then put my ears to it, when alone, in hopes it would answer me; and I have been very much concerned when I found it remained silent. (Equiano 68)

The "talking book" scene has long captured the imagination of literary critics, and there is much more going on here than the mere comedy of an illiterate person literally speaking to a book and then listening for a voice to make a reply. It is, therefore, important not to gloss over this scene as lighthearted comedy with our students. Most American students encountering writings by an African (particularly an eighteenth-century writer of African descent like Equiano) almost always comment with amazement at the skill and lucidity of the piece, so when they encounter the "talking book" scene Equiano's "illiteracy" is taken for granted as a condition of an African of the historical period to be illiterate. It never occurs to my Western-educated students that West Africans were often very literate, able to read and write in Arabic as well as in other languages brought into the region by trade, religion, and settlement. If, however, we take Equiano's "talking book" scene for granted and assume he genuinely was unfamiliar with the technology of writing and the written word, then I suggest to my students that they consider the scene from the perspective of *cultural* literacy and then connect that aspect of interpretation with their own knowledge of writing and Western philosophical discourses concerning writing. By couching interpretation of the scene in these terms, I can better lead them to understanding it in terms of Equiano's disorientation and social dislocation.[8] Adam Potkay argues that the scene of the "talking book" positions Equiano as an outsider, as someone foreign to eighteenth-century British culture and that the scene functions as a "reflection on the daunting but ultimately not prohibitive chasm that separates the orality of his childhood from the literate culture to which he crossed over" ("Olaudah" 677).

In Potkay's essay, he states that "[i]t is in light of Equiano's ultimately theological curiosity that his 'great curiosity to talk to books' must be read: indeed, the book that Equiano as *yet unwittingly desires to read is not just any book, nor just a synecdoche for Gates's 'Western letters,' but specifically the Bible, a book that claims to express the genesis of all things*" (678; emphases added). Here Potkay makes a compelling argument. Equiano's assumed outsider status and his inability to "hear" the Bible he wished to discourse with highlights, as it did with other black writers before him, his "alienation from Western literary culture, an alienation relieved by adding his own distinctive books to the culture" ("Olaudah" 678). Further, we know it is most likely the Bible he is trying to hear because the tropological revision this scene represents is one in a long chain of references by previous eighteenth-century black-Atlantic writers to talking books, a chain that extends back to sixteenth-century European travel writings as well. Each of these earlier accounts, an apparent tradition that Equiano is referencing, all feature the Bible as the "talking book."

In a similar vein, Henry Louis Gates Jr. has made a strong case that the book's silence in the "talking book" scene symbolizes the ideal that the displaced African's "countenance and discourse stand in Western texts as signs of absence, of the null and void" (156).[9] Indeed, the Western literary and philosophical tradition had long defined Africa and African peoples as sites of absence, and this scene does strongly point to the problem of absence (that is, the absence of an authoritative speaker) in relation to text and reader.

Gates and Potkay make similar arguments concerning their readings of this passage, but in each case it is assumed that the absence and alien status the scene represents are flaws inherent to Equiano and markers of his illiteracy. These readings, though, inherently assume a dualism that Equiano seeks to dismantle as part of his own Christian argument against slavery. It is an equally valid reading, and perhaps a more revealing one, to suggest that, rather than attributing the silence to his ignorance, the text itself is a site of absence—that through a double-voiced presentation Equiano suggests that the particular Bible to which he places to his ear is absent of the divine spirit he wishes to encounter, and that this is the source of his own disappointment. What the reader of Equiano's narrative encounters here is an instance of what Gates refers to as tropological revision, "the manner in which a specific trope is repeated, with differences, between two or more texts" (xxv). This is a type of intertextuality, and in Equiano's case, it is an instance of directly borrowing a trope from another black writer (and as we will later see, white European writers) but changing it to create or signify complexity. At the time of the writing of his *Interesting Narrative,* Equiano is clearly well versed in the Afro British and Western literary tradition. And the trope of the "talking book" as a feature in the burgeoning Black Atlantic literature of his time is clearly well known to him.[10] The use of this trope, once again, is not meant to signify absence of subjectivity or ignorance on the part of Equiano, but absence or error attributable to the culture that has made him a captive and slave. (Indeed, for what was the punishment for original sin but the *absence* of God!)

Equiano's reworking of the trope of the "talking book" permeates the entirety of the narrative and problematizes claims to Christian salvation by those who participate in the slave trade. This idea informs Equiano's understanding of both the Bible and the nature of textuality as a moving presence in his own work as well. Equiano attributes a spiritual presence to objects he encounters in his third chapter, and particularly to the Bible that refuses to talk to him. This attribution of spiritual presence affords him (and us as readers) an opportunity to explore his work as a truly philosophical text that reveals the cross-cultural attitudes toward the metaphysics of presence that he shared with his captors as well as other Afro British and African American writers.[11] Through his engagement with this philosophical tradition, by incorporating this recurring trope into his book, he seeks to build a stronger case for the immediate abolition of the slave trade as the corrective to a sin shared by the entire culture. In abolishing slavery, political actors will experience the true presence of God rather than the pretend spirituality they practice by mouthing the words of the Bible but never experiencing a divine presence.

The "Talking Book" and Dialectic

Critics often speak of the Olaudah Equiano in the *Interesting Narrative* as a literal representation of the author of the book at various stages in his life rather than a *re-creation* of a life by a writer who is quite educated and engaged in constructing an argument. It should be observed that whether or not Equiano tells the literal truth about the events of his life in the *Narrative,* the "talking book" scene is a retelling of an episode that occurs in various forms no less than three times prior to the publication of Equiano's autobiography. Between 1770 and 1789 we see various versions of the "talking book" experience being related by early black Atlantic writers, indicating that during that nineteen-year period, black people in Britain and British America were reading each others' works, relating similar stories of their encounters with texts (particularly the Bible), and thinking through the intellectual problems associated with reading and textuality as a value in Western culture.

For instance, there are a number of similarities between James Albert Ukawsaw Gronniosaw's, Olaudah Equiano's, and John Marrant's narratives, particularly the "talking book" scenes, which can easily be discerned when read side by side. Quobna Ottobah Cugoano states early in his *Thoughts and Sentiments on the Evil of Slavery* that he is familiar with the writings of both Albert Gronniosaw and John Marrant, both of whom feature a "talking book" scene (Cugoano 23–24). Interestingly, Cugoano's own "talking book" scene is much like Marrant's in that it features a Native American encounter with the Bible in which a Native American places his own ear to the Bible only to find it silent (Cugoano 63–64). Vincent Carretta reveals that much of Cugoano's account cited above is directly quoted from William Robertson's 1777 book, *The History of America,* and, further, that Robertson is drawing his account of this moment from the writings of sixteenth-century Spanish historians (Cugoano 165n108).[12] So not only is Cugoano relating a "talking book" scene in his own work, but referencing a scene with a history in earlier European depictions of "primitives" encountering the technology of writing (particularly the Bible) for the first time. Ironically, Cugoano appropriates this specific "talking book" scene that extends back to sixteenth-century Spanish historical accounts in order to align himself within the tradition of eighteenth-century African American and Afro British writers who related their own autobiographical accounts of the "talking book." His gesture is a self-conscious reworking, or signifying, on the trope of the "talking book."

As we can see in the various black writers (and even accounts of Native American encounters with the Book), divine presence is lacking when one who is unfamiliar with the written word places his ear to the "talking book." It is a disappointing discovery and part of an intertextual meditation on the nature of textuality and presence that occurs early in Western philosophy: Equiano, for instance, critiques the texts and writing in the way that Plato does in the Phaedrus: It does not speak back! Or, rather, as Plato would suggest, it is only able to repeat itself over and over, without the conversation or revision of which human speech is capable. That is, it cannot engage in the dialectic in the way a living person can. This, of course, is a problem for Christian Platonists in need of reconciling Christianity with platonic philosophy. For the displaced African, and Equiano in particular, these two ways of understanding the "text" are at odds with one another. Is the text an empty repetition? Or does it embody a presence that can be engaged? Equiano is seeking the presence that was absent as he constructs his own narrative, the presence in the text that Saint John promises from the Bible, but that Equiano fails to find in his first encounters with it.

So Equiano, like some of his early black Atlantic colleagues, presents the contemporary reader with a fundamentally different understanding of textuality. The text seems to have some connection with objective, corporeal, and final meaning (i.e., God, the Author, etc.), but in a postmodern context this would not be the case. There is no final authoritative and autonomous embodiment/corporeality to the text, but rather the reading that one brings to it. In some extreme cases, students bring an "anything goes" sort of attitude to their readings of texts. But, again, this view of reading a holy text is not consistent with early Christian hermeneutics. Students tend to respond positively to the suggestion that reading and writing are cultural practices situated in particular periods, and that interpretation, therefore, requires a deep understanding of the expectations and assumptions of the period under investigation. This is not so difficult an argument so long as adequate examples are provided. So, for instance, "presence," meaning some sort of divine presence, is *always* assumed in the *reading* of the scripture, as posited by Augustine of Hippo. Augustine clearly argues that divine assistance is a necessary part of understanding the meaning of the Bible (4–6). Corporeality is, therefore, a central part of biblical textuality and interpretation. Even more to the point of Equiano's goals, divine presence, as it relates to the dialectic a reader engages with in an encounter with the Bible and biblical directives, is essential to moral arguments necessary to put an end to the slave trade.

Equiano's Frontispiece and Spiritual Authority

Equiano not only seeks to discover this missing voice but to also have his own texts contain an embodiment (a voice) that is his own, lending credibility, if not a type of corporeality, to his Christian, antislavery arguments that are a part of his efforts at moral suasion. For Equiano, only an embodied text, one that "speaks" to the reader with a corporeal authority, will carry the weight to make moral suasion. This tactic would thereby effectively move his readers to political action in the same way that the Protestant Christian conception of faith through the embodied word of God brings forth the change from sinner to saved. But as a writer, especially an African, he had to deal with the cultural biases and prejudices of eighteenth-century British and British American culture that assumed a *lack* of either learning or authority in the body of an African. John Bugg's important analysis of Equiano's five-year book tour through Britain and Ireland explains that not only did the tour help Equiano sell books, but the author, during the tour, "figures himself as a virtual talking book," a powerful supplement to his ontologizing of voice. Remarking on Equiano's outrage at the lack of legal recognition within British law, Bugg explains, "The idea that without testatory rights slaves, and in Equiano's case even ex-slaves, have no juridical existence shapes his merging of voice and being throughout *The Interesting Narrative*" (1428).

Selling books was crucial, but establishing a sense of authentic *being* was also important, and Equiano did this in textual form as well as in person. His person and persona were the proof he was an African, but also that Africans were capable of letters and learning. From the frontispiece onward, Equiano argues that being "learned" is not a prerequisite for inclusion in the human family or Christian community. In fact, the non-learned could not only be both human and Christian, but also authorities within the Christian community. It is significant that the Bible in the frontispiece to Equiano's narrative is open to the Book of Acts 4:12. Most commentators note that this picture is to signify his identification as a Christian and to place significant emphasis on his body position, clothes, and style of the woodcut.[13] However, specific attention to the text of the passage he is holding needs to be examined to understand more fully how the frontispiece relates to the autobiography in general and to the "talking book" scene in particular. In the precise text of the Bible he holds, Saint John is speaking to the priests, captains of the temple, and Sadducees who have captured John and Peter to interrogate them after they have miraculously healed a man who could not walk from birth. In this verse, Peter says, "Neither is there salvation in any other [than Jesus]: for there is none other name among men, whereby we must be saved." If one stops reading there, this would seem to be a simple proclamation of Christ as the sole means to spiritual salvation, and that Equiano includes it in his text as evidence of his belief in salvation through Christ.

But this text invites the reader to go further and read the next verse, which reveals context and an interesting statement on the question of authority within the Christian community: "Now when they saw the boldness of Peter and John, and perceived that they were *unlearned and ignorant* men, they marveled; and took knowledge of them, that they had been with Jesus" (emphases added). It is also important to note that these uneducated fishermen were also chosen, along with James, to see Jesus in his transfigured form at the top of a mountain where Jesus conversed with the spirits of Moses and Elias (Matthew 17:1–8, Mark 9:2–8, Luke 9:28–36). So, in addition to being a proclamation of faith, this text appearing within the frontispiece is also Equiano's way of signifying that the "unlearned" and "ignorant" may be favored and ascribed authority, even to the marvel of worldly powers.

The frontispiece goes even further by representing the figure of an African who, through the word of God as embodied by the Scriptures, claims his rightful place in Christian society as a voice of authority, not *despite* his origins but *because* of them. The frontispiece functions as an act of ventriloquism that echoes throughout the narrative and implies a radically different reading of the "talking book" scene than the usual interpretation of Equiano as the ignorant outsider.

Equiano's initial engagement with the text of the Scriptures reveals a rejection of the oral/literacy and presence/absence split that was then such a significant part of the Western tradition of philosophy and literature. In fact, within a Christian theological context, it was *reasonable* for Equiano to expect a voice since an embodied text through which the literal voice of God speaks is a part of a Christian hermeneutics and is a part of an encounter with the divine.

Teaching Questions and Practical Methods

A whole course could be structured around *The Interesting Narrative of the Life of Olaudah Equiano.* It is full of interesting possibilities for helping students think about the nature and power of narrative and its role in the construction of social reality, and, more particularly, how many eighteenth-century writers addressing the issue of slavery struggled to define themselves and their own social milieu through biblical interpretation. The "talking book" scene has served as the frame for an entire module on slavery and narrative that addressed a series of related questions that were discussed over several class periods: how do eighteenth-century writers use earlier source texts to construct their own autobiographical narratives? What are the implications of such usage? Since narratives are what human beings use to help make sense out of or construct social reality, what can intertextual references that we can identify tell us about the process of composition and reader expectations? Do recurring themes and their changes over time make an argument for a "living" text? What is the signifying power of the embodied text in Equiano's narrative? And, does the trope of the "talking book" reveal a Platonist ambivalence about the authority of the written text as illustrated by the repeated theme of books that refuse to talk back to illiterate listeners?

Whenever I put together a syllabus that includes *The Interesting Narrative of the Life of Olaudah Equiano* (and other early black autobiographies, for that matter), I like to include a variety of texts by transatlantic writers, both black and white, who were addressing issues of religion, slavery, and society. So a module of two or three weeks would include writings by many of the individuals mentioned above. In addition to Olaudah Equiano, we would read Cotton Mather, Edmund Gibson (Lord Bishop of London), Jupiter Hammon, Quobna Ottobah Cugoano, John Marrant, James Albert Ukawsaw Gronniosaw, and Venture Smith so that students would have an opportunity to encounter a variety of proslavery as well as antislavery writings from roughly the same time period. Throughout the module, as we discussed the shorter texts, I found it important to emphasize the similarities among all of the works and to try to understand where the points of agreement and disagreement arise. It is also important to note where the theological beliefs of the individual writers intersect and converge. For instance, though Equiano's narrative is a sustained antislavery argument, he nevertheless has much in common theologically with Edmund Gibson and Cotton Mather. The same goes especially for Jupiter Hammon, also, though he is much less invested in ending the slave trade than Equiano. This comparison is an especially interesting one for students because Hammon was both a slave and a devout Calvinist Christian.

In addition, I encourage teachers and student readers of Equiano's text to become familiar with the various biblical quotes and allusions he uses throughout his narrative as well as key biblical references in the other works. This exercise is not always very easy since many, and sometimes most, of the references to Scriptures are unidentified by the writers who often opt for paraphrases, which requires a high degree of familiarity with the text of the Bible. One particularly useful exercise I have successfully employed when teaching Equiano (and other early transatlantic writers as well) is to have students download a plain-text copy of *The Interesting Narrative* from a web site like Project Gutenberg, split the text into a number of sections equal to the number of students in the class, and make each of them responsible for searching out and annotating as footnotes any biblical references they find in their assigned section.[14] As part of the assignment, students are required to explain the context and meaning of the reference as it appears in the Bible and then explain why the author of the eighteenth-century text used it where he or she did in his or her text. This assignment not only familiarizes students with the tremendous amount of biblical knowledge a writer like Equiano possessed, but also gives them a high degree of competency in the text they are reading. After such an assignment, students find they can write more focused interpretive essays with deeper, more substantive insights into Equiano's methods of argumentation. After using this exercise in a number of semesters, this assignment results in a thoroughly annotated plain-text version of Equiano's narrative that can be used to help prepare future lectures. What teachers end up with is a wealth of information gathered together by students' original research, which ultimately improves one's knowledge of Equiano's text. Once the sections are reassembled, the annotated version of the text can be redistributed to students, reedited, and improved upon for later assignments and future semesters. This assignment can be easily applied to many writers from the early transatlantic period, especially as more plain-text transcriptions of writings from the era become available.

While this approach to teaching Equiano's narrative requires a good bit of background knowledge of the historical period and a number of the religious arguments and ideas related to slavery, the effort is well worth it. My own students, after engaging in this literature in this way, often remark how grateful they are to have had experience learning about the history of transatlantic slavery and black autobiography by studying these overlapping fields of knowledge. They have also picked up on the fact that the assignment forces them to study texts very closely. Students often have to read their section of the text multiple times and very thoroughly in order to become familiar enough with the language to pick up on subtle clues regarding context and usage. This focus on content also helps them to discover and pose new questions about the text that they may never have considered, and these inquiries can be used to guide class discussion. One student of mine even remarked in writing how she felt after completing a very similar assignment: "After completing this project, aside from feeling like a huge weight was gone from my shoulders, I actually felt *proud.* It's not often that I complete a paper and feel proud. . . . This assignment actually made me pay attention to the text I was working with. I actually read the whole thing multiple times. I've never done that before."

Notes

1. Vincent Carretta's book *Equiano, the African: Biography of a Self-Made Man* (2005) is the most extensive, as well as controversial, study of Equiano's life to date. Here he makes the claim that according to baptismal and naval records, Equiano may have been born in South Carolina rather than Africa as he claims in his *Interesting Narrative.* Chapter 4 of Henry Louis Gates Jr.'s *The Signifying Monkey: A Theory of African-American Literary Criticism* (1988) has an extensive section on Equiano's talking book scene that examines its intertextual connections to previous black literary texts and tropological revision. Srinivas Aravamudan's book *Tropicopolitans: Colonialism and Agency, 1688–1804* (1999) discusses Equiano's *Narrative* in the context of nation and nationalization in Chapter 6, titled "Equiano and the Politics of Literacy." Elizabeth Jane Wall Hinds's article "The Spirit of Trade: Olaudah Equiano's Conversion, Legalism, and the Merchant's Life" examines Equiano's critique of the slave trade as a free-trade argument couched in economic priorities and legal theory. Adam Potkay has written about Equiano's narrative as a spiritual autobiography in "Olaudah Equiano and the Art of Spiritual Autobiography." He also critiques postcolonial theory as a means for understanding Equiano in "History, Oratory, and God in Equiano's *Interesting Narrative.*" Rebuttals by Srinivas Aravamudan and Roxann Wheeler in the same issue of *Eighteenth-Century Studies,* titled "Equiano Lite" and "Domesticating Equiano's *Interesting Narrative,*" respectively, contest Potkay's arguments against postcolonial theory. Another interesting and useful essay that deals with teaching Equiano's narrative as a spiritual autobiography is Eileen Razzari Elrod's "Moses and the Egyptian: Religious Authority in Olaudah Equiano's *Interesting Narrative.*"

2. I purposely use the writer/reader configuration here, though I am fully aware that this sort of binarism is exactly what a deconstructive reading is meant to undermine. What I am doing here is illustrating the way *Equiano* would have thought of the hierarchy of language in his own context.

3. John Bugg discusses this particular point of moral suasion, in relation to Equiano's 1789–94 book tour, in his article "The Other Interesting Narrative: Olaudah Equiano's Public Book Tour."

4. As the verses from Exodus make clear, "And if a man smite the eye of his servant, or the eye of his maid, that it perish; he shall let him go free for his eye's sake. And if he smite out his manservant's tooth, or his maidservant's tooth; he shall let him go free for his tooth's sake."

5. Allen Dwight Callahan, in his book *The Talking Book: African Americans and the Bible* (2006), relates the story of a nineteenth-century American scholar named William Brown Hodgson who struggled to translate a manuscript written by a West African named London, who was a slave on a Georgia plantation. London was a Mandingo and a Muslim who could write in Arabic, but Hodgson was unable to discern what dialect the manuscript was written in. While trying to sound out the Arabic text, he realized that "the lines of the Arabic script were from neither an Arabic text nor an Arabic translation of an English text," but that London had used Arabic letters to transliterate African-American speech into script: "fas chapta o jon / inde be ginnen wasde wad / and wad was wid god / ande wad was wid god / ande wad was god" (Callahan 1–2). From this account, Callahan points out that, "African Americans first encountered the bible as strangers in a strange land of slavery, through the strange language of English letters. . . . London, an African in America and a slave, was a literate Muslim. Yet his very literacy bears witness to his encounter with the Bible not as a written text but as spoken word" (2). The account of the white American scholar not only highlights both the literacy of many West Africans in other languages and their ability to memorize Scripture, but also their ability to translate that knowledge into forms baffling to whites who encountered it—a mirror version of the "talking book" scene we are used to discussing in relation to slave encounters with the Bible!

6. In this point, I am in agreement with Adam Potkay when he writes, "Equiano's narrative presupposes as a condition of its intelligibility a world very different from, and in many ways antagonistic to, the world inhabited by many of his recent critics: his is a Christian, an oratorical, and a colonial world" ("History" 602). Indeed, critics must be sensitive to Equiano's historical context, particularly the significant impact Christianity played in his sense of personhood and literary aesthetic. However, Potkay's dismissal of the tools of postcolonial criticism closes the door to important insights that can and have led to significant contributions to Equiano studies. My own analysis will, to some extent, examine the use of such processes as "creolization," "parodic subversion," and "talking back" which, rather than being "faint" (602), as Potkay claims, are central to understanding Equiano's engagement with Western concepts of the metaphysics of presence, an engagement that is implicit in the very orality/literacy split that critics, including Potkay, examine in their own analyses of Equiano's *Narrative.* To be Christian *and* oratorical, as Potkay rightly points out, is a feature of Equiano's work that deals with the metaphysics of this identity in Western culture.

7. In more contemporary philosophical discussions dealing with the problem of presence and spirit, Luce Irigaray refers to the "spirit and flesh" as the "sensible transcendental," in which she figures the divine as immanent (Ingram 54). Though it has been customary for many Christians and theologians to think of God as a remote figure, it was of incredible importance in the eighteenth century for Protestant Christians in particular to envision God as an immanent presence, particularly as one listened to a particularly powerful sermon or read from the Bible in solitude. And as Penelope Ingram writes in her study of Luce Irigaray's theory of the immanent transcendental in feminist theory, "It is through the formulation of the concept of the immanent divine, the divine as a sensible transcendental, with its potential to dismantle dualisms, therefore, that we can understand the necessity for, and the value of, theorizing the role of the divine within feminist practices" (55). The idea of the sensible transcendental is equally useful for understanding how many Christians, and Equiano in particular here, understood their relationship with God. Though Irigaray proposes a feminist formulation of divinity, the ideas she works with are equally useful to a postcolonial understanding of the Western notion of the divine to the "native" or "outsider."

8. As I point out in a previous note, this is a similar sort of confusion and social dislocation that the nineteenth-century scholar, William Brown Hodgson, experienced when faced with the text of the first verse of *The Gospel According to Saint John* written in African American dialect with Arabic script. It was literally unintelligible to him until he spoke the words, phonetically, out loud—in a real sense revealing a slave's written text to be a "talking book" for the European.

9. It is significant to point out that, throughout Gates's chapter on the "talking book," he further explains the problem of absence that Africa and Africans signify in eighteenth-century philosophical discussions.

10. Henry Louis Gates Jr. identifies James Albert Ukawsaw's *A Narrative of the Most Remarkable Particulars in the Life of James Albert Ukawsaw Gronniosaw,* John Marrant's *The Lord's Wonderful Dealings with John Marrant, A Black,* and Quobna Ottobah Cugoano's *Thoughts and Sentiments on the Evil and Wicked Traffic of the Slavery and Commerce of the Human Species* as three texts by eighteenth-century black writers who discuss the "talking book" in their autobiographies. These works predate Equiano's *Interesting Narrative.*

11. Gates refers to Equiano's anthropomorphizing the book as naïve, a response I think is understandable. However, when we consider the problem of presence and embodiment in Western philosophical discourse, what Equiano suggests in his gesture has long been part of a serious argument within philosophy and rhetoric.

12. The quotation begins at the top of page 174 of Robertson's *History.*

13. Srinivas Aravamudan discusses the religious significance of his attire, explaining that "Equiano is dressed not as an exclusively religious man, but as an evangelical lay preacher, mediating between religion and its potential adherents" (244). Aravamudan also discusses a fascinating revision of the frontispiece that appeared in a 1791 unauthorized New York edition in which Equiano's facial features and hair are altered to make him appear more multiracial or "typically African American" (*Tropicopolitans* 247–48). Vincent Carretta gives an interesting reading of the frontispiece, arguing, "It is both the first and the last illustration of the trope of the 'talking book' that the author uses to emphasize the significance of literacy and acculturation in his autobiography" (*Equiano* 290).

14. *The Interesting Narrative of the Life of Olaudah Equiano* can be downloaded for free from the Project Gutenberg website: http://www.gutenberg.org/ebooks/15399.

Works Cited

Aravamudan, Srinivas. "Equiano Lite." *Eighteenth-Century Studies* 34.4 (2001): 615–19.

———. *Tropicopolitans: Colonialism and Agency, 1688–1804.* Durham: Duke UP, 1999.

Augustine. *On Christian Teaching.* Oxford, UK: Oxford UP, 1997.

Bugg, John. "The Other Interesting Narrative: Olaudah Equiano's Public Book Tour." *PMLA* 121.5 (2006): 1424–42.

Callahan, Allen Dwight. *The Talking Book: African Americans and the Bible.* New Haven, CT: Yale UP, 2006.

Carretta, Vincent. *Equiano, the African: Biography of a Self-Made Man.* Athens: U of Georgia P, 2005.

Cugoano, Quobna Ottobah. *Thoughts and Sentiments on the Evil of Slavery.* Ed. Vincent Carretta. New York: Penguin, 1999.

Elrod, Eileen Razzari. "Moses and the Egyptian: Religious Authority in Olaudah Equiano's *Interesting Narrative.*" *African American Review* 35.3 (2001): 409–25.

Equiano, Olaudah. The Interesting Narrative *and Other Writings.* Ed. Vincent Carretta. Rev. ed. New York: Penguin, 2003.

Gates, Henry Louis, Jr. *The Signifying Monkey: A Theory of African-American Literary Criticism.* New York: Oxford UP, 1988.

Gibson, Edmund. *A Letter from the Lord Bishop of London, to the Clergy of his Diocese.* London, 1742.

———. *Two Letters of the Lord Bishop of London to the masters and mistresses of families in the English plantations abroad; exhorting them to encourage and promote the instruction of their Negroes in the Christian faith.* London: Joseph Downing, 1727.

The Holy Bible: Authorized King James Version. Nashville, TN: Holman, 1989.

Ingram, Penelope. "From Goddess Spirituality to Irigaray's Angel: The Politics of the Divine." *Feminist Review* 66 (2000): 46–72.

Mather, Cotton. *The Negro Christianized: An essay to Excite and Assist the Good Work, the Instruction of Negro-Servants in Christianity.* Boston: B. Green, 1706.

Potkay, Adam. "History, Oratory, and God in Equiano's *Interesting Narrative.*" *Eighteenth-Century Studies* 34.4 (2001): 601–14.

———."Olaudah Equiano and the Art of Spiritual Autobiography." *Eighteenth-Century Studies* 27.4 (1994): 677–92.

Robertson, William. *The History of America.* Vol. 2. Dublin, 1777.

Wall Hinds, Elizabeth Jane. "The Spirit of Trade: Olaudah Equiano's Conversion, Legalism, and the Merchant's Life." *African American Review* 32.4 (1998): 635–47.

Wheeler, Roxann. "Domesticating Equiano's *Interesting Narrative.*" *Eighteenth-Century Studies* 34.4 (2001): 620–24.

Part 4

Pedagogy, American Studies, and *The Interesting Narrative*

"Neither a Saint, a Hero, Nor a Tyrant": Teaching Equiano Comparatively

Keri Holt

"So, does Olaudah Equiano remind you of anyone?"

I posed this question to my Early American Literature survey class, feeling somewhat bad for opening the day's discussion with such an obviously leading question. My students stared back at me, testing the silence to see if I would eventually break down and give them the answer they assumed I was looking for. In truth, I was not looking for anything specific. While I expected that someone would probably link Equiano with Mary Rowlandson's captivity narrative or the work of Phillis Wheatley, I was curious to see what other connections my students would come up with. And so I waited, watching them rifle through the pages of their brick-like anthologies and shift uncomfortably in their seats until a few hands finally went up. "This might be really off base," said one student sitting in the back of the room, "but this guy really reminds me of Ben Franklin, especially with all his talk of improvement and reputation and stuff."

I was trying something new in my approach to teaching Equiano that day. I had been teaching the survey course regularly for the past few years, and I usually introduced Equiano's *Interesting Narrative* as part of a special section on the syllabus titled "Voices of Difference" or "Another View," grouping Equiano together with writers such as Samson Occom, Phillis Wheatley, and Judith Sargent Murray in order to highlight the diversity of voices and perspectives that shaped the early American public sphere. By drawing specific attention to the writings of women, Native Americans, and African American slaves in a single thematic unit, I felt it would be easier for my students to think critically about the status of these marginalized subject positions in the early eighteenth century, as well as to examine the different rhetorical strategies these writers used to critique and, at times, subvert, the structures of domination, exclusion, and exploitation shaping their experiences. Furthermore, by grouping these texts together, I also hoped to counteract my students' tendency to view the literature of this period in monolithic terms, as an era dominated by the perspectives of white, male writers such as William Bradford, John Winthrop, Cotton Mather, J. Hector St. John de Crèvecoeur, and, of course, Benjamin Franklin.

While this technique was effective in disrupting and revising my students' prior conceptions of eighteenth-century America, the more I taught the course the more I became concerned about my "battering ram" approach. Introducing students to different racial, gender, and class perspectives through a barrage of "otherness" meant inadvertently encouraging them to see the world in binary terms—as black versus white, slave versus free, male versus female, rich versus poor, and so on—when I actually wanted them to recognize the ways in which these texts represented the eighteenth-century Atlantic World as a complex and contradictory space, where identities and power relations were defined through dynamic cross-identifications, overlappings, and interactions. Rather than examining the ways in which the works of Equiano, Wheatley, or Occom took part in the social, political, and philosophical debates of the eighteenth century, however, my students were approaching these writers *solely* as voices of difference, exclusion, and dissent. The proof of the pudding emerged in their papers, where, time and again, my students characterized figures such as Equiano as isolated crusaders for racial justice and equality, forever speaking out against the "dominant" world from which they were excluded.

Finding ways to avoid these kinds of generalizations is one of the fundamental challenges of teaching a survey course. Given the sheer amount of material to be covered (my own course extended from Columbus to the Civil War), distortions and oversimplifications inevitably occur. Paul Lauter, editor of the *Heath Anthology of American Literature,* has written on the problems of adequately representing the size and scope of American literary history, particularly when it comes to incorporating texts that have long been excluded from the canon. On the one hand, the push to include the work of formerly "marginalized" writers over the past thirty years has made it possible to introduce students to the diversity and complexity of American literary history (or, as Lauter describes it, "the conflicted relationships of *pluribus* and *unum*" [332]). On the other hand, as numerous critics have noted, the process of including these new voices also runs the risk of creating a "canon of separation" which (depending on how such texts are categorized and taught) has the potential to perpetuate the idea that "minorities are in fact different from the mainstream populace" (Ruland 357). Additional concerns arise when trying to account for variety within these "other" literary traditions. As Richard S. Pressman notes, as the literary canon continues to expand and diversify, it becomes increasingly important (and also increasingly difficult) to ensure that the work of minority writers is not "subsumed" into a "homogenized mass" (65).[1]

Returning to my own pedagogical endeavors, when teaching Equiano I needed to find a way to accomplish two related, yet somewhat contradictory goals—how to push my students to recognize the ways in which his text was fundamentally shaped by his experiences as a black slave while, at the same time, teaching them how to see Equiano as more than just a voice of difference and alterity. As it turned out, the comparison posed by that first student—the one who linked Equiano's *Interesting Narrative* with Franklin's *Autobiography* based on their shared interest in issues of "improvement and reputation"—proved to be immensely generative in addressing these concerns. Since then, I have regularly drawn on this comparative model when teaching Equiano's work, and in the essay that follows, I would like to present some of the specific opportunities and possibilities that arise when teaching *The Interesting Narrative* alongside Franklin's *Autobiography.* Such a comparison is hardly revolutionary. Critics have often drawn attention to similarities between these works, particularly with respect to their methods of self-presentation and rhetoric of liberty, commerce, and individualism. While these arguments have generated compelling discussions in scholarly circles, however, there is even more to be gained by moving this comparative analysis from the journals to the classroom, enabling students to better recognize the lively critical dimensions of both texts.[2]

As a general rule, comparative discussions are particularly effective in survey courses: they help students learn how to read individual texts closely (with an eye for their formal and aesthetic particularities) and, at the same time, contend with the social and political contexts in which they were produced. By placing *The Interesting Narrative* in dialogue with Franklin's *Autobiography,* for instance, students become able to identify and analyze the use of distinctive tropes and stylistic features in both works, such as the use of book-related metaphors to describe life experiences and the strategic (and at times, radically different) invocations of God and Christianity. Discussions of these formal characteristics give rise to further questions about the social, political, and economic conditions in which these texts operated and intervened, particularly with regard to eighteenth-century conceptions of race, the history of the Atlantic slave trade, the emergence of new forms of industry and capitalist development, the influence of Enlightenment philosophy and political theory, and the uncertain and fluctuating status of identity and national affiliation in the transatlantic world.

Of course, such issues and questions can be raised by comparing *The Interesting Narrative* with any number of texts. What makes a comparative reading of Equiano and Franklin particularly useful in the classroom is the disarming mixture of similarity and difference that students must confront when placing these texts in dialogue with one another. When asked to compare them, students typically have no trouble identifying similar features and interests, particularly regarding (again, as my one student so eloquently put it) their mutual focus on "improvement and reputation and stuff." Students, however, invariably grow uncomfortable with the prospect of drawing too many parallels, an uneasiness which arises from their fundamental sense that Equiano and Franklin are *not,* in fact, the same at all. Despite the many thematic and stylistic similarities they can point out—such as the two authors' shared interest in the ideals of individualism, liberty, and civic virtue, their emphasis on cultivating and controlling their public images, their strategies of imitation, their obsession with the logic and language of commerce and business, and so on—students are nevertheless fully aware that Franklin and Equiano are writing from vastly different perspectives and experiences. Franklin writes from the position of a free white American statesman who enjoys international fame and respect and Equiano writes as a free African American who spent a good portion of his life in bondage and who continues to occupy an extremely precarious and unprotected social and political position.

As they work through a comparative analysis, students recognize that they need to find some way to account for these different subject positions, and it is precisely this process of contending with these "similarities with a difference" that leads them toward a more rigorous and sophisticated consideration of the Atlantic World. How, for instance, does Equiano's and Franklin's similar use of a Lockean language of liberty and self-improvement work differently when employed by an ambitious black slave as opposed to an ambitious white printer? Likewise, how must we read their strategies of imitation differently when considering Franklin's desire to imitate the example of figures like Socrates or Addison and Steele alongside Equiano's attempts to copy the "society and manners" of his white masters? What do these comparisons suggest about the different power dynamics shaping Equiano's and Franklin's experiences, and how do they help us think more critically about the racial and social hierarchies of the mid-eighteenth century? What happens to the "up by the bootstrap" narratives of individual industry and agency that each uses to describe his rise to independence when one is about the story of a former apprentice establishing his own business and the other of a slave purchasing his own freedom? Each text affirms a discourse of progress and self-determination, but with different goals and consequences. Equiano's version, for instance, paradoxically becomes a calculated critique of the racial biases and limitations at stake in the narrative of individual potential and advancement.

Confronting such questions inevitably illustrates just how problematic it is to read Equiano and Franklin solely in terms of "black-and-white" notions of the political, social, and ethical conditions of their time. As Dana D. Nelson writes, one of the challenges of these texts is enabling students to recognize how "identities, like cultures, are negotiated not hermetically and in isolation, but in relation to others . . . and how the formation of those identities shore up, respond to, and react against [one another]" (247). Through a comparative approach, students become less inclined to view Equiano simply as a voice of racial difference, exclusion, and dissent, and, instead, examine how he participates in and transforms the discourse of Enlightenment individuality, how he engages with the politics and epistemology of a new economic order rooted in free market economic practices, or how he takes part in the spiritual and oratorical discourse of the eighteenth century.[3] This comparative approach also helps students transform the way they read Franklin's *Autobiography,* helping them recognize the extent to which Franklin's text is just as much shaped and bounded by racial assumptions he might not overtly address. In contrast, then, to their tendency to view Franklin as the definitive and absolute voice of historical, ethical, and national truths, students grasp how Franklin represents one perspective among many. If a comparative analysis encourages students to see Equiano as more than just a marginalized "black" voice, it likewise discourages them from continuing to see Benjamin Franklin as *the* voice of the early American period.

This exercise is not meant to downplay the category of race, nor is it meant to de-emphasize Equiano's status as an African American writer or his influence within an African American literary tradition. To the contrary, one of my primary goals when teaching Equiano is to give students a sense of how the narrative structures and the rhetorical strategies deployed in *The Interesting Narrative* lay a foundation for a tradition of African American writing, particularly with regard to the representation and critique of slavery, racism, and the complex dimensions of black subjectivity as it is depicted in the text. As Henry Louis Gates Jr. writes, "Equiano's strategies of self-representation and rhetorical representation [have] heavily informed, if not determined, the shape of black narrative before 1865" (*The Signifying Monkey* 153). Once again, pairing Equiano's *Interesting Narrative* with Franklin's *Autobiography* offers an extremely useful way to illustrate the form, function, and force of some of these critical strategies, particularly as to the representation of "double consciousness" and Equiano's use of the rhetorical strategy of "signifyin(g)." While these characteristics can certainly be illustrated by comparing Equiano with other black writers such as Phillis Wheatley, Ignatius Sancho, or Frederick Douglass, juxtaposing Equiano's text with Franklin's autobiography often makes it easier for students to recognize the dual subject positions Equiano continually tries to occupy, as well as the strategies of repetition and performance he uses to articulate his experiences as a black slave living in the eighteenth-century Atlantic World. In the end, the process of comparing Equiano with a canonical writer like Franklin who, in many ways, seems to embody the persona, ideals, and perspectives that Equiano seeks to imitate and critique, offers a valuable means of highlighting the multiple and, at times, competing "topographies of loyalty and identity" (Gilroy 16) that shape Equiano's experiences, providing a particularly useful frame of reference for those students encountering *The Interesting Narrative* for the first time.[4]

In the following sections, I have chosen three specific points of comparison for working with Equiano and Franklin which tend to generate particularly lively and effective class discussions, namely 1) their opening rhetorical stances, 2) their respective accounts of self-improvement, and 3) their shared interest in cultivating a particular public reputation. In presenting these points, I do not mean to offer a finalized set of discussion outlines for teaching these texts. Rather, I hope these brief sections will illustrate some of the potential ideas and directions which can emerge when comparing Equiano and Franklin while also providing a starting point for pursuing comparative readings in your own classrooms.[5]

Introductory Remarks: Who's So Vain? And Why?

My students almost always begin their comparisons by turning to the opening paragraphs of Equiano and Franklin, noting (with classic undergraduate vagueness) that "both writers talk about vanity." Indeed, they are not wrong, but a closer look reveals important differences in the way each writer addresses the issue. While Equiano makes a concerted effort to disavow the "imputation of vanity" attributed to "those who publish their own memoirs," Franklin openly admits the vanity of his autobiographical endeavors, even going so far to suggest that any attempt to deny the vanity of his project would, in fact, be a vain attempt to showcase his modesty. Consider the following passage from Equiano:

> I believe it is difficult for those who publish their own memoirs to escape the imputation of vanity; nor is this the only disadvantage under which they labour, it is also their misfortune that whatever is so uncommon is rarely, if ever, believed; and what is obvious we are apt to turn from with disgust. . . . It is therefore, I confess, not a little hazardous, in a private and obscure individual, and a stranger too, thus to solicit the indulgent attention of the public; especially when I own I offer here the history of neither a saint, a hero, nor a tyrant. I believe there are a few events in my life which have not happened to many . . . [and] when I compare my lot with that of most of my countrymen, I regard myself as a *particular favourite of Heaven,* and acknowledge the mercies of Providence in every occurrence of my life. If, then, the following narrative does not appear sufficiently interesting to engage general attention, let my motive be some excuse for its publication. I am not so foolishly vain as to expect from it either immortality or literary reputation. If it affords any satisfaction to my numerous friends, at whose request it has been written, or in the smallest degree promotes the interest of humanity, the ends for which it was undertaken will be fully attained. (Equiano 32; emphases in original)

And from Franklin:

> Having emerged from the poverty and obscurity in which I was born and bred, to a state of affluence and some degree of reputation in the world, and having gone so far thro' life with a considerable share of felicity, the

> conducting means I made use of, which, with the blessing of God, so well succeeded, my posterity may like to know, as they may find some of them suitable to their own situations and fit to be imitated. . . . And lastly, (I may as well confess it, since my denial of it will be believ'd by no body) perhaps I shall a good deal gratify my own Vanity. Indeed I scarce ever heard or saw the introductory words without vanity I may say, etc. but some vain thing immediately follow'd. Most people dislike vanity in others whatever share they have of it themselves, but I give it fair quarter wherever I meet with it, being that persuaded that it is often productive of some good to the possessor and those that are within his sphere of action. And therefore in many cases it would not be quite absurd if a man were to thank God for his vanity among the other comforts of life. . . . And now that I speak of thanking God, I desire with all humility to acknowledge that I owe the mention'd happiness of my past life to his kind Providence which led me to the means I us'd and gave them success. (Franklin 488–89)

Comparing the different rhetorical stances of these opening remarks—one humble and apologetic, the other bold, proud, and contrarian—offers a useful starting point for considering the different expectations, limitations, and pressures that shape Equiano's and Franklin's manners of expression. On a first reading, students have no trouble addressing the different power relations and subject positions influencing these variations in tone and language. It is not particularly difficult, for instance, for students to consider why a black writer of the eighteenth century might find it effective to adopt a humble and submissive tone when writing for a white audience, and why a writer like Franklin would be more able to adopt a direct and self-focused pose. By delving a little deeper into these opening remarks, however, students can also begin to develop a better grasp of how both writers engage with some of the same expectations and conventions of the eighteenth-century Atlantic literary world and, more important, how they employ similar strategies for criticizing and undermining many of its assumptions and structures.

In opening this discussion, I ask students to take a step back from Franklin's and Equiano's differences and consider what is implied by the fact that both feel the need to begin their narratives by addressing the charge of vanity in the first place. What does their shared attention to this rhetorical gesture say about the values, priorities, and expectations of their readers? And, moreover, what do their different responses suggest about the way these texts might be trying to critique and transform those expectations? Approaching the passages from this angle leads to a conversation about the social and literary conventions of the eighteenth-century world, particularly with respect to the principles and practices of civic virtue, the concept of the public sphere, and the qualities of modesty and disinterestedness typically expected from writers of the period.[6] In addition, however, comparing these texts can also help clarify how their authors challenge such conventions, and it is here where a close reading of the critical and rebellious character of Franklin's opening comments can lead students to a better understanding of the critical and rebellious character found in *The Interesting Narrative.*

By acknowledging that he has written his autobiography, in part, to "gratify [his] own vanity," Franklin refuses to adopt the expected stance of impartiality that governed the conventions of public writing in his time. Instead, he exposes this conventional assertion of modesty as an insincere performance, most likely directed toward self-serving ends. How then, I ask students, might we read Franklin's comments in relation to Equiano's narrative—a text that adopts the same rhetorical gesture of modesty that Franklin criticizes in his own work? What is the difference between reading Equiano's claim sincerely and reading it as Franklin might—as a kind of self-interested performance? If we do read Equiano's assertion of modesty as a performance, what does he gain by staging this position? Must we read this part of the text as a self-effacing statement that he must adopt given his status as a black writer writing for a white audience? Or are there other ways to read his denial of vanity? Is Equiano, perhaps, making radical claims for equality by mimicking the polite rhetoric expected of his literary peers?

I also ask students about other rhetorical forms Equiano might have drawn upon in framing his life narrative and what might have prevented him from adopting the kind of rhetorical stance that Franklin used. In addressing these questions, students begin to see *The Interesting Narrative* as a much more active and aggressive text that can be just as critical as Franklin's *Autobiography*—albeit with different objectives. In their respective discussions concerning the teaching of Equiano's work, Srinivas Aravamudan and Roxann Wheeler note that one of the most important challenges when teaching *The Interesting Narrative* is helping students recognize the many ways his text "talks back" to its audience (Aravamudan, "Equiano Lite" 616). As Wheeler writes, "[m]ost of us teach Equiano because he is a literate former slave who is also a lively contemporary observer, political activist, businessman, and Christian" (622), and placing *The Interesting Narrative* in dialogue with the *Autobiography* offers an excellent means of illustrating how Equiano's text operates as an assertive voice intended both to prompt and take part in a forceful critical conversation.

Keeping Up Appearances: The Importance of Looking Earnest

Establishing a reputable character is the secret to success for both Franklin and Equiano. Each works his way toward independence and self-sufficiency by cultivating a reputation founded on honesty, industry, creativity, and trustworthiness. While these identities are not necessarily meant to be deceptive, both, in many ways, are carefully constructed performances—cultivated not merely for personal edification, but to advance a particular set of self-interested objectives. Franklin and Equiano are masters of managing their public images, and both deploy those images in very strategic ways. Consider, for instance, the following set of passages. The first two selections, drawn from *The Interesting Narrative,* identify moments where Equiano describes the methods he uses to earn the trust and respect of his master. In the first quotation, Equiano describes his duties and responsibilities and how he endeavors to present himself as a hard-working, honest, and indispensable slave. The second passage, which occurs several chapters further into the text, illustrates how Equiano subsequently relies upon his honest, hard-working reputation to defend himself when he is later accused of plotting an escape.

> I had the good fortune to please my master in every department in which he employed me; and there was scarcely any part of the business or household affairs, in which I was not occasionally engaged. I often supplied the place of a clerk in receiving and delivering cargoes to the ships, in tending stores, and delivering goods, and besides this, I used to shave and dress my master when it was convenient, and take care of his horse, and when it was necessary, which was very often, I worked likewise on board of different vessels of his. By these means I became very useful to my master, and saved him, as he used to acknowledge, above a hundred pounds a year. (Equiano 103)

> I then appealed to the captain, whether ever he saw any sign of my making the least attempt to run away, and asked him if I did not come on board

> according to the time for which he gave me liberty. . . . To my no small surprise, and very great joy, the captain confirmed every syllable I said, and even more for he said he had tried different times to see if I would make any attempt of this kind, both at St. Eustatia and in America, and he never found I made the smallest; but on the contrary, I always came on board according to his orders. . . . This soon gladdened my poor heart beyond measure . . . and I immediately made him this reply: "Sir, I always had that very thought of you, indeed I had, and that made me so diligent in serving you." He then gave me a large piece of silver coin, such as I had never seen or had before, and told me to get ready for the voyage, and that he would credit me with a tierce of sugar and another of rum; he also said that he had two amiable sisters in Philadelphia, from whom I might get some necessary things. (126)

This second set of passages, taken from Franklin's *Autobiography,* likewise depicts moments where Franklin describes his methods and motives for cultivating his public reputation. In the first passage, he describes how, as a young man, he learns to manipulate his word choices to create an "appearance" of modesty (and thus better advance his own positions) and, in the second, he describes the various steps he takes to ensure that people recognize him as a reliable and industrious businessman when he begins to embark on his own printing career.

> I [gained] the habit of expressing myself in terms of modest diffidence, never using when I advance any thing that may be possibly disputed, the words, "certainly," "undoubtedly," or any others that give the air of positiveness to an opinion; but rather I say "I conceive," or "I apprehend" a thing to be so and so, "It appears to me" or "I should think it so for such and such reasons," or "I imagine it to be so" or "it is so if I am not mistaken." This habit I believe has been of great advantage to me, when I have had the occasion to inculcate my opinion or persuade men into measures that I have from time to time been engaged in promoting. (Franklin 498; quotation marks added)

> I now opened a little stationer's shop. I had in it blanks of all sorts the correctest which ever appeared among us. . . . I had also paper, parchment, chapmen's books, etc. . . . I now began gradually to pay off the debt I was

> under for the printing-house. In order to secure my credit and character as a tradesman, I took care not only to be in reality industrious and frugal, but to avoid all appearances of the contrary. I dressed plainly, I was seen at no places of idle diversion. I never went out a-fishing or shooting; a book, indeed, sometimes debauch'd me from my work; but that was seldom, snug, and gave no scandal: and to show I was not above my business, I sometimes brought home the paper I purchased at the stores, tho' the streets on a wheelbarrow. Thus being esteemed as a thriving, industrious young Man, and paying duly for what I bought, the merchants who imported stationary solicited my custom, other propos'd supplying me with books, and I went on swimmingly. (530)

In both selections, Equiano and Franklin describe their efforts to cultivate virtuous and industrious personas. Once again, a close reading of Franklin can help students elucidate some of the critical dimensions of Equiano's work. In the passages above (and throughout the *Autobiography*), Franklin describes the deliberate steps he takes to ensure that others see him as "a thriving, industrious young man." He is equally direct in acknowledging his self-interested reasons for doing so (in this case, to attract clients and gain greater influence over his peers). Franklin is a master of managing his public image, and because he draws such attention to the careful ways he develops and deploys his various "appearances" (both physical and rhetorical), students typically have no problem examining how he uses such an image to strategic ends.

Unlike Franklin, however, Equiano does not portray the performative dimensions of his public character in such direct terms. As a result, students often have a harder time recognizing how he also makes strategic use of his own appearance. I have found that many of my students often take Equiano's words at face value, reading him as a figure sincerely dedicated to the values of hard work, obedience, and loyalty, and firmly committed to earning his freedom by strictly "honest" means. Such a literal interpretation is not necessarily off the mark. Throughout *The Interesting Narrative,* Equiano does go to great lengths to convince readers of his legitimate devotion to the ideals of industry, frugality, loyalty, modesty, and honesty that he seeks to exemplify. What students often have a harder time recognizing, however, is the extent to which this representation can also be read as an equally calculated performance, designed (just like Franklin's account) to advance a particular agenda—in this case to obtain freedom, redefine public perceptions of racial difference, and critique the racist assumptions and attitudes informing the practice of slavery.

Teaching students how to recognize and interpret the performative elements of *The Interesting Narrative* can be challenging, particularly given the fast pace of a survey course where students are often encountering Equiano for the first time. Reading Equiano in conjunction with Franklin offers a useful way for students to approach the strategic use of public image. The *Autobiography* provides a model for approaching the performative aspects of *The Interesting Narrative* and, at the same time, pushes students to recognize that rhetorical strategies are not merely reserved for use by "famous" writers in canonical texts. Just as Franklin is able to further his own wealth and influence by representing himself as a modest, frugal, and industrious figure, Equiano has much to gain (both for himself and others) by representing himself as a virtuous and hard-working slave. Each is a calculated form of self-creation and promotion.[7]

Following Franklin, then, I ask my students to think about what Equiano has to gain by representing himself in the way that he does. There are numerous directions to pursue when considering Equiano's carefully constructed image. On the one hand, one might begin by asking students how Equiano's strategies of self-representation enable him to undermine the slave system from the inside out. As numerous critics have asserted, Equiano is able to gain his freedom by rigidly adhering to the bonds imposed by his masters, rather than relying on active resistance or rebellion.[8] I ask students why this method is effective and what the long-term consequences of this strategy may be, both in regard to *The Interesting Narrative* and when considering Equiano's influence on other African American literary works. To what extent can we read Equiano's performance as a form of subversive trickery or "signifyin(g)," intended to undermine the logic and legitimacy of the bonds he wants to escape? And, to what extent is this also a potentially problematic form of representation, one which runs the risk of perpetuating and reinforcing certain racial stereotypes and which is later actively critiqued by subsequent African American writers?

Another way of tackling the issue of performance is to consider how Equiano's efforts to portray himself as a virtuous and knowledgeable slave allow him to reconfigure the way in which readers view black subjects. As Susan Marren and others have argued, Equiano's careful self-portrayal as an intelligent, loyal, and conscientious slave ultimately allows him to "fashion . . . a 'transgressive' narrative self" which "challenges his readers to scrutinize the very social structures that their preoccupation with racial difference had sought to mask" (Marren 94). In other words, by carefully representing himself as a virtuous individual who espouses the principles of honesty, individual agency, and public responsibility embraced by eighteenth-century society, Equiano is able to transform the ways in which his audience views black subjects. In this regard, students can begin to consider how Equiano's strategies of self-representation become a means of "illuminating a space of possibility within which subsequent black narrators might envision themselves as viable subjects" (Marren 95).

It is also interesting to go a bit beyond the texts and address some of the ways these two writers sought to promote themselves in their public lives. The famous portrait of Franklin clad in a coonskin cap that he wore to play the role of the "American" while seeking aid for the Revolutionary War in France would be a relevant image to examine in this context. Just as Franklin went to great lengths to portray himself as the quintessential American, not just through his writings, but through his public behavior and physical appearance, so too did Equiano pay particular attention to the way in which he appeared to the public, beyond simply the words of his text. John Bugg's and Vincent Carretta's respective accounts of the tireless and inventive ways Equiano sought to promote *The Interesting Narrative* through book tours, anonymous letters to the newspaper, and aggressive subscription campaigns offer an excellent way to introduce students to the ways in which Equiano, much like the Parisian Franklin, carefully managed and manipulated his public image to achieve particular ends (Carretta, "Property of the Author" 131). Also of interest would be the portrait of Equiano featured in the frontispieces for both the 1789 London edition and the 1791 New York edition of *The Interesting Narrative.* Asking students to read the details and implications suggested by these portraits (so carefully positioned in the opening pages of the text) provides a wonderful opportunity for them to explore further the complex dimensions of self-representation at stake in the text, particularly with regard to the ways in which Equiano's portrait (more so than Franklin's) is subject to, yet also critical of, certain eighteenth-century political and cultural expectations regarding race, class, and civility.

The Secret to My Success: Strategies of Self-Improvement

A third point for discussion when comparing *The Interesting Narrative* and the *Autobiography* concerns their accounts of self-improvement. Both writers tell of their efforts to become independent and successful through their initiative and industry. Of course, the stakes are higher for one than the other: while Franklin wants to escape the bonds of tradition to become an independent thinker and businessman, Equiano hopes to obtain a more fundamental freedom by escaping the bonds of slavery. Nevertheless, both rely on the same rhetoric of individual virtue and agency to tell their stories, which, in turn, shed light on the assumptions, biases, and critiques in their tales of success. Once again, I offer some specific passages for considering these ideas. The first set, taken from Equiano's *Narrative,* are a series of quotations selected from the first half of the book where Equiano describes his growing desire to "improve" himself (and, thus, increase his chances of becoming free) by imitating the manners and morals of his various masters, whom he refers to here as his "new countrymen" (see below).

> I now not only felt myself quite easy with these new countrymen, but relished their society and manners. I no longer looked upon them as spirits, but as men superior to us; and therefore I had the stronger desire to resemble them; to imbibe their spirit, and imitate their manners; I therefore embraced every occasion of improvement; and every new thing I observed I treasured up in my memory. (Equiano 77–78)

> I thought now of nothing but being freed and working for myself, and thereby getting money to get a good education; for I always had a great desire to at least be able to read and write; and while I was on shipboard I had endeavored to improve myself in both. (91)

> My mind was therefore hourly replete with inventions and thoughts of being freed, and, if possible, by honest and honorable means; for I always remembered the old adage, and I trust it has ever been my ruling principle, "that Honesty is the best policy"; and likewise that other golden precept—"To do unto all men as I would they should do unto me" . . . I therefore

looked up with prayers to God for my liberty and, at the same time, did all that was possible on my part to obtain it. In process of time I became master of a few pounds and, in a fair way of making more . . . and, from great attention to [my master's] orders and his business, I gained him credit and, though his kindness to me, I at last procured my liberty. (119)

In this second set of quotations, taken from the *Autobiography*, Franklin similarly describes the steps he takes to "improve" himself. In the first example, he describes the specific methods he uses to educate himself and make better use of his time and money while working as a printer's apprentice for his brother. The next two quotations illustrate the ways in which Franklin sought to improve both his social and financial standing through his adherence to a personal and practical moral code.

> [I] propos'd to my brother, that if he would give me weekly half the money he paid for my board, I would board myself. He instantly agreed to it, and I presently found that I could save half what he paid me. This was an additional fund for buying books: But I had another advantage in it. My brother and the rest going from the printing-house to their meals, I remain'd there alone, and dispatching presently my light repast . . . had the rest of the time till their return, for study, in which I made the greater progress. (Franklin 497)

> The library afforded me the means of improvement by constant study. . . . Reading was the only amusement I allow'd myself. I spent no time in taverns, games, or frolics of any kind. And my industry in my business continu'd as indefatigable as it was necessary. I was in debt for my printing-house, I had a young family coming on to be educated, and I had to contend with for Business two printers who were establish'd in the place before me. My circumstances, however, grew daily easier: my original habits of frugality continuing. . . . I from thence consider'd industry as a means of obtaining wealth and distinction. (538)

> I have always thought that one man of tolerable abilities may work great changes, and accomplish great affairs among mankind, if he first forms a good plan, and, cutting off all amusements or other employments that

> would divert his attention, makes the execution of that same plan his sole study and business. (549)

In all of these passages, Franklin and Equiano provide strikingly similar descriptions of their desire and efforts to "improve" themselves. Both want to become more literate, independent, respected, and self-sufficient, and both try to realize these goals by imitating the example of others and cultivating frugal and practical business habits. Moreover, as is evident in the passages cited above, both narratives exhibit a great deal of faith in the power of the individual to achieve success through initiative, industry, and virtue. For this reason, my students often argue that Franklin and Equiano represent the embodiment of the "American Dream"—that ever-popular (and ever-problematic) notion that, with hard work and dedication, anyone can make something of him or herself.

Getting students to think critically about the "truth" of this narrative is one of the constant challenges of teaching American literature. The appeal and cultural embeddedness of this "up-by-the-bootstraps" narrative make it a hard one to dislodge, and, students often turn to it as the default theme for all American writing, particularly when studying earlier texts. As they move from Winthrop's call for the early settlers to "labour and suffer together . . . [to] be as a city upon a hill" (93) to Crèvecoeur's claim that an American "whatever be his talents or inclinations . . . may procure an easy, decent maintenance by his industry" (56), to Emerson's assertion that "self-reliance . . . must work a revolution in all the offices and relations of man" (32), students invariably want to read the literature of the early United States as the starting point for a patriotic American master narrative founded on the idea of overcoming adversity to achieve personal freedom and success. As a result of this tendency, one of my primary goals when teaching a survey course is to help students learn to read these texts closely and carefully enough to question this style of broad, thematic interpretation. In this regard, comparing the *Autobiography* and *The Interesting Narrative* is particularly effective, precisely because this comparison does not let students entertain such romantic notions about American individualism, industry, and identity for long. For as much as Franklin and Equiano seem to embrace and embody this narrative of individual agency, a close reading of the two helps students recognize some of the ways in which *The Interesting Narrative* aggressively criticizes this notion of equal opportunity by exposing its racial limitations and exploitative power structure.

Beginning with the initial observation that *The Interesting Narrative* and the *Autobiography* both seem to share a faith in the promise of individual improvement and success, I ask students to consider the extent to which this narrative actually works out in either text. While it is pretty clear that Franklin attains the independence and success he seeks (at least, as far as he is concerned), Equiano's "success" is a little more troubling. On the one hand, Equiano does end up earning his independence, eventually buying his own freedom "very honestly and with much industry" (135). On the other hand, however, the question arises—are we really meant to read Equiano's path to independence as a story of "success"? And, does Equiano really earn his independence when he must obtain it by purchasing it in the economic marketplace?

The fact that Equiano's story of hard work, self-improvement, and frugality is ultimately directed toward the purchase of his physical freedom—in contrast to Franklin, who seeks a very different set of freedoms (namely to pursue his own interests, build his own capital, and express his own ideas)—helps students recognize how *The Interesting Narrative* might offer an ironic critique of this narrative of self-improvement, rather than an earnest endorsement of it. While independence might emerge as a fundamental and obtainable right in a narrative like the *Autobiography, The Interesting Narrative* portrays "independence" in very different terms, as a commodity that most non-white subjects were not authorized to obtain. The very fact that Equiano can only obtain his freedom by purchasing it exposes the ideological inconsistencies and racial limitations of the Enlightenment ideology of individualism and independence. As the narrative continually asks its readers—how can freedom ever be "honestly" bought?[9]

Another way to approach a comparative discussion of Franklin's and Equiano's narratives of self-improvement is to consider the differences between Franklin's slow but steady rise to success and Equiano's much more uneven and uncertain path. *The Interesting Narrative,* as Cathy Davidson notes, is a text characterized by "profound disruption" that is constantly overshadowed by a "sense of ever-imminent crisis" (20). For as much as Equiano tries to portray his path to independence as a careful, step-by-step progression ("In process of time I became master of a few pounds and, in a fair way of making more . . . and, from great attention to orders and his business . . . I at last procured my liberty" [119]), *The Interesting Narrative* is filled with near-constant setbacks, such as when he is unexpectedly sold by a master who "take[s] all [his] wages and prize money"

(93), when he is robbed of his entire stock of limes and oranges "without the least redress" (117), and when he is cruelly beaten "to no purpose" by a drunk he encounters in Georgia who leaves him "nearly dead" (129). Despite his commitment to virtue and hard work, Equiano's ideals rarely pay off—not, at least, in the way they do for Franklin.

The various ups and downs depicted in *The Interesting Narrative* invariably prompt a discussion of the different degrees of agency and control Equiano and Franklin exhibit in their respective texts. Although both attempt to tell similar stories of individual advancement, *The Interesting Narrative* presents a world that is defined by chance rather than agency. In contrast to Franklin (a figure who regularly represents himself as an individual able to take charge of his own environment), Equiano emerges as a figure who lacks the kind of individuality and authority needed to make a "Franklinian" narrative of success possible. It is precisely by illustrating the failure of this narrative that Equiano articulates, as Davidson writes, "the inherent insecurity of being an African or of African descent in a world where black people are enslaved" (19).

The most damning critique of this narrative of individual improvement emerges when Equiano describes the precarious situation of all free black men in the eighteenth-century Atlantic World. In Chapter 6, he tells the story of a man named Joseph Clipson, "a very clever and decent free young mulatto-man who [had] sailed a long time with us" (120). Although "all knew this young man from a child that he was always free, and [that] no one had ever claimed him as their property," Equiano reports that a captain from Bermuda claimed Clipson was "not free" and immediately seized and forced him into slavery, "without giving the poor man any hearing on shore or suffering even to see his wife and child" (121). In reporting this story, Equiano again illustrates the extent to which black subjects did not possess individual identity and agency in the eyes of the law and the general public. Even when "free," black men could not capitalize on their individual industry and honesty, precisely because they could never possess the rights or opportunities needed to make their independence and financial success secure. As Equiano himself writes,

> These things opened to my eyes a new scene of horror, to which I had been before a stranger. Hitherto I had only thought slavery dreadful, but the state of a free Negro appeared to me now equally so at least, and in some

> respects even worse, for they live in constant alarm for their liberty, which is but nominal, for they are universally insulted and plundered without the possibility of redress. (122)

Through this example, the "universal" character of individualism suggested by a text like the *Autobiography* emerges, instead, as a very exclusive discourse of success.

In closing, while there are numerous ways to address the critical and perfomative elements of *The Interesting Narrative,* reading this text in conjunction with Franklin provides a particularly effective way for students to recognize the aggressive and challenging elements of Equiano's tale. Returning once again to Equiano's self-effacing introduction, there is a tendency, I think, for students to read Equiano as a writer trapped by circumstance—unable to express himself as clearly or freely as he might like due to his status as a black author writing in a white world. Rather than approaching Equiano as a persecuted and disenfranchised victim, the process of comparing Equiano and Franklin allows students to see him as an active and assertive writer who is every bit as capable of using and controlling language for strategic ends. While there are important differences in the form, function, and circumstances of these texts, both works are actively and imaginatively engaged in addressing the ideals and assumptions of the Atlantic World in which they take part. In noting this point, students can thus come away from *The Interesting Narrative* by recognizing it not as the history of "a saint, a hero, nor a tyrant" (Equiano 31) but as a complex and sophisticated work of social critique.

Notes

1. Debates over how best to diversify the canon without, simultaneously, "enshrining difference" tend to crop up around the publication of new (or revised) literary anthologies (Lauter 331). For some particularly helpful examples, see Joe Lockhard and Jillian Sandell, Richard Ruland, Paul Lauter, and Richard S. Pressman.

2. Numerous scholars have offered comparative readings of Franklin and Equiano, some using the comparison as the primary focus and others noting comparative elements as part of a larger argument. For a few specific examples, see Dana D. Nelson, Susan Marren, and Ross J. Pudaloff.

3. Examples of these readings can be found, respectively, in Srinivas Aravamudan (*Tropicopolitans*), Ross J. Pudaloff, and Adam Potkay.

4. This notion of doubleness and the concept of competing experiences of identity and affiliation draws heavily on the work of Paul Gilroy, whose concept of the "Black Atlantic" is useful for introducing students to the complex and shifting senses of location, identity, and affinity experienced by black subjects in the Atlantic World.

5. In working through this comparison, it is important to emphasize that Franklin and Equiano did not have a direct influence on one another. Indeed, their narratives were published at different times—Equiano's *Interesting Narrative* in 1789 and the first part of Franklin's *Autobiography* in 1793—making any intentional connections or borrowings between the two texts unlikely. Nevertheless, asking students to trace the similarities and differences within these works can be a useful exercise for helping them understand the process (and the value) of pursuing a text-based analysis, as opposed to reading works solely in terms of authorial intention. Moreover, pursuing a comparative reading, without reference to biographical connections, can also help students to locate these two narratives as part of a shared historical and discursive framework.

6. To provide students with an overview of the concept of the public sphere and the anonymous and disinterested dimensions of eighteenth-century public discourse, I often draw on the ideas presented in the work of Michael Warner, Jay Fliegelman, Christopher Looby, and Nancy Glazener.

7. Critics have written at length about the performative dimensions of *The Interesting Narrative,* noting specifically how Equiano "cultivate[s] careful personae that ingeniously mimic—and subvert—dominant discourses" (Carretta and Gould 4). See also Houston A. Baker Jr., Keith A. Sandiford, and Henry Louis Gates Jr. (particularly *The Signifying Monkey*).

8. For a few examples of versions of this argument, see Srinivas Aravamudan (*Tropicopolitans*), Joseph Fichtelburg, and Henry Louis Gates Jr. (*Figures in Black*).

9. Susan Marren and Ross J. Pudaloff both offer useful readings of how *The Interesting Narrative* exposes the ethical and ideological contradictions of slavery through its account of how Equiano "buys" his own freedom, and their discussions offer helpful ideas for preparing class discussions.

Works Cited

Aravamudan, Srinivas. "Equiano Lite." *Eighteenth-Century Studies* 34.4 (Summer 2001): 615–19.

———. *Tropicopolitans: Colonialism and Agency, 1688–1804.* Durham: Duke UP, 1999.

Baker, Houston A., Jr. *Blues, Ideology, and Afro-American Literature: A Vernacular Theory.* Chicago: U of Chicago P, 1984.

Bugg, John. "The Other Interesting Narrative: Olaudah Equiano's Public Book Tour." *PMLA* 121.5 (Oct. 2006): 1424–42.

Carretta, Vincent. "'Property of the Author': Olaudah Equiano's Place in the History of the Book." *Genius in Bondage: Literature of the Early Black Atlantic.* Ed. Vincent Carretta and Philip Gould. Lexington: UP of Kentucky, 2001. 130–50.

Carretta, Vincent, and Philip Gould. Introduction. *Genius in Bondage: Literature of the Early Black Atlantic.* Ed. Vincent Carretta and Philip Gould. Lexington: UP of Kentucky, 2001.

Crèvecoeur, J. Hector St. John de. *Letters from An American Farmer.* 1782. Ed. Susan Manning. New York: Oxford UP, 1999.

Davidson, Cathy. "Olaudah Equiano: Written by Himself." *Novel: A Forum on Fiction* 1–2 (Fall 2006–Spring 2007): 18–51.

Equiano, Olaudah. The Interesting Narrative *and Other Writings.* Ed. Vincent Carretta. New York: Penguin, 1995.

Emerson, Ralph Waldo. "Self-Reliance." *Self-Reliance and Other Essays.* New York: Dover, 1993. 19–38.

Fliegelman, Jay. *Declaring Independence: Jefferson, Natural Language, and the Culture of Performance.* Stanford: Stanford UP, 1993.

Franklin, Benjamin. *The Autobiography.* 1791. *The Norton Anthology of American Literature.* Ed. Nina Baym. 4th ed. Vol. I. New York: Norton, 1994. 487–600.

Fichtelburg, Joseph. "Word Between Worlds: The Economy of Equiano's *Narrative.*" *American Literary History* 5 (1993): 459–80.

Gates, Henry Louis, Jr. *Figures in Black: Words, Signs, and the "Racial" Self.* New York: Oxford UP, 1987.

———. *The Signifying Monkey: A Theory of African-American Literary Criticism.* New York: Oxford UP, 1989.

Gilroy, Paul. *The Black Atlantic: Modernity and Double Consciousness.* Cambridge, MA: Harvard UP, 1993.

Glazener, Nancy. "Benjamin Franklin and the Limits of Secular Civil Society." *American Literature* 80.2 (June 2008): 203–31.

Lauter, Paul. "On the Implications of the *Heath Anthology:* Response to Ruland." *American Literary History* 4.2 (Summer 1992): 329–33.

Lockhard, Joe, and Jillian Sandell. "National Narratives and the Politics of Inclusion: Historicizing American Literature Anthologies." *Pedagogy: Critical Approaches to Teaching Literature, Language, Composition, and Culture* 8.2 (2008): 227–54.

Looby, Christopher. *Voicing America: Language, Literary Form, and the Origins of the United States.* Chicago: U of Chicago P, 1998.

Marren, Susan. "Between Slavery and Freedom: The Transgressive Self in Olaudah Equiano's Autobiography." *PMLA* 108.1 (Jan. 1993): 94–105.

Nelson, Dana D. "Reading the Written Selves of Colonial America: Franklin, Occom, Equiano, and Palou/Serra." *Resources for American Literary Study* 19.2 (1993): 246–60.

Potkay, Adam. "History, Oratory, and God in Equiano's *Interesting Narrative.*" *Eighteenth-Century Studies* 34.4 (Summer 2001): 601–14.

Pressman, Richard S. "Is There a Future for the *Heath Anthology* in the Neo-Liberal State?" *Symploke* 8 (Jan. 2001): 57–67.

Pudaloff, Ross J. "No Change Without Purpose: Olaudah Equiano and the Economies of Self and Market." *Early American Literature* 40.3 (2005): 499–527.

Ruland, Richard. "Art and a Better America." *American Literary History* 3.2 (1991): 337–59.

Sandiford, Keith A. *Measuring the Moment: Strategies of Protest in Eighteenth-Century Afro-English Writing.* Selinsgrove, PA: Susquenanna UP, 1988.

Warner, Michael. *Letters of the Republic: Publication and the Public Sphere in Eighteenth-Century America.* Cambridge, MA: Harvard UP, 1992.

Wheeler, Roxann. "Domesticating Equiano's *Interesting Narrative.*" *Eighteenth-Century Studies* 34.4 (Summer 2001): 620–24.

Winthrop, John. "A Model of Christian Charity." 1630. *Puritan Political Ideas.* Ed. Edmund S. Morgan. Indianapolis: Hackett, 2003. 75–93.

Equiano's *Interesting Narrative* and the Difficulties of Teaching the Early American Literature Survey Course

Michael Pringle

The undergraduate early American literature class poses unique problems for a professor teaching within the conventional literary historical periods: the era is not particularly "early" in relation to the British and European literature to which students have been exposed; the "American" designation is dubious for many of the texts they will read; and the category of "literature" necessarily must be expanded to include personal journals, relations, memoirs, pamphlets—in short, the primal stuff of history. Course readings will challenge students' deeply internalized myths of America's founding and force them to grapple with the nebulous categories of "history" and "literature": therefore, teaching such a course requires a clearly defined methodology to help students contextualize antebellum American texts within an English-designated course. The problem is that the struggle for disciplinary clarity often comes at the expense of exploring the subtle ways genre distinctions fail us, and tends to privilege one discipline over another. How much can we poach on "historical" territory? How far can we muddy the waters and still provide a rich and useful coverage of the era? While there is no single, definitive methodology that will solve the stickier genre troubles for all teachers of early American literature, the demotion/promotion of portions of *The Interesting Narrative of the Life of Olaudah Equiano, or Gustavus Vassa, the African. Written by Himself* (1789) from historical narrative to fiction provides a particularly useful way of framing the discussion.[1]

The upper-division early American literature course is necessarily a forum for discussing the nature of how the stuff of history becomes narrative, and how fiction becomes history. Perhaps in no other literature class do we expose students to so many non-literary texts in the form of relations, accounts, journals, personal narratives, and (of course) histories. I teach at a small liberal arts college, and we delineate the early American literary historical period from the Colonial period to the 1840s. The course could very easily be taught as a history class; indeed, I inevitably draw a group of history majors when I teach it. It is essential, therefore, that I have a clearly defined methodology for distinguishing what it is precisely that makes mine a literature course, without giving short shrift to the many primary historical texts. Equiano's *Interesting Narrative* comes conveniently at midterm in a survey course set up on a literary historical model, and it offers an exemplary test case for trying out some of the theoretical concepts students have been exploring in earlier texts. At mid-semester they have already worked through the structure of historical texts such as Cabeza De Vaca's *Relation,* Bradford's *Of Plymouth Plantation,* Rowlandson's captivity narrative, and Franklin's *Autobiography;* likewise, they have also studied overtly literary texts such as Bradstreet's poetry, Wigglesworth's "Day of Doom," and Taylor's poetry. Equiano's narrative marks a boundary in the course, the pivotal moment when we move from poetry and personal narrative to the study of prose fiction. Because the *Interesting Narrative* employs both personal narrative and fictional narrative prose, it is both useful and problematic in marking the shift.

There are a number of possible ways to frame the discussion, and the fact that it is an American literature class places some institutional limits on interdisciplinary range. Nonetheless, to remain too firmly entrenched in a literary bunker raises some significant hurdles. One time-honored way to deal with the issue is to privilege the literary works and introduce the historical contexts as essential background material for fully grasping the great literature of the later periods. To understand Hawthorne's "The Maypole of Merry-Mount" or *The Scarlet Letter,* for example, one has to have read *Of Plymouth Plantation,* "A Model of Christian Charity," and Rowlandson's *A Narrative of the Captivity and Restoration of Mrs. Mary Rowlandson,* among other texts. The problems with such an approach are manifold. Most notably it devalues the majority of the course readings as simply contextual preparation for enjoying a few canonical works at the end of the semester. Furthermore, less canonically accepted works, such as Rowson's *Charlotte Temple,* or Foster's *The Coquette,* do not fit comfortably into such a schema. English majors trained in a formalist tradition wince when they read the sentimental excesses of such works and justifiably wonder why we would read a novel that so obviously fails to meet the traditional standards of literary excellence in a literature class.

When pointing out that we need to read *Charlotte Temple* because it was the most popular novel of its century and that it engages essential issues of its day, I justify the choice by citing its historical importance. Yet privileging the historical value of the sentimental novel necessarily calls into question how "The Maypole of Merry-Mount" could be more highly valued than other historically important texts from our course readings, such as Jefferson's first draft of "The Declaration of Independence" or Paine's *Common Sense.* Because this is a claim few of us would justify, we need to frame the objectives of the course differently. Another way to define the class is to claim that we will bring the tools of literary analysis to "important" texts of the Colonial, Early Federal, and Romantic literary eras. Hayden White's *Metahistory* (1973) provides the classic analytical framework for the close reading of "historical" narratives as literary constructs. Rendering historical texts into the divisions of "plot," "characterization," and "narrative" provides a comforting model for an English professor, and yields some undeniable advantages in framing an early American literature course. This pedagogical strategy helps reinforce the close-reading skills prized at our institution, it gives equal weight to texts regardless of genre, and it helps provide clear transitions between literary and historical texts. Such an approach is also amenable to a variety of cultural and poststructural methods of dealing with textual matter. To point to just one example, it is easy to transition from White's concept of history as narrative story to Bakhtin's concept of dialogism and heteroglossia. Treating "objective" history as another kind of narrative fiction makes for an easy transition into the concepts of deconstruction, new historicism, and cultural criticism.

The toolbox of theoretical approaches we bring to our courses can certainly enrich the ways we teach, but it is important to keep in mind that our theoretical choices have pedagogical consequences. When teaching a novel such as *Charlotte Temple,* for example, I tend to treat it as one facet of a broader discursive movement concerning gender roles and social justice. The problem with such an approach is that it tends to lead everywhere, and the boundaries of literary criticism crumble to a rubric of cultural context. The rabbit hole has no end, and to privilege the historical and cultural contexts can lead to as many problems as privileging only the literary aspects of the course. If the clear distinctions of "history" and "literature" of previous generations seem too rigid to those of us schooled in a postmodern climate, we should also consider the value of such boundaries and think through the ramifications that breaking down the genre barriers and blurring distinctions will have on course structure and, consequently, our students.

The very instability of Equiano's *Narrative* in terms of genre, discipline, nationality, and authenticity makes it an ideal text for discussing the ways differing disciplinary approaches and expectations intersect and sometimes clash. Of course, if we are not to blur the boundaries too much, we must clarify as much as possible of where they lie. At mid-semester students have been briefly exposed to some of the ideological, cultural, gender, and class assumptions that undergird the structure of "literary history" via critics as diverse as Harold Bloom, Jane Tompkins, Terry Eagleton, and Stephen Greenblatt. While it is impractical to cover in one semester the last thirty years of debate on literary history, it is feasible to take specific examples of critical approaches I find helpful into this early American literature course. For example, fresh critical approaches applied to sentimental fiction by literary historians have expanded the concepts of how literature and culture intersect. Nina Baym, Jane Tompkins, and Cathy Davidson, among others, have struggled to show the institutionalized biases against sentimental fiction, and due to their work, critics that judge works such as *Uncle Tom's Cabin* or *Charlotte Temple* as unimportant seem fairly antique. Jane Tompkins points out that the modernist certainty of what constituted "good" literature and "mawkish" literature blinded critics to *Uncle Tom*'s complexity, and "how it connects with the beliefs and attitudes of large masses of readers so as to impress or move them deeply" (xiv). Tompkins manages to explore the cultural tensions with which the novel is in dialogue without wandering too far afield, and in the process of retelling the literary history of the mid-nineteenth century changes the way we read and understand sentimental fiction.

Although what "everybody knows" about sentimental fiction today makes critics interpret literary facts differently, we cannot definitively argue that our interpretive scheme is any more objective than was the modernists' literary history of mawkish, silly, sentimental women's stories. We can follow the lead of literary historians such as Tompkins and Davidson, however, by invoking a fuller historical context in our criticism and by analyzing the ways authors use fiction to do social work. Asking what the category of "history" can mean to a person born in slavery and stripped of familial, cultural, and national heritages, for instance, expands the conceptual framework for how we apply the term. The fictional creation of a genesis, family, and home that opens the *Interesting Narrative* can be framed as an act of reclamation and resistance, as well as a manifesto for political change in regard to the abolition movement. Pedagogically speaking, this critical investigation means asking why an author makes certain choices from more than one perspective (artistic, personal, rhetorical, political, etc.). This strategy helps us move beyond labeling the text as being historically "inaccurate" to exploring the work's construction in light of a number of differing purposes.

From a literary perspective, we notice that some early portions of the narrative employ sentimental passages to move readers that might have come straight from the page of popular eighteenth-century fiction. An example of such "purple prose" comes when the protagonist has been separated from his sister: "Yes, thou dear partner of all my childish sports! thou sharer of my joys and sorrows! happy should I have ever esteemed myself to encounter every misery for you and to procure your freedom by the sacrifice of my own" (680).[2] Like the sentimental novelists, Equiano employs emotion to draw the reader into sympathizing with his larger cause, and adds interest to his tale in a vernacular familiar to his audience. I tend to compare this stylistic choice to novels such as Rowson's *Charlotte Temple* and Foster's *The Coquette,* with their focus on bringing awareness of gender inequities: "Is she gone! Gone in this most distressing manner? Have I lost my once loved friend: lost her in a way I could never have conceived possible? Our days of childhood were spent together in the same pursuits, in the same amusements" (Foster 902). The Equiano quote is from the (most likely) fictionalized portion of the narrative, but is "fiction" just a euphemism for "hoax" here? How much do the fictional elements of the work diminish its value as a historical narrative, if at all? How much does it matter that Equiano was an eyewitness to many such scenes? It helps in pursuing these questions to point out that no one has yet found a way to avoid narrative "emplotment" altogether, nor to provide an entirely objective way to delineate history.

It is easy to become discouraged by the problems of subjectivity with which literary history presents us, and it is possible to become paralyzed by the wave of subjectivity that has crashed over the postmodern community. One response to this condition is to simply accept that there is no recoverable past in any objective sense, and to revel in our present subjectivity by imposing it at will on "history." If no amount of rigorous historical research can yield an objective historical moment, then why try? Since "we can never be anything other than participants in the stories we are driven to tell" (Nelson 17), we should concentrate on making them pertinent to our contemporary condition rather than trying to make them correspond with an impenetrable past. While I cannot demonstrate any "objective" access to the past, I heartily disagree with Cary Nelson's position. Because historical evidence is slippery, it *increases* our responsibility to try to historicize rather than decreases it. Lee Patterson describes this job well:

> Literary historians know, perhaps too well, that there is no magical elixir (least of all "theory") that will enable them to tell the truth about either literature or history. But they must also not ignore the scrupulousness and inclusiveness that attend a commitment to the theoretically problematic yet ethically indispensable desire to get it right. (261)

Much of the shift in the way we view literary history has to do with the shift in how we view power relationships in early America, which draws on a complex picture inherent in a Foucauldian concept of power as network rather than as a single locus. Of course, bringing up Foucault's notion of power also invokes his use of the terms "discourse" and "discursive," which largely frames the work of Davidson and Tompkins. The "field of discourse" pertinent to their investigations is extremely wide, ranging from personal diaries, letters, and wills to public sermons, court decisions, newspaper articles, public records, and contemporary histories of the era. While the use of such sources is not entirely novel in literary history, the range of such sources has increased and become more prevalent in contemporary literary histories. Texts that seemed marginal and unimportant to other historians take on central importance in cultural treatments of early American power relations, and it is that expansion of what is important and what informs the understanding of our early history that makes the field so interesting. In cultural, discursive studies we cannot escape the influence of Foucault: "One impoverishes the question of power if one poses it solely in terms of legislation and constitution, in terms solely of the state and state apparatus" (158). Current literary historians frame questions of power and resistance in ways that help us read Equiano with fresh eyes.

Because of the wider range of critical strategies now taught, as well as the more complex integration of culture and history into literary studies, we presently occupy a key moment to appreciate more fully Equiano's narrative strategies.

Brian McHale has analyzed the many problems to be found in narrative history in our current "postmodern condition," and he concludes that for all its faults narrative is still the best option. "Reflecting on the role of narrative in the organization and transmission of literary-historical knowledge, I have come more and more to emphasize the narrativity, the storytelling character, of my own pedagogical practice" (7). Stephen Greenblatt calls such emplotment "cultural poetics," and he readily confesses the fictional aspects of exploring the complex interactions between fiction and social institutions. Greenblatt is notoriously anecdotal, but is unapologetic about his narrative strategy: "I remain possessed by stories and their complex uses" (1). While critics no longer lay claim to "objective" history, and the new historicist foregrounds her or his own ideology, as well as trying to uncover past ideological struggles, any attempts to "historicize" literature are still "stories" that will be subject to the vicissitudes of time and social conditions. When compared to earlier course readings that were "emplotted," such as Morton's biased account of the incidents of Merry-Mount and Rowlandson's providential view of the Native Americans, the fictionalized elements of Equiano's narrative seem to qualify as "historical." He was in an excellent position to know slaves who had been taken prisoners in Africa and who had survived the Middle Passage, and he knew firsthand the ins and outs of slave trading ships through his employment as a first mate in Mr. King's service. Why then should the simple slip into the first-person point of view of "the African" disqualify his text as "history" and relegate it to "fiction?" The resulting discussion of the power of fiction to encapsulate historical "truth," the need for transparency and openness in historical texts, and the interplay between fiction and history generally proves productive in approaching the blurred edges of literary and historical boundaries without erasing them.

Because the *Interesting Narrative* stands as one of the early accounts of an African taken into slavery and sold in the New World, it remains of great historical importance. It has justly become required reading in early American literature courses, and my students generally compare it favorably to the grim, heavily typological Puritan narratives. They often praise Equiano's descriptive passages and his ability to involve emotionally the reader in the narrative: a frequent comment is that he gives the reader a strong sense of what it must have felt like to be a slave in the eighteenth century. Recent scholarship, most notably Vincent Carretta's *Equiano, the African: Biography of a Self-Made Man* (2005), has made a strong case that Equiano had never been in Africa; rather, he was born in South Carolina:

> Reasonable doubt raised by the recent biographical discoveries inclines me to believe that the accounts of Africa and the Middle Passage in *The Interesting Narrative* were constructed—and carefully so—rather than actually experienced and that the author probably invented an African identity. But we must remember that reasonable doubt is not the same as conviction. (xiv)

Nonetheless, the evidence is compelling, and it seems likely that Equiano's history of growing up in Africa, of the slave trade there, of the Middle Passage, and of being sold in the West Indies is actually "fiction" (perhaps better described as "historical fiction" or "biographical fiction") while the later portions of his work comport with the known facts of his life. After my students have read the first half of the narrative I tell them about the likelihood that it was not autobiographical, and ask them if it matters whether or not what is recorded in the text actually happened to Equiano (the *Norton* commentary on authenticity seems to slip by all but the most scrupulous readers).[3] After reading this commentary, it seems as though the editors wish to downplay the controversy surrounding the text, but I believe that the issue of biographical accuracy offers a goldmine of pedagogical possibilities, and I press my students to confront it. Does it matter? A few feel a sense of betrayal while some actually like it better as historical fiction/biography, but the answer is always nearly unanimous: YES, it matters.

The contradictory mixtures of "borrowed" biography and historical accuracy, personal aggrandizement (he does make himself an African prince, after all), and frank admissions of the humiliations he suffered make it a complex text to categorize. In limited ways, it is similar to popular memoirs that proved to be hoaxes, and several recent incidents suggest that the distinction between fiction and history is very important to Americans. For example, James Frey's "factual" autobiography, *A Million Little Pieces,* caused quite a stir in 2005 when it was discovered that he had fictionalized the more lurid sections of the work to increase the book's appeal. Readers were scandalized, feeling that the tale of redemption that had so moved and motivated them was really a cheap scam. Not least among these outraged readers was Oprah Winfrey, who had originally praised the book (thus greatly increasing its sales), and later vigorously denounced the book and author for cheating readers. While there were a few attempts—primarily by university professors—to question whether or not it mattered if the story were strictly factual if it achieved its objective as moral exemplum, the resounding answer was

YES, it matters! Another instance of popular interest in the subject may be found in the movie *The Hoax,* which chronicles the false autobiography of Howard Hughes. Yet another example is the work of Laura Albert, who published "memoirs" for a decade under the pen name of Jeremiah "Terminator" LeRoy. Although Albert claimed the pseudonym was simply artistic license, she was convicted of fraud in 2007 and had to pay reparations for her hoax. These examples have stirred enough popular interest that the majority of students in the class know of some, or all, of them, and they offer a way to make the issue feel contemporary as we discuss Equiano's text.

The outrage contemporary readers felt at these falsified memoirs is echoed in the sense of betrayal some readers feel towards the *Interesting Narrative.* As Adam Potkay notes, "few of us can really or finally transcend the customary world of authors and concrete events—especially when it come to autobiography" (604). Potkay resolves the problem by placing a higher value on rhetoric: "*The Interesting Narrative* is far less significant as a factual account of one man's life than as a rhetorical performance of considerable skill" (604). Yet the question will not so easily go away, because it does matter to many readers that he represents himself as something he was not. How much do the cultural conditions that Equiano was held in slavery, that he was in a position to know intimately about the horrors the Middle Passage (one of his more moving chapters), and that he had a right to resist his oppressors in whatever way possible also matter? His historical condition as a slave born in America trying to escape from bondage makes it difficult to judge Equiano in the same way as Frey or Albert (who were simply seeking notoriety and money), but does this point distinguish his use of false autobiography from theirs? Does, as Potkay claims, the text's political success in aiding abolition absolve any stretching of the truth?

Another point of view (similar to that of the *Norton* introduction) is that the actual facts of Equiano's youth do not matter much at all, so long as he gets the communal story right.

> The matter will continue to be debated, but for present purposes it does not matter. If Equiano was born in West Africa, he is telling the truth—as he remembered it, modified by subsequent experience—about his enslavement and voyage on a slave ship. If he was born in South Carolina, he could have known what he knew only by gathering the lore and experience

> of people who had been born in Africa and made the dreaded Middle Passage aboard the slave ship. He thus becomes the oral historian, the keeper of the common story, the griot of sorts, of the slave trade, which means that his account is no less faithful to the original experience, only different in its sources and genesis. (Rediker 109)

While the narrative will not resolve into a single category, trying out the labels of "autobiographical hoax" versus "keeper of the common story" elicits some excellent classroom discussion, and at midpoint in the semester the students have the vocabulary and historical context to debate the topic in some depth. I assemble students into groups (selected by their own preferences) to make an argument for the best label (drawn from other texts we have read to that point) for Equiano's work. Abolitionist tract? Literary fiction? Autobiographical hoax? Communal account? Captivity narrative? Travel narrative? Ethnography? The subsequent debates go straight to the heart of the subjective view of literary history and genre distinctions. The best outcome is when students realize the text will not fit into any of the selected boxes.

Historical context is essential for reading this text—though I confess to never being able to supply enough within the time constraints of a survey course. In parallel to the charged topic of hoaxes today, the eighteenth-century criticism of Equiano's work was political and social dynamite, and the proslavery contingent staged the most belligerent attacks on the veracity of the narrative. The narrative's importance to the abolitionist cause can scarcely be overestimated, and their fierce defense of the text's truthfulness in reference to the horrors of slavery coincided with their need to bring those terrors into public view (both Carretta and Rediker are good sources for historic context). Equiano's engaging style and compelling story made it highly popular, and his narrative served as a perfect instrument for abolitionist groups to sway public opinion towards ending the slave trade. That, of course, was also Equiano's aim in the narrative, but not his only one. The charged political and cultural elements surrounding the text no doubt affected the way later scholars refused to pursue doubts concerning the narrative's factuality (which, in turn, highlights the persistence of racial tensions in the West). Recent hoaxes like LeRoy's or Frey's cause outrage in readers, but the depth of emotional, political, and social investment in those works pales in comparison to the exponentially higher eighteenth-century investment in Equiano's narrative.

The importance of its "truthful" status raises interesting questions in light of the text's efforts to do social work. Do the higher cultural stakes make Equiano's falsification even more troubling? Does the fact that the proslavery advocates were partially correct about the narrative's reliability lend credence to their arguments? Did he have a moral right to re-create a stolen past? Or, did the abolitionists have it right—did Equiano tell an essentially true story that the world needed to hear? From the abolitionist's point of view, the *Interesting Narrative* largely functioned as a captivity narrative. Forced into this genre mold, it was essential to organized abolitionists that Equiano not be a trickster figure nor fictionalize any elements of his story. The text served its contemporary political purpose, but what is its status now? The larger sweep of "history" can do strange things to facts, and the question of what we are prepared to recover infringes on our reading. For example, in one hundred years when teacher-scholars analyze this particular historical moment (and we are no longer alive to feel betrayed by Frey), how will literary historians like Tompkins or Davidson discuss the top-selling nonfiction book of 2005 to understand the interests and anxieties of individuals in this decade? The sensational aspects of its partial fictionality will likely be relegated to a footnote. While it is useful to compare Equiano's text to other captivity narratives (such as Cabeza De Vaca's, Morton's, and Mary Rowlandson's texts), it defies the category in as many ways as it emulates it. The potent blending of fact and fiction around this emotionally and politically charged narrative serves to engage thoroughly students in the more academic questions of "literariness" and "historicity."

If students do not come up with it themselves during the discussion, I draw on the parallel of Benjamin Franklin's use of an alter ego in the *Autobiography.* The similarities between Equiano's and Franklin's texts are strong throughout, and Franklin's earliest use of a persona is, for multiple reasons, surprisingly close to Equiano's. Finding himself apprenticed to his abusive brother, Franklin tricks James into publishing his essays under the pen name of "Silence Dogood." "Tho' a brother, he considered himself as my Master, and me as his apprentice; and accordingly expected the same Services from me as he would from another; while I thought he demean'd me too much in some he required of me" (484). Demeaned, and even beaten, Franklin avenges himself on James by fooling him into accepting essays for publication in his paper under an assumed identity. "Silence Dogood" is an obvious pseudonym and Franklin acknowledges the deceit when it served his purpose, neither of which is true for Equiano; nonetheless, Equiano also uses a fictional persona to wreak a little vengeance on demeaning and abusive masters. There is a "trickster" element for both writers, but Equiano did not have the luxury of revealing his trick, because the stakes were higher in maintaining his pretense. The false persona was important not only to Equiano personally but essential to finding an audience and exposing the larger historical truths of the barbarity of the peculiar institution.

Like Franklin, Equiano assumes a tone of scientific detachment at times, and some passages read like descriptive travel narratives. In a creative, fictional scene his alter ego (the captured young African prince) describes in lush detail the African countryside before being taken onboard a European slaving vessel. There, the empirical, "age of reason" tone turns the tables on whites, and they become the terrifying savages under scrutiny by a more civilized race. The nightmarish scene of a slaving ship full of "cargo" reverses the contemporary stereotypes, and the humane narrator fears the violent barbarians in charge of it all. He wonders, "[W]ere we not to be eaten by those white men with horrible looks, red faces, and long hair" (683). The narration includes such a wealth of detail—smells, sounds, deck conditions—that it reeks of authenticity (it was, indeed something Equiano had seen with his own eyes), and the terror of the scene makes the fear of cannibalism seem justified. "I had never seen among any people such instances of brutal cruelty; and this was not only shown towards us blacks, but also to some of the whites themselves" (683). The fictional narrator allows Equiano to describe a white ethnography from the slave's perspective, but despite the fictionality of the plot, the early, highly accurate description of the Middle Passage remains historically important. Furthermore, the fictional plot reveals a harsh reality that too many contemporary readers were willing to ignore or deny. Not quite fictional history, not quite historical fiction, the narrative is *sui generis,* and hops boundaries to achieve differing narrative goals.

We currently inhabit a rare moment when something old has become new, and the *Interesting Narrative* is once again a politically and socially charged text. The issues of authenticity surrounding Equiano's work offer teachers of the Early American survey course an entry point into some of the more complex issues of genre and interdisciplinarity. It provides the perfect test case to toss out the really big questions: What is literature? And, what is history? While I do not find it beneficial to tell students categories are unimportant, via Equiano's work we thoroughly test the limitations of genre and disciplinary boundaries.

After the "labeling" exercise, the classroom will have fallen into differing camps and students will have formulated and defended their positions. The strongest students quickly discover the weaknesses of their own positions. By the time we leave Equiano's narrative, all will have discovered the limitations of any one label for, or approach to, this multivalent work. This parallels my own tenuous position, for while I set any text within the rubric of "discursive practices" in a given time period, I ground my course as "literary" and work from that bias to explore a work's respective relationships to "history." The reasons for doing so are largely institutional because there are no compelling reasons inherent in some texts to privilege a "literary" approach; however, the distinction is important. I respect students' instinctive need for boundaries, and believe they need an organizing set of concepts to make sense of early American literature. Although I push them to recognize how arbitrary and fragile those boundaries sometimes are, it is not my intention to erase them. Equiano gives us a complex narrative that resolves into a compelling story and an important historical document no matter how many ways an instructor parses and presents it. It is a remarkably flexible and fortuitous text to occupy the mid-semester slot of the Early American survey course.

Notes

1. Questions about Equiano's narrative, most notably Vincent Carretta's *Equiano, the African: Biography of a Self-Made Man* (2005), indicate he was born in South Carolina, not Africa.

2. I have cited the *Norton Anthology of American Literature,* volume A, throughout this essay, because it is the text I use in the upper-division survey course.

3. The seventh edition *Norton* commentary reads:

> Recent scholarship has questioned these claims, suggesting that Equiano may have been born in the Carolinas. If this is true, it would mean that the narrative constitutes his decision to assume an African heritage, the testimony of someone from a marginalized group who speaks for the entire group's history. To make his own life appear more representative, Equiano thus merges his personal story with that of the voiceless African who has had to endure the horrors of the Middle Passage. (W. Franklin 674)

Works Cited

Baym, Nina. "Melodramas of Beset Manhood: How Theories of American Fiction Exclude Women Authors." *American Quarterly* 33.2 (1981): 123–39.

Carretta, Vincent. *Equiano, the African: Biography of a Self-Made Man.* Athens: U of Georgia P, 2005.

Davidson, Cathy N. *Revolution and the Word: The Rise of the Novel in America.* New York: Oxford UP, 1986.

Equiano, Olaudah. *The Interesting Narrative of the Life of Olaudah Equiano, or Gustavus Vassa, the African. Written by Himself. The Norton Anthology of American Literature.* Ed. Nina Baym, Jerome Klinkowitz, Arnold Krupat, Mary Loeffelholz, and Patricia B. Wallace. 7th ed. Vol. A. New York: Norton 2003. 675–709.

Foster, Hanna Webster. *The Coquette. The Norton Anthology of American Literature.* Ed. Nina Baym, Jerome Klinkowitz, Arnold Krupat, Mary Loeffelholz, and Patricia B. Wallace. 7th ed. Vol. A. New York: Norton, 2003. 807–904.

Foucault, Michel. *Power/Knowledge: Selected Interviews and Other Writings.* Ed. Colin Gordon. New York: Pantheon, 1980.

Franklin, Benjamin. *The Autobiography. The Norton Anthology of American Literature.* Ed. Nina Baym, Jerome Klinkowitz, Arnold Krupat, Mary Loeffelholz, and Patricia B. Wallace. 7th ed. Vol. A. New York: Norton, 2003. 473–587.

Franklin, Wayne. "Olaudah Equiano." *The Norton Anthology of American Literature.* Ed. Nina Baym, Jerome Klinkowitz, Arnold Krupat, Mary Loeffelholz, and Patricia B. Wallace. 7th ed. Vol. A. New York: Norton, 2003. 674–75.

Frey, James. *A Million Little Pieces.* New York: Doubleday, 2003.

Greenblatt, Stephen. *Marvelous Possessions: The Wonder of the New World.* Chicago: U of Chicago P, 1991.

The Hoax. Dir. Lasse Hallström. Miramax, 2006.

McHale, Brian. *Constructing Postmodernism.* New York: Routledge, 1992.

Nelson, Cary. *Repression and Recovery: Modern American Poetry and the Politics of Cultural Memory, 1910–1945.* New York: Routledge, 2001.

Patterson, Lee. "Literary History." *Critical Terms for Literary Study.* Ed. Frank Lentricchia and Thomas McLaughlin. Chicago: U of Chicago P, 1989. 250–62.

Potkay, Adam. "History, Oratory, and God in Equiano's *Interesting Narrative.*" *Eighteenth-Century Studies* 34.4 (2001): 601–14.

Rediker, Marcus. *The Slave Ship: A Human History.* New York: Penguin, 2007.

Tompkins, Jane. *Sensational Designs: The Cultural Work of American Fiction, 1790–1860.* New York: Oxford UP, 1986.

White, Hayden. *Metahistory: The Historical Imagination in Nineteenth-Century Europe.* Baltimore: The Johns Hopkins UP, 1973.

The Difference Teaching Equiano Makes: Notes on Teaching *The Interesting Narrative* in the Undergraduate American Literature Survey

Lisa M. Logan

> So we must admit to our students that the study of literary works, great ones or otherwise, will neither make them behave more ethically nor lead them to THE TRUTH. Why, then, teach literature *anyway?* Because, I would posit, *literary study* is the only discipline that teaches difference—from the linguistic difference between, say, the indefinite article and the definite one . . . or to the difference, constructed in language between one individual and another. . . . [I]n the end any poem or novel or autobiography that is of more than passing interest always escapes the system imposed on it, opening itself up to yet another system or set of norms down the road. In this context, the much maligned language-game know[n] as "close reading" is perhaps our first obligation to students. Close reading simply means reading attentively and bringing to the text in question as much knowledge and practice as possible.
>
> **—Marjorie Perloff (January 5, 2009)**

> Attention is "the taking possession by the mind, in clear and vivid form, of one out of what seem several simultaneously possible objects or trains of thought. . . . It implies withdrawal from some things in order to deal effectively with others, and is a condition which has a real opposite in the confused, dazed, scatterbrained state which in French is called 'distraction.'"
>
> **—William James (1890)**

I teach American Literature I, which the University of Central Florida's undergraduate catalog defines as "[m]ajor American writers from beginning through Whitman." Such description invites the kinds of questions literary scholars ask undergraduates to think about critically: What and/or who is American? What texts qualify as American literature? When did such literature "begin"? And what on earth is a "major" writer? During regular fifteen-week semesters, when we have time to read entire texts rather than excerpts from large anthologies, I approach this course using real and fictionalized personal narratives, which we consider as a sort of "literature of witness" and an extended dialogue about these questions. My current course description follows:

> American Literature I surveys texts produced in what is now the United States from colonial settlement through the mid-19th century, a period when concepts of an American landscape, nation, citizens, and literature were being consciously formulated. We will examine how this literature depicts an animated and evolving conversation about definitions of American nation, geography, self, and literature by comparing texts by men and women writers from different socioeconomic, ethnic, and cultural backgrounds. Because the production of literatures is imbedded in particular historical moments, we will consider these texts in and be responsible for understanding the specific contexts from which they emerged. Primarily, we will explore the ways that the assigned texts struggle with definitions of "America" and "Americans" and what is at stake—for us and for the writers we read—in those definitions.

Given this emphasis on personal narratives, we use online editions of texts and smaller anthologies, such as Henry Louis Gates Jr.'s *The Classic Slave Narratives* and William L. Andrews, Sargent Bush Jr., Annette Kolodny, Amy Schrager Lang, and Daniel B. Shea's *Journeys in New Worlds: Early American Women's Narratives.* To get a feel for how personal narratives and histories operate, I begin with online excerpts from Cabeza de Vaca's *Narrative,* John Smith's *Description* or *General History,* and Bradford's *Of Plymouth Plantation;* in each case we consider how the narrator constructs a self with relation to the "American" landscape and the people he encounters. Students learn to recognize that none of these writers is "American," and that America as an idea emerges from Western Europeans who write for specific purposes. Using *Journeys in New Worlds,* we read Rowlandson's *The Sovereignty and Goodness of God* and other eighteenth-century representations of the self found in that volume, including the *Journal of Madam Knight* and *Some Account of the Fore Part of the Life of Elizabeth Ashbridge.* We also read Franklin's *Autobiography,* Samson Occom's *A Short Narrative of My Life* (online), and the subject of this essay, *The Interesting Narrative of Olaudah Equiano.* Equiano's text reinforces the difficulty of the term "American," as it resists firm placement in African, U.S., African American, British, and Caribbean literary canons.

Personal narratives of the early Americas pose many challenges for twenty-first century students, including the difficulties of early modern language, spelling, and capitalization; the discomfiting prominence of religion; the emotional opacity (for a generation accustomed to blogs, tweets, text messaging, Oprah, and reality TV); and, of course, the question of why in the first place our English Department maintains a "Literature before 1865" requirement. From a pedagogical perspective, one might describe the source of the consistent and recurring challenges in working with personal narratives as their "difference." For example, they are generically "different." While the modern memoir genre attracts a popular readership, students of literature at my public university of fifty thousand expect to read stories (all of which are frequently called "novels") or poems (decidedly not stories but still literary because of the way they look on the page). As well, seventeenth- and eighteenth-century personal narratives operate according to different assumptions about the purpose and value of literature itself. Students often respond with uncertainty when these early texts convey clear political or religious motives, which violate their sense of how "art" should work. I remind them that literature emerges from specific contexts and that all of us—readers and writers—live in a world in which political, social, and cultural institutions shape not only our lives but our capacity to imagine. Over the years several students have buttressed their objections to reading personal narratives by disqualifying these texts as literature (which, I infer, is loosely defined by its resemblance to a novel); diaries, memoirs, autobiographies, and travel journals are, according to these students, more appropriate for history courses because they reveal information about life in a past time.

If students are able to understand literary productions as cultural artifacts, these objections diminish. Therefore, I often require that students view digitized versions of first editions in the *Early American Imprints* (Evans) database; facsimiles of original title pages, dedications, illustrations, and subscriber lists render visible the cultural work these texts performed when they were first published. The size, binding, and typeface are compelling illustrations of how texts circulated among early audiences. For unpublished texts, copies of manuscript pages can anchor students in the rhetorical situation of the writer. The size and shape of the paper, the presence of inkblots, and the handwriting itself add another layer to our interpretive processes. By performing close readings of textual apparatus and treating texts as cultural artifacts worthy of rhetorical analysis, we anticipate patterns of language within the text proper that may have gone unnoticed.

To this end, I assign a rhetorical analysis of the front matter of published works. This exercise familiarizes students with the ways that print matter engaged particular audiences. Focusing on the front matter only, students read closely the advertisements, subscriptions, illustrations, dedications, and prefaces that accompany the text proper and come to a better understanding of how texts operated in a public sphere. To facilitate their work, I assign Trish Roberts-Miller's excellent online introduction to rhetorical analysis, "Understanding Misunderstandings," which explains in accessible language the rhetorical triangle, implied and actual authors, and logos, pathos, and ethos. Most students report that Roberts-Miller's online handout empowers them. Undergraduates lack experience with the processes literary scholars use to unpack texts and often suspect that their professors' analyses "take things too far." This pedagogical exercise demystifies close reading, showing with clear examples how to think beyond merely what a text says to how it works.

Second, I use a generic "blueprint" for reading personal narratives, developed from Margo Culley's introductory essay to her edited collection of women's diaries, *A Day at a Time.* This blueprint addresses the most frequent response I hear from students regarding their initial readings of diaries, autobiographies, and journals: Okay, so now what? That is, faced with a textual entity that fails to operate in familiar ways, students want to know what exactly to look for and how to talk about what they find. Students learn to frame their textual encounters as literary responses with the following questions: What role does the audience assume for the writer? How does she address the diary/audience? What things are repeated? If actions are repeated, how do they create the structure of text? What organizing ideas shape the narrating "I"? What symbols come to represent the subject? And, what "silences" are found in the text—places where the text *doesn't say* something?

These questions serve as a literary Global Positioning System for personal narratives, which Sidonie Smith and Julia Watson have called a "transparently simple" and yet "amazingly complex" genre (15). Grounding students in close reading of language patterns, these questions remind us that literary analysis uses language as data to illuminate texts—however strange or unfamiliar. By focusing on strategies for reading (rather than on covering specific texts), the course prepares our graduates to teach American literature to high school or community college students. Knowing how to ask literary questions, students can manage even unfamiliar works with confidence.

Finally, Smith and Watson include a "Tool Kit: Twenty Strategies for Reading Life Narratives." Particularly relevant to this essay, the sections "Authorship and the Historical Moment" and "The Autobiographical I" provide explanations and sample questions for unpacking the historical situation of text, author, and reader and for analyzing voice in the narrative. These tools reinforce our emphasis on the historical and cultural contexts of personal narratives. Students inevitably begin with the issues they grapple with most: authorship, including authorial intent, origins, and truth value, or "what *really* happened." Drawing on Cathy N. Davidson's *Revolution and the Word,* I help them to understand authorship as part of the eighteenth-century book business. Emphasizing the production and circulation of texts as well as the "autobiographical I" reminds us that personal narratives construct selves, or characters, and that our job in a literature class is to understand how and why those constructed selves operate—then and now.

With these three frameworks, we approach Equiano's *Interesting Narrative.* New research suggesting that Equiano may have been born in South Carolina has intensified student concerns about authorship and authenticity and jeopardized Equiano's narrative ethos with this twenty-first-century readership.[1] Despite the inconclusiveness of the research even according to those who have conducted it, students are poised for scandal.[2] Many contend that if Equiano was not a native of present-day Nigeria, as he maintains, then he presented a fictionalized account of his childhood in Africa and his experience during the Middle Passage, which makes him an unreliable narrator and unworthy of their trust. I anticipate these responses by directing students in the reading guide I provide to Brycchan Carey's website, which presents a point-by-point overview of the evidence on both sides of this birthplace debate and a lucid explanation of the implications for each point. As well, the recent discovery of a portrait at the Royal Albert Memorial Gallery adds to confusion by casting doubt on whether the portrait that appears in eighteenth-century editions is Equiano's own.[3] Too much focus on the factual content of the narrative mirrors the strategies used by Equiano's eighteenth-century detractors, who attacked his personal credibility to minimize his arguments against slavery.[4] An inordinate concern with factual truth seems to arise often when studying texts by women and people of color, and it can deflect us from literary concerns.[5] All too frequently, these considerations about factual authenticity, while important, use precious class time that could be better used to consider how the texts themselves operate. Perhaps some students privilege concerns about authenticity because that kind of discussion enables a more general discussion than one that focuses on the close analysis of language. That is, close analysis demands their labor in the classroom. Yet, curiously, the most vociferous authorship-based objections I have experienced in the classroom occur around texts by women and people of color.[6] Equiano's text confronts readers, demanding that we identify with the stolen African slave boy amidst white savages; he presents Western culture as alien, unnatural. The experience of reading Equiano reminds me of bell hooks's questions about location or the situatedness of subjects.

> Within complex and ever shifting realms of power relations, do we position ourselves on the side of colonizing mentality? Or do we continue to stand in political resistance with the oppressed, ready to offer our ways of seeing and theorizing, of making culture, towards that revolutionary effort which seeks to create space where there is unlimited access to the pleasure and power of knowing, where transformation is possible? (145)

These questions push us past easy dismissals of the narrative as inauthentic to how the narrative challenges both eighteenth- and twenty-first-century cultural norms. How does Equiano position himself "on the side of colonizing mentality" and how does he "stand in political resistance"? Moreover, how do we as readers do so? Equiano's narrative takes up a history of the Middle Passage and the transatlantic slave trade that undergraduates (and their professors) in American universities may be more comfortable forgetting. Many first-time readers of Equiano accept that slavery is part of the history of the Americas but believe that the United States has moved on to a fairer, more color-blind society (ostensibly evinced by the election of President Barack Obama). bell hooks, invoking South Africa's Freedom Charter and the "struggle of memory against forgetting," suggests that remembering is an important process in the movement against oppression. She argues that the "politicization of memory" can "illuminate and transform the present" (147). From a pedagogical perspective, Cathy N. Davidson positions the debate brilliantly: "[W]hat do we learn *because* of the specific questions we ask and, equally important, what do we *not* learn because we have chosen to ask those questions?" ("Olaudah Equiano"18).

The question of the author's factual origins opens a space for important discussions about what is at stake in complicating (versus simplifying) identity by situating it. As many scholars have noted, Equiano does not fit neatly into one category—African, American, British, or some hyphenated combination of some or all of those categories. When studying so many authors in a survey course, students can be quick to pigeonhole—Mary Rowlandson is a religious fanatic, Sarah Kemble Knight a racist, classist complainer, Samson Occom a sellout, and Benjamin Franklin a hypocrite. Yet one of the reasons literature, especially early literature of the Americas, is so crucial to study is that it challenges us, as Marjorie Perloff writes, with difference, demanding that we question our snap judgments and move past what a text *says* to careful analysis of how its language works. That is, we all think we know how to read; but the study of literature requires us to try harder, to push past the surface, and, often, to notice how two or more competing ideas coexist in a text. For example, Equiano both castigates and embraces aspects of Western culture. As a narrator, Equiano enacts the close reading process by asking readers to view Western culture and the particulars of the transatlantic slave trade with new eyes, those of an African. This narrative perspective constitutes a kind of analysis that defamiliarizes the world that his audience—and we—knew about but failed to read as closely as we could.[7] For literary scholars, *The Interesting Narrative* demonstrates, as Davidson observes, that "a text can be simultaneously polemically powerful and unresolved" ("Olaudah Equiano" 22). Susan M. Marren writes that Equiano's text constructs a

> narrative self . . . [that] challenges his readers to scrutinize the very social structure that their preoccupation with racial difference had sought to mask . . . [and] interrogat[es] the boundaries that separate the apparently distinct, apparently oppositional categories into which Western culture has organized itself: black/white, male/female, master/servant, Christian/heathen, civilization/savagery, freedom/slavery. (94–95)

From its frontispiece and dedication and throughout his travels on twenty-six different ships, the narrative interrogates boundaries.[8] In British and American editions, the title page identifies its author and subject as "Olaudah Equiano, or Gustavus Vassa, the African," citing both his African and European names.[9] Many editions included an engraved portrait of Equiano, a person of obvious African descent dressed in proper British attire and holding a Bible open to Acts 4:12 ("Neither is there salvation in any other: for there is none other name under heaven given among men, whereby we must be saved.").[10] Commentary on the frontispiece abounds, much of it emphasizing Equiano's "difference." Molesworth argues that this image "signifies doubly: in addition to portraying the author as a modern apostle, the portrait offers the Bible as the very instrument whereby the author's pious 'acts' . . . are accomplished" (125). Holbrook Gerzina contends that, like Equiano's multiple names, the portraits are "emblematic . . . of his hybridized national identity" (47). Carrigan finds that the title page "deeply problemati[zes] the conception of self as singular, complete, and static" (44). Bozeman claims that Equiano is "neither the singular African nor Briton" but "inhabit[s] an interstitial landscape caught between an identity to which he can never fully return and one in which he will never be allowed to fully partake" (61). Certainly, the engraving renders visually the cognitive dissonance many eighteenth-century readers felt about an educated, erudite African. The portrait affirms Equiano's complex identity, visually enacting the deconstruction of "apparently oppositional categories": black/white, African/English, master/servant, Christian/heathen, freeman/slave.

The engraving also provides a good opportunity to introduce students to double-consciousness, a fundamental concept in African American literature. I provide W. E. B. Du Bois's definition of double-consciousness and ask students to identify aspects of the portrait that support Equiano's self-construction as an African and as a British citizen.

> [T]he Negro is a sort of seventh son, born with a veil, and gifted with second-sight in this American world,—a world which yields him no true self-consciousness, but only lets him see himself through the revelation of the other world. It is a peculiar sensation, this double-consciousness, this sense of always looking at one's self through the eyes of others, of measuring one's soul by the tape of a world that looks on in amused contempt and pity. One ever feels his two-ness,—an American, a Negro; two souls, two

> thoughts, two unreconciled strivings; two warring ideals in one dark body, whose dogged strength alone keeps it from being torn asunder. (Du Bois)

In this exercise, I ask students to think about the choices they make about self-presentation when sitting for important photographs. By recalling what elements of their appearance they plan, from facial expression to setting to clothing, hair, and glasses, students easily apprehend how portraits (like the texts we read) operate as constructions of self. Although Equiano is not American, his position as a minority in dominant culture, his experience "looking at [him]self through the eyes of others, of measuring one's soul by the tape of a [white] world" impacted his decisions in writing and publishing *The Interesting Narrative.* This conversation anticipates a concern that arises much later in their reading, when students wonder why Equiano adopted so much of the culture that oppressed him and was himself complicit in the trading and keeping of slaves. Helpful for thinking through these issues are bell hooks's reflections on "the reality of what it means to be taught in a culture of domination by those who dominate" (150). hooks notes the importance, as a person of color, to "separate useful knowledge" from other "ways of knowing that would lead to estrangement, alienation, and worse—assimilation and co-optation" (150). In what ways do Equiano's acquisition and mastery of Western knowledge empower him? In what ways does Equiano's Western knowledge permit or prevent him from maintaining an oppositional perspective on colonization and slavery? Such questions help us to situate Equiano as a worker, writer, and self-publisher who toured behind various editions of his wildly popular (in Great Britain, at least) text.[11]

Equiano's narrative deconstructs disciplinary boundaries as well, including history and literature, and its "hybrid form" complicates generic categories. As Davidson notes, "[t]he text combines (in unequal parts) slave narrative, sea yarn, military adventure, ethnographic reportage, historical fiction, travelogue, picaresque saga, sentimental novel, allegory, tall tale, pastoral origins myth, gothic romance, conversion tale, and abolitionist tract" ("Olaudah Equiano" 19).[12] *The Interesting Narrative* is at once none and all of these genres, eluding our systems of categorization. Similarly, the text escapes national boundaries, as the case could be made for teaching it in American, British, and "World" literature courses offered at my university. One result of the hemispheric work of the text is that large anthologies excerpt only those sections that contribute to a particular literary history. For example, in American anthologies, the most frequently excerpted portions of the text concern Equiano's youth, kidnapping, and forced march in Africa; the Middle Passage and subsequent voyages throughout the Americas; and his struggle for and acquisition of freedom. The narrative movement created by these excerpts suggests two quintessential American stories, the ex-slave narrative and the adventure story. In the latter, the hero—Columbus, Smith, Bradford, Ashbridge, Franklin—arrives by boat and makes his or her own way in the New World.[13]

Indeed, some have argued that we view the pervasive imagery of the ship and the ocean in *The Interesting Narrative* as metaphors for the position of the narrator. As Janelle Collins notes, the sea in European literature is often "a site of adventure, opportunity, exploration, and profit. In contrast, the sea in Middle Passage literature always symbolizes captivity and barbarity" (213). Equiano's narrative uses the sea in both ways. *The Interesting Narrative* first presents the sea and the ship through Equiano's terrified child's eyes. In Chapter 2, the sea is a site of brutality and betrayal, for "riding at anchor, and waiting for its cargo" (Equiano 38) is the slave ship, where Equiano is overcome with "terror," "horror," "anguish," and "despair" (38–39). On the slave ship "white men with horrible looks, red faces, and loose hair" beat, flog, rape, tease, and torture "a multitude of black people of every description chained together" (39). However, Equiano also acquires education, opportunity, and, finally, liberation through his work on ships at sea. Equiano survives the Middle Passage, learns reading, writing, and arithmetic, ship navigation, Christianity, and commerce, and, finally, purchases his freedom.[14] But that freedom is always tenuous, as the narrative points out, because the ghost of slavery follows him continuously. Equiano's entry into the Americas by the slave ship contrasts well with Benjamin Franklin's *Autobiography.* In that text, the young Franklin enters Philadelphia from the Delaware River by boat, his pockets "stuffed out with shirts" as he takes his emblematic walk down Second Street, three great puffy rolls under his arms. Franklin associates his entry into a new world with abundance and possibility, while Equiano finds starvation and limitation. Through the metaphor of the ship upon the ocean, Equiano's text illustrates how self-ownership and self-construction are intersectional and complicated processes, especially for people who live in the margins. Davidson writes,

> Given the inherent insecurity of being an African or of African descent in a world where black people are enslaved, watchfulness is a precondi-

> tion of Equiano's existence. His is not a Moses-like journey from slavery to freedom, but rather, an episodic and often anxious narrative meandering—from freedom to kidnapping by other Africans, from one form of African slavery into a far more barbarous enslavement by European slavers in the hold of a ship bound for Barbados, from one owner to another, from a promised freedom to disappointment, from ferocious activity to save money to buy his liberty to a manumission marred by the constant threat of re-enslavement. ("Olaudah Equiano" 19)

Like Franklin, Equiano demonstrates assiduous frugality and determination, yet he ultimately resigns his sea ventures because of the difficulties of being a person of African descent in the Atlantic World.[15]

Equiano's decision to quit the sea can be read against another iconic scene in Franklin, when the Philadelphia printer wheels a barrow full of paper through the streets. Franklin writes that "to secure my Credit and Character as a Tradesman, I took care not only to be in *Reality* Industrious & frugal, but to avoid all *Appearances* of the Contrary" (73). Students view Franklin's concern with appearances as the charade of a consummate politician who matches his performance to audience expectations. In Equiano's *Narrative,* no performance of industry can overcome his physical appearance as an African in a white world. Equiano works and studies hard, avoids drink, and practices frugality, whether as a seller of glass tumblers or a merchant seaman. Yet his identity as an African marks his difference and prevents his success.

Ironically, as an African child, he was destined for but kidnapped before he received the mark of embrenche, which was carved into the faces of chiefs and elders in his tribe. As a free black in the Atlantic World, Equiano, who styles himself "Freeman" and "African," is frantic to preserve himself from physical marks of slavery on his body. Threatened with flogging during a brief stay in Georgia, Equiano writes that he "dreaded, of all things, the thoughts of being striped, as I never in my life had the marks of any violence of that kind" (108). He determines that he "would sooner die a free man, than suffer myself to be scourged, by the hands of ruffians, and my blood drawn like a slave" (108). Although Equiano eludes the scars of public flogging, he is nonetheless marked by Western ideas about Africans and "race." Fed up with "so many impositions in my commercial transactions in different parts of the world . . . [Equiano] became heartily disgusted with the seafaring life," and "determined not to return to it, at least for some time" (166).

During most of the narrative, Equiano is "'situated' at sea and therefore unrooted, in a state of continual movement" (Carrigan 45). As Gretchen Holbrook Gerzina points out, "Particularly for black slaves and free men and women the ocean [w]as a symbol of movement" (42).[16] Black sailors experienced "relative freedom from national boundaries" (48) and unusual mobility, privilege, and wealth compared to most slaves.[17] Marion Rust argues that Equiano "obtains the greatest authority" (23) on water, a "transitional medium in both physical and spiritual terms" (24). "Rules that exclude him from full membership in London society do not apply there" (23). However, we mistake Equiano's milieu if we equate the movement the sea enables with freedom. Robert Reid-Pharr articulates the tenuousness such mobility proffered: "On board ships, slaves fought in the wars of free and republican nations. The protocols of race were thrown by the wayside one moment, then taken up with a vengeance the next" (xiii). As Equiano's text reveals, "the environment aboard ships could be toxic and often deadly" (xiii). Again, Reid-Pharr articulates this duality:

> As a practical matter of survival, eighteenth-century sailors, both bond and free, had to overcome not only the sea, the elements, and the ships themselves, but also the rather complex social structures that these ships bore from one continent to another. . . . [T]his meant that his freedom was always in process, as it were, was always being negotiated with every new relationship, including those that he formed with his captors. (xvi)

Equiano himself expresses the complexity of his position, which he must constantly renegotiate, by recounting a stormy night on Montserrat:

> While I thus went on, filled with the thoughts of freedom, and resisting oppression as well as I was able, my life hung daily in suspense, particularly in the surfs I have formerly mentioned, as I could not swim. These are extremely violent throughout the West-Indies, and I was ever exposed to their howling rage and devouring fury in all the islands. (89)

Here Equiano uses the metaphor of the sea to express his own situatedness. Holding "freedom, and resisting oppression" in his mind even as his "life hung daily in suspense," Equiano makes his careful way through "extremely violent" surfs. Like the unpredictable white people, who by turns offer him opportunity and hold him in chains, or perhaps the savage slave traders who handled him on the slave ship, the surfs buffet the ship with "howling rage" and "devouring fury." Equiano, who mastered English and ship navigation, cannot swim; instead, he survives by wearing a jacket that keeps him a bit above water and by calling on a man near him who was a good swimmer. Equiano's navigation of this near-drowning parallels his negotiation of Western culture, which he accomplishes with resourcefulness, self-education, and the goodwill of certain well-meaning white individuals.

In that same chapter, Equiano relates "a very curious imposition on human nature" that occurs at St. Kitts, in which a white man wishes to marry a free black woman who "had land and slaves in Montserrat" (88). Since the clergyman will not defy the "law of the place" forbidding a racially mixed marriage in a church, the parties move the ceremony to the water. The wedding, a personal act of resistance to institutionalized oppression, occurs aboard two boats, the clergyman and parson on one, the couple seeking marriage on another. As Paul Gilroy notes, ships are "cultural and political units rather than abstract embodiments of the triangular trade . . . a means to conduct political dissent and possibly a distinct mode of cultural production" (17). On two tiny boats, the parties enact their personal defiance and political dissent. Following the ceremony, the happy couple climbs aboard Equiano's ship where his "captain treated them extremely well, and brought them safe to Montserrat" (Equiano 88). Yet soon thereafter, "a very clever and decent free young mulatto-man" is stolen by a Bermuda captain and "forcibly taken out of our vessel" (90). Such are the "violent surfs" of Western culture through which Equiano sails.

Reading the sea and the ship metaphorically illuminates the text and its hero's capacity to traverse national, generic, and disciplinary borders. Citing Equiano's traversal of three continents on twenty-six ships, William Boelhower treats "the ship figure as semiotic operator in producing Atlantic space." Boelhower analyzes the ship and the modern world map in a transatlantic context, as "critical conduits for the flow of peoples, goods, and ideas back and forth between Europe, Africa, and the Americas" (33). Just as the ship represents movement, Equiano's account questions the relationship between human identity and nation. For example, the words "country" or "countrymen" are used thirty-two times. Equiano identifies himself on the title page as "the African," uses his African name, which he tells his readers means "fortunate," and dedicates his work as "an instrument towards the relief of his suffering countrymen" (7). He ruminates on nationalism, pondering "whether the love of one's country be real or imaginary, a lesson of reason or an instinct of nature" (32). Whatever its source, Equiano identifies himself as African via the use of the words "country" or "countrymen" fourteen times in Chapter 2, the account of the slave ship and the Middle Passage, but soon thereafter states that he was "almost an Englishman" and "quite easy with these new countrymen" (56). As he learns to read the Bible, he is "wonderfully surprised to see the laws and rules of my own country written almost exactly" there (68). Later in the narrative, when he accompanies Dr. Irving to Jamaica to begin a plantation, he assists Irving in procuring slaves who were "all of [his] own countrymen" (155). This enterprise positions him alongside the English Irving, who purchases slaves by boarding a "Guineaman" and carrying them across the ocean to perform his labor. When Equiano leaves Irving's service, he notes that "[a]ll of my poor countrymen, the slaves, when they heard of my leaving them, were very sorry, as I had always treated them with care and affection, and did everything I could to comfort the poor creatures, and render their condition easy" (159–60). As Laura Doyle observes, Equiano demonstrates whites' dependence on blacks in the Atlantic (184); Equiano's knowledge of sailing and the transatlantic trade insure Irving's success. These narrative elements place Equiano's text within "hemispheric studies," in which "nation-state borders are repeatedly transgressed, blurred, and negated, and differences between individuals and groups residing in disparate countries are frequently represented as nonexistent, minor, or irrelevant" (Nwankwo 582).

Reading Equiano closely, we learn to hold apparently conflicting ideas together: Equiano is cargo and merchant, African and British, a sailor who cannot swim, an ex-slave who purchases slaves himself, an African who embraces much of the culture of his captors and persecutors. Often, students respond to Equiano's conversion (to Christianity and Briton) with disbelief—he cannot really be a Christian, a slaveowner, a person who swallows the "master's tools" hook, line, and sinker. Perhaps he writes with irony, sarcasm, and caginess, some suggest. Equiano's *Narrative* exemplifies the process of how we need to read closely, attentively, and with the sense that, as a product of humans, literature opens up the difficult possibility that conflicting ideas can coexist. In some ways, Equiano's several roles as slave, ex-slave, and slave trader, exemplify his potential to become Henry A. Giroux's "oppositional intellectual": "homeless—in exile and living on the border, occupying an unsutured, shifting, and fractured social space in which critique, difference, and a utopian potentiality can endure" (74). Moving among masters, nations, oceans, audiences, as goods and as agent, Equiano the narrator reaches out across shifting and fractured time and space to remind us that difference matters.

Notes

1. Vincent Carretta, drawing on historical documents in Great Britain and the United States (baptismal record, British naval muster lists, etc.), has raised questions about Equiano's birthplace based on his findings. However, not all scholars are convinced. John Bugg states that "[s]o alluring is this supplement to Equiano's evident self-fashioning that the evidence seems secondary" ("The Other Interesting Narrative" 1424). Bugg writes unequivocally that "there is no 'Vassa' on the muster roll" (1425). See Carretta ("Deciphering") for that scholar's most recent iteration of his position and his response to Bugg. Additionally, Davidson summarizes her unpublished conversations with several scholars on the debate ("Olaudah Equiano" 24, 27–33).

2. See Davidson's essay for an overview of what is at stake in these arguments for and against Equiano's birthplace in South Carolina.

3. Brycchan Carey's website includes reproductions of both images and explains the controversies about Equiano's African or South Carolinian origins and the two portraits using clear and accessible prose. See Carey's links for "Where was Equiano Born?" and "The Equiano Portraits" at http://www.brycchancarey.com/equiano/index.htm.

4. Carretta (*Equiano*) discusses early positive reviews and finds that "the apologists for slavery left the authority of the work and the binomial identity of its author unchallenged, watching the book become a bestseller" (97). Carretta writes that the author's "true identity" raised questions when Equiano toured Edinburgh before the publication of the fifth Edinburgh edition of *The Interesting Narrative.* As a result, according to Carretta, Equiano responded to these attacks on his origins in the preface to the fifth edition.

5. Teaching "Captivity and the National Imagination" with UCF historian, Rosalind J. Beiler, has heightened my attentiveness to distinctions between historical and literary questions and evidentiary claims and given rise to a coauthored handout I use in literature classes that outlines the primary differences.

6. Some of the most vociferous objections on the basis of authorship I have encountered in the classroom occurred around Harriet Jacobs's *Incidents in the Life of a Slave Girl.* Jacobs's black female narrator radically challenges dominant cultural ideas about race, gender, and authority that persist even today. Jean Fagan Yellin has devoted an entire scholarly career to documenting the biographical details of Jacobs's life for a skeptical academy. For a discussion of how marginal positions create sites of resistance, see hooks's essay "Choosing the Margin as a Space of Radical Openness" (149).

7. Marren uses the term "defamiliarize" in her excellent essay (98).

8. Boelhower provides a useful list of the ships Equiano names (31).

9. Bozeman believes that Equiano uses the name imposed upon him as a slave to promote his book to a "consumer base that has come to know him as Equiano. As a financial move, the decision to lead in the title with 'Equiano' again allows the author to declare himself on his own terms" (65).

10. Ito outlines the differences between the first American edition and several British editions. He notes that the narrative was probably read as part of the debate about abolition in Britain and was "immensely popular in England," while it "left little, if any, impression on American readers, for whom it functioned as post-revolutionary rhetoric" (83). As well, Ito examines the subscriber lists to show that British subscribers were prominent individuals while American subscribers were mostly artisans.

11. In "The Other Interesting Narrative," John Bugg details Equiano's book tours.

12. Carrigan maintains that *The Interesting Narrative* belongs to the "postcolonial life-writing" genre (42).

13. This informal survey included Bedford, Heath, and Norton anthologies of American literature.

14. As Carretta notes, Equiano eventually was ranked as an "able seaman, the highest-paid, most skilled and prestigious rank below an officer in the Navy" ("Olaudah" 102).

15. Bozeman discusses Equiano's "middle-class values" (65, 68).

16. Holbrook Gerzina also argues that the ocean is often a symbol for religious conversion. Her description of the historical situation of black slaves and free men and women in eighteenth-century England is especially helpful (45–46).

17. Gerzina relies on Bolster for some of her claims.

Works Cited

Andrews, William L., Sargent Bush Jr., Annette Kolodny, Amy Schrager Lang, and Daniel B. Shea, eds. *Journeys in New Worlds: Early American Women's Narratives.* Madison: U of Wisconsin P, 1990.

Boelhower, William. "'I'll teach you how to flow': On Figuring Out Atlantic Studies." *Atlantic Studies* 1.1 (2004): 28–48.

Bolster, W. Jeffrey. *Black Jacks: African American Seamen in the Age of Sail.* Cambridge, MA: Harvard UP, 1997.

Bozeman, Terry S. "Interstices, Hybridity, and Identity: Olaudah Equiano and the Discourse of the African Slave Trade." *Studies in the Literary Imagination* 36.2 (2003): 61–70.

Bugg, John. "Deciphering the Equiano Archives: Reply to Vincent Carretta." *PMLA* 122.2 (2007): 572–73.

———. "The Other Interesting Narrative: Olaudah Equiano's Public Book Tour." *PMLA* 121.5 (2006): 1424–42.

Carey, Brycchan. Home page. 20 February 2010. http://www.brycchancarey.com.

Carretta, Vincent. "Deciphering the Equiano Archives." *PMLA* 122.2 (2007): 571–72.

———. *Equiano, the African: Biography of a Self-Made Man.* Athens: U of Georgia P, 2005.

———. "Olaudah Equiano or Gustavus Vassa? New Light on an Eighteenth-Century Question of Identity." *Slavery and Abolition* 20.3 (1999): 96–105.

Carrigan, Anthony. "Negotiating Personal Identity and Cultural Memory in Olaudah Equiano's *Interesting Narrative.*" *Wasafiri* 21.2 (2006): 42–47.

Collins, Janelle. "Passage to Slavery, Passage to Freedom: Olaudah Equiano and the Sea." *Novel: A Forum on Fiction* 39.1 (2005): 209–23.

Culley, Margo. Introduction. *A Day at a Time: The Diary Literature of American Women from 1764 to the Present.* Ed. Margo Culley. New York: Feminist P, 1985. 3–28.

Davidson, Cathy N. "Olaudah Equiano, Written by Himself." *Novel* 40.1–2 (Fall 2006–Spring 2007): 18–51.

———. *Revolution and the Word: The Rise of the Novel in America.* New York: Oxford UP, 1986.

Doyle, Laura. *Freedom's Empire: Race and the Rise of the Novel in Atlantic Modernity, 1640–1940.* Durham: Duke UP, 2008.

Du Bois, W. E. B. *The Souls of Black Folk.* 1903. Bartleby.Com Website. 15 May 2010 <http://www.bartleby.com/114/1.html>.

Equiano, Olaudah. *The Interesting Narrative of the Life of Olaudah Equiano, or Gustavus Vassa, the African. Written by Himself.* Ed. Werner Sollors. New York: Norton, 2001.

Franklin, Benjamin. *The Autobiography and Other Writings.* Ed. Kenneth Silverman. New York: Penguin, 1986.

Gates, Henry Louis, Jr., ed. *The Classic Slave Narratives.* New York: Signet, 1987.

Gilroy, Paul. *The Black Atlantic: Modernity and Double Consciousness.* Cambridge, MA: Harvard UP, 1993.

Giroux, Henry A. "Higher Education Under Siege: Implications for Public Intellectuals." *Thought and Action: The NEA Higher Education Journal* 22 (Fall 2006): 63–78.

Holbrook Gerzina, Gretchen. "Mobility in Chains: Freedom of Movement in the Early Black Atlantic." *South Atlantic Quarterly* 100.1 (Winter 2001): 41–59.

The Holy Bible: King James Version. U of Michigan Digital Library. 2000. May 2010 <http://quod.lib.umich.edu/cgi/k/kjv/kjv-idx?type=DIV1&byte=4870983>.

hooks, bell. "Choosing the Margins as a Space of Radical Openness." *Yearning: Race, Gender, and Cultural Politics.* Boston: South End, 1990. 145–54.

Ito, Akiyo. "Olaudah Equiano and the New York Artisans: The First American Edition of *The Interesting Narrative of the Life of Olaudah Equiano, or Gustavus Vassa, the African.*" *Early American Literature* 32.1 (1997): 82–101.

James, William. "Attention." *The Principles of Psychology. Classics in the History of Psychology Website.* Online. Ed. Christopher D. Green. 20 Feb. 2010 <http://psychclassics.asu.edu/James/Principles/prin11.htm>.

Marren, Susan M. "Between Slavery and Freedom: The Transgressive Self in Olaudah Equiano's Autobiography." *PMLA* 108.1 (1993): 94–105.

Molesworth, Jesse M. "Equiano's 'Loud Voice': Witnessing the Performance of *The Interesting Narrative.*" *Texas Studies in Literature and Language* 48.2 (2006): 123–44.

Nwankwo, Ifeoma C.K. "The Promises and Perils of US African American Hemispherism: Latin America in Martin Delaney's *Blake* and Gayl Jones's *Mosquito.*" *American Literary History* 18.3 (2006): 579–99.

Perloff, Marjorie. "The Centrality of Literary Study." U of Chicago P Blog. 20 February 2010 <http://pressblog.uchicago.edu/2009/01/05/audacity_of_literary_studies.html>.

Reid-Pharr, Robert. Introduction. *The Interesting Narrative of the Life of Olaudah Equiano, or Gustavas Vassa, the African,* by Olaudah Equiano. Ed. Shelly Eversly. New York: Modern Library, 2004. vii–xxi.

Roberts-Miller, Trish. Home page. "Understanding Misunderstandings: How to Do a Rhetorical Analysis." 14 March 2010 <http://www.drw.utexas.edu/roberts-miller/handouts/rhetorical-analysis>.

Rust, Marion. "The Subaltern as Imperialist: Speaking of Olaudah Equiano." *Passing and the Fictions of Identity.* Ed. Elaine K. Ginsburg. Durham: Duke UP, 1996. 21–36.

Smith, Sidonie, and Julia Watson. *Reading Autobiography: A Guide for Interpreting Life Narratives.* Minneapolis: U of Minnesota P, 2001.

U of Central Florida Undergraduate Catalog. 14 March 2010 <http://www.catalog.sdes.ucf.edu/UCFUGRDCatalog0910.pdf>.

Captives, Slaves, and Writers: Teaching *The Narrative* of Olaudah Equiano as Captivity Narrative

Abby Chandler

The 1789 publication of *The Interesting Narrative of the Life of Olaudah Equiano or Gustavus Vassa* (hereafter Equiano's *Narrative*) introduced an important player in the abolition movement taking place on both sides of the Atlantic Ocean in the late eighteenth century. For the first time, abolitionists hoping to outlaw the transatlantic slave trade had a readily available eyewitness to the brutalities suffered by slaves transported to the Americas. "I was soon put under the decks," writes Equiano, "[where] I received such a salutation in my nostrils as I had never experienced in all my life" (Equiano 33). Equiano's vivid descriptions made it possible for abolitionists to argue that the slave trade was a devastating experience for its forced participants and not one easily dismissed or forgotten. In addition to detailing his experience of the Middle Passage, the *Narrative* also provided readers with descriptions of Equiano's life as a slave and his eventual bids for literacy, religious salvation, and personal freedom, among other significant aspects.

Like many scholars of early American history, I teach a survey course whose chronology ranges from the period prior to European contact to the conclusion of Reconstruction in 1877. Some students of this survey course are history majors who need the class as a prerequisite for upper-level course work, some are non-majors interested in history, and others are non-majors for whom the class is a requirement to be survived as painlessly as possible. Most of these students have little knowledge of the colonial period, but its very unfamiliarity often serves as a draw. This is not the quantum leap from Jamestown and Plymouth to the American Revolution they remember from high school. The opening classes introduce students to the players present in North and South America by the seventeenth century: Native Americans, Europeans, and Africans. While students occasionally complain that they signed up for *American* history, not a course on French, Spanish, or African history, this approach provides a vivid depiction of the complex cultural exchanges of the early modern Atlantic World. It also serves as a reminder that globalization was not created in the twenty-first century and that its challenges have always been part of American history.

Students first encounter Olaudah Equiano during the lecture on the African presence in the Western hemisphere as they prepare for class by reading the excerpt from Equiano's *Narrative* published in the course textbook, *America Firsthand,* vol. 1*: Readings from Settlement to Reconstruction.* This lecture discusses the changing slave trade, the horrors of the Middle Passage, and the growth of slavery in the Western hemisphere in the sixteenth and seventeenth centuries. From a chronological standpoint, reading Equiano's *Narrative* at this stage in the class is problematic as Equiano was part of the British abolition movement at the turn of the nineteenth century. Nevertheless, I find that the benefits of assigning Equiano at this point in the course outweigh the chronological issues. As the book's title suggests, *America Firsthand* is a collection of documents chosen to give students eyewitness views of historical events from a wide range of perspectives. Semester after semester, it is cited in student-teacher evaluations as a favorite part of the course by most students. This text also provides further pedagogical benefits as many of its documents offer the opportunity for rich comparative analysis, thereby making it possible to draw comparisons and connections throughout the entire course.

The excerpt from Equiano's *Narrative* published in *America Firsthand* describes his trip to North America on a slave ship. Having students read it in the second week of class highlights a point Equiano himself was eager to make: that the Middle Passage was equally horrifying to all those who experienced it. Passages like the one quoted above describing the stench below the deck of a slave ship have much the same effect on twenty-first-century students than they had on eighteenth-century readers. All the statistics in the world cannot replace firsthand accounts. Documents like these add a necessary level of urgency to a course about events and people now long gone but still relevant.

Having students read Equiano's *Narrative* in the early stages of an American history class also poses certain geographic issues to address. Olaudah Equiano himself spent very little time in North America as he was taken to Britain a few years after his arrival in the Western Hemisphere. Once he eventually gained his freedom, he chose to remain in Britain and become part of the flourishing British abolition movement at the turn of the nineteenth century. Without doubt, British scholars and teachers have a stronger claim to Equiano's history than their American counterparts. Nevertheless, he has long been appropriated by scholars of African American history as one of their own. Carla Mulford's essay collection *Teaching the Literatures of Early America,* for example, includes an essay by Amy E. Winans entitled "Diversity and Difference in African American Writings" that cites Equiano's *Narrative* as a frequent source used in classes on Africans in the American colonies. To point out a second example, Henry Louis Gates Jr. published a now well-known collection in 1987 titled *The Classic Slave Narratives,* which includes Equiano's *Narrative* as well as the text of the British and Caribbean writer Mary Prince and African American writers Frederick Douglass and Harriet Jacobs. Prince's account was first published in 1831 and describes her experiences as a slave in the West Indies. Douglass originally published his autobiography, *Narrative of the Life of Frederick Douglass, an American Slave,* in 1845, and it became a best seller with more than thirty thousand copies sold by 1850. Jacobs first began publishing serial accounts of her experiences in Horace Greeley's *New York Tribune* in the late 1840s. Her description of sexual abuse was deemed too shocking for book form, and *Incidents in the Life of a Slave Girl* was not published in book form until 1861. This twenty-five-year-old anthology compiled by Gates, therefore, shows another instance in which scholars have already placed Equiano in the canon of African American letters and in African American Studies courses.

Gates places Equiano's *Narrative* as the forerunner to these nineteenth-century slave narratives, "a *genre* of literature that at once testified against their captors and bore witness to the urge of every slave to be free" (ix; emphasis in original). By writing the first-hand account of a slave's struggle for freedom, he provided both literary and life models for other enslaved Africans in which nationality played a secondary role to ethnic identity. In addition, Gates sees Equiano's ability to read and write as a second model for African Americans: freedom was not fully attained until the ex-slave acquired literacy. Equiano's example was clearly embraced by many African Americans, as Marion Wilson Starling estimates that a total of 6,006 ex-slaves would eventually tell their stories through interviews, essays, and books (Gates ix). Equiano, himself, clearly preferred Britain to the United States and to the Caribbean. Nevertheless, his long commitment to the abolition movement suggests a man willing to have his life story used on both sides of the Atlantic Ocean in service to a valiant cause, whether recruiting future abolitionists in the late eighteenth century or teaching students in the twenty-first century.

While acknowledging Equiano's *Narrative* as a likely forerunner to the nineteenth-century slave narratives, I argue that, through my placement of Equiano's *Narrative* in this survey course, this text should also be read for its roots in the literary styles of the seventeenth and eighteenth centuries. Interpreting Equiano's autobiography only as the forerunner to a coming genre tells an incomplete story in the classroom. It is also necessary to provide students with the underpinnings beneath his world. The abolitionist movement came to fruition in the nineteenth century, but its founders frequently drew upon the writings from previous generations. Like contemporary writers today, their work was shaped by earlier writings which they responded to, incorporated, and rejected. This point is one easily extended across disciplines as students majoring in English will recognize evolving literary styles and the concept of intertextuality while students majoring in science are familiar with the importance that their discipline places on building upon previous experiments and discoveries to create new knowledge.

The captivity narrative was one of the most popular literary genres in the American colonies in the late seventeenth and eighteenth centuries. While the concept of the captivity narrative dates back to the medieval period, this essay focuses on the unique American variant of the genre. Lisa Voigt notes that early modern audiences had "a desire for captivity accounts in new and exotic locales [coupled with] eyewitness information about cultures and lands where Europeans hoped to extend commercial and territorial dominion" (1). The earliest of these narratives were oral accounts, told by Europeans captured by Native Americans or Native Americans captured by Europeans. Other captivity narratives featured Europeans taken captive by European, Islamic, or African pirates and privateers as ocean travel became more common. By the early seventeenth century, some European explorers had begun to publish their accounts, as we see in John Smith's *The Generall Historie of Virginia, New-England, and the Summer Isles,* first published in 1624. These early accounts placed the captivity experience as part of a larger narrative. While Smith describes being taken captive by the Powhatan tribe, his overall narrative details all of his North American experiences. Other accounts written by Spanish and Portuguese explorers taken captive at this period were written in a similar fashion.[1]

The turn of the eighteenth century, in contrast, saw the development of the captivity narrative as a specific literary genre in the New England colonies, one with a particular style of narration, intentions, and goals. Unlike narratives written by John Smith, Jose de Santa Rita Durao, and Juan Ortiz, these tales were largely intended to be read by a New England audience already residing in North America. Highlighting the challenges of living in a region continually at war was, consequently, less of an issue for presses hoping to sell their publications. Instead, these texts served as literary pulpits for the Puritan ministers who often edited these tales. As Anglo-American colonization increased in New England in the late seventeenth century, so did tensions with neighboring Native Americans tribes. These tensions eventually resulted in a long series of wars ranging from King Philip's War in the 1670s to King William's War in the early eighteenth century. Between 1675 and 1763, approximately 1,641 colonists were taken captive in New England (Vaughan and Clark 3; Little 91). Many of these captives returned to the English settlements while others were permanently absorbed into the families of their Native American or French captors. Similar to the argument found in this essay, my introduction of the New England captivity narratives opens with a wider discussion of the captivity narrative and its role in European history.

As a way of addressing the often negative portrayals of Native Americans in these works, students are reminded that these captivity narratives were written to document and to discuss the phenomenon of cultures coming into conflict with one another. An excerpt from the writings of Father Paul Le Jeune, a Jesuit missionary who lived among the Huron in the 1630s and 1640s, another text published in *America Firsthand,* provides students with an opportunity to examine the differences found in this literary genre. In their analysis of this text, students discover that while Le Jeune is often perplexed by the Huron, his long and peaceful relationship with them allows room for a more evenhanded portrayal (22–27). It is therefore important to highlight in the classroom the diversity that exists in this genre and to discuss with students the fact that not all writers of captivity narratives represent the "other" culture they come into contact with as uncivilized, unsophisticated, and alien.

The first of the New England captivity narratives to be published was Mary Rowlandson's *The Sovereignty and Goodness of God* (hereafter Rowlandson's

Sovereignty) in 1682.[2] Rowlandson was a minister's wife, living in Lancaster, Massachusetts. After Lancaster was attacked in February 1676, Rowlandson and her children were captured by the Wampanoag and Narragansett. Her youngest daughter died, and she was separated from her other children. After eleven long weeks, Rowlandson was ransomed back to her husband, Joseph Rowlandson. It is unclear precisely why Rowlandson decided to commit her story to paper, but her conclusion suggests she felt others would benefit from the lessons she has learned: "We must rely on God himself and our whole dependence must be upon Him. If trouble from smaller matters begins to arise in me, I have something at hand to check myself and say, why am I troubled?" (75). Rowlandson's *Sovereignty* was followed by a long series of books, pamphlets, and sermons, all detailing the experiences of their narrators. All of these texts proved immensely popular and Rowlandson's *Sovereignty* has never been out of print since 1770.

We find additional variations in this genre when we recognize that most of these other captivity narratives depict women captives, including the tale of Hannah Swarton, captured from her home in Casco, Maine, in 1690. Swarton's husband and oldest son were killed, and she was separated from her younger children. Unlike Rowlandson, Swarton was taken north to Canada, where she was sold to a French family. Her captivity also lasted years, rather than months. Swarton did not have a well-connected minister husband at home advocating for her release. Negotiating for the release of captives taken prisoner by the French or Native Americans was a veritable cottage industry in the Northeast at the turn of the eighteenth century. It was also an industry shaped by the hierarchy of Puritan society: ministers and their families were usually among the first captives ransomed back to English settlements (Melvoin 240–42). As an inconsequential Maine settler with no family members left to speak for her, Swarton's captivity lingered longer than most.

One of the few captivity narratives written by a man was John Williams's "The Redeemed Captive Returning to Zion" which described his family's experiences after their town of Deerfield, Massachusetts, was attacked in 1704 by a mixed group of French, Abenaki, Huron, and other Native American groups. While attacks on English settlements were common in this period, the Deerfield attack became particularly well known likely because its victims were determined for their story to be told (Melvoin 21). Even today, the attack on Deerfield is remembered each year with an event jointly sponsored by the Pocumtuck Valley

Memorial Association and Historic Deerfield. Williams's youngest children were killed in the family home, and his wife died on the long journey north to Canada. Like Rowlandson, Williams was separated from his remaining children, although he was occasionally allowed to see them. Williams was eventually ransomed and returned to Deerfield, where he published an account of his captivity while rebuilding his life.

As this sampling of texts illustrate, the New England captivity narratives were distinctive from other captivity tales for several reasons. They dealt with a specific geographic place and time: the New England colonies during the long series of wars with Native Americans in the late seventeenth and eighteenth centuries. They were written for an audience based in New England, one already intimately familiar with the events being described. They also follow a certain, specific narrative trajectory: the narrator is captured by Native American or French raiders, the narrator endures challenges to both faith and stamina, and the narrator is eventually set free, all, according to the writer, by the grace of God. After the narrator returned to English settlement, he or she "almost invariably offered his experience as a lesson to neighbors of the ephemeral security of this world and the awesomeness of God's sovereignty" (Vaughan and Clark 5). This narrative pattern appears consistently throughout many New England captivity narratives. While there can be little doubt about the belief in the importance of this message from narrators like Rowlandson, colonial publishers clearly both recognized and encouraged this winning formula.

My interpretation of Olaudah Equiano's *Narrative* as an outgrowth of the captivity narrative genre and my teaching of the *Narrative* as a text within this literary space emerged while I was first teaching the United States history survey as a graduate student. After using the *America Firsthand* document collection for a couple of semesters, I began reflecting both on the similarities found in Equiano's *Narrative* and the "Narrative of the Life of Mary Jemison," another document published in *America Firsthand,* and the pedagogical benefits in conducting this comparative reading of historical documents in my survey course. As I learned in my readings of these texts, Jemison was taken captive by Native Americans in 1758 as part of the larger French and Indian War occurring between 1754 and 1763. She later dictated her story to James Seaver, and the account was published in 1824. Both tales pay particular attention to the agonies suffered as these individuals who are now slaves and captives enter into dramatically different lives.

Turning to Chapter 2 of the *Narrative,* for instance, readers encounter Equiano's description of his capture and time on board a slave ship. This discussion is continued in Chapter 5 when Equiano works for a slave trader: "I was often a witness to cruelties of every kind. . . . [They] cut and mangle the slaves in a shocking manner, on the most trivial of occasions, and altogether treat them like brutes" (75). As most slaves rarely came back in contact with the Atlantic slave trade after their initial sale, Equiano's prolonged proximity allowed him ample opportunity for reminding readers about Africans' brutal initiation into slavery.

In turn, Jemison's "Narrative" provides vivid details about her first weeks as an Indian captive. Afraid of counterattacks, most Native American groups with recent captives moved away as swiftly as possible, killing anyone who could not keep up with the group. Mary Jemison was the only member of her family chosen to become a captive; her parents and siblings were killed along the way. While the decision to kill some captives was made for the survival of the group as a whole, most captivity narrators use these deaths to remind readers about the "savage" nature of their Native American captors. The group may be better able to survive as a whole, but the rupturing of individual family units is a common theme in many of the captivity narratives.

The descriptions of the days and months following the captive's or slave's initial entry into bondage highlight another similarity between Equiano's *Narrative* and the New England captivity narratives. All of these works pay careful attention to the Christian faith of their narrators. However challenged, the narrator perseveres through faith and determination. This same faith is eventually rewarded by freedom, a message enthusiastically proclaimed to the readers of these texts. Equiano makes clear that his conversion to Christianity stemmed from his liberation from slavery and from the slave trade: "I felt an astonishing change; the burden of sin, the gaping jaws of hell . . . which had weighted me down before, now lost their horror" (143). Having become free, he now commits his life to arguing against the eighteenth-century transatlantic slave and to spreading the word of God. Mary Rowlandson concludes her *Sovereignty* in a similar spirit: "Thus hath the Lord brought me and mine out of that horrible pit. . . . it is the desire of my soul that we may walk worthy of the mercies received" (76). Like the older tales of Catholic saints, these accounts by Rowlandson, Equiano, and other writers were intended to provide both comfort and inspiration for religious readers.

One of the great challenges when teaching about colonial slavery is explaining how different it was from slavery in the decades prior to the Civil War. Most students are familiar with the rigid forms of nineteenth-century slavery, whether through the slave narratives of Frederick Douglass and Harriet Jacobs or through their high school textbooks or films such as *Gone with the Wind.* In contrast, slavery in the colonial period was still evolving. I utilize a variety of methods to address this significant evolution; often, I have my students analyze relevant documents that address the history of slavery in the colonies into lectures on relevant topics. These exercises allow the students to discover the fact that the first Africans arrived in Virginia and Maryland as indentured servants, not slaves. Slavery did not become firmly established in the Chesapeake region until the late seventeenth century. The handful of African indentured servants who received their freedom at the end of their indentures went on to found small free African communities across the south. Prior to beginning my academic career, I spent several years in the museum field and still incorporate the study of material culture (better known among my students as "history through stuff") into the classroom. Actual artifacts from seventeenth-century free African communities are hard to come by outside a museum. However, the 1996 reissue of James Deetz's classic *In Small Things Forgotten: An Archaeology of Early American Life* includes a chapter on archaeology digs conducted by Deetz on the remains of those same communities (212–52). Its discussion of the objects found during these digs helps students to envision what these communities may have been like. The use of material culture in the classroom provides a crucial nuance for students accustomed to thinking of history solely in terms of written documents: even largely illiterate peoples can still leave traces in the historical record (Deetz 212–52).

Any discussion of *colonial* slavery leads easily into a discussion on Equiano's *Narrative* as the product of a specific colonial literary genre, the captivity narrative. As we observed earlier in this essay, the captivity narrative formula was clearly a successful one. Channeling its narrative arc allowed Equiano to create a story line familiar to white readers, even if its events were unfamiliar. Likewise, the emphasis on the Middle Passage and the slave trade in the *Narrative* can spark a discussion of the early stages of the abolition movement. Most students do not realize that the American slave trade was abolished in 1808, some fifty years before the abolishment of slavery in the United States.

Another way of teaching students about Equiano's representation of the eighteenth-century Atlantic World lies in comparing his narrative to another eighteenth-century memoir written by a freed slave, the 1798 "Memoirs of the Life of Boston King, a Black Preacher, Written by Himself, during His Residence at Kingswood-School." King was born a slave in South Carolina around 1760 to parents originally from Africa. He was apprenticed to a carpenter and became a skilled tradesman. Like many African Americans during the Revolutionary War, he chose to join the British army as it promised freedom to all slaves who fought for the Loyalist cause. After the war, King and his wife moved to Nova Scotia and then to Sierra Leone. Similar to Equiano, he was educated, deeply committed to his religion, and advocated for the abolition of slavery. An excerpt from King's "Memoirs" is also published in *America Firsthand* and includes a description of King's own final conversion to the Christian faith, one that King also directly connects to obtaining his freedom from slavery. As readers of King notice, he decided one night to run away by swimming across a river and making his way to New York City, where he had friends waiting. Before departing, he attended a prayer service, where he thought "the Lord heard me and would mercifully deliver me" (120–21). After successfully crossing the river without detection from the guards posted there, King "fell down upon [his] knees and thanked God for the deliverance." Like Equiano, King reminds his readers that freedom from captivity results directly from one's own faith in God and the Christian religion.

This last point segues nicely into a wider discussion of literature and publishing practices in the seventeenth and eighteenth centuries. As paper and ink were expensive in the colonies, publishing a book was a risky endeavor. Much like today, publishers only took on projects that likely guaranteed them a return on their investment. Analyzing similar narrative patterns in the individual writings of Olaudah Equiano, Mary Rowlandson, and Boston King allows students to consider the decisions made when writing, editing, and publishing a best seller in a different time period. The message that salvation, whether from captivity, slavery, or challenges found in ordinary life, came through religious faith clearly resonated with colonial readers. However, these tales were not solely religious in nature. They also provided readers with details of unknown worlds, whether life with a Native American nation in the late seventeenth century or the practices of people living in the interior of Africa. If religion played an important role in the colonial world, so did a growing curiosity about unfamiliar places. The captivity narrative genre allowed publishers to capitalize successfully on both of these elements.

Despite their status as colonial best sellers, neither the captivity narrative genre nor Equiano's *Narrative* are without their controversies, whether we discuss the eighteenth century or the contemporary moment. The *Narrative* opens with a description of his childhood in the "remote and fertile" province of Essaka (12). According to the account found in the *Narrative,* he was kidnapped by traders at the age of eleven and eventually taken to the coast to be sold as a slave. After surviving the Middle Passage, Equiano arrived in Barbados and was eventually taken to Virginia, where he was sold to a naval lieutenant who took him to England. The description of the voyage to Barbados is one of the most haunting in Equiano's *Narrative* and the segment most likely to be anthologized. However, recent scholarship has called into question the veracity of Equiano's account. Baptismal records suggest that he was born in South Carolina and, consequently, that he never crossed the Atlantic Ocean on a slave ship (Carretta 3–9). While the *Narrative* states that Equiano reached England in 1757, naval and newspaper records suggest instead that he arrived there in 1754.

The authorship of many of the captivity narratives has also been called into question by modern scholars. Mary Rowlandson, Hannah Swarton, and Mary Jemison all describe their experiences in the first person. Rowlandson, for instance, reflects that "Now is that dreadfull hour come, that I have often heard of (in time of War . . .) but now mine eyes see it" (29). Teresa Toulouse points out that while Rowlandson composed her tale herself, it was most likely heavily edited by both her clergyman husband and Increase Mather (7). Hannah Swarton's account was ghostwritten by Cotton Mather as part of his *Magnalia Christi Americana* in 1698. For her part, Jemison was illiterate, and her memoirs were dictated to James E. Seaver in the 1820s. In all three cases then, it is impossible to tell where the female narrators leave off and where their male editors begin.

The issue of authenticity and the written word still lingers today, particularly with the recent controversies over fictitious memoirs such as James Frey's *A Million Little Pieces,* Misha Defonseca's *Misha: A Memoir of the Holocaust Years,* and Margaret B. Jones's *Love and Consequences: A Memoir of Hope and Survival.* The surfacing of these more contemporary controversies over accuracy in the text allows for instructors to draw connections between the captivity narratives mentioned above (including the scenes of captivity found in Equiano's *Narrative*) and the more recent texts. Given these current tensions, it is not surprising that students are often disoriented and dismayed by the suggestion that these tales may not directly reflect the experiences of their narrators. As we do not know whether Olaudah Equiano was enslaved in Africa or the extent to which James Seaver shaped Mary Jemison's story, I find questioning the truth of these narratives rarely constructive for any length of time. While concluding from the historic record that Equiano was probably born in North America, Vincent Carretta chose to write his biography as if Equiano was born in Africa, arguing that Equiano deserved the history he had chosen for himself (8–9). I address this issue by focusing instead on the question of why these texts are told in the way they are told. If the Middle Passage was such a traumatic experience, why did Equiano elect to give himself such a history? What were the benefits of such a decision? And what are the possible dangers of including this traumatic event in his *Narrative?* These focused questions encourage students to consider these texts as crafted for specific purposes and as ones grounded in specific historical moments.

Olaudah Equiano's *Narrative* was first published in 1789 when the organized abolition movement in Britain was barely a decade old. The first society for the abolition of African slaves was founded by a group of Quakers in 1783. Their cause was introduced to Parliament on June 17, 1783, by Sir Cecil Wray. Despite the backing of Wray and a handful of other politicians, the early abolitionists were met with scorn and discouragement. After Equiano joined the movement in the mid-1780s, he began publishing columns arguing for abolition in two London newspapers, the *Public Advertiser* and the *Morning Chronicle.* Nevertheless, these papers reached an audience limited to their circulation numbers. Publishing his *Narrative* in 1789 allowed Equiano to make a longer, more detailed plea for the slave trade to end to a much wider audience. Given the ultimate purpose of the *Narrative,* it may not have mattered to the abolition movement whether Equiano himself had survived the Middle Passage. What did matter, however, was the fact that thousands of Africans were still experiencing its brutality. If Equiano's descriptions could bring its horrors home to countless middle- and upper-class white readers on both sides of the Atlantic Ocean, then it was appropriate for him to write the story of a young boy enslaved in Africa and horrified by his experiences during the Middle Passage. It also provided an additional layer of authenticity to his tale by giving him an "ordinary" slave experience. He was an African slave who gained his freedom and then, briefly, worked in the slave trade in the 1760s. Regardless of circumstances, his life story was uncommon for anyone in the eighteenth century, whatever his or her race. Unless an individual migrated (forced or otherwise) to the Americas, most people did not travel extensively, let alone to the Arctic Ocean and Istanbul.

Vincent Carretta also offers an additional explanation for why Equiano began his tale in Africa: "creating or recreating an African past allowed him to forge a personal and national identity other than the one imposed on him by Europeans" (9). At various points in his life, Equiano made occasional attempts to return to Africa. He had been frustrated in 1779 when the Anglican Church had rejected his offer to serve as a Christian missionary in Africa. At least this way, he could claim roots in Africa. The early chapters of the *Narrative* describe his family background, particularly focusing on a sister who was sold into slavery at the same time as Equiano. The fragility of slave life made family ties particularly important to Africans in the Atlantic World, whether they were ties of blood or friendship. This emphasis on family connections also provides another link to the captivity narratives where they are equally prized and equally fragile.

Providing historical contexts for both Equiano's *Narrative* and the captivity narratives also helps when discussing their authorship. The early stages of the abolition movement occurred at a difficult point in England's history when questions of power and empire were being actively debated in Parliament. Similarly, the late seventeenth century was regarded as a crisis period by many political and religious leaders in New England. By this time, English colonization in the region was in its second and third generations. The urgency that had spurred the establishment of Puritan churches and Puritan settlements had largely faded, and children often did not share their parent's ardent religious commitments. The outbreak of the long series of wars from King Philip's War in the 1670s to King William's War in the early eighteenth century, as noted above, was seen as a judgment on the growing lack of commitment to the Puritan church. The publication of Mary Rowlandson's *The Sovereignty and the Goodness of God* in 1682 came as a great reassurance to the Puritan clergy. Here was an ordinary woman, albeit a minister's wife, who had survived great hardship and deprivation, all through her commitment to God. Rowlandson was proof that they had not failed in their mission. Ministers like Cotton and Increase Mather almost immediately went looking for similar stories: "[T]hese texts [are linked] to fears, beliefs, and positions espoused by colonial male elites whose dominance is threatened during a specific historical period" (Toulouse 5). The output of captivity narratives in both published works and sermons over the next fifty years clearly indicates that there was no shortage of them. Any unease felt by men like the Mathers about appropriating these women's stories was washed away by religious and political expediency.

Despite the initial similar descriptions of capture and entry into captivity, Mary Jemison's "Narrative" stands apart from the captivity narratives produced in New England at the turn of the eighteenth century. Jemison was originally from

Pennsylvania, and her captivity resulted from the Seven Years' War rather than any of the New England conflicts. Jemison also decided as an adult to remain permanently with her Seneca family, despite repeated opportunities to return to white society. The New England captives who chose not to return to their Anglo-American families were rarely acknowledged during the colonial period. John Williams's "The Redeemed Captive" only briefly mentions his daughter, Eunice, who eventually married an Abenaki man. Eunice's decision baffled and saddened her family, who felt she was betraying both her religion and her heritage. The New England captivity narratives emphasize the difficulties of life among Native Americans, particularly for women. In contrast, Jemison observes that Seneca women's "task is probably not harder than that of white women . . . and their cares certainly are not half as numerous, nor as great" (33). Bringing Jemison's "Narrative" into the twenty-first century classroom provides an important contrast to the New England captivity narratives. It also introduces an evolving discussion on how minority groups have been portrayed in the writing of United States history.

The impetus behind Jemison's "Narrative" was very different than the impetus behind the New England captivity narratives. Secure in the knowledge that white society dominated the eastern seaboard, early nineteenth-century American playwrights and writers often romanticized the lives of eastern Native American groups in the colonial period. Among the most popular of these tales were James Fennimore Cooper's series of novels known collectively as *The Leatherstocking Tales,* which began with *The Pioneers* in 1823. Published in 1824, Jemison's "Narrative" can easily be interpreted as part of this movement. Captivity narratives brought back into print in the late twentieth century were now studied for their detailed descriptions among the Native Americans in the early years of contact between Native and European cultures. As part of this movement, John Demos's *The Unredeemed Captive* finally provided John Williams's daughter, Eunice, with her own captivity narrative in 1994.

There is another element to be considered when introducing students to books written in the captivity narrative genre. The W. H. Smith bookstore chain in Britain introduced a new fiction prize in 1992. Entitled the "Thumping Good Read" award, it was intended for books that readers simply wanted to read, rather than the more literary choices considered for Britain's Booker or Whitbread awards.[3] It is likely that had such an award existed at the turn of the eighteenth century, the tales of Mary Rowlandson, Hannah Swarton, and, for that matter, Olaudah Equiano, would have been considered. They were all books intended to capture readers' attention through vivid storytelling and a careful balance of perfect detail and images left to the reader's imagination. It is important to remember that the captivity narratives were also best sellers in their day, and they still make good reading. While the intense pace of a survey class does not allow time for leisurely consideration, an upper-level course could begin a section on captivity narratives by assigning a first segment to be read without the usual expectations of thoughtful note taking. Instead, simply ask students to read the story as they might a piece of modern popular fiction. History at its best is as much a visceral process as an intellectual one, and this allows time for this particular window onto the past.

As always, it is difficult to gauge immediate student response to lectures and discussion topics. A customary first writing assignment for this particular survey class asks students to analyze three documents from *America Firsthand* they feel are linked by a common theme. In every class, papers on the captivity narrative genre are extremely popular, perhaps because the framework provided by the captivity narrative's story pattern is helpful to students occasionally lost in the verbose language and unfamiliar words of the colonial period. Looking for the specific plot turns of the captivity narrative provides a road map when first reading Equiano's *Narrative,* Rowlandson's *Sovereignty,* or King's "Memoirs." Having found those landmarks, students can move more fully into the particular experience of the Middle Passage or an eleven-week captivity among the Narragansett in greater depth. As my class transitions to the nineteenth century, students are introduced to new literary genres, including the slave narratives mentioned earlier in this essay. Henry Louis Gates Jr. has observed that "so similar was the structure of these narratives that it sometimes seems . . . that the slave authors were tracing a shared pattern, and then cutting that pattern from similar pieces of cloth" (x). Once again, a familiar framework has provided the necessary support for understanding the details of a strange, new world.

Notes

1. See Lisa Voigt's *Writing Captivity in the Early Modern Atlantic: Circulations of Knowledge in the Iberian and English Imperial Worlds* for further discussion of Iberian captivity narratives and for examples to be used in the classroom.

2. Mary Rowlandson's narrative has been published under a variety of titles. While the editors of *The Norton Anthology of American Literature* refer to this text as *A Narrative of the Captivity and Restoration of Mrs. Mary Rowlandson,* I have chosen

to refer to her narrative as *The Sovereignty and Goodness of God* as that is the title commonly used by the colonial historians cited in this essay.

3. The award was ended in 2004, but the phrase "Thumping Good Read" entered the English language enough to be used as a category in the now equally defunct *A Common Reader Catalog.*

Works Cited

Carretta, Vincent. *Equiano, the African: Biography of a Self-Made Man.* Athens: U of Georgia P, 2005.

Deetz, James. *In Small Things Forgotten: An Archaeology of Early American Life.* New York: Doubleday, 1996.

Defonseca, Misha. *Misha: A Memoir of the Holocaust Years.* Bluebell, PA: Mt. Ivy P, 1997.

Demos, John. *The Unredeemed Captive: A Family Story from Early America.* New York: Knopf, 1994.

Equiano, Olaudah. *The Interesting Narrative of the Life of Olaudah Equiano, or Gustavus Vassa, the African. Written by Himself. The Classic Slave Narratives.* Ed. Henry Louis Gates Jr. New York: Penguin, 1987. 1–182.

Frey, James. *A Million Little Pieces.* New York: Anchor, 2005.

Gates, Henry Louis, Jr. Introduction. *The Classic Slave Narratives.* Ed. Henry Louis Gates Jr. New York: Penguin, 1987. ix–xviii.

Jemison, Mary. "A Narrative of the Life of Mary Jemison." *America Firsthand.* Ed. Robert D. Marcus, David Burner, and Anthony Marcus. 7th ed. Vol. 1. Boston: Bedford/St. Martin's, 2007. 29–34.

Jones, Margaret B. *Love and Consequences: A Memoir of Hope and Survival.* New York: Riverhead, 2008.

King, Boston. "Memoirs of the Life of Boston King, a Black Preacher, Written by Himself, during His Residence at Kingswood-School." *America Firsthand.* Ed. Robert D. Marcus, David Burner, and Anthony Marcus. 8th ed. Vol. 1. Boston: Bedford/St. Martin's, 2009. 117–21.

Le Jeune, Paul. "The Jesuit Relations and Allied Documents: Travels and Exploration of the Jesuit Missionaries in New France." *America Firsthand.* Ed. Robert D. Marcus, David Burner, and Anthony Marcus. 8th ed. Vol. 1. Boston: Bedford/St. Martin's, 2009. 22–27.

Little, Ann M. *Abraham in Arms: War and Gender in Colonial New England.* Philadelphia: U of Pennsylvania P, 2007.

Mather, Cotton. "A Narrative of Hannah Swarton Containing Wonderful Passages Related to Her Captivity and Deliverance." *Puritans among the Indians: Accounts of Captivity and Redemption, 1676–1724.* Ed. Alden T. Vaughan and Edward W. Clark. Cambridge, MA: Harvard UP, 1981. 145–58.

Melvoin, Richard. *New England Outpost: War and Society in Colonial Deerfield.* New York: Norton, 1989.

O'Callaghan, E. B. *Laws and Ordinances of New Netherland, 1638–1674.* Albany: Weed, Parsons, 1868.

Rowlandson, Mary. *The Sovereignty and Goodness of God. Puritans Among the Indians: Accounts of Captivity and Redemption, 1676–1724.* Ed. Alden T. Vaughan and Edward W. Clark. Cambridge, MA: Harvard UP, 1981. 29–76.

Smith, John. *The Generall Historie of Virginia, New-England, and the Summer Isles by John Smith, 1624.* Ed. A. L. Rowse. Cleveland: World, 1966.

Toulouse, Teresa. *The Captive's Position: Female Narrative, Male Identity, and Royal Authority in Colonial New England.* Philadelphia: U of Pennsylvania P, 2007.

VanDerBeets, Richard. *The Indian Captivity Narrative: An American Genre.* New York: UP of America, 1984.

Vaughan, Alden T., and Edward W. Clark. Introduction. *Puritans among the Indians: Accounts of Captivity and Redemption, 1676–1724.* Ed. Alden T. Vaughan and Edward W. Clark. Cambridge, MA: Harvard UP, 1981. 1–28.

Voigt, Lisa. *Writing Captivity in the Early Modern Atlantic: Circulations of Knowledge and Authority in the Iberian and English Imperial Worlds.* Chapel Hill: U of North Carolina P, 2009.

Williams, John. "The Redeemed Captive Returning to Zion." *Puritans Among the Indians: Accounts of Captivity and Redemption, 1676–1724.* Ed. Alden T. Vaughan and Edward W. Clark. Cambridge, MA: Harvard UP, 1981. 165–226.

Winans, Amy E. "Diversity and Difference in African American Writings." *Teaching the Literatures of Early America.* Ed. Carla Mulford. New York: MLA, 1999. 27–47.

Transatlantic Transformations: Olaudah Equiano's *Narrative* and Caryl Phillips's *Cambridge*

Eric D. Lamore

Some readers have established parallels between *The Interesting Narrative of Olaudah Equiano, or Gustavus Vassa, the African. Written by Himself* and Caryl Phillips's novel *Cambridge.*[1] These comparative readings, however, reflect a need to examine further this intertextual relationship. These readers of Equiano's and Phillips's texts fail to explicate fully the sophisticated ways in which Phillips responds to Equiano in his twentieth-century literary text nor do they pursue any discussion relating to the meaningful teaching of these two texts in the contemporary literature classroom. The reworking of Equiano by Phillips in *Cambridge,* therefore, stands as a more complicated relationship that deserves a more complete analysis. This significant pairing of texts, I maintain, offers teachers of a variety of courses the opportunity to examine with their students the representations of slavery in literature, the dynamics of the transatlantic slave trade, the history of slavery in the Caribbean, and other pedagogical topics still relevant to our students. In this essay, I propose a pedagogical sequence that places Equiano's *Narrative* in conversation with Phillips's *Cambridge.*

One benefit of spending classroom time and intellectual energy analyzing both Equiano's *Narrative* and Phillips's *Cambridge* is the flexibility that such a pedagogical pairing of texts offers instructors. While I wish to investigate this intertextual relationship in the context of American studies, these texts fit particularly well in courses that examine early American literature, British literature, African American literature, colonial and postcolonial literature, the literature of the early black Atlantic, and special-topics courses such as the African American Slave Narrative and the Neo-Slave Narrative, and Representations of Slavery in Caribbean Literature, among others.[2] By reading Equiano's *Narrative* alongside

Phillips's *Cambridge* in the classroom, we also advance discussions beyond investigations that place Equiano's seminal text in the genres of the spiritual autobiography, apologia, transatlantic travel writing, and the African American slave narrative, beyond analyses that investigate how Equiano draws on, in different ways, eighteenth-century discourses on Africa and the Judaeo-Christian Bible to shape his text, and beyond discussions that actively debate whether or not Equiano was born in Africa or in the Carolinas and the implications of these significant positions, to cite just a few recent threads in Equiano studies. Even though these topics are significant ones to tackle with contemporary students in the classroom, this literary and pedagogical project seeks not only to expand the ways in which we teach the *Narrative* but also to uncover how more contemporary historical and cultural contexts continue to shape our understanding of Equiano's eighteenth-century text.

Set on an unnamed island in the Caribbean during the early nineteenth century between the eradication of the transatlantic slave trade and the abolition of slavery in the British colonies, *Cambridge* offers readers a fragmented novel that pushes them to be ever conscious of movement across time and space and how the narrative shifts (a total of five times). The perspectives of a third-person omniscient prologue, a first-person travel diary/journal of a wealthy Englishwoman, a first-person narrative of the slave Cambridge, an "objective" colonial newspaper account of the aforementioned African slave, and a third-person omniscient epilogue constitute the five radically different sections of the novel. As Gail Lowe holds, "The juxtaposition of these narratives forces the reader to mediate between the self-contained realities of their different worlds, and provides rich opportunities for the ironic exposure of willful self-delusion of the slave-owning communities" (123).

For readers more familiar with Equiano's *Narrative* than with Phillips's *Cambridge,* it is productive at this point to look at specific parts from both texts to illustrate what Evelyn O'Callaghan has referred to as the "disconcertingly echoic experience" (39) that occurs when a reader moves from one text to the other. Equiano's and Cambridge's reflections on African nations illustrate the degree of similarity in this case of intertextuality. Before documenting his forced removal from his Eboe nation and his survival of the Middle Passage in the *Narrative,* Equiano requests the patience of his eighteenth-century reader because he fears he has given too many details concerning the "account of the manners and customs of my country" (Equiano 31–32). As he continues, he reflects, "[F]or, whether the love of one's country be real or imagined, or a lesson of reason, or an instinct of nature, I still look back with pleasure on the first scenes of my life" (32).

With Phillips's text, we encounter the fictional character Cambridge, another African who eventually acquires literacy, as he momentarily embraces his African nation before slavers capture him: "Whether affection for one's country is real or imagined, it is not an exaggeration to proclaim that at this moment instinct of nature suffused our [Cambridge and his countrymen's] being with an overwhelming love for our land and family, whom we did not see again" (137). Here we not only find numerous layers of direct lifting from the 1789 *Narrative,* but we also see, in Phillips's text, how Cambridge appears even to provide an answer to the catalogue of possibilities the eighteenth-century writer lists concerning the source of either "love" in Equiano or "affection" in Phillips "for one's country." Of course, this intertextuality translates productively into a classroom activity. When reading these two texts in the classroom, students can be assigned to catalogue all of the precise similarities between Equiano and Cambridge. Careful readers find several other meaningful parallels between Cambridge, the "disobedient" slave on a nineteenth-century Caribbean sugar plantation whose name serves as the title of the novel, and Equiano. Both individuals, for instance, experience forced removal from their native African (Eboe) nation(s), survive the Middle Passage, come into contact with whites who strip them of their African identities through renaming on multiple occasions, document their experiences learning the English language, work under cruel and inhumane conditions in the Caribbean, seek salvation in reading and studying the Bible, contemplate becoming missionaries in Africa, and engage in interracial marriages, among other layers. Mapping these similarities in the classroom hones students' close-reading skills; at the same time, this intellectual exercise encourages them to begin to read comparatively and to make connections between more than one literary text through the use of concrete evidence from Equiano's and Phillips's texts.

Reading interviews with Phillips stands as another productive pedagogical exercise because this contemporary writer consistently offers significant commentary on his writing that can be directly applied to the intertextual relationship between *Cambridge* and Equiano's *Narrative.* For example, Phillips, in a 1995 interview, points to what he calls "received history" and how he works in his texts to "digest" "first-person voices" in order to "rework" this same "received history" he has encountered in historical documents (Sharpe 157). In another part of the same interview, Phillips admits that he "enjoy[s] reading first-person historical material," yet he also works to subvert "the form, because all too often there's a self-serving nature behind these narratives" (158).

Phillips's commentary in this interview provides teachers and students with an insight into, even a theory of, his writing. Instructors can focus on defining with their students specific key words or phrases: "received history," "rework," "first-person historical material," "subverting," "self-serving," and "form," for example, all allow for extensive and important classroom discussions that seek to explain and expand on how we, as readers, understand these terms to form a critical bridge that connects the ideas from the interview with the novel, *Cambridge,* and, eventually, the novel with Equiano's *Narrative.*

In a second interview, one from 1991, the same year *Cambridge* was published, Phillips shifts from commenting on strategies that inform his creative process to biographical information on the cultural adjustments he faced after he was born on the island of St. Kitts and soon after moved with his family to Great Britain. Phillips states that growing up in Britain was a difficult experience on several levels: walking down the street he would be "stopped by the police on the street asking me where I was going, where I had been" (Bell 580), and attending Oxford University brought about "frustration" because "there were so few black faces around me to reinforce my sense of self" (579). These experiences, among others, motivated Phillips to engage in his writing with problems that accompany "being a West Indian in Britain" (588). In addition, Phillips acknowledges how transplantation and membership in a diasporic community frequently result in individuals "question[ing] their identit[ies]" (599) and wrestling with the "question of home" (599). Teachers can utilize these interviews to analyze the displacement of Cambridge (in both England and in the Caribbean) and how one layer of the novel allows readers to establish a biographical interpretation in additional parts of the text. Furthermore, in my experience teaching *Cambridge* on a number of occasions, I have found that students become more engaged in the novel by studying the interviews and even watching You Tube posts that feature Phillips reading from his texts or further commenting on his writing. This pedagogical exercise, in my estimation, personalizes Phillips for contemporary students.

Nonetheless, even though these interviews contain significant information that applies directly to *Cambridge,* a pedagogy that only introduces students to the interviews runs the risk of having student readers develop an interpretation that equates the author's testimony with the "meaning" of the text. Key parts from *Cambridge* not only resist this type of reading and but also require that readers tease out what Roland Barthes refers to as the "multi-dimensional space" (1468) that exists in texts. Barthes's point concerning the multidimensionality of texts even anticipates difficult questions that readers of *Cambridge* are likely to ask should they continue to focus on a biographical reading. How are we, as readers, for instance, to interpret the "Emily sequence," the bulky 122-page section of the novel narrated by a white, wealthy Englishwoman and daughter of a Caribbean sugar plantation owner? Or, how are we to make sense of the three-and-a-half-page section of the novel presented as an article lifted from a colonial newspaper? These other substantial parts of the novel call for additional interpretive and pedagogical strategies.

The pedagogical pairing of Equiano's *Narrative* and Phillips's *Cambridge* ultimately succeeds when student readers are invited to concentrate on how the more contemporary literary text comments forcefully on British colonialism in the early nineteenth-century Caribbean. One productive way to address the clear presence of the British colonial system and the representation in *Cambridge* of the ideologies of certain British expatriates who have traveled from the metropole to the settler colony can be accomplished by engaging students in the analysis of "how language usage and 'historical' representations work to enforce certain ways of being in the world for members of a dominant group" (Mulford, "Resisting Colonialism" 79).

To frame successfully this type of discussion first requires students to pay close attention to *Cambridge*'s one-and-a-half-page prologue, which introduces the "almost thirty" (4), wealthy, and privileged British woman, Emily Cartwright, whose father plans to force her into a marriage with a "fifty-year-old widower with three children" (3) when she returns from her stay on his sugar cane plantation. The narrator also notes, in this prologue, that the "truth" (3) concerning her visit to the Caribbean is that "she was fleeing the lonely regime which fastened her into backboards, corsets, and stays to improve her posture" (3). Approaching this part of the novel armed with a modern assumption that everyone has the right to marry whomever she or he pleases, most student readers allow the seductive prologue to entice them into sympathizing with this character because, as Jenny Sharpe observes, readers first encounter her in a society that refuses to grant her complete independence (160).

Encouraging this type of interpretation of the prologue sets up what should be a deliberately jarring experience for many contemporary students as they encounter the Emily sequence. In this section of the novel, Emily travels from England to the Caribbean and promises to document her observations in her journal to show her father "what pains and pleasures are endured by those whose labour enables him to continue to indulge himself in the heavy-pocketed manner to which he has become accustomed" (7). Even though Emily fashions herself as one capable of offering an objective and detached critique of the exploitive labor system that allows her absentee father to gamble to excess, as she lands close to the island Phillips employs a striking metaphor of the colonial relationship that previews what follows. In Emily's words: "A few yards short of the shore I discovered there was yet another journey to be made, for it proved inadvisable to beach the small craft in such shallow waters. I therefore completed the rest of the journey on the back of a negro" (20).

As Emily documents her observations of the plantation, she introduces readers to several ways in which the British Empire exercises control and maintains its authority on the Caribbean island even though, as she puts it, the colonial settlers wish to occupy the island because they are "on a civilizing and economic mission" (24). The walls of her father's "Great House" reveal that the island's landscape has been geographically and strategically documented in "many prints and maps, some which relate to navigation, a great number being of local interest and depicting the division of lands and the breadth and extent of the estates" (29), and the veranda of this same house contains a "spy-glass so that one might observe in one direction the labourers at work in the fields" (29). Moreover, these "truths" (38), as Emily sometimes refers to them and which she promises to impart to her father in her journal (and by extension to the reader) about the African slaves on the sugar cane plantation, reinforce, as Gail Lowe observes, that the laborers are "represented as a subhuman species of peoples, and she [Emily] upholds the familiar stereotypes about their animal and childlike nature, their petty thieving, and their wanton sexual behavior" (124).

This context prepares student readers to investigate the extensive parallels found in both Equiano's narrative and in Phillips's representation of the fictional character Cambridge. Perhaps the most significant intertextual dimension that needs to be discussed in the classroom lies in how Phillips critiques Equiano's ability to escape successfully from the eighteenth-century transatlantic slave trade, to enter into the eighteenth-century public sphere, and to present the details of his success story in the form of a highly successful autobiography. For the field of postcolonial and colonial studies, Helen Tiffin has coined the term "counter canonical discourse," a strategy the postcolonial writer employs to critique colonial writings and the ideologies contained therein through the "mapping of the dominant discourse, a reading and exposing of its underlying assumptions, and the dis/mantling of these assumptions" (101). I maintain that Tiffin's theory provides the most instructive approach for our contemporary students to understand how Phillips "maps," "exposes," and "dismantles" the underlying logic of success found in Equiano's *Narrative* in his writing of *Cambridge.*

Despite the availability of this instructive theory, certain literary anthologies that include Equiano's *Narrative* make it difficult to discuss his extensive representations of the eighteenth-century Caribbean. Even though a literary anthology such as Nellie McKay and Henry Louis Gates Jr.'s *The Norton Anthology of African American Literature* includes portions from Chapters 1, 2, 3, and 4 from Equiano's *Narrative,* this selection firmly positions this eighteenth-century literary text as an important one in the African American slave narrative tradition. Including these parts from Equiano's *Narrative* ultimately minimizes the prevalent interactions among different cultures and peoples in the eighteenth-century Atlantic World and reduces the complexity found in Chapters 5 and 6 (among others) that document Equiano's experiences in the Caribbean. Therefore, teachers of Equiano's *Narrative* need to attend more closely to Chapters 5 and 6 to assist their students in understanding how Phillips "maps," "exposes," and "dismantles" the ideology of success found in the *Narrative.*

In these chapters, Equiano works for the Quaker, Robert King, and, when King permits him, for Captain Thomas Farmer in the Caribbean and other parts of the Americas. Equiano's job consists of maneuvering small boats and selling goods for King throughout many different Caribbean islands, and he writes about the presence of slavery and other pertinent topics on the islands of Montserrat, St. Kitts (Phillips's birthplace), St. Eustatia, Barbados, and Martinique. Readers of the Caribbean sequence from Equiano's *Narrative* quickly observe his incorporation of the Judaeo-Christian religious tradition in these chapters. The ambitious Equiano starts to yearn for his freedom, and he consistently hopes for the Judaeo-Christian God to assist him in his industrious pursuits so that he can earn the required amount to purchase his manumission from King.

While one may point out that this clear dedication to acquire capital and his participation in selling human beings (African slaves, specifically) as one of his "goods" runs counter to several tenets found in the Judaeo-Christian religious tradition, Equiano merges, in this part of his *Narrative,* the deity's role in allowing him to make money and the importance of his exercising his industry as he acquires additional goods. We see another manifestation of this same logic when Equiano holds that "I therefore looked up with prayers anxious to God for my liberty; and at the same time I used every honest means, and endeavoured all that was possible to obtain it" (89). Here Equiano hopes that he will obtain "liberty" through his firm belief in the involvement of the Judaeo-Christian God and honest means to secure his liberty. In other parts of his *Narrative,* he emphasizes the significance of "honest means" (88, 89) and hard work in acquiring his freedom. Earning money from these jobs, continually asking the Judaeo-Christian God for his help, and embodying his philosophy on the importance of "honest means" and hard work allow Equiano to purchase his freedom in Chapter 7 of the second volume. This freedom, in turn, not only allows but motivates Equiano to construct his *Narrative* as a critique of the transatlantic slave trade and the cruel institution of slavery.

Focusing entirely on Equiano's representation of work in his sophisticated *Narrative,* however, downplays the author's obvious success at being able to enter into the public sphere and to sell and to market his text. Students of Equiano can classify him as "the first successful professional writer of African descent in the English-speaking world" (Carretta, *Equiano* 366) and as an individual who "could have easily garnered more than a thousand pounds in total gross profits from the nine editions of his *Interesting Narrative*" (301). Equiano's achievements in the eighteenth-century transatlantic world, therefore, include his ability both to experience freedom and financial success well outside of the slave trade and the institution of slavery.

Turning back to *Cambridge,* we see that Phillips, in certain parts of his novel, dismantles the thinking found in Equiano's text which holds that, for an ambitious African slave, the Judaeo-Christian religious tradition, honest means, and hard work bring about freedom and success. In the section of the novel featuring Cambridge's narrative, for instance, readers learn that the character is robbed of a significant amount of money, which he inherited from his deceased master. The robbers are white men who board the same ship, learn of Cambridge's inheritance, and, after stealing his money, sell him to plantation owners in the Caribbean. Strikingly, Cambridge, in contemplating these dreadful circumstances, remarks, "I faced these white men, with more knowledge of their country than they could possibly imagine, believing that through hard work and faith in the Lord God Almighty, my bondage would soon cease" (157).

Thus, despite becoming a slave for the second time in his life, Cambridge remains stubbornly loyal to the ideology that Equiano embraces throughout parts of his *Narrative.* After being sold to a West Indian sugar cane plantation overseer, Cambridge's "faith" in "God Almighty," dedication to "hard work," and his attempts to create a more equitable culture on the plantation bring about disastrous consequences. In Phillips's novel, the white planters on the sugar plantation ultimately hang Cambridge for his murder of the white overseer, Mr. Brown. The circumstances leading to Cambridge's final, deadly confrontation with Brown—and thus to his own death—include his refusal to supervise his fellow Africans for the white overseer, his efforts to spread Christianity to other slaves, his consistent reading of the Bible, and, most important, his attempts to stop Brown's continued sexual abuse of Cambridge's wife. The white British planters turn the hanging of Cambridge into a public spectacle and permanently silence him because he refuses to play by their rules on the plantation. Unlike Equiano, who more successfully navigates what Phillips refers to as "the ethnic difficulties of belonging" (Phillips, *Extravagant* "Preface" xiv) in several points in the early Atlantic World, Cambridge devises a strategy in hopes of achieving this state of belonging on the early-nineteenth-century plantation, but he ultimately fails in this attempt.

In the short section of the novel following Cambridge's first-person narrative, the reader encounters a colonial newspaper column. This part of the novel offers students another opportunity to examine what Mulford calls the relationship between historical representation and language. While only three and a half pages long, this section requires close reading and pushes student readers to continue exercising their critical and comparative reading skills. One part of the journalistic account silences the deceased slave, Cambridge, and permanently positions him as "insane" and "particularly obnoxious" (171), details that clearly undermine and diminish his attempt to bring justice and social equality to the plantation. As student readers examine this section further, they notice some striking observations concerning Cambridge's murder of the overseer, Mr. Brown. The earlier representation Cambridge provides of himself, written in a first-person account that mimics the rhetoric of the slave narrative, mirrors Equiano's self as an individual with agency—one who travels throughout England to lecture on slavery and the slave trade and how its abuse of human beings runs counter to biblical teaching. In his first-person account, Cambridge also says that he initially approached Mr. Brown "[i]n a simple and Christian manner" (167) to request "that he behave towards myself and my *wife* with a decency that one would have afforded a dog" (167; emphasis in original). According to Cambridge, he ends up killing the overseer in self-defense when Brown violently attacks him shortly after this confrontation.

Contradicting Cambridge's narrative, the journalistic account claims that the slave's mind was "destroyed by fanciful notions of a Christian life of moral and domestic responsibility which he, in common with his fellow slaves, was congenitally unsuited to" (172–73). The unnamed journalist then positions Mr. Brown, the overseer who frequently beat Cambridge and sexually abused his wife, as a dutiful Christian man who, mortally wounded by Cambridge, attempted to deliver a prayer before his soul "flew to meet his God" (173). Then, the journalist continues, "his murderer [Cambridge] was left standing alone, with the stain of human blood upon him" (173). To this sentence the writer adds a footnote: "The negroes say that no grass has ever grown in the spot where the blood dropped since the time of the murder" (173). The failure of grass to grow in this spot now serves, according to this account, as a permanent reminder of what happens to literate Africans who transgress the rules of the sugar cane plantation. Cambridge's actions in the novel, however, cast him as a more radical, Equiano-like figure who not only reads and studies his Bible to bolster his antislavery arguments but openly questions white authority figures in face-to-face confrontations, even refusing to participate in trading slaves and to oversee his fellow Africans.

The journalistic section of the novel also erases the humane and compassionate portrayal of Cambridge in his autobiographical section, effectively robs Cambridge of his agency, and positions the slave, one who worked so hard to dismantle the institution of slavery in both Great Britain and on a Caribbean island, as an individual corrupted and tainted by his acquiring literacy and learning the principles of the Judaeo-Christian Bible. Unlike the representation of Equiano in his narrative, Phillips refuses to grant Cambridge complete freedom outside the Caribbean, and it is obvious that the murder of this same "fictional" character permanently denies him access to the nineteenth-century public sphere and to market actively and successfully any autobiographical account he wishes to write and distribute.

On yet another level, this section of *Cambridge* introduces students to the rhetoric of apologists who attempted to preserve the slave trade and slavery, as well as interrogates the notion of "objective" journalism. This journalistic account permanently silences Cambridge, shapes this African-turned-Englishman as a hostile individual, and, at the same time, as Evelyn O'Callaghan argues, uncovers one of the mechanisms through which the British colonial system silences the colonized through language (46). In other words, Phillips not only demands that the contemporary reader revisit this specific period in Caribbean history, which followed the dismantling of the transatlantic slave trade, but he also works to document the significance of language used by both the colonizer and those who are colonized. Unlike the celebration and effective uses of literacy evinced in Equiano's *Narrative,* Phillips offers an alternative representation of Caribbean history and culture in which an ambitious African's acquisition of literacy, understanding of the Judaeo-Christian Bible, and ability and desire to think and speak critically of a society results in his permanent removal from that society, preventing him from gaining access to the public sphere.

Even more striking, however, is the following detail Phillips provides concerning Cambridge: according to the slave's testimony, his hair "took on a grey aspect, and [his] strength began to fade" (159) as he lived on the plantation. This detail is not insignificant. Indeed, having Cambridge notice his gray hair only reinforces the way in which Phillips reworks and rewrites Equiano's *Narrative.* It signifies Phillips constructing an older Equiano figure who cannot escape the colonial culture and rigid hierarchy of the nineteenth-century plantation, however much he tries and despite subscribing to the same ideology as Equiano.

This reading of *Cambridge,* therefore, positions some parts of this text as a postcolonial critique of those portions from Equiano's *Narrative* which hold that by subscribing to the Judaeo-Christian religious tradition (the same religious tradition of the white owners) and maintaining a diligent work ethic, a slave may gain freedom. Although Cambridge tries to negotiate carefully within the context of slavery and the plantation culture, while rejecting participation in the oppression of his fellow Africans, his plan ultimately backfires: he does not experience complete freedom. Equiano, on the other hand, sells his fellow Africans, stands and watches as African women are raped by slave traders, and uses his position as a clerk to acquire his freedom and preserve his life. Students frequently question Equiano's participation in the slave trade, and it would appear that Phillips offers one explanation for why Equiano admits that, when he sees African women being raped, he was "obliged to submit to at all times, being unable to help them" (77). Cambridge, who *does* speak out against a similar outrage, meets a very different fate from that of Equiano.

Once the several layers of similarity and difference among the two texts are discussed, however, it is essential to encourage students to take a further interpretive step and answer the following question: *why* would a contemporary Afro British and Caribbean writer wish to revisit the Middle Passage, the early black Atlantic, and the several texts and perspectives that constitute the sophisticated text *Cambridge?* In reflecting on this complicated question, we see that Phillips insists throughout *Cambridge* that twentieth-century readers (this novel was originally published in 1991) and now twenty-first-century readers must remember the presence of slavery in the Caribbean, the complex dynamics of this institution, and its lingering effects in contemporary Caribbean and European cultures.

Furthermore, Phillips recovers, as we have observed above, the voice and subjectivity of an African who works vigorously to cultivate a more nuanced understanding of slavery in the context of British culture, an act that literally costs him his life after he is forced back into slavery in the Caribbean. As we see from the autobiographical testimony concerning his experiences in Great Britain, Cambridge even outlines the need to address publicly discrepancies within British culture. Cambridge's desire to confront British society and interrogate its beliefs leads him to conclude that "time and energy must immediately be given over to correcting the situation of the poor, oppressed, needy, and much-degraded negroes" (148). Of course, Equiano's petition to the British Parliament, which appears beside his famous frontispiece, makes nearly the same point: that the "chief design [of his 1789 *Narrative*] is to excite in your august assemblies a sense of compassion for the miseries which the Slave-Trade has entailed on my unfortunate countrymen" (7). Similarly, within the British sequence of Cambridge's autobiography, contemporary readers discover in Phillips's representation of Cambridge a nineteenth-century character using his literacy to argue, in different ways, against slavery and the slave trade.

Through his character Cambridge, Phillips participates in what Barbara T. Christian has referred to as the "revisioning of the literary tradition" (250) of previous works in the African American literary canon. While Christian's remarks in her essay "Does Theory Play Well in the Classroom?" pertain to her readings of Toni Morrison's *Beloved* and other texts in the African American literary canon, her theory concerning the process of rewriting literary texts and the significance of "filling in the silences" (250) of marginalized communities offers another productive way to approach the intertextuality found in Equiano's and Phillips's narratives in the classroom. Despite critiquing the logic of Equiano in certain parts of his novel, Phillips, like Equiano, works in other parts of his text to establish the significant roles that Africans played in dismantling the slave trade. As Stuart Hall points out in the valuable documentary *A Son of Africa:* "The way in which the history of abolition is written, the historiography, has sort of written out black agency as if abolition was principally the gift of liberal and reforming whites to the slaves and that the slaves themselves did not play much of an active part."

Echoing the comments from Hall, Phillips underscores this same frustration with the historiography of abolition and the passion for recovering the agency of Afro British figures who worked against the slave trade. In an interview, he comments on Hugh Thomas's book *The Slave Trade* because this historian "downplays the role of black people in stirring the moral imagination of England" (Yelin 50). Phillips adds that Thomas "only mentions Equiano (or any of the huge numbers of black people who were active on their own behalf) in passing, in the context of abolition" (Yelin 50). The representations of Africans, whether they were individuals struggling to survive in the Caribbean, as we will see below in selected parts from Equiano's *Narrative,* or working to eradicate the slave trade and/or the institution of slavery, as we see in both literary texts, deserve to be discussed in the classroom. Comparatively analyzing these diverse representations of active Africans in Equiano's and Phillips's texts encourages students both to understand the varieties of slaves' experience in the Atlantic World and to avoid formulating a problematic master narrative that purports to document the parameters of the life of a Caribbean slave. Further, teaching the novel *Cambridge* can enable twenty-first-century students to comprehend how language becomes the means by which the title character's life and life narrative are resurrected following their deliberate erasure by colonial masters and institutions.

In fact, one may explore in the classroom how Equiano also represents, in specific parts of his narrative, the language of displaced and struggling New World Africans. In Chapter 5, for example, Equiano documents his conversation with a "poor Creole negro" whom he "knew well, who, after having been often thus transported from island to island, at last resided in Montserrat" (82). Because of such passages in *The Interesting Narrative,* we may include Equiano in the same category as Stuart Hall and Caryl Phillips—i.e., as cultural critics who document and recover in their works the heretofore silenced voices of victims of the slave trade and the institution of slavery.

A productive way to conclude conversations in the classroom on Equiano's *Narrative* and Phillips's *Cambridge* lies in encouraging students to reflect on the canonical status of each text. The term "canonical" applies to our current discussion of Equiano's *Narrative* because this seminal text has appeared and continues to appear in popular textbooks such as *The Longman Anthology of British Literature, The Norton Anthology of American Literature, The Heath Anthology of American Literature, The Norton Anthology of African American Literature,* Vincent Carretta's *Unchained Voices: An Anthology of Black Authors in the English-Speaking World of the Eighteenth Century,* Myra Jehlen and Michael Warner's *The English Literatures of America, 1500–1800,* Carla Mulford's *Early American Writings,* Adam Potkay and Sandra Burr's *Black Atlantic Writers of the Eighteenth Century: Living the Exodus in England and the Americas,* Susan Castillo and Ivy Schweitzer's *The Literatures of Colonial America* (Drexler and White 19), Henry Louis Gates Jr.'s *The Classic Slave Narratives,* and Gates and William Andrews's *Slave Narratives.* As we see in the texts listed above, consistent critical dialogue in the fields of eighteenth-century studies, early black Atlantic studies, African American studies, and early American studies has solidified Equiano and his text in more than one literary canon.

When students are asked to articulate the place of these texts in an appropriate canon, they engage in significant intellectual work. Indeed, when instructors give students the opportunity to step back from the nuances of the literary text in order to examine the multilayered justifications of scholars and textbook editors for placing such texts in a particular canon or canons, they learn about another layer of the literary text. Curiously, both Equiano's and Phillips's texts resist placement in a single literary canon, and this point reinforces the reason why instructors need to discuss canonicity with students. Reading Equiano's *Narrative* allows our students to pose and to answer difficult yet rewarding questions about its canonicity: does Equiano's *Narrative* deserve a place in the African literary canon because of the writer's descriptions of his youth? Or, does Vincent Carretta's superb archival work on Equiano's place of birth obligate readers to place it in the canon of U.S. literature and, more specifically, in the tradition of the African American slave narrative? To frame this significant issue in slightly different terms, how much attention should readers give to the portions from the *Narrative* that focus on Equiano's presence in London, in the Caribbean, in the United States, in various parts of Europe, and even aboard a ship, a cosmopolitan eighteenth-century space that resists nationalistic and geographical classifications, in articulating justifications for the text's canonical status?

This same line of inquiry produces complicated questions concerning the canonicity of Phillips's *Cambridge.* Would it be an accurate and productive classification, for instance, to include Phillips's *Cambridge* as a work of American literature now that this author works in the Department of English at Yale University, that portions of Phillips's 1993 novel, *Crossing the River,* are included in McKay and Gates's *Norton Anthology of African American Literature,* and that, in *Cambridge,* Emily consistently refers to "tropical America" (16, 99), "our American empire" (33), the "production of American sugar" (38), "tropical American holdings" (50), "this small island in the Americas" (78), and the "tropical backwater of the Americas" (118)? On the other hand, should *Cambridge* reside in the Anglophone Caribbean literary canon because of Phillips's birthplace and the setting of the novel on an unnamed Caribbean island? Or, should we be content with classifying Phillips as a contemporary Equiano figure who successfully straddles the United States, the Anglophone Caribbean, and the British literary canons?[3]

These questions generate fruitful discussions on how specific evidence from the text supports and resists such classification choices and the significant interpretative strategies that shape productive discussion and debate in the field of literary studies: should we, as readers, place more value on the primary text, the cultural and historical contexts that shape this primary text, or the author's life? And, what specifically are the respective limitations in focusing on each of these dimensions in the text? Clearly, as these numerous questions imply, the value in teaching Equiano's *Narrative* alongside Phillips's *Cambridge* lies in pushing students to understand and articulate how these complex literary texts question and even critique the legitimacy of canonicity derived solely and often reductively from national and geographical boundaries.

We can pinpoint the significance of Phillips's reworking of Equiano's autobiography by understanding how this contemporary Afro Caribbean and British writer constructs a narrative about an African who can never fully maneuver outside of the transatlantic slave trade nor permanently gain his freedom. *Cambridge,* as we have observed, offers readers a more complicated narrative of the transatlantic slave trade and ultimately interrogates Equiano's ideology of success. This particular reading of Phillips's *Cambridge* advances the field of Equiano studies by providing a more complete understanding of the circulation and appropriation of Equiano's autobiography in contemporary contexts. Furthermore, this transatlantic comparative literary and pedagogical investigation productively complicates the tradition of studying and teaching American literature by solely utilizing the geography of the United States to determine what is and what is not significant to this body of literature. Finally, this reading highlights the need for teacher-scholars in American studies to work beyond and against disciplinary, geographical, and temporal boundaries.

Notes

1. See, for instance, Fernando Galván's essay "Between Othello and Equiano: Caryl Phillips's Subversive Rewritings," C. L. Innes's "Transnational and Black British Writing: Colonizing in Reverse," and Evelyn O'Callaghan's "Historical Fiction and Fictional History: Caryl Phillips's *Cambridge*" for treatments of this intertextual relationship.

2. For instructors of British literature, it is significant to point out that after publishing *Cambridge,* Phillips, in 1997, compiled an important anthology titled *Extravagant Strangers: A Literature of Belonging.* Curiously, Phillips takes his title from act 1, scene 1 of Shakespeare's *Othello* to focus on the key issue that drives his project. In this particular scene, Roderigo focuses on the otherness of Othello to explain to Brabantio, Desdemona's father and an authoritative figure in Venice, why he should be alarmed that the "Moor" has taken his daughter. Roderigo constructs Othello as an "other" by equating the character to an "extravagant . . . stranger" (1.1.136), by framing Desdemona's "revolt" (1.1.134) with the eventual tragic figure as "gross" (1.1.134), and by using the adjective "wheeling" (1.1.136), a word implying that an individual has no permanent home, to describe Othello. This title not only reveals Phillips's meticulous reading of Shakespeare but also provocatively links Othello to other "extravagant and wheeling stranger[s]" who may be found in the British literary canon. *Extravagant Strangers: A Literature of Belonging* explores the works of British writers who were not born in Britain and how "the question of 'belonging' surfaces in their

work[s] in a variety of ways . . . depending upon race, class and gender, [and] the degree to which they feel alienated from British society" (Phillips, *Extravagant* "Preface" xiv).

Placing Equiano as the third writer in his anthology and providing significant information about his life, Phillips pays particular attention to Equiano's involvement in dismantling the eighteenth-century transatlantic slave trade, his sophisticated writing skills, and, as one would expect given the nature of this anthology, his place as an individual not fully part of British society ("Olaudah Equiano" 9–10).

All of the texts I have mentioned—from the essays cited in note 1 to *Othello* to Phillips's anthology—are productive ones to use in the classroom.

3. Even though I offer this specific point in the form of a question, I am indebted to Andrew Warnes for this observation.

Works Cited

Barthes, Roland. "The Death of the Author." *The Norton Anthology of Theory and Criticism.* Ed. Vincent B. Leitch. New York: Norton, 2001. 1466–70.

Baym, Nina, ed. *The Norton Anthology of American Literature.* 6th ed. New York: Norton, 2003.

Bell, C. Rosalind. "Worlds Within: An Interview with Caryl Phillips." *Callaloo* 14.3 (1991): 578–606.

Carretta, Vincent. *Equiano, the African: Biography of a Self-Made Man.* New York: Penguin, 2006.

———, ed. *Unchained Voices: An Anthology of Black Authors in the English-Speaking World of the Eighteenth Century.* Lexington: U of Kentucky P, 1996.

Castillo, Susan, and Ivy Schweitzer, eds. *The Literatures of Colonial America.* Malden, MA: Blackwell, 2001.

Christian, Barbara T. "Does Theory Play Well in the Classroom?" *Critical Theory and the Teaching of Literature: Politics, Curriculum, Pedagogy.* Ed. James F. Slevin and Art Young. Urbana, IL: NCTE, 1996. 241–57.

Damrosch, David, and Kevin J. H. Dettmar, eds. *The Longman Anthology of British Literature.* 3rd ed. New York: Pearson, 2006.

Drexler, Michael J., and Ed White. "Canon Loading." *Beyond Douglass: New Perspectives on Early African-American Literature.* Ed. Michael J. Drexler and Ed White. Lewisburg, PA: Bucknell UP, 2008. 1–19.

Equiano, Olaudah. *The Interesting Narrative of the Life of Olaudah Equiano, or Gustavus Vassa, the African. Written by Himself.* Ed. Werner Sollors. New York: Norton, 2001.

Galván, Fernando. "Between Othello and Equiano: Caryl Phillips's Subversive Rewritings." *Refracting the Canon in Contemporary British Literature and Film.* Ed. Susana Onega and Christian Gutleben. Amsterdam: Rodopi, 2004. 187–205.

Innes, C. L. *The Cambridge Introduction to Postcolonial Literatures in English.* Cambridge, UK: Cambridge UP, 2007.

Jehlen, Myra, and Michael Warner, eds. *The English Literatures of America, 1500–1800.* New York: Routledge, 1997.

Lauter, Paul, ed. *The Heath Anthology of American Literature.* 5th ed. Boston: Houghton, 2006.

Lowe, Gail. "'A Chorus of Common Memory': Slavery and Redemption in Caryl Phillips's *Cambridge* and *Crossing the River.*" *Research in African Literatures* 29.4 (1998): 122–41.

McKay, Nellie Y., and Henry Louis Gates Jr., eds. *The Norton Anthology of African American Literature.* 2nd ed. New York: Norton, 2003.

Mulford, Carla, ed. *Early American Writings.* New York: Oxford UP, 2002.

———. "Resisting Colonialism." *Teaching the Literatures of Early America.* Ed. Carla Mulford. New York: MLA, 1999. 75–94.

O'Callaghan, Evelyn. "Historical Fiction and Fictional History: Caryl Phillips's *Cambridge.*" *The Journal of Commonwealth Literature* 28.2 (1993): 34–47.

Phillips, Caryl. *Cambridge.* New York: Vintage, 1991.

———. *Crossing the River.* London: Bloomsbury, 1993.

———. "Olaudah Equiano." *Extravagant Strangers: A Literature of Belonging.* Ed. Caryl Phillips. New York: Vintage, 1997. 9–10.

———. Preface. *Extravagant Strangers: A Literature of Belonging.* Ed. Caryl Phillips. New York: Vintage, 1997. xiii–xvi.

———, ed. *Extravagant Strangers: A Literature of Belonging.* New York: Vintage, 1997.

Potkay, Adam, and Sandra Burr, eds. *Black Atlantic Writers of the Eighteenth Century: Living the New Exodus in England and the Americas.* New York: St. Martin's, 1995.

Sharpe, Jenny. "Of This Time, of That Place." *Transition* 68 (1995): 154–61.

A Son of Africa. Dir. Alrick Riley. Aimimage Productions, 1996.

Thomas, Hugh. *The Slave Trade: The Story of the Atlantic Slave Trade, 1440–1870.* New York: Simon, 1999.

Tiffin, Helen. "Post-Colonial Literatures and Counter-Discourse." *The Post-Colonial Studies Reader.* Ed. Bill Ashcroft, Gareth Griffiths, and Helen Tiffin. 2nd ed. New York: Routledge, 2006. 99–101.

Yelin, Louise. "An Interview with Caryl Phillips." *Conversations with Caryl Phillips.* Ed. Renée T. Schatteman. Jackson: UP of Mississippi, 2009. 46–52.

Contributors

SRINIVAS ARAVAMUDAN earned his Ph.D. at Cornell University in 1991 and has taught at the University of Utah and at the University of Washington. He joined the Duke English Department in Fall 2000. He is currently Professor of English and Literature and Dean of Humanities at Duke. He specializes in eighteenth-century British and French literature and in postcolonial literature and theory. He is the author of essays in *Diacritics, ELH, Social Text, Novel, Eighteenth-Century Studies, Anthropological Forum, South Atlantic Quarterly, boundary 2,* and other venues. His study *Tropicopolitans: Colonialism and Agency, 1688–1804* (Duke UP, 1999) won the outstanding first book prize of the Modern Language Association in 2000. He has also edited *Slavery, Abolition and Emancipation: Writings of the British Romantic Period: Volume VI Fiction* (Pickering and Chatto, 1999). His book *Guru English: South Asian Religion in A Cosmopolitan Language* was published by Princeton University Press in January 2006 and republished by Penguin India in 2007. He is working on two book-length studies, one on the eighteenth-century French and British oriental tale, tentatively titled *Enlightenment Orientalism: Resisting the Rise of the Novel,* and another study, *Sovereignty and Anachronism: Hobbes and the Democratic Tradition.* His edition of William Earle's antislavery romance, *Obi: or, The History of Three-Fingered Jack,* appeared in 2005 with Broadview Press.

SARAH BROPHY is Associate Professor of English and Cultural Studies at McMaster University, Hamilton, Canada. Her research interests include British literature since 1945, black British literature, gender/sexuality, health and embodiment, autobiography, and cultural studies. She is the author of *Witnessing AIDS: Writing, Testimony, and the Work of Mourning* (U of Toronto P, 2004) and of articles in *Contemporary Women's Writing, Literature and Medicine, scrutiny2,* and *PMLA.*

Vincent Carretta, Professor of English at the University of Maryland, specializes in eighteenth-century transatlantic historical and literary studies. He has recently held fellowships from the John Simon Guggenheim Memorial Foundation, the Library Company of Philadelphia, the John Carter Brown Library, the Massachusetts Historical Society, the University of London, the W. E. B. Du Bois Institute for Afro-American Research at Harvard University, and the School of Historical Studies at the Institute for Advanced Studies, Princeton. Author of more than one hundred articles and reviews, Carretta has also written and edited twelve books, most recently *Equiano, the African: Biography of a Self-Made Man* (U of Georgia P, 2005), *The Life and Letters of Philip Quaque: The First African Anglican Missionary* (Georgia, 2010), co-edited with Ty M. Reese, and *Phillis Wheatley: Biography of a Genius in Bondage* (Georgia, 2011).

Tess Chakkalakal is an Assistant Professor in the Departments of Africana Studies and English at Bowdoin College. Her essays on early African American literature have appeared in *South Atlantic Quarterly* and *Studies in American Fiction,* as well as in several edited volumes. She is currently completing a book on nineteenth-century African American literature titled *Novel Bondage: Slavery, Marriage, and Freedom in Nineteenth-Century America.* She is co-editor of a critical edition of the novels of Sutton E. Griggs (forthcoming from West Virginia University Press) and is co-editing a collection of critical essays on Griggs's life and work.

Abby Chandler completed an M.A. in public history from the University of Massachusetts at Amherst in 2002. From there, she went on to a doctoral degree in history at the University of Maine which she finished in 2008. Her dissertation is titled "At the Magistrate's Discretion: Sexual Crime and New England Law, 1636 to 1718." She now teaches at the University of Massachusetts at Lowell.

Angelo Costanzo is Professor Emeritus of English at Shippensburg University of Pennsylvania. He has written extensively on Olaudah Equiano in several journals and textbooks. His publications include *Surprizing Narrative: Olaudah Equiano and the Beginnings of Black Autobiography* (Greenwood, 1987) and an edition of *The Interesting Narrative* (Broadview, 2002).

Jessica L. Hollis is currently a Visiting Assistant Professor at Ohio University. She specializes in the literature and culture of the long eighteenth century. Her work has appeared in *Eighteenth-Century Studies* and *Women's Writing* and is forthcoming in a volume titled *Teaching the Transatlantic Eighteenth Century* (edited by Cristobal Silva and Jennifer Frangos). She is working on a manuscript titled *Geographies of Commerce: Space, Class, and Gender in the Eighteenth Century.*

Keri Holt is an Assistant Professor in the English Department at Utah State University, where she teaches courses in late eighteenth and nineteenth-century American literature. She received her Ph.D. from Brown University in 2008. Her research interests include early American regionalism and hemispheric studies, and she has written articles on Royall Tyler's *The Algerine Captive,* as well as on the work of western writer Timothy Flint. She is currently at work on a book titled *Out of the Many–One: Reading the Federal Republic,* which explores the intersections between literature and the political philosophy of federalism between the founding of the republic and the beginning of the Civil War.

Emily M. N. Kugler received her Ph.D. in literature from the University of California, San Diego, and is an Assistant Professor at Colby College. Her research and teaching interests focus on placing texts in a transnational context and examining them through the lenses of gender, ethnic, and postcolonial studies. Her areas of specialization include the history and theory of the novel, drama, English interactions with the transatlantic and Mediterranean worlds, and political theory (with an emphasis on social contract, sovereignty, slavery, and citizenship). Her current book project, *The Sway of the Ottoman Empire on English Identity in the Long Eighteenth Century,* analyzes how the period's popular culture was impacted by cross-border exchanges, especially with groups in the transatlantic and Mediterranean regions.

Eric D. Lamore is an Assistant Professor of English at the University of Puerto Rico at Mayagüez, where he teaches courses in American studies, African American studies, and Caribbean studies. He is co-editor of *New Essays on Phillis Wheatley* (U of Tennessee P, 2011) and is working on a book titled *The Early American Georgic: A Reassessment.*

Lisa M. Logan is Associate Professor of English at the University of Central Florida, where she teaches American literature, women's studies, and feminist theory. She is the author of *Resources for Teaching the Bedford Anthology of American Literature, Volume 1* (2006) and several pedagogical articles on American literature. Her research considers how early women writers in the Americas envisioned "place" in their personal narratives. She has published essays on Mary Rowlandson, Harriet Prescott Spofford, and several other American women writers.

Cedrick May is Associate Professor of English at the University of Texas at Arlington. He is the author of *Evangelism and Resistance in the Black Atlantic, 1760–1835* (U of Georgia P, 2008). He is currently at work on a book manuscript titled "The Voyages of Phillis Wheatley," as well as a second project on the metaphysics of presence in early African-American writings.

Adam Potkay is William R. Kenan Professor of Humanities at the College of William and Mary in Virginia. His books include *The Fate of Eloquence in the Age of Hume* (Cornell UP, 1994), *The Passion for Happiness: Samuel Johnson and David Hume* (Cornell, 2000), and, co-edited with Sandra Burr, *Black Atlantic Writers of the Eighteenth Century: Living the New Exodus in England and the Americas* (St. Martin's, 1995). His most recent book, *The Story of Joy from the Bible to Late Romanticism* (Cambridge UP, 2007), is a winner of the Harry Levin Prize of the American Comparative Literature Association for best book in literary criticism and history, 2007–2008.

Michael Pringle is an Associate Professor of English at Gonzaga University, where he teaches literature classes and specializes in early American literature.

Phillip M. Richards has written widely on early black Anglo-American literature, contemporary black literary scholarship, and the racial world of Cleveland in the fifties and sixties. He is the author, most recently, of *Black Heart: The Moral Life of Recent African American Letters* (Peter Lang, 2006) and *An Integrated Boyhood: Growing up in Black Cleveland* (Kent State UP, 2011).

John Saillant was awarded degrees in American civilization from Brown University and is professor of English and history at Western Michigan University, where he teaches English, history, Africana studies, and comparative religion. He is the author of *Black Puritan, Black Republican: The Life and Thought of Lemuel Haynes, 1753–1833* (2003). Works he has edited, co-edited, or co-authored include *"Face Zion Forward": First Writers of the Black Atlantic, 1785–1789* (Northeastern UP, 2002), *Migration in Modern World History* (Wadsworth, 2000), and *Afro-Virginian History and Culture* (Garland, 1999). His essays and transcriptions of rare documents have appeared in a number of scholarly journals. He lives in Kalamazoo, Michigan, with his family.

Roxann Wheeler is an Associate Professor of English at The Ohio State University where she teaches theory and eighteenth-century literature and culture at the undergraduate and graduate levels. She is currently working on a book about class and racism in eighteenth-century Britain. Her book, *The Complexion of Race: Categories of Difference in Eighteenth-Century British Culture,* was published by the University of Pennsylvania Press in 2000, and her recent essays include "Powerful Affections: Slaves, Servants, and Labors of Love in Defoe's Writing" (in *Defoe's Footprints: Essays in Honor of Maximillian E. Novak* [U of Toronto P, 2009]) and "Racial Legacies: The Speaking Countenance and the Character Sketch in the Novel" (in *A Companion to the Eighteenth-Century English Novel and Culture* [Wiley-Blackwell, 2006]).

Index